CROSSING THE FINISH LINE

CROSSING THE FINISH LINE

COMPLETING COLLEGE AT AMERICA'S PUBLIC UNIVERSITIES

William G. Bowen, Matthew M. Chingos,
and Michael S. McPherson

PRINCETON UNIVERSITY PRESS   PRINCETON AND OXFORD

Copyright © 2009 by Princeton University Press
Published by Princeton University Press, 41 William Street,
Princeton, New Jersey 08540

In the United Kingdom: Princeton University Press, 6 Oxford Street,
Woodstock, Oxfordshire OX20 1TW

Library of Congress Cataloging-in-Publication Data

Bowen, William G.
Crossing the finish line : completing college at America's public universities /
William G. Bowen, Matthew M. Chingos, and Michael S. McPherson.
p.   cm.
Includes bibliographical references.
ISBN 978-0-691-13748-3 (hardcover : alk. paper)
1. College graduates—United States—Social conditions.   2. Minority college
graduates—United States.   3. Public universities and colleges—United States.
4. Educational attainment—United States.   5. Educational equalization—United
States.   I. Chingos, Matthew M., 1983–   II. McPherson, Michael S.   III. Title.
LC208.8.B68   2009
378.1′69120973—dc22   2009007506

British Library Cataloging-in-Publication Data is available

This book has been composed in Adobe New Baskerville by Princeton Editorial
Associates, Inc., Scottsdale, Arizona
Printed on acid-free paper. ∞

press.princeton.edu

Printed in the United States of America

3 5 7 9 10 8 6 4

Contents

The following materials are available at http://press.princeton.edu/titles/8971.html.

Acknowledgments

As a friend is fond of saying, this is the section of the book in which it is customary for authors to display their clean linen in public. Our difficulty is that in this instance the size of the wash is truly enormous. Research of the kind reported here, based in large part on the construction and analysis of elaborate new databases, inevitably requires the participation of a great many people and numerous organizations. It also requires trust, much patience, persistence, and willingness to subordinate personal predilections to the overall needs of the project. In looking back over the four years that it has taken to build the new databases, complete the research, and write this book, the authors can only marvel at their good fortune in having been privileged to work with so many talented, unselfish, and just plain nice people. We hope that those mentioned here (often in cryptic fashion) will understand that our thanks go far beyond our capacity to express them in these few pages.

We begin by acknowledging the contributions of two key collaborators who have been part of the research team from the start: Eugene M. Tobin, an accomplished historian and program officer at The Andrew W. Mellon Foundation, who authored the separate essay describing the evolution of America's flagship universities (Appendix A), and Susanne C. Pichler, the exceptionally talented librarian of the Foundation, who found obscure materials, checked references, oversaw the work done by her two library colleagues (Lisa Bonifacic and Ellen Nasto) in creating both the bibliography and tables, drafted paragraphs, and in countless other ways made the book better. Several very smart research associates made original contributions in analyzing specific questions: Murrayl C. Berner did much of the work involved in assessing the predictive power of high school grades and test scores and in estimating the extent of what we call "undermatching"; Christopher L. Griffin Jr. used hazard rate analysis to identify the semesters in which transfers and withdrawals were most likely to occur; and Francie Streich and Jennifer Bendewald at the Spencer Foundation in Chicago worked tirelessly on the financial aid analysis. Julia H. Gluck worked with us in the early days on background aspects of the study and on data collection from the flagship universities. Gabrielle Holburt worked on data collection from the state systems and on framing our study of high schools. We were very fortunate in persuading Dyuti Bhattacharya to join us later, first on a part-time basis when she was still a senior at Barnard, then on a full-time basis; Dyuti took responsibility for a number of complex tasks near the end of the study and has also been our primary point of contact with Princeton University Press.

Other colleagues at the Mellon and Spencer Foundations have helped in many ways: Johanna Brownell at the Mellon Foundation has taken responsibility for putting the manuscript, complete with tables and figures, into shape for submission and has also done an excellent job of editing; Johanna's counterpart at Spencer has been Judy Klippenstein; Jackie Ewenstein made a major contribution by handling negotiations concerning permissions and other legal matters, and Jackie's successor, Rebecca Feit, carried on this important work; Lewis Bernard and Taylor Reveley (both Mellon trustees) made many helpful suggestions, and Taylor played a key role in encouraging Virginia colleges and universities to participate in the study; Ira Fuchs, Philip Lewis, Don Randel, Michele Warman, and Harriet Zuckerman at Mellon made useful comments and provided invaluable moral and logistical support. We must say a special word of thanks to Marlon Palha, our colleague in the IT arena, who has saved us from so many crises and managed always, in his remarkably cheerful way, to meet the needs of a project totally dependent on reliable access from all locations to master files lodged on a New York server.

James Shulman, president of ARTstor and a long-time participant in related research projects in higher education, contributed his usual trenchant comments, and his colleague, Neil Rudenstine, chairman of ARTstor and president emeritus of Harvard, was always available to discuss perplexing issues.

We were also very fortunate to engage the interest of a number of scholars at other institutions who read much (and in some cases, all) of the manuscript and made innumerable suggestions for improvements. This group included Sandy Baum at the College Board; David Breneman and Sarah Turner at the University of Virginia; Jesse Rothstein, Cecilia Rouse, Deborah Prentice, and Paul Benacerraf at Princeton; Saul Geiser, research associate at the Center for Studies in Higher Education at the University of California–Berkeley, and Richard Atkinson, former president of the University of California; Nicholas Lemann, dean and Henry R. Luce Professor at the Columbia University Graduate School of Journalism; Eric Wanner, president of the Russell Sage Foundation; and Shirley Ort at the University of North Carolina–Chapel Hill.

We also express our thanks to the leaders of key Washington-based educational organizations who encouraged their member universities to participate in the study—Nils Haaselmo, Robert Berdahl, and John Vaughn at the Association of American Universities, and Peter McPherson and David E. Shulenberger at the Association of Public and Land-grant Universities. For reasons explained in the preface, much of the value of this study derives from the inclusion of rich data from four state systems, and this would have been impossible had it not been for the active support of William (Brit) Kirwan in Maryland; Erskine Bowles and Harold Martin in North Carolina; Eric Fingerhut, Gordon Gee, and Nancy L. Zimpher in Ohio; and Daniel J. LaVista at the State Council of Higher Education for Virginia. In addition, we thank June Atkinson of the Department of Public Instruction in North Carolina and Elizabeth Glennie of the North Carolina Education Research Data Center for facilitating access to high school data in their state. The utility of the databases we have built also derives from the willingness of Gaston Caperton at the College Board, Richard Ferguson at ACT, and Sylvia Hurtado at the Higher Education Research Institute at the University of California–Los Angeles to contribute data that could be linked to the institutional records we obtained from individual universities and state systems.

In addition to contributing critically important data, Presidents Caperton and Ferguson, along with their colleagues at the College Board and ACT, were very helpful in carefully and critically reviewing content pertaining to the tests administered by their organizations and to testing in general. Special thanks are due to Wayne Camara, Andrew Wiley, and Laurence Bunin at the College Board and to Ranjit Sidhu at ACT for the painstaking care with which they commented on Chapter 6, in particular. In addition, and with our encouragement, the College Board asked Professors Paul Sackett and Nathan Kuncel in the Department of Psychology at the University of Minnesota to comment in some detail on related issues, both methodological and other, and to point us to relevant research. We did our best to take advantage of these comments and leads, but we would not want readers to think that the College Board, ACT, or these individuals necessarily agree with our final formulations.

This "high-level" support provided by presidents and chancellors of universities and university systems was essential in allowing us to access and organize the individual student records that are the core of the empirical work reported in the study. But the successful construction of the databases depended, finally, not only on the willingness of leaders of individual universities to participate in the study but on the hard work of the small army of people at these universities who worked tirelessly to provide the raw material that our staff then assembled in New York. We next list individuals at the individual universities who did this work, often at nights and on weekends. We also list the names of key staff members at the organizations that provided secondary ("linked") data. Although we do not list the names of the presidents and chancellors who authorized the participation of their universities, we should note that some of them went to considerable lengths to convince their own constituents that this study was sufficiently important that they simply had to go through "the hoops" necessary to release their data. We are very grateful to all of these individuals, and we hope that the results of the study will justify their commitment to the project.

INDIVIDUALS AT FLAGSHIP UNIVERSITIES

Thomas Hill, Kathleen Jones, and Julia Sullivan: Iowa State University
Julie Carpenter-Hubin, Stephanie Houdeshell, and Linda Katunich: The Ohio State University
Anne Kepler, John Romano, Tina Storms, and J. James Wager: Pennsylvania State University
Sarah Bauer, Brent Drake, Larry Eddy, Jacquelyn Frost, Rab Mukerjea, and Edward Vahary: Purdue University
Tina Grycenkov and Robert Heffernan: Rutgers, The State University of New Jersey
Paula Pelletier and Emily Thomas: Stony Brook University–State University of New York
Gregg Thomson: University of California–Berkeley
David Darling, Frank Kong, Janina Montero, and Judith Richlin-Klonsky: University of California–Los Angeles
Joe Glover, Cynthia King, Elaine Stuckman, and Victor Yellen: University of Florida
Carol Livingstone and Ruth Watkins: University of Illinois at Urbana-Champaign
Tom Kruckeberg, Tom Rocklin, and Pete Sidwell: University of Iowa
Angela Hamlin, Sharon La Voy, Denise Nadasen, and William Spann: University of Maryland–College Park
Paul Courant, Phil Hanlon, and Ruth Kallio: University of Michigan
Richard Howard and John Kellogg: University of Minnesota–Twin Cities
William Nunez and Mary Werner: University of Nebraska–Lincoln
Kitti Ballenger, Weiguo Jiang, and Lynn Williford: University of North Carolina–Chapel Hill
J. P. Monroe: University of Oregon
John Dollard and Linda Hardwick: University of Texas–Austin
Cameron Howell and George Stovall: University of Virginia
Andrew Hummel-Schluger and Todd Mildon: University of Washington
Clare Huhn and Jocelyn Milner: University of Wisconsin–Madison

INDIVIDUALS IN STATE SYSTEMS

Kara Bonneau: North Carolina Education Research Data Center
Darrell Glenn and Andy Lechler: Ohio Board of Regents

Tod Massa: State Council of Higher Education for Virginia
Gayle Fink: University System of Maryland
Diana Haywood, Scott Jenkins, and Alan Mabe: University of North
   Carolina

INDIVIDUALS AT ORGANIZATIONS
THAT PROVIDED SECONDARY DATA

Dave Shawver and Robert Ziomek: ACT
Sherby Jean-Leger and Andrew Wiley: College Board
William Korn: Higher Education Research Institute
Pam Gilligan, Darrell Pierre, and Elizabeth Stefanik: National Student
   Clearinghouse

In addition to providing data, the following leaders of participating universities and university systems organized campus visits and discussions that were very helpful in giving us a better feel for local circumstances and the perceptions of those working "on the ground" to improve outcomes: Erskine Bowles, Harold Martin, and Shirley Ort in North Carolina; Alan G. Merten at George Mason; Freeman Hrabowski and Brit Kirwan at the University of Maryland and the University of Maryland–Baltimore County; Daniel J. LaVista at the State Council of Higher Education for Virginia and Charles Steger at Virginia Polytechnic Institute and State University; and Gordon Gee at Ohio State University. In addition, Heather Wathington at the University of Virginia took the lead in organizing a sub-study of black graduates of historically black colleges and universities (HBCUs) and of state system universities in North Carolina that is still in progress. Similarly, social psychologists Deborah Prentice of Princeton and Nancy Cantor of Syracuse are leading an ongoing companion study of factors leading students at several participating universities from different backgrounds to withdraw or not in the face of personal difficulties of one kind or another.

Thanks to the generosity of participating universities and organizations in contributing both data and much of the work required to organize the records made available to us, this was not an expensive research project (by modern-day standards!). However, we record our thanks to The Andrew W. Mellon Foundation and the Spencer Foundation for defraying the costs of the research associates who worked on the project and of some administrative and incidental expenses.

We also thank Peter Dougherty and his colleagues at Princeton University Press, who—once again—have provided both encouragement and highly professional assistance beyond what authors have any right to expect from their publisher. It has been a real pleasure to work with Victoria Hansard, Neil Litt, and Jessica Pellien at Princeton University Press and with Peter Strupp and his team at Princeton Editorial Associates.

On a more personal note, Bill Bowen thanks those who are by now, after many seemingly interminable projects, the usual suspects—especially Mary Ellen. Matt Chingos thanks, for their love and encouragement, Abigail, his parents (all four of them!), his grandparents, and Tim. Mike McPherson recalls with loving gratitude his late wife, Marge, whose support in his work and partnership in their common lives meant so much.

Finally, the authors cheerfully subscribe to the convention of acknowledging our responsibility for whatever errors of omission and commission remain after all of the efforts of so many people to correct our mistakes. And the three of us do so collectively. This has been a wonderful partnership from beginning to end, and the alphabetical listing of our names is meant to connote that we share fully in responsibility for the conclusions drawn and the views expressed.

Preface

A READER'S GUIDE TO THIS BOOK

FOR REASONS DISCUSSED at length in Chapter 1, educational attainment in the United States today is highly consequential. Important are both the overall level of educational attainment and disparities in educational outcomes by race/ethnicity, gender, socioeconomic status (SES), and the kind of university a student attends. These outcomes and the forces that drive them are enormously important not only to prospective students and their parents, institutional decision makers, and policy makers but to all who care about both the economic prospects for this country and its social fabric—which is so strongly shaped by the pronounced differences in educational levels seen in relation to how one grows up. In this study, we focus on patterns of educational attainment at public universities, which educate more than two-thirds of all full-time students seeking bachelor's degrees at four-year colleges and universities.

Because our audience is the generalist as well as the specialist, we have worked hard to make the detailed findings reported in the body of the book accessible. Even so, we recognize that, as one reader put it, there is just too much here to digest in a single sitting—he said it took him four "bites of the apple." Accordingly, a brief chapter-by-chapter reader's guide seems in order (with a discussion of databases and data-related issues at the end).

• Chapter 1 begins by describing recent trends in the overall level of educational attainment in the United States, the reasons we should be concerned about the dramatic slow-down in the building of human capital over the past 35 years, the pronounced disparities in educational outcomes that are so evident today, and why we regard these disparities as themselves grounds for serious concern. We then "introduce," as it were, the public universities that are the primary institutional actors in this drama and locate them within American higher education. We also comment briefly on changes in the characteristics of flagship universities over the past 35 years.

• Appendix A is a separate "framing" essay, written by our colleague Eugene Tobin, which describes in far greater detail the evolution of these universities and how they have been shaped by broad demographic trends, reports of national commissions, and policies adopted by particular states (such as the California Master Plan). We refer to this rich historical content at various places in the book, and we believe that many readers will find it of independent interest.

- Chapter 2 provides important context for our detailed examination of educational outcomes at public universities by looking more broadly at bachelor's degree attainment at the national level. In this chapter we describe the overall level of educational attainment in the United States today, based as it is on a combination of high school graduation rates, college enrollment rates, and college graduation rates. We also document the pronounced disparities in outcomes that are seen when we compare, for example, graduation rates by race/ethnicity, gender, and SES (as measured by family income and parental education). A brief analysis of trends addresses the important question of whether the disparities we see today have narrowed or widened over the past 25 years. The answer is not reassuring.

- Chapter 3 shifts the focus to the much more detailed new data we have assembled on graduation rates at various sets of public universities, highlighting both general patterns and the substantial differences among sub-groups of students and across universities that differ in their selectivity. A key question is to what extent the substantial differences that we often observe in "raw" outcomes can be explained by related differences in academic preparedness and family circumstances. (The answer is "Only in part.") This chapter also utilizes a hazard rate model to pinpoint semester-by-semester differences in when withdrawals occur. A question of great interest to those concerned with persistence is how much emphasis should be placed on student departures during the first two years of college. Do large numbers of withdrawals continue to be observed in subsequent semesters? (The answer is a resounding "Yes.") And do these patterns differ among sub-groups of students? (The answer is "Not as much as one might have thought.")

- Chapter 4 investigates differences in other academic outcomes, specifically major field of study, time-to-degree, and college grades. Do students from low-SES backgrounds and racial minorities choose different fields of study than other students? (The differences turn out to be surprisingly modest.) To what extent does time-to-degree vary across these same groups? (The answer is "Substantially.") Do college grades correlate with race/ethnicity, gender, and SES—both before and after adjusting for differences in academic preparedness? (Here the answer differs depending on whether we are considering race/ethnicity or SES.)

- Chapter 5 begins the process of probing factors that drive the differences just described by examining in detail relationships between type of high school attended and college outcomes, both at the flagship universities and in several state systems. We do our best to control for differences in the earlier academic preparation of students so that we do not inadvertently credit high schools with accomplishments in college that are due primarily to the characteristics that entering high school students brought with them from the eighth grade. The key question is to what extent (and in what ways) high schools themselves matter. Perhaps the most important part of this analysis is the discussion of "undermatching." Evidence suggests that there are a surprisingly large number of students whose pre-collegiate preparation seems to qualify them to attend strong four-year colleges but who do not do so. A question with strong policy relevance is whether we might improve the overall level of educational attainment and narrow disparities in outcomes by reducing the number of undermatches.

• Chapter 6 focuses on the predictive power of three frequently used measures of student potential: high school grades, SAT/ACT tests, and subject-specific achievement tests. Which of these measures is the best predictor of graduation rates? Do we need all three? And do the answers to these questions depend on the characteristics of the student population being studied and the characteristics of the institution the students attend? Should we be concerned about the "signaling" effects for high schools of reliance on different types of tests? How do test scores and high school grades correlate with race/ethnicity, gender, and SES? We conclude that all of these predictors have value but that some universities might be able to improve educational outcomes—and perhaps simultaneously enroll more diverse student bodies—by shifting the weights they assign to these various measures.

• Chapter 7 compares the educational outcomes of students who transfer into four-year programs with those of students who enter as first-time freshmen. Are there significant differences in outcomes? Do students who start out in two-year programs pay a significant "price" for that decision in terms of the likelihood that they will eventually earn bachelor's degrees? Could we enhance the overall effectiveness of the higher education system (and reduce disparities in outcomes) by improving the alignment between two-year college programs and academic expectations in four-year programs?

• Chapter 8 takes a broad look at financial aid programs (national, state, and institutional) and reports research findings by others that relate educational outcomes to patterns of financial aid. Methodological problems are formidable, and data limitations have made it especially difficult to study the effects of job commitments. Still, there seems little doubt that insufficient and overly complicated financial aid, especially grant aid, slows progress toward degrees and reduces the overall educational attainment of needy students. Recent initiatives of the Obama administration are consistent with these lines of argument and may alleviate some of the problems discussed here.

• Chapter 9 complements the broad analysis of financial aid in the previous chapter by asking whether our database provides evidence that need-based grant aid, in particular, affects graduation rates. A key question, with great policy relevance, is to what extent the provision of grant aid affects the graduation rates of students from high-income as well as low-income families. What are the implications of this analysis for merit aid programs and debates over tuition policy?

• Chapter 10 addresses a very different question: to what extent do graduation rates, including four-year graduation rates, vary directly with institutional selectivity *even after controls are introduced for differences in student characteristics?* That is, are comparable students, with essentially the same test scores, high school grades, and family backgrounds, more likely to graduate, and to graduate in four years, if they go to a highly selective institution than to one that is less selective? If so, what factors are driving these patterns (which, in fact, we find to be relentlessly consistent)? How important are peer effects, expectations concerning a "normal" path to graduation, residential patterns, and the availability of various kinds of teaching and other educational resources? This chapter also addresses the question of whether low overall graduation rates are the result of some universities "dipping too low" in deciding which students to admit.

• Chapter 11 looks specifically at the outcomes of "target populations" who most need improvements in educational attainment: minority students, especially black men and Hispanic students, students from low-SES backgrounds, and certain groups of under-achieving students from other families. Is there evidence that some students, especially minority students, are recruited into programs that are too challenging for them (the so-called mismatch hypothesis)? What does the evidence show concerning the effects of particular kinds of institutional interventions designed to increase persistence?

• Chapter 12 pulls together the threads of this analysis by looking ahead and suggesting both the challenges to be recognized and what we regard, based on the available evidence, as promising approaches to doing better. The research that we report in this book convinces us that there definitely are opportunities to reshape national programs— certainly in awarding financial aid—and that there are also practical steps that individual institutions and state systems can take to improve outcomes. Heightened awareness of the seriousness of this set of issues, especially of the need to focus on helping students *finish* the programs that they begin, could itself make a considerable difference.

A note to readers with a special interest in particular topics covered in this study

This book has a definite structure—with context-setting chapters coming first, then chapters that document educational outcomes, then chapters on "levers" that might be used to change outcomes (including high school programs, choices among predictors of college outcomes, financial aid policies, and institution-based interventions), and finally concluding comments. However, we have done our best to make individual chapters more or less self-contained. This approach has the advantage of allowing someone with an interest in a particular topic—such as the problem of "undermatching" or the predictive power of test scores—to turn more or less directly to the relevant chapter without first having to study all previous chapters.

THE PUBLIC UNIVERSITY FOCUS OF THE STUDY— AND TWO NEW DATABASES

We elected to concentrate this research project on students who enrolled at leading public universities—"flagships"—and then to include other students who attended a broader range of public institutions. Our reasons for choosing to focus on public universities are straightforward. They have to do with scale of enrollment, mission (a tradition of emphasizing a commitment to social mobility), and the fact that—because of their geographic dispersion, their larger size, and their generally lower tuition—these universities are going to continue to be the primary entry points for the majority of students pursuing bachelor's degrees, especially for those from modest backgrounds. The private sector also has an important role to play in improving educational attainment, and we will make some comparisons between outcomes in the private and public sectors, but there is no denying the primacy of the public sector in addressing these issues.[1]

The 21 flagship universities included in this study (listed in Chapter 1, with their salient characteristics) are geographically spread across the country and also differ in interesting ways, such as enrollment and selectivity. In an effort to understand patterns of educational attainment at public universities more generally—and how students in a given state sort themselves by type of state university—we also analyzed outcomes at statewide systems of higher education in four states: Maryland, North Carolina, Ohio, and Virginia. (The 47 state system universities that we study are also described in Chapter 1.) We chose these four states largely on opportunistic grounds: they had good data that could be harvested, and they were eager to participate in the study. We were especially pleased to be able to include Ohio so that we would have at least one Midwestern state to study alongside the three Atlantic Coast state systems. The presence in the Atlantic Coast states of a number of HBCUs was an added reason for wanting to study these state systems. (In Chapter 1 we show that a subset of these state system universities, called the SEL Bs, is surprisingly representative of all four-year public universities in the United States.)

We focus on outcomes achieved by individual members of the 1999 entering cohort. The reason for choosing this cohort is that we wanted to follow individual students for at least six years after their initial enrollment in college (so that they would have this amount of time in which to earn their degrees), and we knew that the inevitable logistical problems involved in assembling data from many different institutions and data sources meant that the records for the 1999 entering cohort were the most recent ones that we could be sure would be available to us.

We assembled data from a combination of institutional records and other sources of information about individual students and then created two massive new databases, a "Flagships Database" and a "State Systems Database." The process of building these elaborate databases was exceedingly complex, and we have chosen not to burden this text with a detailed description of what was done and why we made the choices that we did along the way. But because our analysis rests so heavily on the contents of these databases, we have created a long appendix (Appendix B) that explains in great detail (1) the data collection process and the key elements of these two databases, (2) the restriction of our sample of students to include only first-time freshmen and full-time transfer students of traditional college-going age, (3) the imputation of missing values of two key variables—family income quartile and high school GPA, and (4) further restriction of the sample to exclude students with missing values on variables used in particular parts of the analysis. There will be ample opportunities, we are confident, to put these data-rich resources to further use in exploring questions beyond the scope of the present study.

THE PRESENTATION OF FIGURES AND APPENDIX TABLES

The main story lines of this study can be "read" directly from the figures that we have used liberally to highlight key points and relationships. The figures are so important that we have kept them closely aligned to the associated text within each chapter. Although some of the figures require explanation in the text, most of them are stand-alone presentations of data. We frequently compare "raw" relationships between, say, race and graduation rates with "adjusted" relationships that take account of differences in factors such as family backgrounds and high school records that explain part, but rarely all, of the "raw" or simple associations. These adjusted relationships are almost always derived from standard regression equations, and sometimes we present regression coefficients in figures or in the text. But most of the time we present the underlying regression results in appendix tables.

There are so many appendix tables that inserting them in the book, even at the ends of chapters, would be overwhelming. At the same time, readers clearly need access to these tables so that they can judge for themselves whether the arguments in the text are soundly based. In an effort to find a solution to this problem of presentation, we have decided, with the strong support of our publisher, to make the appendix tables available on a Web site maintained by the publisher (available at http://press .princeton.edu/titles/8971.html). Readers interested in this level of detail can of course print out a full set of appendix tables for themselves. We have also put on this Web site the full text of Appendix B, in which we describe in detail the construction of the two key databases on which the regression equations and the figures depend. (Eugene Tobin's historical analysis of the evolution of the flagship universities appears in the body of the book.)

Because we know that by no means everyone will want to print out all the appendix tables or be forced to consult a Web site as they read each page of the book, we have tried to carefully explain in the text the main points we believe come out of the regression equations and the appendix tables. We hope that this "hybrid" approach will not inconvenience readers too much and will succeed in reconciling, at least to some extent, the competing objectives of full disclosure of the evidence on which our analysis rests and publication in standard form of a book that is of manageable size.

ACCOUNTABILITY AND DATA PRIVACY ISSUES

Attempts to address issues of educational attainment have to be seen in the context of broader concerns. American higher education has been challenged in recent years, as never before, to prove that it is producing "good value." Former secretary of education Margaret Spellings and her Commission on the Future of Higher Education were unrelenting in their effort to get colleges and universities to focus more on how they are doing. Whatever one thinks about the debate over measures of "learning outcomes," we agree with a number of commentators that certain fundamental measures, such as graduation rates, time-to-degree, and the success of graduates in completing applicable licensing exams, are much less problematic and should be made publicly available by colleges and universities. It is encouraging to note that, led by the APLU (the Association of Public and Land-grant Universities, formerly NASULGC) and other higher education groups such as NAICU (the National Association of Independent Colleges and Universities), there is a growing willingness on the part of colleges and universities to provide online information that gives applicants and their parents a direct sense of how students admitted to particular programs have fared.

In September 2008, the University of California (UC) released a draft "accountability framework" of more than 200 pages that provides a massive amount of data on graduation rates, costs and financial aid, undergraduate experiences, research support, and the outcomes of graduate and professional degree students—all with comparisons among not only UC campuses but also other public and private universities. In releasing this document, the president of the UC system, Mark G. Yudof, said: "The American people have made it quite clear that they want a visible accountability that they can see of their larger institutions. It doesn't really matter whether you want to do it—you're going to have to do it."[2] These are highly positive developments, in our view, and we hope that the detailed data on graduation rates and time-to-degree reported in this study will encourage more colleges and universities to be forthcoming about such outcomes.[3] This information will have value, however, only if it is actively used by large numbers of prospective students and their families, who can then "vote with their feet." There is much to be said for what one reader has called "consumer accountability." Colleges and universities could also do much more than many do at present to evaluate the effectiveness of their own programs.

Data do matter. In commenting on the disastrous consequences of the Paris peace talks held at the end of World War I, Freud wrote that Woodrow Wilson "repeatedly declared that mere facts had no significance for him." "Noble intentions" were what counted. Thus, although Wilson went to France intent on bringing a "just and lasting peace" to Europe, in Freud's opinion he "put himself in the deplorable position of the benefactor who wishes to restore the eyesight of a patient but does not know the construction of the eye and has neglected to learn the necessary methods of operation."[4]

We are entirely on Freud's side of this argument. So is Bill Gates. At the Bill and Melinda Gates Foundation's 2008 Forum on Education, he said: "Without evidence, innovation is just another word for 'fad.'"[5] In carrying out the research undergirding this book, we have sought to leverage our comparative advantage, which is in building large, linked databases and seeing what lessons can be learned from them.

In building these databases—in ways described in detail in Appendix B—we have had many experiences with FERPA (the Family Educational Rights and Privacy Act) and numerous discussions with general counsels of colleges and universities. We are pleased to report that a number of colleagues in academia clearly understood that it is both possible and highly desirable to protect privacy while simultaneously conducting the outcomes-based research advocated by so many, including former secretary Spellings. Others, unfortunately, seemed to believe that admonitions to protect student privacy prevented, for all intents and purposes, the linking of records that is necessary if research is to take into account, for example, differences in family backgrounds. One person confessed, "The safest course of action is simply to do nothing." That may be true, but we believe it is an absurd (irresponsible) stance. The Department of Education and, if need be, the Congress, will need to continue to rethink the balancing of interests so that responsible efforts to pursue serious scholarly work will not be retarded by unnecessarily (foolishly) restrictive notions of how to protect student records from abuse. Fortunately, efforts have recently been made to create more "research-friendly" regulations.[6]

More generally, it is our hope that the Department of Education (primarily through its Institute of Education Sciences, or IES) will continue to improve the collection and presentation of data needed to evaluate policies and policy proposals. In recent years the IES has made definite progress in advancing these objectives, and these efforts need to continue. Educational data are worth a major investment, as we hope the results of this study will help demonstrate.

Note: For reasons explained in the preface, the large number of appendix tables to which we refer in the text are on the Princeton University Press Web site http://press.princeton.edu/titles/8971.html rather than in the book itself.

CROSSING THE FINISH LINE

Educational Attainment: Overall Trends, Disparities, and the Public Universities We Study

THE SUBJECT OF this book—educational attainment in the United States —could hardly be more timely. Academics, framers of public policy, and journalists are united in bemoaning the failure of the United States in recent years to continue building the human capital it needs to satisfy economic, social, and political needs. In their book *The Race Between Education and Technology*, Claudia Goldin and Lawrence Katz applaud America's astonishingly steady and substantial educational progress during the first three quarters of the 20th century—and then are just as emphatic in calling attention to the dramatic falling off in the rate of increase in educational attainment since the mid-1970s.[1] The chairman of the Federal Reserve Board, Ben S. Bernanke, in remarks delivered at Harvard on Class Day 2008, told the assembled graduates that "the best way to improve economic opportunity and to reduce inequality is to increase the educational attainment and skills of American workers."[2] The *New York Times* columnist David Brooks has referred to "the skills slowdown" as "the biggest issue facing the country."[3] In writing about how to increase growth in America, David Leonhardt, also at the *New York Times,* says simply: "Education—educating more people and educating them better— appears to be the best single bet that a society can make."[4]

Bernanke was wise to couch his argument in terms of educational *attainment* (which we generally equate with earning a degree) rather than just enrollment or years of school completed, for the payoff to completing one's studies is much higher than the payoff to having "just been there" another year—the so-called "sheepskin" effect.[5] In our view, too much discussion has focused on initial access to educational opportunities ("getting started") rather than on attainment ("finishing"). It is noteworthy that in his first speech to a joint session of Congress (and then in his budget message), President Barack Obama emphasized the importance of *graduating from college, not just enrolling.*[6]

In any case, as Bernanke and others have stressed, the key linkage is between the formation of human capital and productivity. In his Class Day remarks, Bernanke observed: "The productivity surge in the decades after World War II corresponded to a period in which educational attainment was increasing rapidly." Technological change and the breaking down of barriers to the exchange of information and ideas across boundaries of every kind have unquestionably increased the value of brainpower and training in every country. As President Obama has said: "In a global economy where the most valuable skill you can sell is your knowledge, a good education is no longer just a pathway to opportunity—it is a prerequisite."[7] Leonhardt adds: "There really is no mystery about why education would be the lifeblood of economic growth. . . . [Education] helps a society leverage every other investment it makes, be it in medicine, transportation, or alternative energy."[8] Nor are economic gains the only reason to assert the importance of educational attainment. The ability of a democracy to function well depends on a high level of political engagement, which is also tied to the educational level of the citizenry. A high level of educational attainment fosters civic contributions of many kinds.[9]

Even though our emphasis on "finishing" is meant to be a useful corrective to the sometime tendency to focus simply on "starting," we hasten to add that there are of course dimensions of college success beyond just graduating that must also be kept in mind. The kind and quality of the undergraduate education obtained are plainly important. It would be a serious mistake to treat all college degrees as the same or to put so much emphasis on earning a degree that other educational objectives are lost from sight. This is why some are skeptical of the weight given by the National Collegiate Athletic Association to graduation rates (whatever the subject studied and whatever the rigor of the graduation requirements) in assessing the academic performance of scholarship athletes. As in platform diving, differences in the "degree of difficulty" of various courses of study deserve to be acknowledged, and considerable weight should be given to academic achievement in assessing educational outcomes. For these reasons, we examine fields of study chosen by students and grades earned, as well as graduation rates. However, much as there is to be said for such finer-grained analyses, we believe it is valuable to place special emphasis on graduation rates as presumptively the single most important indicator of educational attainment—which is what we do in this book.

EDUCATIONAL ATTAINMENT IN THE UNITED STATES

These basic propositions explain why there is reason for serious concern about the slow-down in the rate of increase in the overall level of educational attainment in the United States. The facts are sobering. As Goldin and Katz report on the basis of an exhaustive study of historical records, the achievements of America in the first three quarters of what they call "the Human Capital Century" are impressive indeed. This country's then unprecedented mass secondary schooling and the concurrent establishment of an extensive and remarkably flexible system of higher education combined to produce gains in educational attainment that were both steady and spectacular (see Figure 1.1, which plots years of schooling by birth cohorts from 1876 to the present). Unfortunately, this truly amazing record of progress came to a halt about the time when members of the 1951 birth cohort (who were 24 years old in 1975) were attending college.[10]

We see this same "flattening" when we use data from the *Current Population Survey* to track the educational attainment of 25- to 29-year-olds from 1968 to 2007 (Figure 1.2). Although there was a modest increase in educational attainment in the 1990s, the curve is flat for the years thereafter. The failure of educational attainment to continue to increase steadily is the result of problems at all stages of education, starting with pre-school and then moving through primary and secondary levels of education and on into college (see the discussion in Chapter 2 of "losses" of students at each main stage of the educational process). Our focus on completion rates at the college level should certainly not be read as dismissing the need to make progress at earlier stages. In any case, it is noteworthy that over this 40-year period the completion rate (the fraction of those who started college who eventually earned a bachelor's degree) changed hardly at all, while time-to-degree increased markedly.[11]

This is not a pretty picture when looked at through the lens of America's history of educational accomplishments during the first 75 years of the 20th century. It is an equally disturbing picture when juxtaposed with

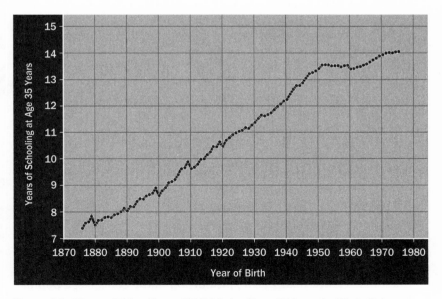

Figure 1.1. Years of Schooling of U.S. Native-Born Citizens by Birth Cohorts, 1876–1975

Source: Goldin and Katz, figure 1.4.

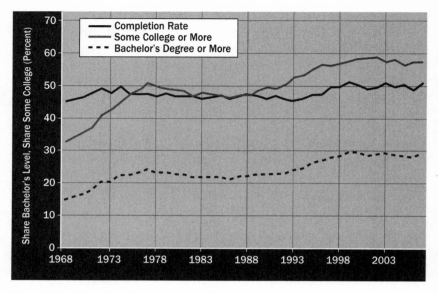

Figure 1.2. Educational Attainment of 25- to 29-Year-Olds, 1968–2007
Source: Current Population Survey.

the remarkable gains in educational attainment in other countries. As is increasingly recognized, the United States can no longer claim that it is "first-in-class" in terms of continuing progress in building human capital. The 2008 annual stock-taking document produced by the Organization for Economic Co-operation and Development (OECD) reported that the 2006 higher education attainment rate for 25- to 34-year-olds in the United States is nearly identical to that of 55- to 64-year-olds, a group 30 years their senior. In 2006, the United States ranked 10th among the members of the OECD in its tertiary attainment rate. This is a large drop from preceding years: the United States ranked 5th in 2001 and 3rd in 1998. Moreover, in the United States only 56 percent of entering students finished college, an outcome that placed this country second to the bottom of the rank-ordering of countries by completion rate.[12] In recognition of this reality, President Obama has set an ambitious goal for American higher education: "By 2020, America will once again have the highest proportion of college graduates in the world."[13] And the situation in the United States is even more worrying when the focus is on degrees in the natural sciences and engineering. According to a report published by the National Science Board, "The proportion of the college-age population that earned degrees in NS&E fields was substantially larger in more than 16 countries in Asia and Europe than in the United States in 2000."

In that year, the United States ranked just below Italy and above only four other countries. Twenty-five years earlier, in 1975, the United States was tied with Finland for second place (below only Japan).[14]

A central question is why educational attainment in the United States has been on a plateau in recent years. In seeking to answer this question, a key analytical tool is the wage premiums earned by college graduates and high school graduates. Data painstakingly assembled by Goldin and Katz (presented in Figure 1.3) show that both of these premiums fell sharply between 1915 and 1950, moved somewhat erratically between 1950 and 1980, and then increased sharply from 1980 to 2005—with the wage premium for college graduates increasing much faster than the premium for high school graduates. By 2005, the wage premium for college graduates had returned to the high-water mark set in 1915.[15]

In looking inside these ratios, Goldin and Katz found that the growth rate of demand for more educated workers (relative to less educated workers) was fairly constant over the entire period from 1915 to 2005. It was the pronounced slow-down in the rate of growth in the supply of educated workers (especially native-born workers) that was primarily responsible for the marked increase in the college graduate wage premium. In recent years, growth in the supply of college-educated workers has been sluggish and has not kept up with increases in demand—especially inceases in the demand for individuals with strong problem-solving skills

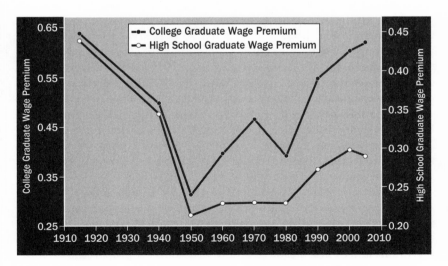

Figure 1.3. Wage Premiums of College Graduates and High School Graduates, 1915–2005
Source: Goldin and Katz, figure 8.1.

and degrees from the more selective undergraduate programs and leading professional schools.[16] The real puzzle is why educational attainment has failed to respond to the powerful economic incentives represented by the high college graduate wage premium. We would have expected rising returns on investments in a college education to have elicited a solid increase in the number of students earning bachelor's degrees.[17] But this has not happened.

To be sure, some commentators have suggested that the perception that there are superior economic returns to investments in higher education is mistaken; however, careful statistical work by several leading economists strongly suggests that these worries are misplaced. Indeed, research reported and reviewed by David Card (among others), suggests that returns for prospective college students who might be added "at the margin" are at least as high as the average for all students.[18] As Goldin and Katz put it, there may be some "natural limit" to the share of high school graduates who can benefit from earning a college degree—the optimal graduation rate is surely not 100 percent—but there is no evidence that we are anywhere close to such a limit now.[19]

Thus, the sluggish response of educational attainment to economic incentives remains puzzling, and we are driven back to the need to understand the forces responsible for what appears to be a "supply-side" block. One possible explanation for the surprisingly stagnant state of overall educational attainment in the United States can be rejected out of hand: the problem is not low aspirations. Students of all family backgrounds have high (and rising) educational aspirations. The Education Longitudinal Study of 2002 shows that in 2002, 80 percent of 10th-graders expected to earn a bachelor's degree or higher—with 40 percent expecting to earn a graduate or professional degree. In 1980, just half as many 10th-graders had similarly high aspirations. Especially noteworthy is the evidence of rising aspirations among students of low socioeconomic status (SES): whereas in 1980, 22 percent of these 10th-graders aspired to a bachelor's degree or higher, in 2002, three times as many (66 percent) had such aspirations. In 2002, 77 percent of black 10th-graders aspired to earn a bachelor's degree or higher. The conclusion is simple: there are no longer pronounced aspiration gaps by race or SES.[20]

The presence of high aspirations does not mean, however, that anything like all high-aspiring students know how to translate their aspirations into realities. On the contrary, there is much evidence of limited knowledge of how to prepare for college and how to enroll, which we will present in due course. More generally, problems of "preparedness" have their roots in family circumstances and educational deficits that are evident both in early childhood years and in high school. Subsequently, financial constraints, combined with an aversion to borrowing on the part of some, can inhibit students from finishing college—or even from starting. Also at work are a combination of demographic trends and disparities in educational outcomes related to race and SES.[21]

Before saying more about these disparities and why we consider them so important, we need to fill in one more piece of the larger puzzle. For much of our recent history, the United States has relied heavily on "imports" of well-educated students from other countries to compensate for its own difficulties in graduating enough native-born candidates for advanced degrees and, in particular, for jobs in science and engineering. Census data reveal that in 2000, foreign-born holders of doctorates constituted approximately *half* of all doctorate-holders among employed engineers, scientists, and mathematicians.[22] The percentage of science and engineering Ph.D. graduates who were foreign born increased from 23 percent in 1966 to 39 percent in 2000.[23]

It would be a serious mistake to believe that the United States can continue to rely so heavily on this inflow of talent from overseas. Following 9/11, there was a marked fall-off in foreign enrollments, due in part to visa issues. Visa processing has now become more efficient, and some of the perception problems that inhibited foreign enrollment have lessened. Still, it is unclear what will happen to foreign enrollments, especially to foreign enrollments in graduate programs in science and engineering. A survey released by the Council of Graduate Schools (CGS) in August 2008 indicates that while the number of foreign students admitted to U.S. graduate schools increased in 2008, the rate of increase over the previous year declined for the second consecutive year. Data released by the CGS in November 2008 show that first-time enrollment also grew by just 3 percent.[24]

An important consideration to bear in mind is that universities in other parts of the world, including both Europe and Asia, are making increasingly aggressive efforts to compete for top students from all over the world. India, China, and South Korea are examples of countries actively engaged in improving their own educational systems.[25] In the future, promising students from these countries will have better and better educational opportunities at home. China now takes in more students than it sends abroad; in 2007, its foreign enrollment ranked fifth in the world.[26] The moral of the story is simple: the United States is going to have to do a better job of "growing its own timber"—a phrase popular in South Africa, where the same issues are being debated. Of course, increasing educational attainment at the bachelor's level is not the only—and probably not the most efficient—way of increasing the number of Americans who earn advanced degrees in science and engineering. Serious thought needs to be given to the incentives that influence choice of major among U.S. undergraduates and to the incentives used to encourage students to undertake—and complete—advanced degrees.

EDUCATIONAL DISPARITIES AND WHY THEY MATTER

In seeking to understand patterns of educational attainment so that we can address recent shortfalls in the rate of growth of human capital, a major complication—and a major source of concern—is the existence of large disparities in educational outcomes related to (1) race/ethnicity and gender, and (2) SES, which reflects both family income and parental education. In budget materials related to higher education which were released by the White House and which presented an overview of President Obama's 2010 fiscal budget, these disparities were acknowledged by noting that there is an "opportunity gap," as well as a shortfall in the overall number of college graduates.[27] We document these disparities in detail in Chapters 3 and 4 of this study. For present purposes, it will suffice to compare the national educational attainment rates (defined here as the percentage of eighth-graders who went on to earn a bachelor's degree by age 26) of students from the two groups just mentioned:[28]

1. Thirty-six percent of white women earned a bachelor's degree by age 26 compared with 22 percent of black women and 13 percent of Hispanic women; just under 30 percent of white men earned a bachelor's degree compared with 11–12 percent of black and Hispanic men.
2. Sixty-eight percent of students from families in the top income quartile with at least one parent having received a college degree earned a bachelor's degree by age 26 compared with just 9 percent of those from families in the bottom income quartile with neither parent having received a college degree.

Why do these pronounced disparities (and others not highlighted here) matter so much? First, the deeply rooted differences in academic achievement that are associated with race and ethnicity, when considered alongside demographic trends, have major adverse implications for the country's overall level of educational attainment in the future. The most consequential demographic trend relates to Hispanic students. Between 2004–05 and 2014–15, the nation's public schools are projected to produce nearly 197,000 fewer white non-Hispanic high school graduates (a decline of 11 percent); over this same period, the public high schools will produce almost 207,000 more Hispanic graduates (an increase of 54 percent). If current differences in college graduation rates by race/ethnicity persist, this shift alone implies that there will be a decrease of roughly 5 percent in the nation's overall educational attainment rate (and the drop would be greater were it not for the partially offsetting effect of a projected increase in Asian high school graduates, who have an above-average completion rate).[29]

In August 2008, the U.S. Census Bureau projected that by 2042, Americans who identify themselves as Hispanic, black, Asian, American Indian,

Native Hawaiian, and Pacific Islander will together outnumber non-Hispanic whites. Just four years earlier, officials had projected that this shift would occur in 2050. The *New York Times* reports: "For the first time, both the number and the proportion of non-Hispanic whites, who now account for 66 percent of the population, will decline, starting around 2030. By 2050, their share will dip to 46 percent."[30]

The conclusion is simple: a failure to reduce current disparities in rates of educational attainment by race/ethnicity is bound to exacerbate the problem of a sluggish, at best, rate of increase in human capital formation. It will not do to concentrate efforts on improving outcomes of college-bound upper-class white students, who already have a much higher rate of educational attainment than do other students—if for no other reason than that there are not going to be enough of them.

Second, disparities in educational attainment lead to greater inequalities of all kinds, which in turn have multiple long-term effects. Consistent with the tenor of the findings of Goldin and Katz cited earlier, the Department of Education's 2008 *Condition of Education* report tells us that young adults with bachelor's degrees earned 28 percent more in 2006 than those with associate's degrees and 50 percent more than those with just high school diplomas.[31] In recent years there have been numerous articles in the popular press citing dramatic differences in rates of increase in income between those at the top of the income distribution and everyone else. According to a 2004 Congressional Budget Office study, those in the top quintile were making 63 percent more than in 1979, after adjusting for inflation; comparable increases were 2 percent (bottom quintile), 11 percent (next quintile), 13 percent (middle quintile), and 23 percent (fourth quintile). In 1979, the top 1 percent received 9 percent of total income; in 2004, they received 16 percent. In commenting on these data, Roger Lowenstein emphasizes the strong link with educational attainment and describes the failure of rates of educational attainment to rise in the face of high returns as a "conundrum."[32]

The consequences of failing to deal with these growing inequalities can be profound. As one commentator put it: "There is little question that it is bad for one's health to be poor." More generally, "research indicates that high inequality reverberates through societies on multiple levels, correlating with, if not causing, more crime, less happiness, poorer mental and physical health, less racial harmony, and less civic and political participation." There is evidence "that living in a society with wide disparities—in health, in wealth, in education—is worse for *all* the society's members." Apparently, "relative deprivation" is an important phenomenon, and there is evidence that levels of stress throughout a society tend to be a function of the degree of inequality.[33]

Third, as the arguments in the University of Michigan affirmative action case demonstrate,[34] there is educational value to the presence in class-

rooms and on campuses of a diverse student population, with diversity measured along many dimensions (race/ethnicity, gender, SES, geography).

Fourth, equity and fairness concerns are, to our way of thinking, compelling. The long-term health of our country depends on the existence
of social mobility and a widely shared confidence that students from
racial minorities and poor families have a real opportunity to move
ahead. The increasing inequalities in income and wealth that are so
much in the news these days highlight the importance of ensuring that
educational opportunities close rather than widen disparities in access
to the most powerful as well as the most highly remunerated positions
in society. In the Michigan affirmative action case, Justice Sandra Day
O'Connor broke new ground when she moved beyond the diversity defense of affirmative action to opine that "the diffusion of knowledge and
opportunity . . . must be accessible to all individuals regardless of race or
ethnicity. . . . Effective participation by members of all racial and ethnic
groups in the civic life of our Nation is essential if the dream of one Nation, indivisible, is to be realized."[35]

THE PUBLIC UNIVERSITIES IN OUR STUDY:
THEIR SALIENT CHARACTERISTICS AND "LOCATION"
WITHIN AMERICAN HIGHER EDUCATION

It is against this sobering backdrop—in which present-day realities contrast
so sharply with deeply held aspirations—that we now describe the main institutional "actors" in the story that we are about to tell. As important as the
private sector of higher education is in America,[36] the struggle to improve
educational attainment across the board and to reduce the marked disparities in outcomes that are so troubling will take place mainly within the
public universities. In the vernacular, that is "where the action is" (or at least
most of it). Approximately two-thirds of all full-time students pursuing
bachelor's degrees at four-year colleges and universities attend public universities. As a group, public universities are, of course, subsidized by the
states in which they are located, charge lower tuition to in-state than to out-
of-state students, and enroll undergraduate students who are residents of the
states in which the universities are located (about 80 percent, on average). Most state systems are stratified and include a wide range of public
institutions—both research-intensive public universities (with extensive
Ph.D. programs and professional schools in fields such as law, business, and
medicine) and "comprehensive" colleges and universities that place more
emphasis on undergraduate and master's-level programs.

In pursuing our strategy of focusing on the public sector in general, we
first gathered data on the approximately 125,000 members of the 1999
entering cohort at 21 prestigious research-intensive flagship universities

(listed in Table 1.1).[37] These universities are all members of the Association of American Universities and are widely regarded as leaders in American higher education. They were chosen on the basis of a non-scientific but carefully considered effort to achieve both geographic diversity (the set of institutions being studied includes flagship universities from the West Coast, the Midwest, the South, and the Northeast), and a mix of other characteristics, including differences in racial composition and in degree of selectivity, as approximated by the average SAT/ACT score of enrolled students.[38]

We then added data on the '99 entering cohorts at essentially all public universities in the four state systems of Maryland, North Carolina, Ohio, and Virginia (these 47 additional state system public universities are listed in Table 1.2 and described in more detail in Appendix Table 1.2).[39] The two main differences between the flagships and the state system universities—apart from the much greater geographic dispersion of the flagships, which reflects the different ways in which the two sets of universities were chosen—are in average entering enrollment and selectivity. The average flagship in our study enrolled slightly more than 4,100 first-time full-time freshmen in 1999 as compared with a median enrollment of just 1,400 at the 47 state system universities. The median average SAT/ACT score of the entering freshmen in the flagships was 170 points higher than the median average in the 47 state system universities.

As is evident from Tables 1.1 and 1.2, we divided the universities in our two databases into selectivity clusters based on the average SAT/ACT scores of their entering classes; we refer to these clusters as SEL I, SEL II, and SEL III in the case of the flagships and as SEL A and SEL B in the case of the state systems. Use of a selectivity categorization is not meant to imply that we endorse "the rankings game," which we regard as foolish and hurtful to students trying to find the best fit between their capabilities and interests and the characteristics of institutions to which they choose to apply. There is no denying, however, that there are pronounced differences in outcomes, such as graduation rates, across selectivity clusters. Failure to acknowledge these differences would muddy the analysis of many important questions, such as the effects on outcomes of high school characteristics and differences in the predictive power of SAT/ACT scores and high school GPA. The use of selectivity clusters also allows us to study, on something approaching an other-things-equal basis, the strong relationship between institutional selectivity per se and outcomes such as graduation rates and time-to-degree. Near the end of this chapter we will present additional information on trends in selectivity among the flagships and will also comment more generally on the characteristics of these important universities.

As we now seek to "locate" our universities within the universe of four-year institutions, the first point to note is that the 68 public universities in our study (21 flagships plus other state system universities, including his-

TABLE 1.1
Flagship Universities by Selectivity Cluster

SEL I
University of California–Berkeley
University of California–Los Angeles (UCLA)
University of Maryland–College Park
University of Michigan
University of North Carolina–Chapel Hill
University of Virginia

SEL II
Pennsylvania State University
Rutgers, The State University of New Jersey
University of Florida
University of Illinois at Urbana-Champaign
University of Texas–Austin
University of Washington
University of Wisconsin–Madison

SEL III
Iowa State University
Ohio State University
Purdue University
Stony Brook University
University of Iowa
University of Minnesota–Twin Cities
University of Nebraska–Lincoln
University of Oregon

torically black colleges and universities, or HBCUs) educate a far from trivial share of all students at four-year colleges and universities in this country. Full-time freshmen at these universities make up almost a quarter of full-time freshmen at all four-year public universities (our estimate is 23 percent) and roughly 15 percent of full-time freshmen at all public and private four-year colleges and universities. Of course, these percentages drop appreciably if we choose as a reference point students attending all two-year or four-year colleges: the 15 percent figure falls to about 10 percent.

A next key question is how the characteristics of the public universities that we study compare with the characteristics of the entire set of public and private universities that make up the four-year sector of American higher education. Table 1.3 provides a basis for answering this question. In this table we show summary data for our 21 flagships and the 28 state system SEL Bs and comparable summary data for all four-year public universities and all four-year private colleges and universities.[40] We exclude the 8 state system SEL As shown in Table 1.2 because they are simi-

TABLE 1.2
State System Universities by Selectivity Cluster or HBCU Status

Maryland	**Ohio**
SEL A	*SEL A*
University of Maryland–Baltimore County	Miami University
SEL B	*SEL B*
Frostburg State University	Bowling Green State University
Salisbury University	Cleveland State University
Towson University	Kent State University
	Ohio University
HBCU	Shawnee State University
Bowie State University	University of Akron
Coppin State University	University of Cincinnati
University of Maryland–Eastern Shore	University of Toledo
	Wright State University
North Carolina	Youngstown State University
SEL A	
North Carolina State University	*HBCU*
University of North Carolina–Asheville	Central State University
SEL B	**Virginia**
Appalachian State University	*SEL A*
University of North Carolina–Charlotte	College of William and Mary
University of North Carolina–Greensboro	James Madison University
University of North Carolina–Pembroke	University of Mary Washington
University of North Carolina–Wilmington	Virginia Tech
East Carolina University	
Western Carolina University	*SEL B*
	Christopher Newport University
HBCU	George Mason University
Elizabeth City State University	Longwood University
Fayetteville State University	Old Dominion University
North Carolina A&T University	Radford University
North Carolina Central University	University of Virginia's College at Wise
Winston–Salem State University	Virginia Commonwealth University
	Virginia Military Institute
	HBCU
	Norfolk State University
	Virginia State University

lar in so many respects to the flagships, and we also exclude the 11 state system HBCUs because they have few national counterparts. (In the chapters that follow, we describe the characteristics of these HBCUs within the context of their respective state systems.)

These comparisons are revealing in many ways. We see, first of all, that the flagships differ in almost all respects from both the state system SEL

Bs and all public and private four-year institutions. As we would have expected, the flagships have much larger undergraduate enrollments, higher SAT/ACT scores, lower admit rates, and higher average graduation rates. They also have more diverse student bodies (with white non-Hispanic students comprising only about three quarters of their student bodies), which we think results primarily from the fact that a number of the flagships are in heavily urban areas and in states such as California, with large Asian and Hispanic populations. (Appendix Tables 1.1 and 1.2 provide much more detailed data on the ethnic and racial compositions of the student bodies of the individual universities in our study.)

The more interesting comparisons are between our state system SEL Bs and the rest of the four-year colleges and universities in America. Using median first-year enrollment as one metric, we find that the SEL Bs are, on average, roughly 80 percent larger than the typical public university and almost seven times larger than the typical private college or university—a sector that includes many very small institutions. (To provide some indication of the dispersion around the medians, in Table 1.3 we also report interquartile ranges; the main lesson the ranges teach us is that there is considerably more variation among the private colleges and universities than among the public institutions and that, as one would expect, there is more variation among all four-year public institutions than there is among our state system SEL Bs.)

Much more striking than differences in median enrollment, and perhaps more surprising, is that the SEL Bs are very much like both all public and all private four-year colleges and universities in terms of selectivity. The average SAT/ACT scores and average admit rates (both measured as medians) are very, very similar across these sets of institutions—the average SAT/ACT scores differ by no more than 2 or 3 percent; the SEL Bs admit 77 percent of their applicants, whereas all publics admit 75 percent and all private institutions admit 78 percent. In racial diversity, too, the differences between the SEL Bs and the larger sets of universities are minimal. As one would expect, the SEL Bs and all four-year publics enroll more in-state students than do the private institutions. Finally, the average six-year graduation rate at the SEL Bs (51 percent) is reasonably close to the average for all publics (45 percent) and all private institutions (55 percent). The general conclusion we draw from these data is that, in terms of selectivity, diversity, and graduation rates, the state system SEL Bs in our study are tolerably representative of American higher education.

So, although we do not want to claim too much for the "representativeness" of the results that we report in this book (which certainly do not reflect anything purporting to be a "scientific" sampling effort), we are reassured to find that our population is both consequential in size and—putting the flagships off to one side—surprisingly similar in key characteristics to the rest of American higher education. The SEL B compar-

TABLE 1.3
"Location" of the Public Universities in Our Study within
American Higher Education

	Our Flagships	Our State System SEL Bs	All Four-Year Public Universities	All Four-Year Private Universities
Number of Institutions	21	28	540	1,129
Total Full-Time Freshman Enrollment	94,316	51,736	749,273	392,331
Median Full-Time Freshman Enrollment	4,131 (3,619–5,291)	1,922 (897–2,555)	1,059 (539–2,035)	280 (145–486)
Median SAT/ACT[a]	1195 (1125–1240)	1030 (975–1058)	1018 (970–1090)	1065 (990–1140)
Median Admit Rate (Percent)	64 (54–74)	77 (71–88)	75 (64–85)	78 (68–85)
Median Percentage White	76 (64–81)	83 (77–89)	80 (62–89)	83 (68–91)
Median Percentage In-State	79 (70–90)	90 (86–95)	90 (86–96)	63 (40–82)
Median Six-Year Graduation Rate (Percent)	77 (66–84)	51 (45–61)	45 (35–56)	55 (41–68)

Source: IPEDS (Integrated Postsecondary Education Data System) and College Board Annual Survey of Colleges.

Notes: For full-time freshman enrollment, average SAT/ACT scores, admit rates, percentage of white students, percentage of in-state students, and six-year graduation rates we present interquartile ranges as well as medians (with the figures at the 25th and 75th percentiles shown below the medians).

[a]Median of the average SAT/ACT score for each institution.

isons also reinforce our sense that we were wise to include the four state systems in our study as a complement to the flagships.

THE FLAGSHIPS: TRENDS IN SELECTIVITY AND OTHER CHARACTERISTICS

In contrast to the SEL Bs, the flagships are far from "representative"; the students at these prestigious universities are, by any measure, a special group. They have had strong pre-collegiate preparation, and they enjoy access to educational resources far beyond what can be offered by many other colleges and universities, public and private. For both of these reasons, it is hardly surprising that graduation rates at the flagships are appreciably higher than the rates among students attending all four-year colleges and universities.

As many commentators have noted (see the discussion in Appendix A), the flagship universities have become much more selective over time. At three highly selective universities for which we have been able to assemble consistent data for the years 1974–2006—the University of California–Los Angeles (UCLA), the University of North Carolina (UNC)–Chapel Hill, and the University of Virginia—the fraction of entering students with A or A+ high school grades has risen from roughly 55 percent to about 90 percent over this 35-year period (Figure 1.4). At three somewhat less selective universities (Iowa State and Ohio State Universities and Virginia Tech), the fraction of entering students with A or A+ grades has risen at least as rapidly—from just over 20 percent to roughly 60 percent—at the same time that the fraction with high school grades in the C+ or lower range has fallen from just over 10 percent to nearly zero (Figure 1.5).[41] In Chapter 12 we comment on the policy implications of this pronounced increase in selectivity.

There have been accompanying changes in the SES of students attending these universities as reflected, for example, in the highest level of education obtained by mothers of entering freshmen. In 1972, at the three less selective universities listed in the previous paragraph, more

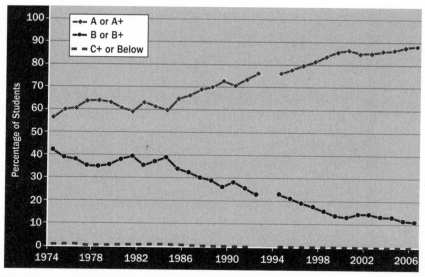

Figure 1.4. Average High School Grade Distribution of Incoming Freshmen at Highly Selective Universities

Source: Higher Education Research Institute (HERI) Freshman Survey.

Note: The universities included are UCLA, UNC–Chapel Hill, and the University of Virginia. These trends were obtained by taking an average of the grades at the three schools. Blanks represent missing data for at least one of the constituent universities for the corresponding year.

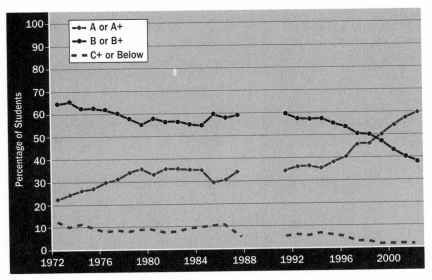

Figure 1.5. Average High School Grade Distribution of Incoming Freshmen at Less Selective Universities

Source: HERI Freshman Survey.

Note: The universities included are Iowa State and Ohio State Universities and Virginia Tech. These trends were obtained by taking an average of the grades at the three schools. Blanks represent missing data for at least one of the constituent universities for the corresponding year.

than 40 percent of these mothers had only a high school degree; by 2002 this percentage had fallen to 20 percent, and by then almost an equal number had a graduate degree. Of course, educational attainment of women has risen dramatically across the board, but not at this rate. There is also evidence that average family income has gone up markedly, much faster than the national average. Today more than 40 percent of the undergraduates at these universities come from families in the top quartile of the income distribution.[42]

These widely recognized trends—both in the degree of selectivity and in the share of students who come from privileged backgrounds—have provoked much debate as to whether these institutions are becoming too "privatized" and are losing their traditional character, what some think of as their role as "people's universities." It is not for us to pronounce on this issue—which is in fact much more complicated than it is sometimes thought to be—but Eugene Tobin's analysis of the evolution of the flagships in Appendix A reminds us of several salient points:

- The flagships are important to American higher education, and to America, for many reasons beyond the education they provide to talented undergraduates. They are major research universities that also have many of the country's leading graduate and professional programs. In addition, they contribute in many ways to the states in which they are located. There are natural—inevitable—tensions between the varied missions of these universities at the same time that they complement each other in many ways. One reason these universities are more selective than ever before is that many of the country's most promising undergraduates want to study in a university that has excellent faculty, a commitment to scholarship, and graduate education that is both important in its own right and necessary to recruit and hold outstanding faculty.

- As enrollment pressures have mounted, along with pressures to excel in research and graduate education, it is natural that many states have opted for greater specialization of function in their overall systems of higher education. The California Master Plan (discussed at length in Appendix A) is a good example of how it is possible to stratify systems of higher education—but the actual experience in California is a good warning that the results obtained (in terms, for instance, of the overall number of bachelor's degrees conferred) do not always match idealized notions of how carefully structured systems of higher education will in fact perform.

- The greater selectivity that we observe today is the result in large part of demographic trends, not conscious policy decisions. The number of prospective students with strong academic credentials has increased faster than places at the flagships, and the result is an entirely predictable increase in the competition for these places. Because family background correlates with academic preparation, the increasing concentration at these universities of students from privileged backgrounds is hardly surprising. But we should also recognize that student bodies at the flagships were never as "representative" of the populations of their states as some would have us believe. In earlier days, large fractions of those eligible to attend leading public universities came, as they do now, from the professional and upper-income families that saw to it that their children had the pre-collegiate preparation necessary to succeed at these universities.

- Finally, it is important to resist the temptation to imagine that there was a "golden age" in which students from every background were taught personally and brilliantly at major flagship universities as a matter of course. One of the most telling vignettes in the account of the evolution of the flagships in Appendix A is the complaint by undergraduates attending universities roughly 100 years ago, in the early part of the 20th century, that they were taught in large lecture courses and "left adrift unaided . . . in an extremely impersonal environment." The more things change, the more they stay the same! And today, resource constraints at even the most prestigious flagships can prevent undergraduates from attending the courses they really want to attend, never mind having direct access to tenured faculty members; in these respects small, highly selective liberal arts colleges have an advantage, which is one reason that they have such high graduation rates.

These observations are intended only to set the stage for the discussion of educational attainment that is to follow by suggesting that in analyzing outcomes of today's undergraduates attending flagship universities it is necessary to have in mind the range of functions these universities are meant to perform and the sometimes conflicting pressures that beat upon them.

We want to end this first chapter by reiterating that the purpose of the research reported in this book is not only to improve our understanding of patterns and relationships but also—as a high priority—to search for clues about ways to make America's colleges and universities more successful in moving entering students on to graduation. Regrettably, if not surprisingly, our studies have not led to the discovery of any simple "quick fixes" or "magic bullets." Many of the patterns we see are remarkably consistent across institutions and settings, and many of them result, we believe, from deep-seated features of American society that will not easily yield to efforts to bring about change. Much patience will be required.

Nevertheless, our work has helped us to identify important steps that colleges and universities, state governments, and the federal government can take to improve college outcomes, especially for disadvantaged students. We also believe that focusing sharply on levels of achievement and success in college may, in and of itself, encourage universities and policy makers to find new ways to make things better. As recent work in the hospital industry shows, simply directing attention to an entrenched problem like hospital-borne infections can stimulate remedial actions at the local level. Lasting improvements will surely require patience (reasonably long time horizons), determination, and willingness to be guided by evidence—as well as the capacity to harvest the low-hanging fruit as promptly as possible. But the goal of helping more Americans from all backgrounds complete college, in a timely way, is well worth the effort that will be required.

CHAPTER 2

Bachelor's Degree Attainment on a National Level

IN THIS CHAPTER we provide a national framework for the far more detailed analysis of bachelor's degree completion in public universities that
is the core of this part of our book. The special characteristics of the flagship universities that we study in such detail set them off in many ways
from higher education in the United States viewed more broadly: they
are much more selective, they enroll more students from privileged backgrounds, and they have resources far beyond what many other colleges
and universities, public and private, can claim. Thus, we would expect
them to have higher graduation rates than is common in American
higher education (as they do). The public universities in the four state
systems that we also study are more typical and thus complement the picture of public higher education presented by our analysis of the flagships.
It is desirable, nonetheless, to start out with a still more inclusive examination of patterns of bachelor's degree attainment at American colleges
and universities so that the results presented in later chapters can be seen
in their proper context. And it is to that task that we turn now.

Data from the nationally representative National Education Longitudinal Study (NELS) of the high school class of 1992[1] tell us that roughly
82 percent of students who had been in the eighth grade in 1988 graduated from high school (excluding those who received a general equivalency diploma, or GED).[2] Of these high school graduates, 58 percent enrolled at a four-year college, and 59 percent of those who started college
earned bachelor's degrees by age 26 (Figure 2.1).[3] The overall bachelor's
degree attainment rate (percentage of all eighth graders who earned a
bachelor's degree), therefore, was 28 percent—a rate that appears to be
slightly below that reported for 25- to 34-year-olds in the United States in
international comparisons and roughly comparable to that of Australia,
Canada, Finland, Iceland, Poland, and the United Kingdom.[4]

DEGREE COMPLETION AND SOCIOECONOMIC STATUS

As important as these overall measures of educational attainment are, it
is just as important to recognize the strong relationship between socioeconomic status (SES) and bachelor's degree attainment. Figure 2.2 shows
how this association relates to both family income and parental educa-

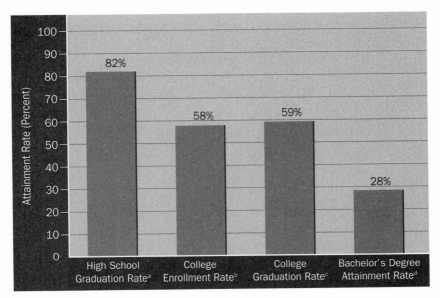

Figure 2.1. Educational Attainment of NELS Students
Source: NELS 1988/2000.
[a] Percentage of entire group who graduated high school by age 20.
[b] Percentage of high school graduates who enrolled in a four-year college by age 26.
[c] Percentage of college matriculants who graduated by age 26.
[d] Percentage of entire group who received a bachelor's degree by age 26.

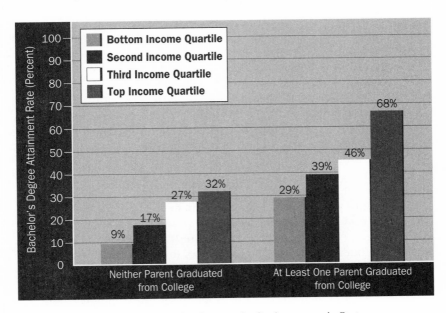

Figure 2.2. Bachelor's Degree Attainment by Socioeconomic Status
Source: NELS 1988/2000.

tion, with attainment rates ranging from 9 percent in the least advantaged group to 68 percent in the most advantaged group.[5] Note that the attainment rate of students in the richest income group whose parents never graduated from college (32 percent) is slightly higher than that of students in the poorest income group who had at least one parent who earned a bachelor's degree (29 percent).

These stark disparities in attainment are the result of similar patterns at each stage of the gradient from high school diploma to bachelor's degree. Figures 2.3a and 2.3b show consistent patterns when we examine educational outcomes in relation first to family income and then to parental education.[6] Compared to students from families in the bottom income quartile, top-income students have high school graduation rates that are 23 percentage points higher, college enrollment rates that are 38 points higher, and college graduation rates that are 32 points higher. The differences in outcomes between the children of the most and least educated parents are equally striking: 17 percentage points in high school graduation rates, 46 points in college enrollment rates, and 33 points in college graduation rates. The compounded effect of these gaps forms the pattern of overall bachelor's degree attainment shown in Figure 2.2 and in the rightmost sections of Figures 2.3a and 2.3b. Students from the top of the family income and parental education distributions were nearly *five times* more likely to earn a bachelor's degree than students from the bottom of these distributions.

Of particular interest to us are the disparities in college graduation rates (among those who started college) by SES. Even among students who matriculate at four-year institutions, low-SES students are substantially less likely than high-SES students to earn a bachelor's degree by age 26. Figure 2.4a shows these statistics broken down by both family income and parents' education.[7] Low-SES students also take additional time to complete their studies. Figure 2.4b shows four-year (and overall) college graduation rates for students who enrolled in a four-year college or university immediately after graduating from high school in 1992, a group with higher overall completion rates than the broader group of students included in Figure 2.4a.[8] These data show that high-SES students are more likely not only to graduate but to graduate more quickly. For example, only 19 percent of the least advantaged group graduated within four years compared to 46 percent of the most advantaged group. Additionally, among first-generation college students in every income quartile, more students graduated in more than four years than in four years or less.

In one sense, narrowing the gap in college completion rates (among those who start college) should be a less daunting challenge than addressing the pervasive achievement gaps in elementary and secondary schools. After all, the students involved have already made it to college

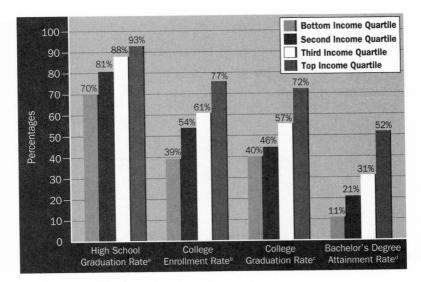

Figure 2.3a. Educational Attainment by Family Income
Source: NELS 1988/2000.
[a] Percentage of entire group who graduated high school by age 20.
[b] Percentage of high school graduates who enrolled in a four-year college by age 26.
[c] Percentage of college matriculants who graduated by age 26.
[d] Percentage of entire group who received a bachelor's degree by age 26.

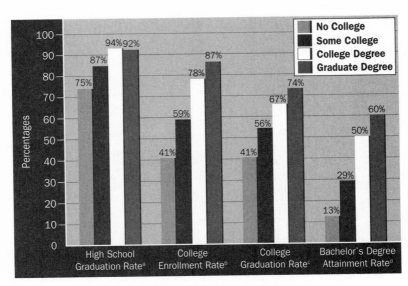

Figure 2.3b. Educational Attainment by Parental Education
Source: NELS 1988/2000.
[a] Percentage of entire group who graduated high school by age 20.
[b] Percentage of high school graduates who enrolled in a four-year college by age 26.
[c] Percentage of college matriculants who graduated by age 26.
[d] Percentage of entire group who received a bachelor's degree by age 26.

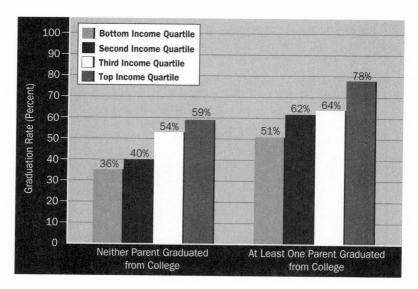

Figure 2.4a. College Graduation Rates by Socioeconomic Status
Source: NELS 1988/2000.
Note: "Graduation rate" is the percentage of students who enrolled at a four-year college who graduated by age 26.

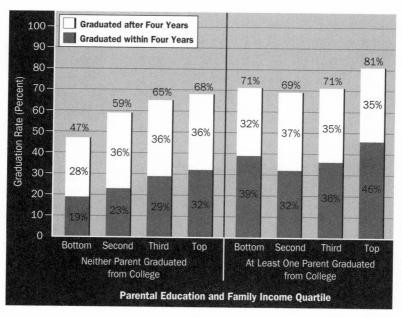

Figure 2.4b. College Graduation Rates and Time-to-Degree by Socioeconomic Status
Source: NELS 1988/2000.
Note: "Graduation rate" is calculated based on 1992 high school graduates who enrolled in a four-year school immediately after graduating.

despite whatever adversity they may have faced earlier. However, the low-SES students who enroll are less well prepared than their high-SES counterparts, as shown by their 12th-grade reading and math test scores.[9] The average score of students from families in the top income quartile was the 73rd percentile compared to the 52nd percentile for students from bottom-quartile families. Children of parents with at least a college degree scored at the 73rd percentile on average; those whose parents did not graduate from college had an average score at the 59th percentile.[10]

Differences in pre-college preparation clearly play a sizable role in explaining differences in college outcomes by SES, but they do not explain all, or even most, of the graduation rate gap. When we control for students' test scores in reading and math, the difference in completion rates between the top and bottom income quartiles falls from 32 to 24 percentage points, and the gap between first-generation and non-first-generation college-goers falls from 22 to 18 points. Thus, *substantial gaps in graduation rates remain after controlling for pre-college test scores.*

The disparities in educational attainment by SES observed in these data are indeed striking, but the surprisingly low attainment rates of high-SES students also deserve emphasis.[11] Figure 2.2 shows an overall bachelor's degree attainment rate of about 68 percent for the highest socio-economic group. Although this rate is high relative to the attainment rates of the other groups, it seems low to us in an absolute sense. Common sense suggests that appreciably more than two-thirds of students from the most advantaged families in the country should be expected to earn bachelor's degrees. The educational attainment rate of high-SES students is certainly less troubling than that of low-SES students from an equity standpoint, but both are important in terms of the stock of human capital in the country and the efficiency with which educational resources are used. This last proposition is especially relevant in the case of public universities, where both high- and low-SES college dropouts consume substantial amounts of public resources. Low-SES students surely consume more public resources in the form of financial aid, but both groups benefit from the large tuition subsidies available to all in-state students at public universities.

Table 2.1 depicts the educational attainment patterns of two top "slices" of the income distribution: students from families with annual incomes (in 2008 dollars) between $118,295 and $157,726 ("high-income") and students from families with incomes in excess of $157,726 ("very high-income").[12] Even the students from families with very high incomes attain bachelor's degrees at a rate of little more than 80 percent, with most of the drop-off occurring during college (nearly 100 percent of these students started college, but only 85 percent of college matriculants in this income group earned a bachelor's degree by age 26). Table 2.1 shows that academic preparation, although clearly an explanatory factor in the aca-

TABLE 2.1
Educational Attainment and Average 12th-Grade Standardized
Test Scores of Upper-Income Groups

	High-Income	Very High-Income
Percentage of 1992 Cohort Who Graduated from High School by 1994	98.2	97.8
Percentage of High School Graduates Who Enrolled in Four-Year Institutions by 2000	88.8	97.4
Percentage of Four-Year College Matriculants Who Received a Bachelor's Degree by 2000	81.3	85.4
Percentage of Cohort Who Received a Bachelor's Degree by 2000	70.7	81.4

	Mean Test Score (Percentile)	Test Score Standard Deviation
All Students	51.6	28.6
All Bachelor's Degree Recipients	72.4	21.7
High-Income, Non–Bachelor's Degree Recipients	56.2	24.0
Very High-Income, Non–Bachelor's Degree Recipients	68.5	27.3

Source: Data from the National Education Longitudinal Study of 1988 (NELS).

Note: "High-income" families have annual incomes of between $118,295 and $157,726; "very high-income" families have annual incomes in excess of $157,726 (all in 2008 dollars). First-generation college students (i.e., neither parent earned a bachelor's degree) are excluded.

demic histories of these students, is certainly not the only one. Although students from wealthy families who did not receive bachelor's degrees had pre-college standardized test scores that were below the mean score of degree recipients, the distribution of their test scores suggests that a considerable number of them were academically capable of earning a degree. The fact that almost all of these students started college but only 80–85 percent finished clearly demonstrates how important it is to understand what happens in college—to learn what explains the college completion patterns of students from high- as well as low-SES backgrounds.

TRENDS

For the U.S. population as a whole, college graduation rates have changed little in the past three decades. As we showed earlier (Figure 1.2), between

1968 and 2007 bachelor's degree attainment increased just enough to keep pace with increases in college enrollment; an important corollary is that time-to-degree has increased substantially, a phenomenon not sufficiently appreciated.[13] A key point is that the relatively modest educational gains that did occur were concentrated among the most advantaged groups. Table 2.2 shows that the most substantial growth (about 8 percentage points) in bachelor's degree attainment between the high school classes of 1972 and 1992 occurred among students in the top income quartile who were not first-generation college students, with virtually all of this growth occurring between 1982 and 1992. More modest growth (4–5 percentage points) occurred among students from families in the top half of the income distribution where neither parent had earned a college degree. The bachelor's degree attainment rate of the other socioeconomic groups remained essentially the same.[14]

Ellwood and Kane calculate *enrollment* rates broken down by family income for the high school classes of 1980–82 (in the High School and Beyond longitudinal study, or HS&B) and 1992 (in the National Education Longitudinal Study, or NELS) and find that the largest increases in enrollment occurred in the top income groups. Table 2.3 shows similar statistics calculated to conform to the conventions of the other figures and tables in this chapter.[15] Table 2.3 demonstrates that the largest increases

TABLE 2.2
Bachelor's Degree Attainment Rates over Time
by Socioeconomic Status (Percent)

		Class of 1972	Class of 1982	Class of 1992
First-Generation	Bottom Income Quartile	12.3	11.1	9.5
	Second Income Quartile	20.2	17.3	17.4
	Third Income Quartile	21.9	21.3	26.9
	Top Income Quartile	27.9	22.1	32.1
Non-First-Generation	Bottom Income Quartile	31.7	31.1	28.9
	Second Income Quartile	38.5	43.8	38.9
	Third Income Quartile	44.2	55.6	46.0
	Top Income Quartile	59.6	60.9	67.7
	Overall Average	25.8	22.3	28.2

Source: National Longitudinal Study of the High School Class of 1972 (NLS), High School and Beyond Study of 1980 Sophomores (HS&B), and the NELS.

Notes: "Attainment rate" is defined as the percentage of the subgroup that completed a bachelor's degree by age 26. First-generation students are those for whom neither parent has a bachelor's degree. Income quartiles are based on discrete survey responses. The percentage in each income quartile (from bottom to top) was as follows: 1972: 26%, 22%, 26%, 25%; 1982: 23%, 28%, 31%, 19%; 1992: 24%, 24%, 20%, 32%.

TABLE 2.3
Four-Year College or University Enrollment Rates over Time
by Family Income (Percent)

	Class of 1982	Class of 1992
Bottom Income Quartile	28.1	28.7
Second Income Quartile	37.1	44.9
Third Income Quartile	46.6	54.0
Top Income Quartile	60.8	73.6
Overall Average	36.7	48.0

Source: HS&B, NELS.

Notes: "Enrollment rate" is defined as the percentage of the subgroup that enrolled in a four-year college or university by age 26.

in college enrollment occurred among students in the top income quartile, with more modest differences in the middle of the distribution and no change in the bottom quartile. Ellwood and Kane argue that the changes in enrollment observed over this 10-year period are the result of

> changes in parental education and the correlation between parental income and parental education. Parental education rose during this period. . . . Simultaneously, the returns to education also rose. As a result, education and income became more highly correlated, with the correlation rising from .3 to nearly .5 in little more than a decade. . . . In effect, parental education, especially college education, increased more for people in the top quartile of income. So students at the top now had a double boost: income and education were more aligned, pushing them to disproportionately higher levels of enrollment.[16]

The same line of argument could reasonably be applied to the changes in graduation rates, given that many of the same factors that drive college enrollment also affect completion. Table 2.4 shows that graduation rates have actually *fallen* among low- and middle-income students at the same time that they have increased among high-income students. Thus, the changes in bachelor's degree attainment between the classes of 1982 and 1992 observed in Table 2.2 are the result of changes in both enrollment and completion rates.[17] Modest increases in enrollment rates for low- and middle-income students were offset by similar decreases in completion rates, resulting in stagnant rates of bachelor's degree attainment. Meanwhile, the attainment rate of high-income students was pushed up by gains in both enrollment and completion—which are themselves rooted, at least in part, in the widely noted increases in inequality in American society.[18]

TABLE 2.4
College Completion Rates over Time by Family Income (Percent)

	Class of 1982	Class of 1992
Bottom Income Quartile	41.6	38.4
Second Income Quartile	54.9	45.2
Third Income Quartile	62.1	56.3
Top Income Quartile	67.4	71.0
Overall Average	57.9	57.3

Source: HS&B, NELS.

Notes: "Completion rate" is defined as the percentage of those who attended a four-year institution who received a bachelor's degree by age 26.

RACE/ETHNICITY AND GENDER

SES is obviously not the only demographic variable in the college enrollment and completion story. Race/ethnicity and gender are also of great interest, and it is instructive to chart the simple relationships evident in the national data between race/ethnicity and gender and college outcomes. At every stage of the progression from high school to college, there are dramatic differences, which are shown in Figure 2.5 for students in the high school class of 1992. As is well known, white students are consistently more successful in both high school and college than are black and Hispanic students.[19] Among black and white students, we see that females of both races outperform males of their race at every stage. Particularly notable are the differences between black males and black females (especially in the case of college graduation rates), which in the NELS data result in an overall bachelor's degree attainment rate of black females that is twice that of black males.[20] Figure 2.5 shows that Hispanic males graduate from high school and enroll in college at slightly higher rates than their female counterparts but that Hispanic females have a higher college graduation rate than Hispanic males. The result of these mixed patterns is that ultimate attainment rates appear to be roughly the same for Hispanic females and males in the NELS data set.

The data collected by the U.S. Census Bureau in the *Current Population Survey (CPS)* make tracking changes over time in educational attainment by race and gender fairly straightforward. Figure 2.6 shows these trends for black and white 25- to 29-year-olds from 1964–2007.[21] The most notable trends are the general increases in attainment over time for both races and genders, although the attainment of white men leveled off in the 1980s while that of white women continued to increase, leading to the greater number of female than male graduates that we observe in

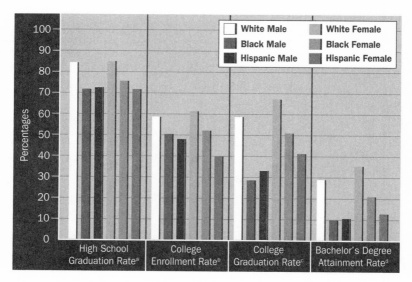

Figure 2.5. Educational Attainment by Race/Ethnicity and Gender
Source: NELS 1988/2000.
[a] Percentage of entire group who graduated high school by age 20.
[b] Percentage of high school graduates who enrolled in a four-year college by age 26.
[c] Percentage of college matriculants who graduated by age 26.
[d] Percentage of entire group who received a bachelor's degree by age 26.

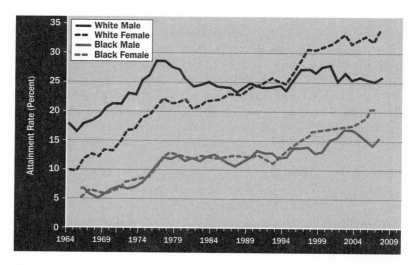

Figure 2.6. Bachelor's Degree Attainment of 25- to 29-Year-Olds by Race and Gender, 1964–2007
Source: CPS; three-year moving average used for blacks.

higher education today. Also worth noting are the far smaller male-female differences among blacks in these *CPS* data than in the NELS data (Figure 2.5). We believe these variations stem from the imprecise nature of statistics based on small cell sizes such as those in the NELS data and from the narrowing of the bachelor's degree gender gap among blacks in the late 1990s.

National data such as those from the NELS survey consistently show large disparities in educational outcomes by SES (defined in terms of both family income and parental education) and by race/ethnicity and gender at every stage from graduating high school to finishing a bachelor's degree. Against this backdrop of national data, we now turn to a detailed examination of college outcomes at the public universities on which we have focused our own research. It is essential to bear in mind that the disparities that we document—among students who have made it to college—are in addition to disparities in high school graduation rates and college enrollment rates. As a result, the findings we present in Chapters 3 and 4 understate the true extent of disparities in educational outcomes because they fail to reflect both the lower high school graduation rates and the lower college enrollment rates that are prevalent among black and Hispanic students, as well as those from low-SES families.

Finishing College at Public Universities

As WE HAVE SEEN, nationally representative data indicate that there are substantial disparities in educational outcomes by socioeconomic status (SES) and race/ethnicity at every stage along the path toward a bachelor's degree: high school graduation, college enrollment, and college completion. The national data demonstrate without question that these disparities are indeed systemic, but the modest size of data sets such as those of the National Education Longitudinal Study, or NELS (12,064 students, of whom 6,529 attended a four-year college at some point) make it difficult to probe the nature and source of these disparities. For example, examining the educational outcomes of certain types of students at certain types of institutions (e.g., black men at selective public universities) is simply impossible with the NELS data; the relevant cell sizes are just too small. The databases we created for this research allow us to examine outcomes in college in far greater detail. Although these databases are not nationally representative in any formal sense, they contain data from a diverse group of 57 four-year public universities, including 21 flagship universities from across the country and four complete state systems of public four-year colleges and universities.[1]

In the next two chapters we examine the college outcomes of 124,522 students who matriculated as first-time, full-time freshmen at these universities in the fall of 1999.[2] We begin by analyzing the single most important college outcome: graduation. Clearly, other post-secondary outcomes, such as academic performance, time-to-degree, and choice of major, are important as well, and we examine them in some detail in the next chapter. But such outcomes generally matter only for students who actually finish college. College dropouts all lack bachelor's degrees, regardless of whether they left with stellar or failing grades or with partially completed coursework toward a degree in English or engineering.

In particular, we focus on six-year graduation rates from the institution where the student initially matriculated.[3] Although it may be desirable for most students to finish their studies in four years, many take more time to do so. At the flagships, 49 percent of students graduate in four years, 24 percent in five years, and 4 percent in six years. The corresponding statistics for the state systems are 38 percent, 38 percent, and 4 percent. Very few bachelor's degree recipients complete their studies at their original institution more than six years after initially matriculating. For example, data from the Ohio system indicate that only 2.7 percent of students who entered college in 1999 graduated between fall 2005 and spring 2007. Put another way, among the first-time, full-time students in the Ohio system who graduated by the end of spring 2007, 95 percent had done so by the end of summer 2005.

As we explained in Chapter 1, we divided the universities in our study into selectivity clusters (SELs) based on the average SAT/ACT score of their 1999 entering classes. Figure 3.1a shows that six-year graduation rates vary markedly and consistently by selectivity, ranging from 86 percent at the most selective flagships (SEL Is) to 51 percent at the least selective universities in the four state systems (SEL Bs). Figure 3.1b indicates that pronounced differences in graduation rates between SEL As and SEL Bs are found in each of the four state systems.[4] These differences are of considerable independent interest, and we consider them in detail in Chapter 10, paying particular attention to the extent to which they reflect selection versus treatment effects. Here we use these clusters in order to determine the extent to which disparities in graduation rates, by SES, race/ethnicity, and gender, vary at different types of universities. A key finding is that disparities in graduation rates, particularly along socioeconomic lines, are amazingly consistent across selectivity clusters.

In this chapter we also examine another question of considerable interest to deans and others concerned with student persistence: the timing of dropouts. To what extent are dropouts concentrated in the first few semesters? Thanks to the extraordinarily detailed data available to us, we are able to track outcomes for sub-groups of students (defined by race/ethnicity and gender and by SES) on a semester-by-semester basis—a luxury not generally available in studies of completion rates.[5]

The cumulative proportion of the entering first-year cohort at the flagships that had withdrawn or transferred to another four-year institution after each semester is shown in Figure 3.2. For example, the pair of points corresponding to semester 2 indicate that, after the second semester (i.e., by the beginning of the third semester), 4.6 percent of students had withdrawn and 3.5 percent had transferred to another four-year institution. (To simplify this analysis, we group together, as "withdrawals" from the four-year sector of higher education, both students who left postsecondary education altogether and the much smaller number who transferred to a two-year institution.) We see that most students who transfer to another four-year institution do so early in their academic careers, with a majority of transfers occurring within the first four semesters. Because this pattern is so predictable and consistent across groups, we do not continue to show transfer-out patterns but rather concentrate on withdrawals.

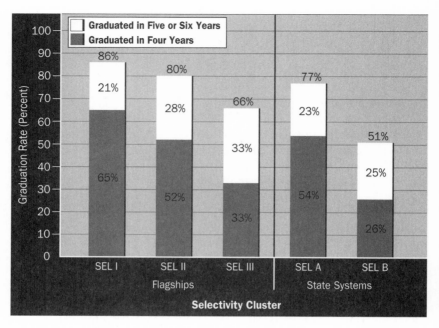

Figure 3.1a. Graduation Rates by Selectivity Cluster, 1999 Entering Cohort
Source: Flagships Database and State Systems Database.

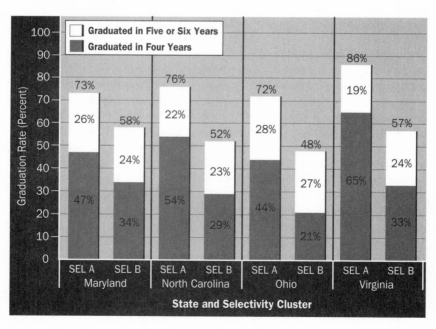

Figure 3.1b. Graduation Rates by State System and Selectivity Cluster, 1999 Entering Cohort
Source: State Systems Database.

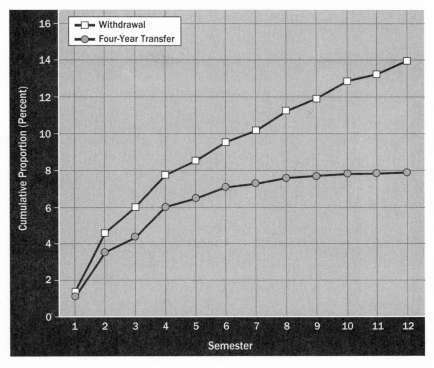

Figure 3.2. Cumulative Withdrawal and Transfer Proportions, 1999 Entering Cohort, Flagships
Source: Flagships Database.

In contrast to transfers, which essentially cease after four semesters or so, withdrawals continue all along the way. There are only modest "spikes" in the number of withdrawals in the second and fourth semesters, and what is striking about Figure 3.2 is how steadily the cumulative withdrawal rate marches upward, semester by semester. In fact, contrary to the claims of those who emphasize the importance of the first few semesters (which are of course highly consequential), *nearly half (44 percent) of all withdrawals occur after the second year.* This important result is a clear reminder that persistence cannot be viewed as simply a function of students' completing their first two years. Similarly, this finding reminds us that although it surely makes sense, as Vincent Tinto notes, to "frontload" some institutional efforts to promote retention, it would be a big mistake to overdo the frontloading.[6]

Withdrawals also occur rather steadily over time at the state system SEL Bs, and the cumulative withdrawal rate at these universities each semester is about twice the rate at the flagships.[7] Figure 3.3 shows the cumulative withdrawal rates for both the state system SEL Bs and the flagships broken down by selectivity cluster. The higher overall withdrawal rates at the less selective institutions are exactly what we would expect given their lower graduation rates, but we also find that withdrawals are concentrated more heavily in the earlier semesters at the less selective universities. For example, both the state system SEL B line and the flagship SEL III line in Figure 3.3 are much steeper than the lines for the SEL I and SEL II flagships over the first four semesters. After that, the lines are largely parallel (i.e., the differences in withdrawal rates do not continue to grow). At the SEL III flagships and the state system SEL Bs, 62 percent of all withdrawals occur within the first two years, compared to only 44 percent at the SEL I flagships and 51 percent at the SEL II flagships. It could be argued that the concentration of attrition in the early years at the less selective universities is a positive outcome in that it reflects decisions about the suitability (or lack thereof) of four-year programs for students before they and their universities have invested so heavily in them.

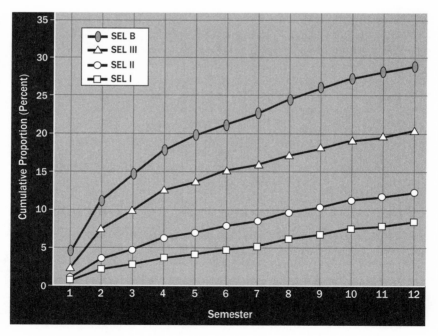

Figure 3.3. Cumulative Withdrawal Proportions by Selectivity Cluster, 1999 Entering Cohort
Source: Flagships Database and State Systems Database.

SOCIOECONOMIC STATUS

At the public universities in our study, we find a strong, highly consistent relationship between a student's socioeconomic background and his or her probability of graduating. Our simplest summary measure of SES divides students into three groups: low-SES students, who come from families in the bottom half of the income distribution in which neither parent had a college degree; high-SES students, who come from families in the top half of the income distribution in which at least one parent had a college degree; and middle-SES students, a grouping that includes those who do not fall into either of the other two categories. We also examine family income and parental education separately.[8]

Figure 3.4 shows the relationship between our combined SES grouping and four-year and six-year graduation rates at the 16 flagship universities and in the three state systems with parental education data available. At the flagships, 83 percent of high-SES students graduate within six years, while only 68 percent of low-SES students do so, a difference of 15 percentage points. The difference in four-year graduation rates is even larger, at 19 points. In the three state systems, high-SES students are 19

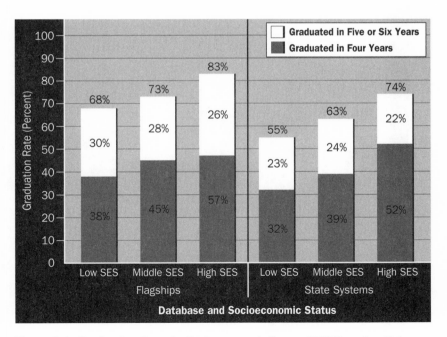

Figure 3.4. Graduation Rates by Socioeconomic Status, 1999 Entering Cohort
Source: Flagships Database and State Systems Database.

percentage points more likely to graduate than are low-SES students (74 percent versus 55 percent).

Figure 3.5 shows similar statistics broken down by parental education. The pattern is similar to the one observed when we examined the combined SES measure in Figure 3.4. The largest gap between adjacent categories is between the "some college" and "college degree" sub-groups. At the flagships, students whose parents obtained a college degree are about 8 percentage points more likely to graduate within six years than those whose parents attended college but never graduated.[9] The difference in four-year graduation rates is 10 points. In contrast, the difference between the "no college" and "some college" sub-groups is small. The pattern in the three state systems is very similar, with a gap between "some college" and "college degree" of 10 points in both six- and four-year graduation rates. We had not anticipated this finding, believing, with many others, that some parental exposure to college would itself affect children's educational attainment. Still, it is not so surprising that students whose parents finished college are themselves more likely to graduate than those whose parents attended college but did not earn a degree. The difference

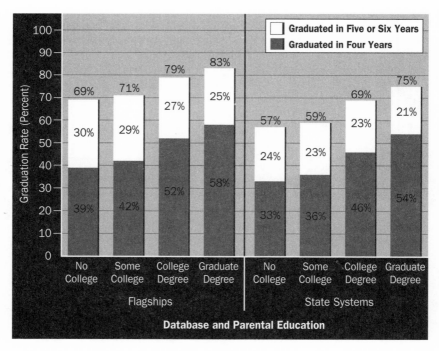

Figure 3.5. Graduation Rates by Parental Education, 1999 Entering Cohort
Source: Flagships Database and State Systems Database.

between the graduation rates of children whose parents hold a college degree and those who earned a graduate degree is modest at the flagships
(4 points) and somewhat larger in the state systems (6 points).

Figure 3.6 presents graduation rates by family income quartile for all
21 flagships and the four state systems (considered together). At the flagships, the gaps between the six-year graduation rates of the bottom and
second quartiles, and between the second and third quartiles, are fairly
modest, at about 3 or 4 percentage points. However, the top quartile has
an appreciably higher graduation rate than the third quartile (a 6-point
difference), which translates into a 13-point difference between the top
and bottom quartiles. Additionally, students from high-income families
graduate more quickly, on average, than students from low-income families. The gap in four-year graduation rates between the top and bottom
income quartiles is 18 percentage points, which is 5 points greater than
the gap in six-year graduation rates. In the four state systems, there is also
basically no difference between the bottom two income quartiles,
whereas the gaps between the second and third and the third and fourth
quartiles are both 7 points. The resulting gap in six-year graduation rates

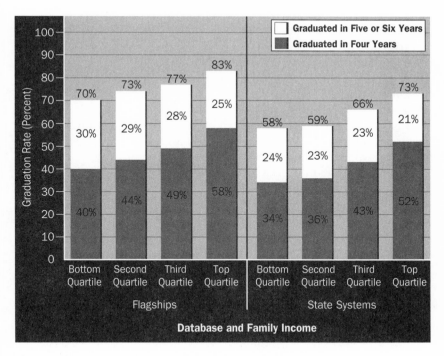

Figure 3.6. Graduation Rates by Family Income, 1999 Entering Cohort
Source: Flagships Database and State Systems Database.

between the bottom and top quartiles in the state systems is 15 points, which is similar to the 13-point gap at the flagships.

Scholars continue to debate whether the association between SES and graduation rates observed in various data sets results from short-term consequences of being poor (e.g., inability to pay for college in the period of enrollment or the need to finance education through loans) or from long-term characteristics that are correlated with both SES and graduation rates (e.g., academic preparation). The natural question to pose is whether there is still a consistent relationship between SES and graduation rates after controlling for academic preparation, other student characteristics such as race/ethnicity and gender, and the university attended. For example, if high-SES students are substantially better prepared for college than low-SES students, the gap in graduation rates between the two groups may shrink or even disappear after these differences are taken into account. Additionally, we want to examine whether parental education and family income each continues to predict graduation rates once the other is held constant.

In order to disentangle the effects of multiple student characteristics on graduation rates, we use a simple multivariate regression analysis that measures the relationships between graduation rates and various student characteristics on an "other-things-equal" basis.[10] Specifically, we include controls for high school GPA, SAT/ACT scores, state residency status, race/ethnicity and gender, and university attended (which ensures that comparisons are made only within universities, not across universities). We then present the differences in six-year graduation rates that remain after differences in these variables are taken into account. Because the results are so similar across selectivity clusters, we present only combined results. Results broken down by database and selectivity cluster are reported in Appendix Tables 3.1a–3.3b.

Figure 3.7 shows differences in six-year graduation rates at the flagships by our combined SES measure.[11] The left-hand panel shows the raw (unadjusted) differences, which are identical to those shown on the left side of Figure 3.4. The right-hand panel then shows the predicted (or adjusted) differences in graduation rates once the various control variables are taken into account. The raw gap of 14 points between high- and low-SES students is reduced by about a quarter, to an adjusted gap of 11 points. These results are remarkably consistent across vastly different types of institutions (Appendix Tables 3.1a and 3.1b). The adjusted graduation rate gap between high- and low-SES students is 9 points at the flagship SEL Is, 12 points at the SEL IIs and IIIs, 11 points at the state system SEL As, and 11–15 points at the SEL Bs.[12] These figures clearly show that differences in the observable background characteristics of the students in our study explain some, but certainly not most, of the SES disparities in graduation rates observed in the raw data.[13]

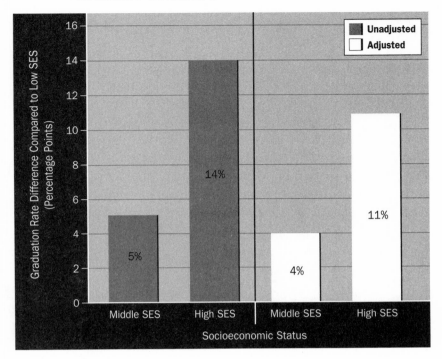

Figure 3.7. Differences in Six-Year Graduation Rates by Socioeconomic Status (Compared to Low SES), 1999 Entering Cohort, Flagships, Unadjusted and Adjusted

Source: Flagships Database.

Note: Adjusted differences control for SAT/ACT scores, high school GPA, state residency status, race/ethnicity, gender, and university attended.

We next examine parental education and family income using the same framework. Because these two measures of SES are correlated (and parental education likely affects graduation rates partly through its effect on family income), we examine them both separately and simultaneously.[14] For example, the middle panel of Figure 3.8 shows the adjusted differences in graduation rates by parental education without controlling for family income, while the rightmost panel adds family income as a control. The relationship between parental education and graduation rates is muted only modestly by controlling for differences in student characteristics; substantial disparities remain. The difference between the "no college" and "graduate degree" groups drops from 14 points in the raw data to an adjusted gap of 9 points. Controlling for family income further reduces this difference by 2 points, but a 7-point gap remains. Additionally, the adjusted results provide further support for the proposition that

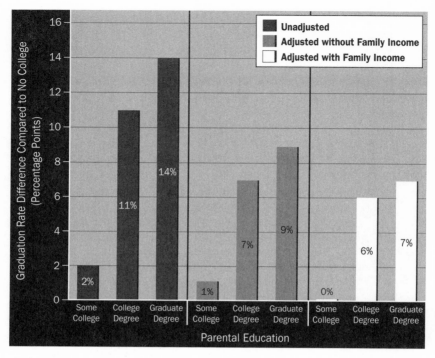

Figure 3.8. Differences in Six-Year Graduation Rates by Parental Education (Compared to No College), 1999 Entering Cohort, Flagships, Unadjusted and Adjusted

Source: Flagships Database.

Note: Adjusted differences control for SAT/ACT scores, high school GPA, state residency status, race/ethnicity, gender, and university attended.

the children of parents with some college experience but no degree have graduation rates essentially identical to those of students whose parents never attended college.

The results for family income, shown in Figure 3.9, are remarkably similar to those for parental education. The adjusted gap between the top and bottom income quartiles is 9 points, and controlling for parental education reduces it by only 3 points—to 6 points. There is basically no difference between the bottom and second quartiles; the graduation rate advantage (both unadjusted and adjusted) is concentrated in the top half of the income distribution. In short, we find that *both parental education and family income are strongly associated with graduation rates even when considered simultaneously and after controlling for related differences in student characteristics, particularly academic preparation.*

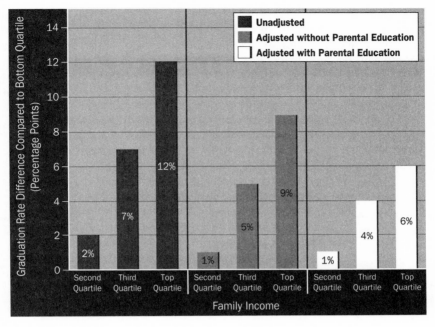

Figure 3.9. Differences in Six-Year Graduation Rates by Family Income (Compared to Bottom Quartile), 1999 Entering Cohort, Flagships, Unadjusted and Adjusted

Source: Flagships Database.

Note: Adjusted differences control for SAT/ACT scores, high school GPA, state residency status, race/ethnicity, gender, and university attended.

Once again, these results do not vary widely across institutional settings. Differences associated with parental education and family income are about as prevalent at the most selective flagship universities as they are at the least selective universities of the four state systems in our study (Appendix Tables 3.2a–3.3b).[15] The fact that these differences appear consistently in essentially every grouping of schools considered here raises the question of whether they also appear at every individual institution. Although many of the schools in the state systems are too small to yield reliable results, we were able to compute adjusted differences in graduation rates at each individual flagship university. At the 16 flagships for which parental education data are available, the adjusted gap between high- and low-SES students ranges from 6 to 17 points at all but one of the schools.[16] The outlier is Stony Brook, where the adjusted gap is a statistically insignificant 2.6 points and where, in the raw data, low-SES students are actually slightly *more* likely to graduate than high-SES students

(62 percent versus 59 percent). We suspect that this unusual pattern has something to do with the special place that Stony Brook holds in the market for higher education in New York in that it competes with many other public and private universities, some of which are highly selective.

These disparities also are quite consistent in every semester; they do not appear to arise disproportionately in any particular semester. Looking at cumulative withdrawal rates by SES, Figure 3.10 demonstrates that the withdrawal rate gap between low- and high-SES students at the flagships initially emerges in the second semester, when an additional 5 percent of low-SES students withdraw compared with only 2 percent of the high-SES group. The semester-by-semester change in the cumulative withdrawal proportion then remains higher for low-SES students than for high-SES students every semester. In short, differences in withdrawal rates by family background do not dissipate; they compound over time to produce a 12-point gap between low-SES and high-SES students by the 12th semester. The general pattern at the state system SEL Bs (not shown) is essentially the same, although the overall withdrawal rates are much higher.[17]

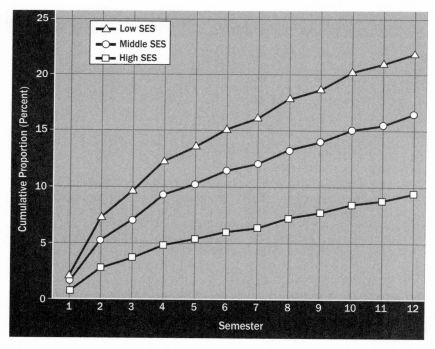

Figure 3.10. Cumulative Withdrawal Proportions per Semester by SES, 1999 Entering Cohort, Flagships
  Source: Flagships Database.

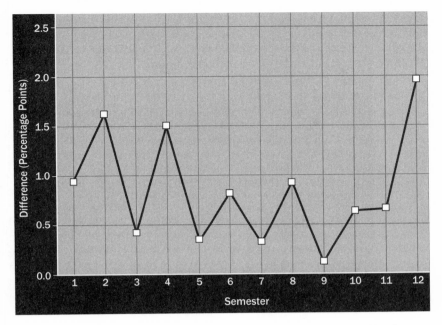

Figure 3.11. Adjusted Withdrawal Differences per Semester (Low SES minus High SES), 1999 Entering Cohort, Flagships

Source: Flagships Database.

Note: Differences control for race/ethnicity, gender, state residency status, SAT/ACT scores, high school GPA, and university attended.

Adjusting for students' academic preparation and demographic characteristics does not alter this finding. We calculated the difference in the probability of dropping out between high- and low-SES students each semester *among students still enrolled that semester,* controlling for race/ethnicity and gender, state residency status, test scores, high school GPA, and university attended.[18] Examining the students still enrolled, low-SES students are consistently more likely to drop out than their high-SES classmates (Figure 3.11). The semester-by-semester differences do not seem particularly large, but they accumulate over time to produce the substantial disparities in six-year graduation rates that we reported earlier. We find this same general pattern of results at the state system SEL Bs (not shown).

The proverbial bottom line is that, with very few exceptions, disparities in educational attainment by SES are pervasive in American public higher education and cannot be explained away by associated differences in academic preparation. Even after accounting for differences in entering credentials, students from lower-income families with less-educated parents are consistently less likely to graduate from college than their classmates from higher-income families with more-educated parents. These differences do not diminish as semesters pass. We now turn to a similar analysis of the relationship between graduation rates and race/ ethnicity and gender.

RACE/ETHNICITY AND GENDER

The fact that educational attainment differs dramatically by race/ ethnicity as well as by gender is well known, and our data produce the expected pattern, with whites and Asians more likely to graduate than blacks and Hispanics and females graduating at higher rates (and much more quickly) than males. However, the more detailed relationships between graduation rates and the intersection of race/ethnicity and gender at these universities are intriguing and deserve closer attention than they sometimes receive. The enormous size of our database allows us to look at race/ethnicity-gender intersections in ways that are impossible with national databases whose cell sizes are too small to permit reliable calculations. In general we focus on outcomes for white and black students, but when we have sufficient data to include Hispanic and Asian students (as is the case for the flagships, but not the state systems), we also present data for these groups.

Differences among the eight race/ethnicity-gender sub-groups at the flagships (shown in Figure 3.12a) can be summarized as follows:[19] Asian females are the most likely to graduate (60 percent do so within four years, 85 percent within six years), and white females perform nearly as well (with a 79 percent six-year graduation rate). The next grouping is perhaps the most surprising: white males, Hispanic females, and black females all have six-year graduation rates between 72 percent and 76 percent. Hispanic and black males have the lowest six-year graduation rates, at 66 percent and 59 percent, respectively. Gender disparities in graduation rates are especially pronounced within the Hispanic and black populations: women are much more likely to earn bachelor's degrees than are men. Additionally, black and Hispanic males take the most time to graduate and are the only sub-groups in which more students graduate in five or six years than in four. Perhaps the single most noteworthy statistic is that only 26 percent of black males attending these leading public universities graduate within four years.

These highly differentiated patterns are remarkably consistent across flagship selectivity clusters, as shown in Figure 3.12b for black and white students only, and in the state systems, as shown in Figure 3.12c. Particularly striking are the low graduation rates for black males at the least

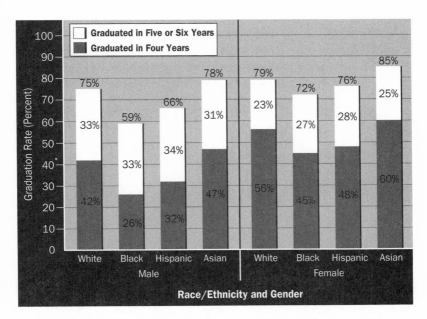

Figure 3.12a. Graduation Rates by Race/Ethnicity and Gender, 1999
Entering Cohort, Flagships
Source: Flagships Database.

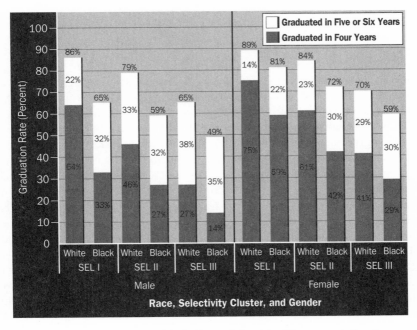

Figure 3.12b. Graduation Rates by Race, Selectivity Cluster, and Gender,
1999 Entering Cohort, Flagships
Source: Flagships Database.

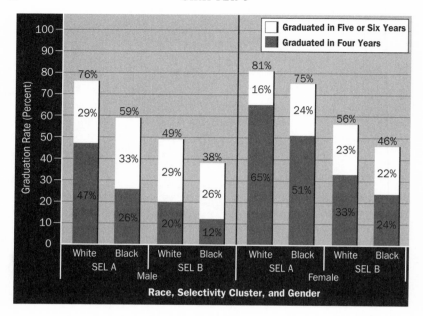

Figure 3.12c. Graduation Rates by Race, Selectivity Cluster, and Gender,
1999 Entering Cohort, State Systems
Source: State Systems Database.

selective (SEL III) flagships, where fewer than half graduate in six years
and only 14 percent graduate within four years, and in the state system
SEL Bs, where 38 percent graduate within six years and 12 percent within
four years. Even the SEL As in the state systems post disappointing results
for black males, with 59 percent graduating within six years and 26 percent within four years. Note, however, that black males at both SEL Is and
SEL As graduate at higher rates than white men at SEL Bs.

These patterns raise the same question discussed earlier, namely, the
extent to which our findings are the result of associated differences in academic preparation and other student characteristics. Disparities by
race/ethnicity in academic preparation in elementary and secondary
schools are certainly well documented, so we should expect to see the
gaps in graduation rates narrow once we account for these differences.
This is indeed what our data show, as depicted in Figures 3.13a and 3.13b.
Differences by race/ethnicity remain, but they are substantially smaller
than the large gaps observed in Figures 3.12a–3.12c. At the flagships,
black males, who are 16 percentage points less likely to graduate than
white males in the raw data, are 6 points less likely to graduate after adjusting for associated differences in the other variables included in the

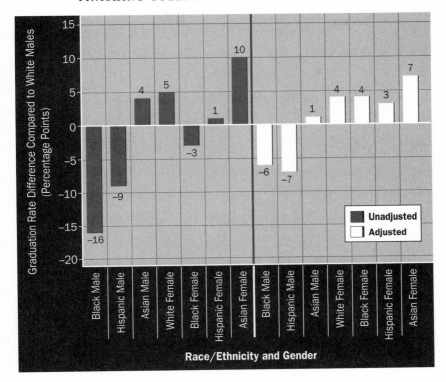

Figure 3.13a. Differences in Six-Year Graduation Rates by Race/Ethnicity and Gender (Compared to White Males), 1999 Entering Cohort, Flagships, Unadjusted and Adjusted

Source: Flagships Database.

Note: Adjusted differences control for SAT/ACT scores, high school GPA, family income quartile, state residency status, and university attended.

analysis, especially high school GPA. For Hispanic males, controlling for background characteristics only reduces the Hispanic-white gap from 9 points to 7 points.[20] However, black and Hispanic females, who are about as likely to graduate as white males in the raw data, are 3–4 points *more* likely to graduate than white males once their demographic characteristics and academic preparation are taken into account.[21] These patterns are fairly consistent across selectivity clusters (Appendix Table 3.6a). The adjusted black-white difference among men is 7 points at SEL I universities and 5 points at the SEL II and III universities. The adjusted figures also show black and white women graduating at roughly the same rates in all three SEL clusters once their background characteristics are taken into account.

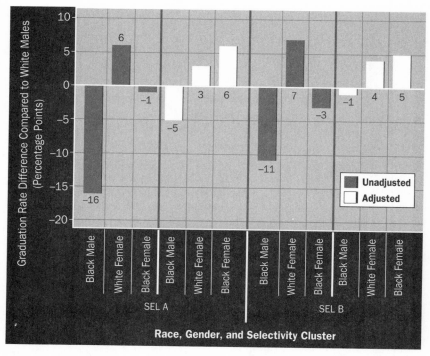

Figure 3.13b. Differences in Six-Year Graduation Rates by Race, Gender, and Selectivity Cluster (Compared to White Males), 1999 Entering Cohort, State Systems, Unadjusted and Adjusted

Source: State Systems Database.

Note: Adjusted differences control for SAT/ACT scores, high school GPA, family income quartile, state residency status, and university attended.

A similar pattern is found at the state system SEL As (Figure 3.13b), with an adjusted black-white difference among men of 5 points and white and black females graduating at rates 3 and 6 points (respectively) greater than those of white men. The state system SEL Bs are the notable exception; there the pattern for women is similar, but the black-white disparity among men is explained entirely by the students' entering characteristics. There is surprising heterogeneity across states and SEL clusters in the adjusted differences by race and gender (Appendix Table 3.6b). For example, in North Carolina and Virginia the adjusted black-white gaps among males at the SEL As are 10 and 6 points, respectively. But this gap is essentially zero within Ohio SEL As and Virginia SEL Bs and is actually reversed at North Carolina SEL Bs, where black men are 9 points more likely to graduate than are white men.[22] The variation in results clearly deserves further attention.

The large disparities in graduation rates between black and white men at the flagships emerge at a later point than do differences by SES (Figure 3.14a).[23] Although an initial gap appears by the end of the 2nd semester and grows, the withdrawal lines diverge most in the 8th through the 10th semesters. We find a similar pattern at the state system SEL Bs (Figure 3.14b), although at these universities black men are *less* likely to withdraw than are white men over the first eight semesters. It is not until the 9th through the 12th semesters that the cumulative withdrawal rate for black men climbs above that of white men.

The adjusted results show a similar pattern. The unadjusted withdrawal gaps found between black and white men at the flagships in the early years of college are largely eliminated once we control for students' entering credentials and demographic characteristics.[24] At the state system SEL Bs, both the unadjusted and adjusted differences are small (and actually favor black students) during this period.[25] That is, differences in withdrawal probabilities between black and white men are negligible through the first seven or eight semesters of college once other relevant characteristics are taken into account (Figures 3.15a and 3.15b). But beginning in the eighth semester at the flagships and in the ninth semester at the state system SEL Bs, black men are more likely to withdraw than are comparable white men. This temporal pattern is the same as the one we observed earlier when examining cumulative withdrawal rates on a simple, unadjusted, basis. Adjusting for differences in family circumstances and other variables does not change the picture substantially, and we are left with the same conundrums mentioned earlier.

We have no convincing way to explain why adjusted differences in withdrawal rates between black and white men occur primarily in semesters 8–12 in the flagships and in semesters 9–12 in the state system SEL Bs. One explanation may be that black men who have not completed their degree requirements after four years are more likely than white men to leave school because of either inadequate financial resources or discouragement. (However, there is no evidence that financial aid declines for black students relative to white students between academic years four and five.) Another conjecture is that black men may be more likely than white men to take temporary leaves before the 8th semester, which would in turn increase the time cost of their finishing. Another perplexing finding that could be related to "stop-out" experiences is that black men at the flagships are almost twice as likely as white men to continue to be enrolled in college at the beginning of the seventh year (4.3 percent versus 2.3 percent at the flagships). To make sense of these patterns requires a more fine-grained analysis of incentives, motivations, and family circumstances than we are able to provide on the basis of our data.

The results in this and the previous section show that, even after controlling for background characteristics and the university attended, there

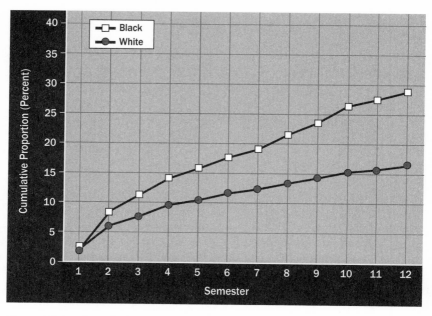

Figure 3.14a. Cumulative Withdrawal Proportions of Males per Semester by
Race, 1999 Entering Cohort, Flagships
  Source: Flagships Database.

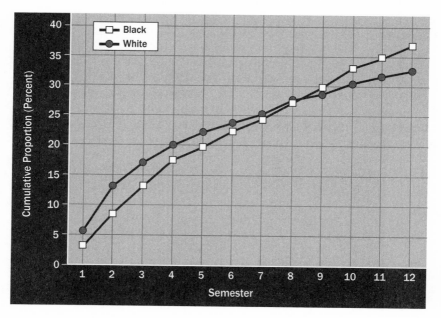

Figure 3.14b. Cumulative Withdrawal Proportions of Males per Semester by
Race, 1999 Entering Cohort, State System SEL Bs
  Source: State Systems Database.

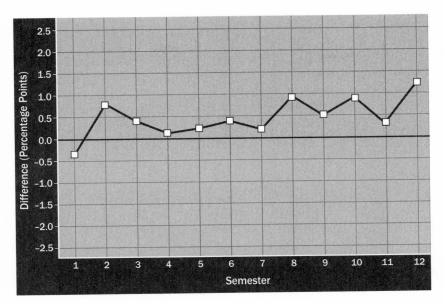

Figure 3.15a. Adjusted Withdrawal Differences (Black Males minus White Males), 1999 Entering Cohort, Flagships

Source: Flagships Database.

Note: Differences control for family income quartile, state residency status, SAT/ACT scores, high school GPA, and university attended.

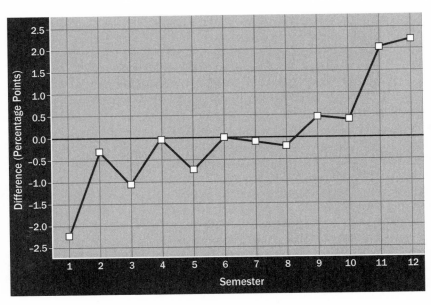

Figure 3.15b. Adjusted Withdrawal Differences (Black Males minus White Males), 1999 Entering Cohort, State System SEL Bs

Source: State Systems Database.

Note: Differences control for family income quartile, state residency status, SAT/ACT scores, high school GPA, and university attended.

is still a strong relationship between a student's probability of graduating and his or her race/ethnicity and gender, family income, and parental education. Each of these characteristics appears to have an independent effect on graduation probabilities, and this is a major "take-away" from the analysis. Moreover, the patterns are highly consistent, especially those for SES. The results for race/ethnicity and gender are equally consistent across the selectivity clusters among the flagships, but the results for race and gender vary widely by state and selectivity cluster in the four state systems.[26]

THE PREDICTIVE POWER OF FIRST-YEAR GRADES

Much happens to students during the time between when they enter college and when they leave (with or without a degree). An intermediate outcome of great interest to many is academic performance in the first year. For example, nearly all College Board and ACT studies of the predictive power of the SAT or the ACT use first-year GPA as the outcome.[27] Just as today's weather is usually the best predictor of tomorrow's weather, we would expect academic performance in the first year to be a strong predictor of academic performance in later years and of graduation rates. This is indeed what we find (Figure 3.16). Graduation rates increase sharply with first-year grades and plateau somewhat only among students with first-year GPAs above 3.0 at the SEL Is and IIs. At the SEL Is, only about half of the students with GPAs in the C to C-minus range ultimately graduate, but there is a graduation rate of about 90 percent among those with at least a B average. Although the lines in Figure 3.16 appear to be more or less as steep at schools in each selectivity cluster, it is important to bear in mind that students at more selective universities earn higher first-year GPAs, on average, than students at less selective universities. Additionally, the lines are steeper for lower first-year GPAs than for higher GPAs. As a result, regression analysis shows that the relationship between first-year GPA and six-year graduation rates is much stronger at the SEL IIIs and SEL Bs than at the SEL Is and SEL IIs (Appendix Table 3.8).

A question it is natural to ask is whether a student's first-year grades provide genuinely new information or represent just an extrapolation of the student's academic record in high school. In our data, high school grades are correlated with first-year college grades (as we would certainly expect), but the correlation coefficient is never larger than 0.46 and is just 0.34 at the SEL I flagships.[28] When we look more closely at the relationship between first-year grades and six-year graduation rates, we find that controlling for high school GPA and for SAT/ACT scores (along with students' demographic characteristics) has a surprisingly modest impact (compare the first and second columns and the third and fourth columns in Appendix Table 3.8).

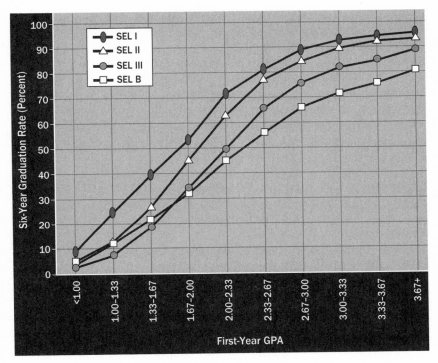

Figure 3.16. Six-Year Graduation Rates by First-Year GPA and Selectivity Cluster, 1999 Entering Cohort
Source: Flagships Database and State Systems Database.

These results suggest that first-year grades do in fact have a powerful "independent effect" on graduation rates. However, grades are of course earned by students, not just assigned to them. Thus, the predictive "effect" of first-year grades potentially captures many factors, the relative importance of which should influence how one interprets these results. For example, if first-year grades are just a proxy for students' overall motivation, it would be difficult to influence grades in a way that would also affect graduation rates (apart from improving motivation). The same would be true if poor grades in the first year result mainly from adverse personal or family events. However, if students who do well in their first year of college do so partly because they took advantage of resources available to them, perhaps encouraging other students to do the same would be beneficial. The key distinction is whether the relationship between grades and graduation rates is primarily the result of *external factors* (e.g., motivation, family events) that affect both first-year grades and graduation rates or of *behaviors in college* (e.g., taking advantage of academic support services, studying more) of first-year students that affect both first-year grades and graduation rates. To the extent that in-college factors drive these results, perhaps policies could be devised to stimulate better outcomes (e.g., identifying and helping students who are struggling academically) and thus improve both first-year academic performance and students' chances of finishing their degrees.

To the extent that first-year grades are related to graduation rates, we might expect to find that disadvantaged students are about as likely to graduate as more advantaged students *with similar first-year grades.* However, it turns out that controlling for first-year grades only modestly reduces the disparity in six-year graduation rates between the top and bottom income quartiles, from 8 to 6 percentage points at the flagships and from 11 to 9 points at the state system SEL Bs (Appendix Table 3.9). Slightly more of the low graduation rates of black and Hispanic men at the flagships are explained by differences in first-year grades. The difference relative to white men falls from 8 to 6 points for black men and 7 to 4 points for Hispanic men (Appendix Table 3.10).

These results suggest that improving the first-year experiences of students from low-income families and those of black and Hispanic men may have the potential to narrow modestly—although not eliminate—disparities in graduation rates between these groups and more advantaged students. Here again, our evidence is more useful in sharpening questions than it is in providing definitive answers. But it certainly would appear that careful exploration of this set of questions, probably using survey data and qualitative techniques, could have a high payoff.

———————

Differences in six-year graduation rates by SES, race/ethnicity, and gender are substantial, as we have just seen. In the next chapter we ask whether there are equally pronounced differences related to choice of major, time-to-degree, and academic performance in college among graduates in these sub-groups and across selectivity clusters. We will find that differences in terms of time-to-degree and academic performance are considerably greater than differences related to choice of major.

CHAPTER 4

Fields of Study, Time-to-Degree, and College Grades

THE PREVIOUS CHAPTER showed that stark disparities in college graduation rates by socioeconomic status (SES), race/ethnicity, and gender persist across a wide variety of settings in American public higher education.
Although these disparities in completion rates (in "finishing") are troubling in and of themselves, they tell us nothing about differences among
students who do graduate.

Differences in the academic experiences of students associated with
family background or race/ethnicity would be of concern even if disparities in graduation rates were not observed. For example, less advantaged
students might feel especially strong pressures to major in fields such as
business that seem to be more directly related to potential jobs even if
they have strong interests in more traditional academic fields. Another
concern—even more serious in our view—is that disadvantaged students
will take additional time to graduate (perhaps due to working many hours
in order to finance their education), thereby both increasing the costs of
going to college and delaying their entry into the job market. Finally, we
might (properly) worry that students from low-SES families or minority
groups will earn lower grades than other students and thus end up as less
competitive candidates in the job market or in the admissions pools for
graduate and professional schools. The main story line growing out of
the data presented in this chapter is that disparities in time-to-degree and
grades earned are indeed serious concerns, and readers may want to devote more time to those sections of this chapter than to the long discussion of choice of major that comes first. It turns out that there are surprisingly few differences of interest in choice of major, and this discussion
is unavoidably dense.

We focus this analysis of outcomes other than graduation rates on college *graduates*. Although this approach ignores the college outcomes of
students who do not graduate—who constitute a substantial minority (or
even a majority) at many of the less selective schools in our study—it allows us to focus on differences in outcomes in addition to those related
to completion rates. Including non-graduates in the analysis would "double count" differences in these outcomes to the extent that they are associated with differences in graduation rates.

In the case of choice of major, our data indicate that including students who declared a major but did not graduate has essentially no impact on the results. We suspect this is because many of the disparities in drop-out patterns arise early on, before students declare a major. When we include the non-graduates in the academic performance analysis, on the other hand, some of the results do change (particularly those that relate grades to SES), as we might expect given the association between college grades and earning a degree.

CHOICE OF MAJOR

We find that choice of major is largely a story of the "dog that didn't bark," but it is also one that debunks the myth that low-SES and minority students are reluctant to pursue "hard" majors such as engineering.[1] Differences in choice of major by SES are generally small, and although there are larger differences by race/ethnicity, they are entirely explained by differences in student characteristics and especially entering credentials. In fact, black graduates are generally *more* likely than comparable white graduates to choose engineering, math, and science majors. We find larger differences by SES, race/ethnicity, and gender in both time-to-degree and academic performance, and these differences are only partly explained by differences in academic preparation. The one exception is differences in college grades associated with SES, which are entirely accounted for by differences in entering credentials.

Figure 4.1 shows the percentage of students at the flagship universities who chose major fields of study in each of seven categories.[2] In light of recurring discussions of the alleged "flight from the arts and sciences," some readers may be surprised to learn that the majority of students (just over 60 percent) chose fields in the arts and sciences. Substantial numbers also chose majors in the communications and education (11 percent), business (14 percent), or "professional and other" fields (12 percent). Among both the flagships and the four state systems in our study, less selective universities tend to award more degrees in professional or vocational fields relative to traditional arts and sciences subjects (Figure 4.2). The least selective universities (state system schools in selectivity cluster [SEL] B) award more than a fifth of their degrees in business and almost as many in each of the categories "communications and education" and "professional and other," but a sizable minority (43 percent) of their graduates majored in the arts and sciences.

We turn next to a detailed examination of patterns in choice of major by SES, race/ethnicity, and gender. The amount of information contained in the figures and appendix tables is daunting due to the fact that the outcome here cannot be summarized by a single number or a simple average but rather consists of the percentage of students majoring in each

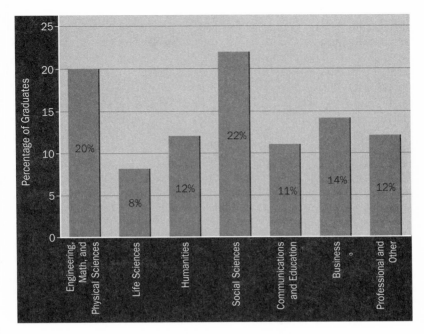

Figure 4.1. Major at Graduation, 1999 Entering Cohort, Flagships
  Source: Flagships Database.

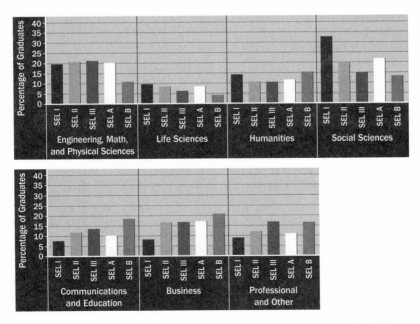

Figure 4.2. Major at Graduation by Selectivity Cluster, 1999 Entering Cohort
  Source: Flagships Database and State Systems Database.

of seven categories of majors (a categorization that is itself already a significant simplification). Although we will point out and identify the patterns we view as most noteworthy, we recognize that other patterns may be of special interest to some readers.

Although there are reasons why one might think that students from different backgrounds would systematically choose various fields of study, the data do not show such clear patterns. There is less of an association between SES and field of study than we would have expected (though there are some differences, to be sure). As mentioned earlier, we might expect low-SES students to be more likely to major in business or other professional programs in response to felt needs to make money immediately after college. The evidence on this question is contradictory. Figure 4.3a shows that, among the college graduates at the flagships and state system SEL As,[3] students from low-SES families are *less* likely to major in business but more likely to major in "professional and other" fields than are students from high-SES families. Our data also offer conflicting evidence on choice of majors in the arts and sciences. Low-SES students are more likely to major in the social sciences but less likely to major in the humanities and engineering, math, and physical sciences.

At the state system SEL Bs (Figure 4.3b), the largest difference in choice of major by SES is in the humanities, which high-SES students were 6 percentage points more likely to choose than low-SES students. Low-SES students were more likely to major in the social sciences, communications and education, and "professional and other" fields—but the differences are even smaller (2–3 points) than they were in the case of the more selective institutions.

In addition to being small, the differences by SES may be related to differences in sorting across institutions rather than within institutions (i.e., students from low-income families are more concentrated in schools that offer "professional and other" programs than in schools that offer engineering or business programs). This consideration is clearly more relevant for fields such as agricultural studies whose curricular "place" varies significantly across institutions (in terms of whether programs are offered at all) than for more traditional arts and sciences fields that are offered everywhere. To examine this possibility, we calculated adjusted differences in choice of major that take account of university attended, high school GPA, SAT/ACT scores, state residency status, race/ethnicity, and gender.

At the flagships and state system SEL As (Appendix Tables 4.1a and 4.1b), the slightly greater propensity of high-SES students to major in engineering, math, and the physical sciences is entirely explained by student characteristics and university attended. On the other hand, high-SES students remain 4–5 points less likely to major in the social sciences and 3–4 points more likely to major in business after the adjustments are

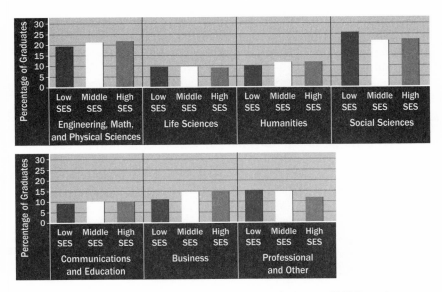

Figure 4.3a. Major at Graduation by Socioeconomic Status, 1999 Entering Cohort, Flagships and State System SEL As
Source: Flagships Database and State Systems Database.

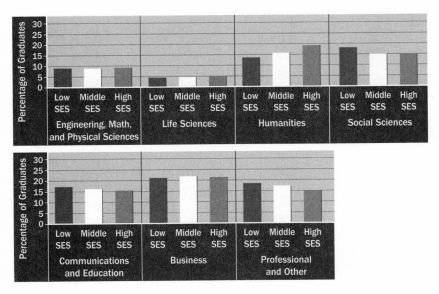

Figure 4.3b. Major at Graduation by Socioeconomic Status, 1999 Entering Cohort, State System SEL Bs
Source: State Systems Database.

made. The finding concerning business appears to be entirely the result of the greater propensity of students from families in the top income quartile to choose this field, for we observe no differences by parental education or for the other income quartiles (Appendix Tables 4.2a–4.3b). It may be that students from high-income families are most familiar with the business world, in part because their parents may themselves have experience and standing in the business community.

At the state system SEL Bs (Appendix Table 4.1b), high-SES students are more likely to major in the humanities and less likely to major in the social sciences, and both of these patterns appear to be related to parental education and not family income. There is no adjusted difference by SES in choice of business majors—an outcome that is the result of a canceling out of parental education and family income effects. Students from families in the top income quartile are more likely to choose

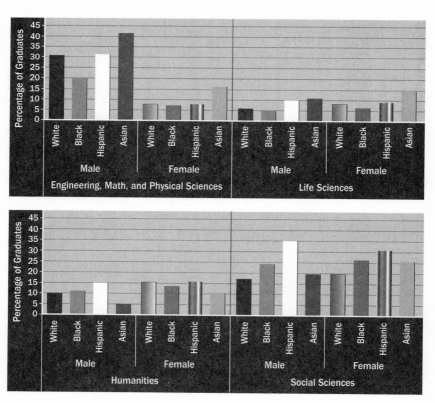

Figure 4.4a. Major at Graduation by Race/Ethnicity and Gender, 1999 Entering Cohort, Flagships and State System SEL As
Source: Flagships Database and State Systems Database.

business, and children of the most educated parents are less likely to choose this field (Appendix Tables 4.2b and 4.3b).

Although differences in choice of major by SES are small both before and after taking student characteristics into account, differences by race/ethnicity and gender are not. Figures 4.4a and 4.4b show major at graduation by race/ethnicity and gender at the flagship universities and state system SEL As. Men are much more likely than women to major in engineering, math, and the physical sciences. Among men, black men are the least likely (20 percent) and Asian men are the most likely (41 percent) to choose this field, with whites and Hispanics falling in between (31–33 percent). Men are also more likely to major in business than are women, but the difference is much smaller. The gender gap is reversed in communications and education and "professional and other" fields, with women modestly more likely to choose these fields.

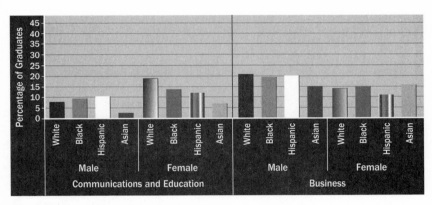

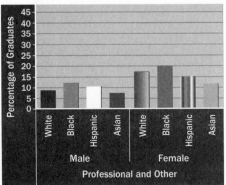

Figure 4.4b. Major at Graduation by Race/Ethnicity and Gender, 1999 Entering Cohort, Flagships and State System SEL As (Continued)
Source: Flagships Database and State Systems Database.

The largest differences by race/ethnicity, in addition to those for men in engineering, math, and physical sciences, are in the social sciences. Black students of both genders are 7 percentage points more likely to choose these fields than whites. Hispanic students are even more likely to major in the social sciences. Other differences also appear—for instance, white women are more likely to choose communications and education than are black women—but these differences are modest.

The patterns observed for black and white students are largely similar for several major categories at the state system SEL Bs (Figure 4.5), but there are also a few notable exceptions. At these schools, white women are substantially more likely to choose majors in communications and education than are black women (25 percent versus 18 percent). White and black men are both very likely to major in business (29 percent and 31 percent, respectively), a major that is also chosen by a substantial percentage of black women (26 percent, compared to 15 percent of white women).

Virtually all of the differences in choice of major by race/ethnicity are explained by differences in entering characteristics (Appendix Tables 4.4a–4.5b). Black students are about as likely as similar white students to

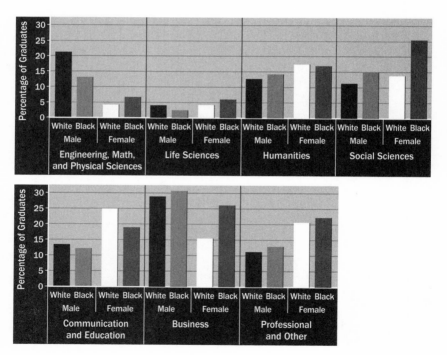

Figure 4.5. Major at Graduation by Race and Gender, 1999 Entering Cohort, State System SEL Bs

Source: State Systems Database.

choose each major category, with the notable exception of engineering, math, and physical sciences, where the gap observed in the raw data is reversed. Black men at the flagships and state system SEL As are 7–8 percentage points *more* likely to choose these fields than are comparable white men; the adjusted white-black difference among women is the same at these universities. At the state system SEL Bs, black students are still at least as likely to major in engineering, math, and physical sciences as are similar white students, but the adjusted differences are smaller, 0.2 points among men and 4 points among women. This finding dispels the myth that minorities are not interested in engineering, math, and science and offers hope that in the future there can be more black and Hispanic engineers and scientists. But this outcome will depend on whether it is possible to correct the underlying forces that cause the raw differences to go in the opposite direction.[4]

In short, the evidence suggests that (1) choice of major appears to be only weakly correlated with SES and (2) although there are strong relationships between major field of study and gender, underrepresented minorities of both genders are more likely to choose engineering, math, and science majors than are white students once their background characteristics are taken into account.

TIME-TO-DEGREE

Our analysis of graduation rates shows that disparities by institutional selectivity, SES, race/ethnicity, and gender are often larger for four-year graduation rates than for six-year graduation rates. The obvious implication is not only that disadvantaged groups are less likely to graduate at all but that those who do graduate take longer to complete their degrees. Time-to-degree should be a concern to students, institutions of higher education, and society at large. Students who take longer to graduate use more of their own time and resources (including family resources) to earn a bachelor's degree. Universities may receive more tuition revenue from students who take longer to graduate, but these tuition dollars are generally only a fraction of the cost of providing an undergraduate education, particularly at public universities where in-state tuition is kept below market rates. Society at large is absorbing much of the cost of increased time-to-degree through the tax dollars that fund these public universities. When resource constraints are challenging (as they are in 2009), a long time-to-degree is especially problematic, and universities are well advised to find ways to encourage more students to complete their programs of study within the traditional four-year time frame. One source of difficulty is that norms seem to have changed, with increasing numbers of students assuming that they will not finish in four years. As

David Leonhardt points out, "Some even refer to themselves as second-
or third-years, instead of sophomores or juniors."[5]

If extended time-to-degree were primarily the result of students' taking one or two semesters off during their college years—perhaps to pursue worthwhile activities—these concerns would not be nearly as salient.
However, this is not the case. Among the graduates of the flagship universities in our study, those who graduated in five years were enrolled for
an additional 1.2 semesters. Students who graduated in six years were enrolled for 2.4 semesters more than were four-year graduates.[6] These data
show that extended time-to-degree is predominantly the result of students' spending additional semesters enrolled in college, not taking time
away from college. Taking into account the fact that some five-year graduates finished in 4.5 years and some six-year graduates finished in 5.5
years, we estimate that between two-thirds and three-quarters of the additional time it took these graduates to earn their degrees was spent enrolled in college.[7] The same pattern appears in data on credits earned
and attempted: relative to four-year graduates, five-year graduates
attempted 12 more credits and earned 9 more; six-year graduates attempted 24 more credits and earned 17 more.[8] The difference between

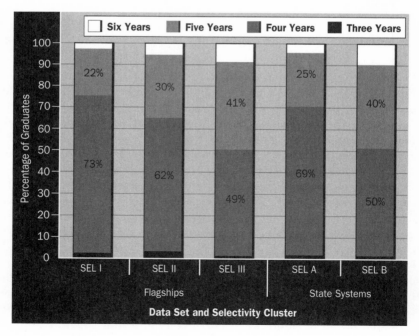

Figure 4.6. Time-to-Degree of Graduates by Selectivity Cluster, 1999
Entering Cohort
Source: Flagships Database and State Systems Database.

credits earned and credits attempted for these two groups of students suggests that, as one would have expected, failing courses is more common among the six-year graduates than among the five-year graduates.

Figure 4.6 shows that the vast majority of graduates at schools in each selectivity cluster finished their degrees in either four or five years, with relatively few finishing in three or six years. However, there are substantial differences in the proportion finishing in four years compared to five years. For example, about 70 percent of graduates finished in four years at SEL I and SEL A universities, whereas only about half finished in the same period of time at SEL III and SEL B schools. Some students are enrolled in five-year programs, which are fairly common in engineering, in particular. Thus, it is no surprise that five-year degrees are most prevalent in engineering (which is separated out from math and physical sciences in Figure 4.7 for this reason). We should emphasize, however, that the participation of some limited number of students, especially engineering students, in five-year programs accounts for only a small fraction of the

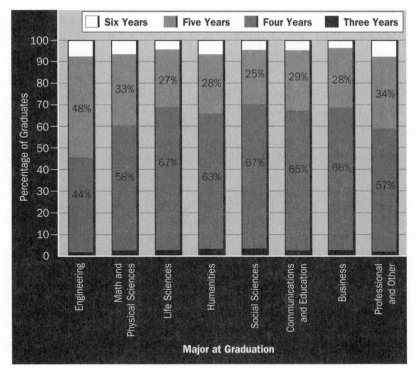

Figure 4.7. Time-to-Degree of Graduates by Major at Graduation, 1999 Entering Cohort, Flagships
Source: Flagships Database.

overall number of five-year graduates. Even in engineering, 44 percent of the graduates at the flagships who majored in this field finished in four years. Time-to-degree varies somewhat across the other fields, but in every case other than engineering four-year degree recipients predominate.

Time-to-degree varies by socioeconomic status (Figures 4.8a and 4.8b), and the largest differences appear at the most selective public universities in our study. At the SEL I flagships, 77 percent of high-SES graduates complete their studies in four years, while only 59 percent of low-SES graduates finish this quickly, a difference of 18 percentage points. The corresponding gap is 11 points at the SEL IIs but only 2 points at the SEL IIIs. In the state systems the pattern is similar, with a gap between high- and low-SES students of 11 points at SEL As and 5 points at SEL Bs.

As in the case of graduation rates and choice of major, we suspect that some of these differences arise from differences in entering credentials, which are more pronounced at the more selective universities.[9] In order

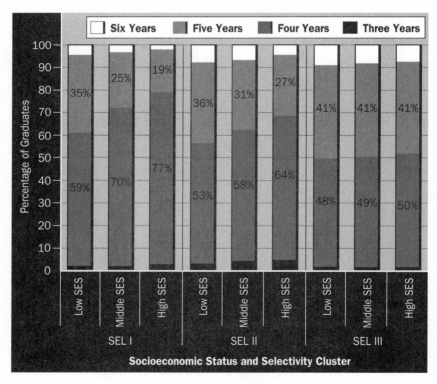

Figure 4.8a. Time-to-Degree of Graduates by Socioeconomic Status and Selectivity Cluster, 1999 Entering Cohort, Flagships
Source: Flagships Database.

to present adjusted differences in a straightforward fashion, we condense our four time-to-degree categories (three-, four-, five-, and six-year graduates) into two groupings: those who finish in four or fewer years and those who do not (the five- and six-year graduates). Because so few students graduate in three or six years, little information is lost by simplifying the analysis in this way. In addition to the standard variables, we also control for choice of major in the adjusted differences.

Figure 4.9 shows unadjusted and adjusted differences in time-to-degree by SES (referring, for simplicity's sake, to those who finish in four years or less as having finished "on time," even though we recognize that there are some five-year programs). Because the results are so similar, we group together the data for SEL I, II, and A universities and those for SEL III and B universities.[10] The left half of Figure 4.9 shows that approximately half of the differences in time-to-degree by SES at SEL Is, IIs, and As are explained by associated differences in entering characteristics; the dis-

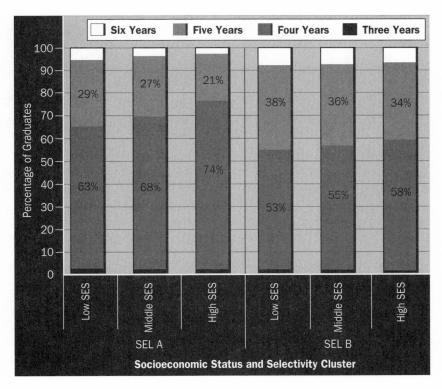

Figure 4.8b. Time-to-Degree of Graduates by Socioeconomic Status and Selectivity Cluster, 1999 Entering Cohort, State Systems
Source: State Systems Database.

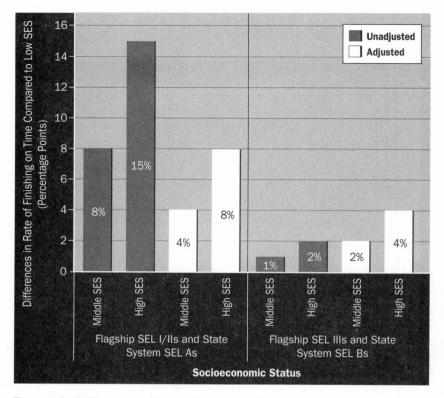

Figure 4.9. Differences in Rates of Graduates' Finishing on Time by
Socioeconomic Status (Compared to Low SES), 1999 Entering Cohort,
Unadjusted and Adjusted

Source: Flagships Database and State Systems Database.

Note: Adjusted differences control for SAT/ACT scores, high school GPA, state residency,
race/ethnicity, gender, major, and university attended.

parity between high- and low-SES students of 15 percentage points drops
to 8 points when controls are added.[11] The small unadjusted differences
at SEL IIIs and Bs increase somewhat when controls are added (as we
might expect given the modestly higher high school GPAs of low-SES students relative to high-SES students at the SEL Bs). Disaggregated results
by selectivity cluster and state system are presented in Appendix Tables
4.6a and 4.6b.[12]

It is important to say as much as we can about what is really driving the
differences in time-to-degree that are related to SES, and we next present data that allow us to separate out the effects of parental education
and family income within the most selective universities (SEL Is, IIs, and

As). *These data strongly suggest that family income, not parental education, is primarily responsible for the overall relationship between SES and time-to-degree.* Once we control for family income (Figure 4.10a), children of parents with college degrees are only slightly (2–3 points) more likely to finish on time than are students from families without college degrees.[13] On the other hand, even after controlling for parental education, family income is still strongly correlated with on-time finishing rates: students from families in the top income quartile are 7 percentage points more likely to finish in four years than are students from families in the bottom income quartile (Figure 4.10b).[14]

We find substantial differences in time-to-degree by race/ethnicity and gender at schools in all selectivity clusters, most of which cannot be explained by differences in entering characteristics. Figure 4.11a shows time-to-degree among the graduates of the flagship universities grouped

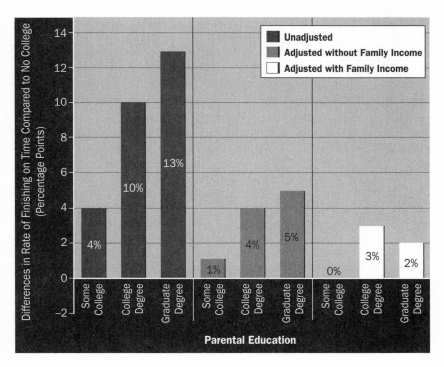

Figure 4.10a. Differences in Rates of Graduates' Finishing on Time by Parental Education (Compared to No College), 1999 Entering Cohort, SEL Is, IIs, and As, Unadjusted and Adjusted

Source: Flagships Database and State Systems Database.

Note: Adjusted differences control for SAT/ACT scores, high school GPA, state residency, race/ethnicity, gender, major, and university attended.

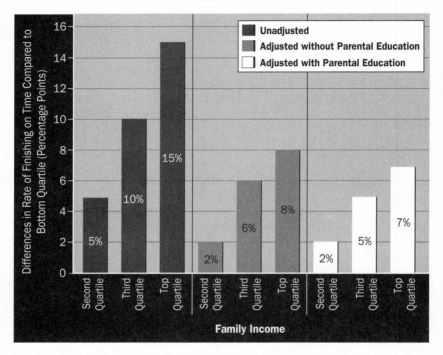

Figure 4.10b. Differences in Rates of Graduates' Finishing on Time by Family
Income (Compared to Bottom Quartile), 1999 Entering Cohort, SEL Is, IIs,
and As, Unadjusted and Adjusted

Source: Flagships Database and State Systems Database.

Note: Adjusted differences control for SAT/ACT scores, high school GPA, state residency,
race/ethnicity, gender, major, and university attended.

by race/ethnicity and gender. Substantially more women than men graduate within four years in all racial groups, with gender differences of 14
percentage points for white graduates and 18 points for black graduates.
White students earn their degrees more quickly than do black students,
with a white-black difference of 9 points among men and 7 points among
women. In the state systems (Figure 4.11b), the pattern is the same, and
white-black differences are larger at state system SEL As (16 points among
men and 10 points among women) than at state system SEL Bs (8 points
among men and 5 points among women).

At the flagships, differences in on-time graduation by race/ethnicity
and gender are largely unchanged by controlling for students' entering
credentials, demographic characteristics, and university attended (Figure 4.12a). The white-black difference among men remains at 12 points,
and the corresponding difference among women is reduced only mod-

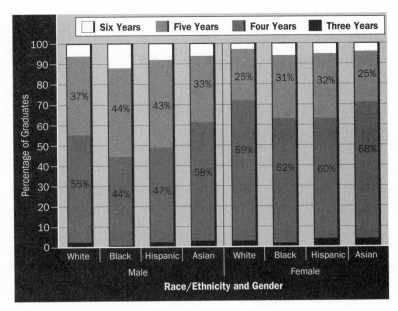

Figure 4.11a. Time-to-Degree of Graduates by Race/Ethnicity and Gender, 1999 Entering Cohort, Flagships
Source: Flagships Database.

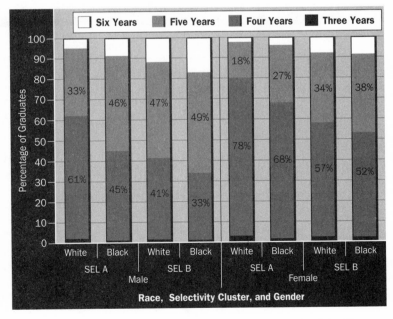

Figure 4.11b. Time-to-Degree of Graduates by Race, Selectivity Cluster, and Gender, 1999 Entering Cohort, State Systems
Source: State Systems Database.

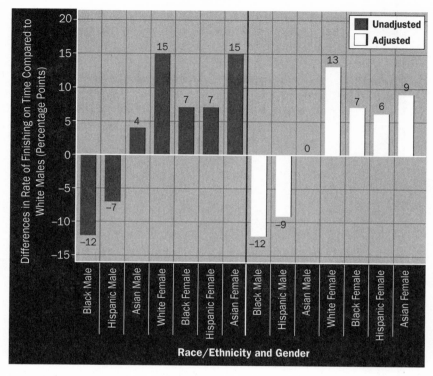

Figure 4.12a. Differences in Rates of Graduates' Finishing on Time by
Race/Ethnicity and Gender (Compared to White Males), 1999 Entering
Cohort, Flagships, Unadjusted and Adjusted
  Source: Flagships Database.
  Note: Adjusted differences control for SAT/ACT scores, high school GPA, family income
quartile, state residency, and university attended.

estly, from 8 points to 6. In the adjusted results, the pattern for Hispanic
students is fairly similar to the pattern for black students. Adjusted differences are quite similar across selectivity clusters, although the difference between white and black men is substantially smaller at SEL IIs than
at SEL Is and IIIs (Appendix Table 4.9a).
   In the state systems, more (and sometimes all) of the white-black
differences in time-to-degree are explained by the control variables—
with the single, and highly important, exception of men at the SEL A
universities, where adding control variables reduces the white-black difference from 17 points to 11 (Figure 4.12b). In sharp contrast, the white-
black gap in time-to-degree for women at the state system SEL A universities is reduced from 12 points to 3. At the state system SEL Bs,
white-black differences in time-to-degree among both men and women

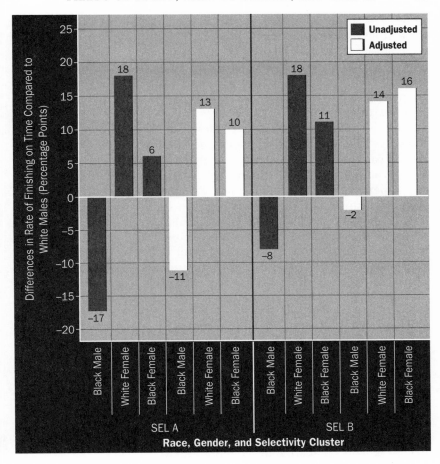

Figure 4.12b. Differences in Rates of Graduates' Finishing on Time by Race, Gender, and Selectivity Cluster (Compared to White Males), 1999 Entering Cohort, State Systems, Unadjusted and Adjusted

Source: State Systems Database.

Note: Adjusted differences control for SAT/ACT scores, high school GPA, family income quartile, state residency, and university attended.

are explained entirely by differences in student characteristics and entering credentials.[15]

ACADEMIC PERFORMANCE

In addition to taking additional time to finish their degrees, low-SES graduates earn significantly lower grades on average than do high-SES graduates.[16] The average low-SES graduate at the flagship universities earns grades that place him or her in the 43rd percentile, whereas the average high-SES graduate ranks in the 53rd percentile. A 10-point difference in rank-in-class is also found at the state system SEL As; the corresponding difference is much smaller at the state system SEL Bs, where, on average, high- and low-SES students earn grades in the 51st and 48th percentiles, respectively.[17]

However, unlike time-to-degree, these differences in grades among graduates of different socioeconomic backgrounds at the flagships and SEL As can be explained almost entirely by differences in entering credentials and major field.[18] We add field of major as a control so that we do not penalize students for choosing harder majors or reward them for choosing majors in which it is easier to get good grades; however, including this control is unlikely to affect our results given the very weak correlations between SES and choice of major found in the previous section.[19]

The difference of 10 percentile points in rank-in-class between high- and low-SES students drops to 2 once differences in entering characteristics, particularly high school GPA and SAT/ACT scores, are taken into account (Figure 4.13). At the state system SEL Bs, we might expect low-SES students to "overperform" relative to high-SES students given the small unadjusted difference, but this is not the case. The 2-percentile point unadjusted difference falls to an adjusted difference of 1 percentile point. The reason is that high- and low-SES students are more similar at the state system SEL Bs than at the other universities in our study. For example, the difference between high- and low-SES students in entering credentials at the flagships is 124 points on the SAT/ACT and 0.10 in high school GPA. At the SEL Bs, low-SES students enter with *higher* high school GPAs (by 0.07 on average) than do high-SES students and with SAT/ACT scores that are only 59 points lower.

When we examine rank-in-class data separately by parental education and family income (Figures 4.14 and 4.15), we find results that are very similar to those found using the combined SES measure. These results are remarkably consistent across selectivity clusters and states, as can be seen in Appendix Tables 4.10a–4.12b. The unadjusted differences tend to be smaller at the less selective flagships than at the more selective flagships, but the adjusted differences are very similar, as is the case in the comparison between SEL As and Bs in the state systems.

The bottom line is that, unlike differences in graduation rates and time-to-degree, differences in academic performance by SES (among those who graduate) are explained almost entirely by differences in students' entering characteristics. These results combined with the similarly small differences in choice of major are heartening in that they suggest that low- and high-SES graduates who started college with similar

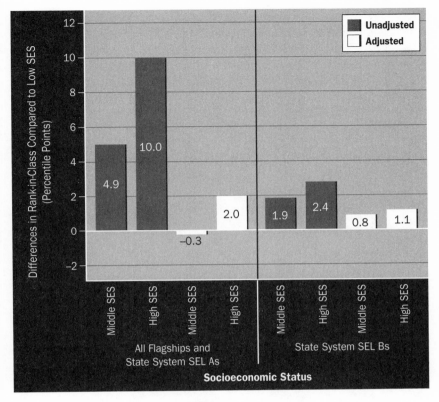

Figure 4.13. Differences in Rank-in-Class at Graduation by Socioeconomic Status and Selectivity Cluster (Compared to Low SES), 1999 Entering Cohort, Unadjusted and Adjusted

Source: Flagships Database and State Systems Database.

Note: Adjusted differences control for SAT/ACT scores, high school GPA, state residency, race/ethnicity, gender, major, and university attended.

credentials may have more similar job market prospects than one might have anticipated. However, this encouraging conclusion must be strongly qualified by the fact that low-SES students are substantially less likely to persist to graduation than are their high-SES classmates, and those low-SES students who do persist to graduation take longer to earn their degrees.

We turn now to differences in rank-in-class that are related to race/ethnicity and gender. Although even larger disparities in performance are observed by race/ethnicity and gender than by SES, we might also expect these differences to dissipate (as did the differences related to SES) once

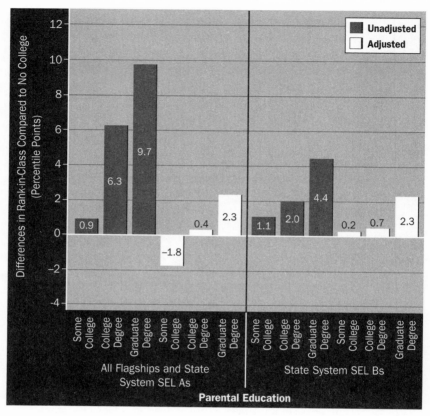

Figure 4.14. Differences in Rank-in-Class at Graduation by Parental Education and Selectivity Cluster (Compared to No College), 1999 Entering Cohort, Unadjusted and Adjusted

Source: Flagships Database and State Systems Database.

Note: Adjusted differences control for family income, SAT/ACT scores, high school GPA, state residency, race/ethnicity, gender, major, and university attended.

students' entering credentials are taken into account. But this does not happen.

The left-hand panel of Figure 4.16a shows the enormous differences in rank-in-class at graduation by race/ethnicity and gender at the flagship universities. Compared to white males, black males rank 22 points lower, Hispanic males 12 points lower, and Asian males 4 points lower. Compared to white females (who rank about 9 points higher than white males), black females rank 24 points lower, Hispanic females 14 points

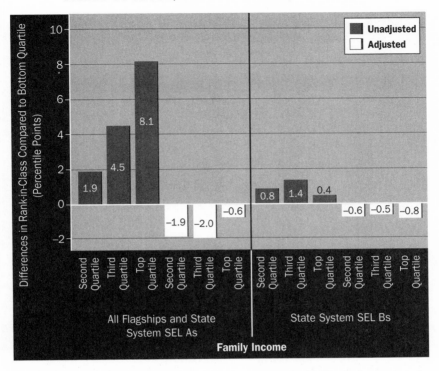

Figure 4.15. Differences in Rank-in-Class at Graduation by Family Income and Selectivity Cluster (Compared to Bottom Quartile), 1999 Entering Cohort, Unadjusted and Adjusted

Source: Flagships Database and State Systems Database.

Note: Adjusted differences control for parental education, SAT/ACT scores, high school GPA, state residency, race/ethnicity, gender, major, and university attended.

lower, and Asian females 6 points lower. The right-hand panel shows that these differences are largely, but by no means entirely, explained by differences in entering characteristics and choice of major. Black, Hispanic, and Asian men all earn grades 5–6 percentile points lower than do comparable white men. Among women the white-black gap in adjusted rank-in-class is still larger, at about 9 points, whereas the white-Hispanic gap is smaller, at about 4 points.

The results for black and white students at the state system SEL As are very similar to those at the flagships, and the results at the SEL Bs are only modestly different (Figure 4.16b). At the SEL Bs, the adjusted white-black difference is about 7 points among both men and women. Looking separately at the flagships by selectivity cluster (Appendix Table 4.13a), the

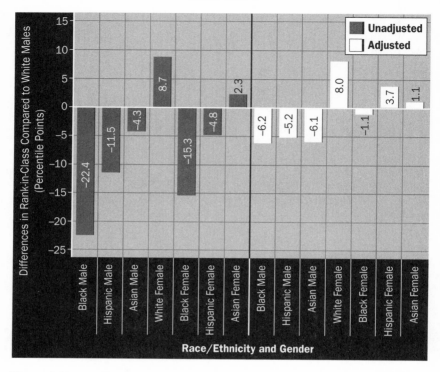

Figure 4.16a. Differences in Rank-in-Class at Graduation by Race/Ethnicity and Gender (Compared to White Males), 1999 Entering Cohort, Flagships, Unadjusted and Adjusted

Source: Flagships Database.

Note: Adjusted differences control for SAT/ACT scores, high school GPA, family income quartile, state residency, major, and university attended.

underperformance of black men relative to white men appears to be greatest at SEL Is and SEL IIIs (7–8 points) and less pronounced at SEL IIs (3 points). The adjusted white-black difference among women is largest at SEL Is (11 points) and smallest at SEL IIIs (7 points). The differences in rank-in-class outcomes vary somewhat by state system and selectivity cluster (Appendix Table 4.13b), and they do not follow a consistent pattern. However, weaker academic performance by black students with the same observable characteristics as their white classmates is found in all states and selectivity clusters, with the white-black difference among men ranging from 4 to 9 points and the difference among women ranging from 5 to 9 points.[20]

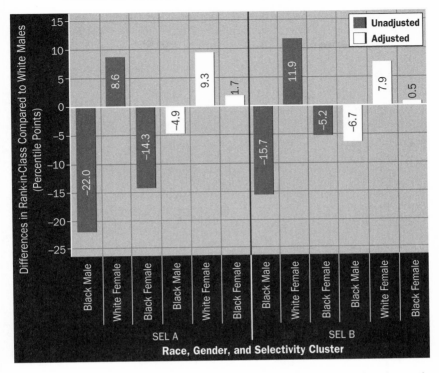

Figure 4.16b. Differences in Rank-in-Class at Graduation by Race, Gender, and Selectivity Cluster (Compared to White Males), 1999 Entering Cohort, State Systems, Unadjusted and Adjusted

Source: State Systems Database.

Note: Adjusted differences control for SAT/ACT scores, high school GPA, family income quartile, state residency, major, and university attended.

SUMMARY OF OUTCOMES BY SES, RACE/ETHNICITY, AND GENDER

All three of the main academic outcomes of college-going—graduating or not, time-to-degree, and rank-in-class at graduation—are strongly associated with SES, race/ethnicity, and gender.[21] That is the inescapable conclusion of the analysis presented in this chapter and the previous one. The other outcome we studied, choice of major, is far less strongly associated with SES, race/ethnicity, and gender than many (including us) have supposed. Nor is it possible to say whether majoring in one field is necessarily better than majoring in another field. We can agree that graduating is better than leaving college without a degree, that it is generally better to finish sooner rather than later, and that it is desirable to have a high class rank on graduation. The purpose of this short summary is to pull together the threads of this analysis by combining the three academic outcomes that can be rank-ordered to allow us to understand, overall, the extent of disparities in college outcomes related to SES, race/ethnicity, and gender. The disparities are substantial.

To accomplish this objective, we created four composite outcomes:

- "Best" outcome (graduate in four years in top half of class)
- "Second"-best outcome (graduate in four years in bottom half of class or in six years in top half of class)
- "Third"-best outcome (graduate in six years in bottom half of class)
- "Disappointing" outcome (no bachelor's degree from either the initial institution attended or a transfer institution)

Four simple figures (Figures 4.17a–4.18b) sum up our analysis. At the flagships and state system SEL As (Figure 4.17a), college students from high-SES backgrounds are almost twice as likely as students from low-SES

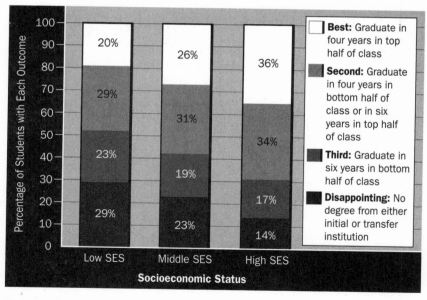

Figure 4.17a. Summary of Outcomes by Socioeconomic Status, 1999 Entering Cohort, Flagships and State System SEL As
Source: Flagships Database and State Systems Database.

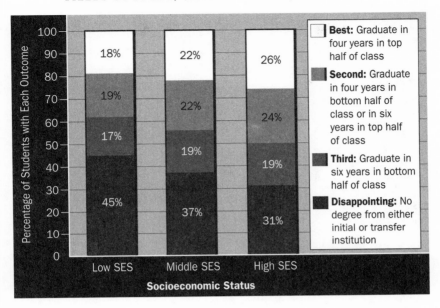

Figure 4.17b. Summary of Outcomes by Socioeconomic Status, 1999 Entering Cohort, State System SEL Bs
Source: State Systems Database.

backgrounds to end up in the "Best" outcomes category (36 percent versus 20 percent) and are only half as likely to end up in the "Disappointing" category (14 percent versus 29 percent). At the state system SEL Bs (Figure 4.17b), the pattern is more or less the same, although many more students fail to graduate at all, with 45 percent of low-SES students and almost a third of high-SES students in the "Disappointing" category.

Looking at race/ethnicity and gender groupings, we see that females do consistently better than males and that white students do consistently better than black students. In fact, only 7 percent of black men at the flagships and state system SEL As (Figure 4.18a) end up in the "Best" outcomes category, versus 25 percent of white men, 13 percent of Hispanic men, and 25 percent of Asian men. Only 16 percent of black women finish in the "Best" category compared with 40 percent of white women, 24 percent of Hispanic women, and 35 percent of Asian women. A sizable percentage of black men (39 percent) end up in the "Disappointing" category compared with 21 percent of white men; again, Hispanics are in an intermediate position, and Asian men (and women) do the best of all on this measure. At the state system SEL Bs (Figure 4.18b), white-black dif-

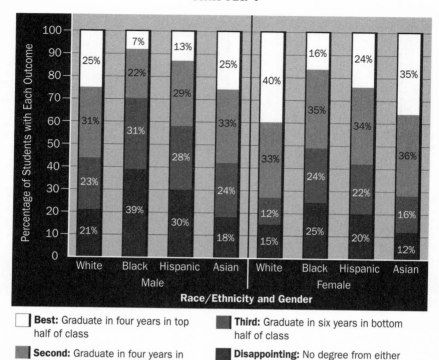

Figure 4.18a. Summary of Outcomes by Race/Ethnicity and Gender, 1999 Entering Cohort, Flagships and State System SEL As
Source: Flagships Database and State Systems Database.

ferences are somewhat smaller in general, but far fewer students graduate at all, with a majority of both black men (59 percent) and black women (51 percent) ending up in the "Disappointing" category.

It is the combined, cumulative effects of weaker academic preparation and greater attendance at less selective institutions that produce these stark disparities. It would be a mistake, however, to attribute all of these differences in outcomes to weaker entering credentials. In fact, we estimate that at the flagships and state SEL As *less than one-third of the overall differences in outcomes by SES can be explained in terms of the lower test scores and lower high school grades of low-SES students* (Appendix Table 4.15a).[22] A higher fraction of the differences in outcomes by race/ethnicity (about half) at these universities can be attributed to the weaker scores and grades of black students (Appendix Table 4.16a). *Still, the evidence shows that outcomes in college are strongly associated with SES, race/ethnicity, and gen-*

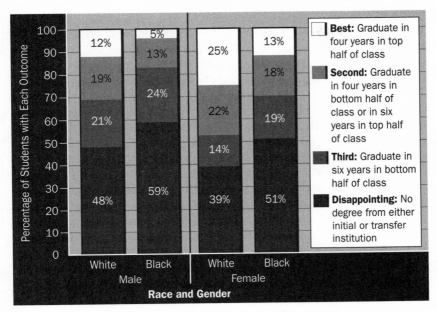

Figure 4.18b. Summary of Outcomes by Race and Gender, 1999 Entering Cohort, State System SEL Bs
Source: State Systems Database.

der, even after controlling for observable differences in student characteristics, including both incoming academic credentials and the universities attended.[23] This evidence signals the huge challenge faced by colleges and universities seeking to reduce national disparities in achievement related to SES, race/ethnicity, and gender.

We should add that if we were able to capture even earlier differences in high school graduation rates and college enrollment rates, the overall disparities in outcomes would be even greater. The data for high school seniors in North Carolina (where we do have college enrollment rates by race/ethnicity and gender though not high school graduation rates) show that only 11 percent of black male high school seniors earned bachelor's degrees within six years of graduating from high school, compared with 21 percent of their white male classmates. As always, women of both races were more successful than men in earning college degrees, but here, too, there were pronounced differences by race: 18 percent of black female high school seniors earned bachelor's degrees within six years, as compared with 31 percent of their white female classmates.[24]

In their general tenor, these results also mirror those for the nation-wide sample of students in the NELS data (discussed at length in Chap-

ter 2). These national panel data allow us to consider, along with differences in college enrollment rates, differences in rates of high school graduation, which, as we just noted, is another stage in the educational
process that leads to still wider ultimate disparities in educational attainment. In short, the empirical findings from our data that we cite in Chapter 3 and this chapter and summarize earlier, striking as they are, *understate* the true extent of disparities in educational outcomes because they
fail to reflect both the lower high school graduation rates and the lower
college enrollment rates that are common among black and Hispanic students and students from low-SES backgrounds.

In the chapters that follow, we attempt to identify some of the deep-
seated forces driving these disturbing results. We start out, in Chapter 5,
by examining in detail the role that high schools play in college access
and success.

CHAPTER 5

High Schools and "Undermatching"

IN SEEKING TO UNDERSTAND the forces that shape educational attainment in the United States, some pride of place needs to be given to secondary schools. Everyone believes that the characteristics of high schools and the experiences of students in high school have much to do not only with immediate secondary school outcomes such as earning a diploma but also with the subsequent educational achievements of those who surmount the hurdle of high school graduation.

There is a considerable body of research analyzing the connections between the high school experiences of students and their later educational outcomes. This literature includes, for example, the widely cited 1999 "Tool Box" publication of Clifford Adelman, then at the Department of Education (DOE). Adelman's research utilized transcript data available from DOE longitudinal studies to examine in detail the role played by the intensity and quality of the high school curriculum—which he regards as prime determinants of how students do in college.[1] There is also the impressive work of the Consortium on Chicago School Research at the University of Chicago, which has had access to a large data set that encompasses all of the Chicago public schools. A 2006 Chicago Consortium study underscored both (a) how greatly outcomes differ across high schools in that large Midwestern city—and, for that matter, across Chicago high schools that at least superficially look quite a bit alike—and (b) how important certain high school results are (especially high school GPA) in determining subsequent college enrollment and graduation patterns.[2] A March 2008 Chicago Consortium study and its successor, an April 2009 study, emphasize that high schools must not only prepare their students for college but also provide the information and support their students need if they are to successfully navigate the college application and admission process.[3] Leading testing services, including ACT, the Educational Testing Service (ETS), and the College Board, also maintain active research and policy analysis operations, focused partly on improving the usefulness of their own instruments but also on broader questions about factors influencing high school success and college readiness.[4]

In this chapter we do not propose to review this body of literature or attempt to reconcile different points of view reflected in it. Rather, we see our task as seeking to make at least a modest contribution to this ongoing conversation about high schools and the post-secondary educational attainments of their seniors by presenting new data. Specifically, we first use a newly created national database describing all U.S. high schools both to describe the kinds of high schools attended by the matriculants at public universities and to examine relationships between graduation rates at these universities and the characteristics of the high schools they attended. Then, in the second section, we present results obtained through a much more detailed examination of the characteristics of North Carolina high schools and how they relate to college enrollment patterns, as well as to graduation rates in that state. Finally, in the third and longest section, we discuss what we have come to call the "under-match" phenomenon, by which we mean the surprisingly large number of high school seniors who were presumptively qualified to attend strong four-year colleges but did not do so, instead attending less selective four-year colleges, two-year colleges, or no college at all.

TYPES OF HIGH SCHOOLS AND COLLEGE GRADUATION RATES AT THE NATIONAL LEVEL

America is known for the variety of its educational institutions at both the secondary school and college levels, which is a legacy of this country's historically decentralized approach to education.[5] With the active cooperation of the College Board and the ACT, we have created a new national high school database that describes every high school in the country (see Appendix C for a description of sources and methods). In Table 5.1 we present a snapshot of the distribution of all high school students by basic characteristics of the high school attended—size of senior class, racial/ethnic mix, urban/suburban/rural location, neighborhood wealth, and academic standing (as measured by SAT/ACT test-taking behavior of seniors, average SAT/ACT scores for those who took one of the tests, and percentages of students taking at least one Advanced Placement [AP] test).[6] This table also presents data showing the corresponding distributions, by type of high school, for the 1999 cohort of high school seniors who went on to matriculate at the two main groups of public universities in our study: the flagship and selectivity cluster (SEL) A universities and the SEL B universities.

It is evident from this table that, as one would expect, students at the more selective universities (the flagships and SEL As) came from high schools that were at least somewhat "above average" in academic standing and wealth. For example, only 18 percent of the matriculants at these universities graduated from high schools in which fewer than half of the seniors took either the SAT or the ACT; in contrast, twice as high a per-

TABLE 5.1

High School Profiles: Percentage Distribution of In-State Students,
National Data (1999 or Thereabouts)

	National *(All Students)*	*Flagship +* *SEL A Students*	*SEL B* *Students*
Size (Number of Seniors)			
Under 100	15	6	6
100–399	59	60	74
400 and Over	26	34	20
Racial/Ethnic Mix (Percent White)			
Under 50	24	15	12
50–84.9	31	39	35
85 and Over	45	46	54
High School Locale			
City	28	29	24
Urban Fringe	40	50	43
Town and Rural	33	22	32
Neighborhood Wealth (Family Income)			
Under 50K	48	29	35
50K–84.9K	42	50	53
85K and Over	11	21	13
Academics (Percent Taking SAT/ACT)			
Under 50	37	18	24
50–65.9	32	34	35
66 and Over	31	48	41
Academics (Mean SAT/ACT Score)			
Under 1000	49	25	38
1000–1099	43	57	55
1100 and Over	8	18	8
Academics (Percent Taking One or More AP Exams)			
Under 25	58	44	52
25 and Over	42	56	48

Source: Flagships Database, State Systems Database, and National High School Database.

centage (37 percent) of all high school seniors attended high schools where a minority of students took the SAT or ACT. Only 25 percent of matriculants at the flagships/SEL As attended high schools where the mean SAT/ACT score (among those who took the tests) was under 1000; in contrast, nearly half of all seniors nationwide (49 percent) attended high schools with mean test scores in this range.

    With regard to neighborhood wealth, only 29 percent of students at the flagships/SEL As came from high schools in which the median family income in the surrounding neighborhood was under $50,000; nationally, 48 percent of all seniors attended high schools in these lower-income neighborhoods. As the data in the table indicate, there were also some differences in the typical racial/ethnic mix of the high schools attended (with students at the flagships/SEL As less likely to come from high schools with predominantly non-white student bodies) and in the size and location of the high schools (with students at the flagships/SEL As less likely to come from small high schools and from high schools in towns and rural areas).

    The distribution by high school of students who matriculated at the SEL B universities generally corresponds to what we would have expected to find. Students at the SEL Bs came from somewhat "less academic" high schools than did students at the more selective institutions. They also came from high schools in neighborhoods where the family income was higher than the national norm for high schools but lower than the family income in the neighborhoods of the high schools that sent more of their graduates to the flagships/SEL As. Students at the SEL Bs were less likely to come from very large high schools and from predominantly minority high schools. Like all students nationally, the SEL B students were more likely than students at the flagships/SEL A universities to come from towns and rural areas.

    We are especially interested in how six-year graduation rates vary according to high school characteristics, and the data summarized in Table 5.2 contain a number of surprises. Most surprising to us is the small degree of variation in graduation rates by size of high school, racial/ethnic mix of high school, and high school location. To be sure, there are substantial differences in graduation rates between the flagships/SEL As and the SEL Bs (a very important pattern that we explore in detail in Chapter 10, where we are concerned with institutional effects), but within each of the two clusters of universities the relationships between graduation rates and these high school characteristics are nearly identical. There is an association between graduation rates and neighborhood wealth, especially within the cluster of flagships/SEL As.

    Graduation rates definitely vary according to our various measures of the "academic" characteristics of the high schools—within both clusters —though the differences are smaller than we might have expected them to be (Figure 5.1). For example, at the flagships/SEL As, where the differences are somewhat more pronounced, six-year graduation rates still differ by only 10 percentage points between students from high schools where the mean SAT/ACT score was under 1000 and schools where the mean was at least 1100. In considering these simple associations, the key

TABLE 5.2

High School Profiles: Six-Year Graduation Rates of In-State Students, National Data (1999 or Thereabouts)

	Flagship + SEL A Students	SEL B Students
Size (Number of Seniors)		
Under 100	74	50
100–399	76	52
400 and Over	80	54
Racial/Ethnic Mix (Percent White)		
Under 50	77	48
50–84.9	80	53
85 and Over	75	52
High School Locale		
City	77	50
Urban Fringe	80	53
Town and Rural	75	53
Neighborhood Wealth (Family Income)		
Under 50K	74	50
50K–84.9K	77	53
85K and Over	82	54
Academics (Percent Taking SAT/ACT)		
Under 50	73	48
50–65.9	75	52
66 and Over	80	54
Academics (Mean SAT/ACT Score)		
Under 1000	72	49
1000–1099	78	54
1100 and Over	82	55
Academics (Percent Taking One or More AP Exams)		
Under 25	73	50
25 and Over	80	54

Source: Flagships Database, State Systems Database, and National High School Database.

question, of course, is to what extent they are driven by the characteristics of the matriculants themselves—that is, we would expect the typical matriculant from a high school with a high overall mean SAT/ACT score to have a higher SAT/ACT score than his or her counterpart from a school where the overall mean was lower. Similarly, our measure of neighborhood wealth is in all likelihood serving as a proxy for the socioeconomic status (SES) of the matriculants themselves, and we know that

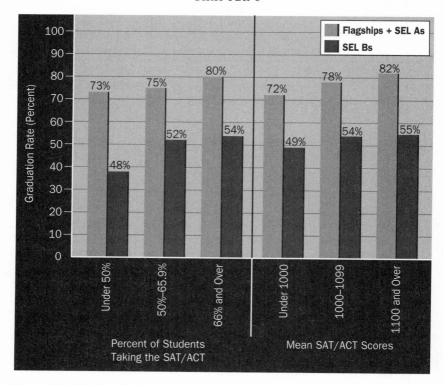

Figure 5.1. Six-Year Graduation Rates by Academic Standing of High Schools
(Percent Taking SAT/ACT and Mean SAT/ACT Scores)
   Source: Flagships Database, State Systems Database, and National High School Database.

students from high-SES backgrounds graduate at higher rates than students from lower-SES backgrounds.

Regression analysis helps us get at the underlying relationships. In general, a 100-point increase in the mean SAT/ACT score of the high school
is associated with an increase of about 4 percentage points in graduation
rates at both sets of universities before adding any controls. When we add
controls for (a) differences in other high school characteristics (size of
school and wealth of neighborhood), (b) individual student characteristics (race/ethnicity, gender, family income, and SAT/ACT scores), and
(c) institution attended, this coefficient declines to about 1 percentage
point (Appendix Table 5.1). We also ran regressions predicting six-year
graduation rates on the basis of the percentage of seniors taking the
SAT/ACT but obtained no interesting results.

Combining the two measures of academic quality is more revealing. We created three "ranks" of high schools: to be classified in the "Rank 1" grouping, a high school had to have a mean SAT/ACT score of at least 1100 and 66 percent or more of its students taking either the SAT or the ACT; "Rank 3" schools were those with mean SAT/ACT scores under 1000 and fewer than half of their students taking one of these tests; the middle ("Rank 2") schools were all others. Students from the Rank 1 schools who attended flagships/SEL As had a six-year graduation rate that was, in the raw data, 11 points higher than the comparable graduation rate for students from the Rank 3 schools and 5 points higher than the comparable graduation rate for students from the Rank 2 schools; adding all the regular controls, including controls for the SAT/ACT scores of the individual matriculants, reduced the difference between Rank 1 and Rank 3 to about 3 points—but it remained highly significant. Students who went to SEL Bs from the Rank 1 high schools also had a graduation rate advantage in the raw data of nearly 10 points over students from the Rank 3 schools. In the case of the SEL Bs, adding the controls made this difference non-significant; however, the difference between Rank 2 and Rank 3 schools continued to be significant (Appendix Table 5.2).

Taken together, these two sets of regressions suggest that the academic characteristics of high schools do affect college graduation rates, though by a modest amount after we account for differences in other variables, especially student characteristics.[7]

EVIDENCE FROM NORTH CAROLINA

Valuable as we believe this unique set of national data to be, it permits us to look only at the high school characteristics of those students who matriculated at one of the universities in our study—not at the college-going patterns of all seniors, grouped by the high schools they attended. In short, the national data allow us to study the relationships between high school characteristics and graduation rates but not enrollment rates. Fortunately, we have been able to complement the evidence from the national data by examining the records of the complete high school population of North Carolina seniors in 1999 (there were about 60,000 seniors who attended more than 300 high schools). Thanks to the co-operation of a great many people, we were able to construct a database that linked these records to later experiences of these seniors in college and to background information of many kinds (including information on race/ethnicity, gender, and SES). Thus, we were able to study the educational paths of well-defined groups of students all the way from high school graduation to enrollment in college (or not) and on to college graduation (or not).[8]

Eighth-Grade Test Scores

In addition to its coverage, the North Carolina database has a second advantage: it includes end-of-eighth-grade math and reading scores for more than 70 percent of the '99 cohort of high school seniors. Of course, we would expect to find differences among high schools in the academic achievements of their entering students, and failure to take account of these differences could lead us to credit particular high schools with subsequent outcomes (for example, above-average college enrollment rates and then above-average college graduation rates) that are really due to the students' own achievements before they even entered high school—a problem that we were able to address only imperfectly when we worked with the national data.

These eighth-grade test scores proved to be powerful predictors of many of the educational outcomes we observe in North Carolina—especially college enrollment rates for students of all races/ethnicities and both genders. To cite the extremes, just 11 percent of students in the bottom quartile of the distribution of eighth-grade scores enrolled at a four-year college compared with 72 percent of those in the top quartile. Also, very large black-white differences in eighth-grade test scores explain the *entirety* of the substantial black-white gap in enrollment rates.[9] The eighth-grade scores also proved to be highly correlated with SAT scores. These results will be of independent interest to some readers, and they are of course consistent with the large body of literature in psychology that stresses how abilities are developed over many years and are strongly influenced by parental behavior in children's early youth.[10]

An obvious next question is "To what extent does the high school matter at all—given the ability of these pre–high school credentials to predict future outcomes?" The short answer is that the characteristics of the North Carolina high schools do indeed matter, even after we take account of differences in prior academic achievements of students and differences in family background of students attending various high schools—and that they matter more for some groups of students than for others. There is no denying, however, that the incoming student profiles "inherited" by high schools, defined both by the mix of their students in terms of race/ethnicity and gender and even more strikingly by eighth-grade test scores, are tremendously consequential determinants of subsequent college enrollment patterns.[11]

High School Characteristics in General

We are especially interested in the associations between the academic characteristics of North Carolina high schools and both enrollment and graduation patterns. However, we need first to consider the effects of other school characteristics. Most of these findings are negative ones, once more of "the dog didn't bark" variety, but that does not diminish their importance. For example, although there is a mild positive association between the size of the high school and college matriculation rates, this relationship disappears entirely when we control for other high school characteristics; there is no evidence in these data that small size, in and of itself, is an advantage. Location also matters less than we might have expected. We do find that students at big-city schools go either to four-year colleges (which they do in large numbers) or to no college at all; students at high schools outside big cities are more likely than others to go to two-year colleges. We find no evidence of lower six-year graduation rates among students from high schools in rural areas (and find that these students have even some modest advantage over students from high schools in most other areas).

As we would expect, high schools in relatively wealthy neighborhoods have somewhat higher college matriculation rates than do other schools. About half of this effect disappears when we add controls for eighth-grade scores (because, as we would expect, these schools enroll students who are, on average, better prepared than most entering high school students), but there is still a matriculation advantage of 4 percentage points associated with going to a high school in a relatively affluent neighborhood. Students from these high schools also graduate at modestly higher rates than do students from other schools. We believe that these relationships are due mainly to the association between neighborhood wealth and both family income and parental education (which of course also affect eighth-grade scores). It is worth noting that we find no consistent relationship between the racial mix of the school (measured by the percentage of black students in it) and either matriculation rates or graduation rates. The patterns are highly erratic, and we suspect that this is because of the complicated interactions in North Carolina between racial mix and the appeal of historically black colleges and universities (HBCUs) to black students.

Academic Levels of High Schools and Enrollment and Graduation Rates

To study the effects of the academic characteristics of high schools on the outcomes of their students, we assigned all North Carolina high schools to one of three academic levels (I, II, and III) on the basis of combinations of four measurable characteristics that seem especially relevant: percentage of seniors taking the SAT, average SAT scores of the students who took the SAT, average "adjusted" SAT scores for all students (SAT scores for SAT-takers, with the scores of those who did not take the SAT predicted based on their scores on state exams in English and algebra taken in 9th or 10th grade), and number of AP courses taken by students.[12] The exact methodology is described in Appendix C.[13]

Looking first at the "raw" relation between the academic level of the high school and the college enrollment rate of high school seniors, we find that appreciably larger numbers of seniors went on to college from Level I high schools than from Level II high schools and that the enrollment rate was lower yet for those from Level III schools (Figure 5.2). These patterns are even more pronounced when we focus on enrollment at four-year colleges than when we look at overall enrollment at both four-year and two-year colleges: 54 percent of seniors from Level I high schools went to four-year colleges versus just 27 percent from Level III schools.

The much smaller fraction of students from Level III high schools who attended four-year institutions then had a six-year college graduation rate that was 12 percentage points lower than the rate among the far larger population of college-going students from Level I high schools (Figure 5.3).

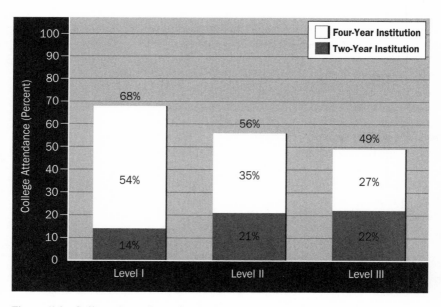

Figure 5.2. College Attendance by Academic Level of High School
Source: North Carolina High School Seniors Database.

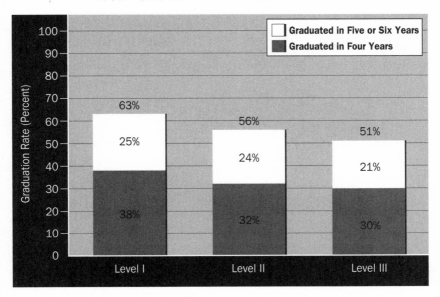

Figure 5.3. College Graduation Rates (at Four-Year Universities) by Academic Level of High School
    Source: North Carolina High School Seniors Database.

Here again we see an initial set of disparities (this time, in matriculation rates by academic level of high school) increase when we move to the next stage of the educational process and consider the outcomes of those who did enroll in college. Combining matriculation rates and graduation rates reveals that 34 percent of all the seniors who attended Level I high schools earned bachelor's degrees within six years compared with just 14 percent of the seniors who attended the Level III high schools.[14] These simple calculations illustrate the advantage of being able to examine both enrollment and graduation rates, which we cannot do with the national data.

   To be sure, this "cumulative" disparity evident in the raw data is affected by many factors for which the high schools can neither be credited nor blamed (with differences in the eighth-grade test scores of their entering students the most prominent variable, along with differences in family backgrounds). More specifically, the differences in enrollment rates are hardly surprising in light of differences among high schools in entering student populations and in other high school characteristics. Adjusting for these differences with regressions changes the picture noticeably but not completely. For simplicity's sake, we compare only Level I and Level III high schools and focus on enrollment at four-year colleges. The very large raw difference in enrollment rates of more than 25 points falls to just over 5 points after we adjust for differences in race/ethnicity, gender, eighth-grade test scores, and other high school characteristics—especially wealth of the neighborhood, which we believe reflects parental incomes and education (Appendix Table 5.3). However, the remaining net difference of 5 percentage points in matriculation rates is, needless to say, far from trivial.[15]

Turning now to college graduation rates, the raw data indicate that six-year graduation rates were 5 to 6 percentage points higher among students who came from Level I high schools than among students from Level III high schools (6 points higher among those who went to SEL A universities and 5 points higher among those who went to SEL Bs). Adding controls for differences in eighth-grade scores and family background eliminates these differences between Level I and Level III high schools at both SEL As and SEL Bs; attending a Level II high school (rather than a Level I high school) did, however, have a significant negative effect on graduation rates at SEL Bs (Appendix Table 5.4).[16]

There is also some evidence that attending a Level I high school is particularly strongly associated with high college graduation rates among students with very good high school records who attended one of the SEL As (Appendix Table 5.5). Students from Level I high schools who had GPAs above 4.0 and attended a SEL A had a graduation rate advantage of 8 percentage points (on an "other-things-equal" basis) over students with comparable grades who attended a Level III high school. Students from Level I high schools with lower GPAs and students from these high schools who attended SEL Bs did not enjoy anything like such a large graduation rate advantage. This relationship is consistent with a proposition advanced by Professor Caroline Hoxby, who has pointed out that the most highly talented students benefit the most from going to an academically strong institution because they are able to take the fullest advantage of the educational resources that are offered. Hoxby made her argument in the context of achievement at the college level, but we see no reason why it should not apply at both high school and college levels.[17]

In sum, the evidence from North Carolina tells us that the academic level of the high school does matter, but that it matters much less than is suggested by looking only at the unadjusted data and much less than most people seem to assume it does—a conclusion that is supported by some of the cross-tabulations of SAT scores, high school GPA, level of high school, and graduation rates reported in the next chapter.

A research task for others is to look in far greater depth than we could at the characteristics of particular high schools that "over-" and "under-achieved" relative to how we would have expected their students to perform on the basis of characteristics known to us. We believe that efforts to improve high schools can benefit greatly from this kind of "micro" analysis and from controlled studies of the effects of introducing various innovations. It is encouraging to see commitments to carrying out just this kind of much-needed research by departments of education in many cities (including our "home" cities of New York, Boston, and Chicago), as well as by independent research groups such as the Consortium on Chicago School Research at the University of Chicago and the newly formed Research Alliance for New York City Schools. The ACT has a long history of working on ways of increasing the quality and rigor of pre-collegiate studies, including its QualityCore program; the College Board has worked extremely hard over many years to encourage the introduction of AP courses and tests. There is no substitute for painstaking work "in the trenches."

It is also clear that, as many have observed, there is much room for improvement—across the board. One of the most sobering findings in the Chicago Consortium study of Chicago public schools was that, overall, "high schools provide few students with the skills, content, and credentials needed for access to 4-year colleges and for success once enrolled. *This is particularly disturbing when one considers that many of these students began high school with relatively high entering achievement test scores and managed to graduate from high school despite high dropout rates in CPS [Chicago Public Schools]. Thus, the low ACT scores and GPAs are not solely the result of students entering high school poorly prepared.*"[18] Recognition of the problem is surely the first step in solving it, but, as the Chicago Consortium recognizes so clearly, it is essential to move beyond recognition to positive steps that will improve outcomes.[19]

UNDERMATCHES: THE BASIC CONCEPT

The last big question that we want to pursue in this chapter is the extent to which the process of sorting students from high school to college aims those high school students who are prepared to take advantage of especially promising educational opportunities to the colleges and universities best able to provide them. High schools have a dual role. They have a responsibility not only to provide their students with strong preparation for success in college—and, as we have seen, some high schools are better at this than others—but also to provide the information and support that students and their families need if they are to translate "preparedness" into enrollment at those colleges and universities that will allow them to take fullest advantage of their talents.

The Chicago Consortium has played a pioneering role in introducing the concept of "match" into this discussion. In their reports titled "Potholes on the Road to College" and "Making Hard Work Pay Off," they use "the concept of 'match' to describe whether a student enrolled in a college with a selectivity level that matched the kind of colleges the student would likely have been accepted to, given his or her college qualifications." A major finding of their March 2008 report is that, across all students (in the Chicago public school system), about two-thirds (62 percent) did *not* "match" in this sense of the term; in their April 2009 report, which focuses just on students in academically advanced programs, they find that "less than half of students from these academically advanced programs ended up enrolling in colleges that match their qualifications."[20] (The Chicago Consortium sometimes uses the term "mismatch" to describe apparent mis-alignments in the matching process, but we prefer to avoid this term because of the connotations it has taken on in the context of debates over affirmative action. We speak, instead, of "undermatches."[21])

Consistent with our general approach, we will not summarize the findings of the Chicago Consortium (because they are already summarized exceedingly well in their report) but rather will seek to augment their findings by adding new evidence based on our own research with North Carolina data. In the main, the two sets of research findings are highly reinforcing—which gives us added confidence in them.

In pursuing our research into the sorting process, we have been concerned, first of all, with the basic question of how many well-qualified students ended up at institutions that are less selective than the ones for which they appeared to be qualified. But we have also wanted to know if there are disproportionate numbers of undermatches among certain groups of students—defined by race/ethnicity, family background, level of high school attended, academic qualifications, and rural or urban location. This last set of questions is highly consequential because of the evidence indicating that students attending more selective institutions graduate at higher rates and in shorter periods of time than do "observationally equivalent" students attending less selective institutions (see Chapter 10). To the extent that race/ethnicity and SES are determinants of where a student enrolls (and whether the student undermatches), we are confronted with issues of unequal access to the most promising educational opportunities as well as with the question of how well society at large succeeds in building as much human capital at the college level as it could build, based on the secondary school achievements of students.[22]

We do not mean to suggest that every student should attend the most selective institution for which he or she might qualify. "Undermatch" is a misleading term if it is interpreted as having this normative connotation, which we certainly do not attach to it. As the Chicago public school study puts it, "Match is just one component of finding the right college fit." Each student needs to find a college that, again in the language of the Chicago study, "meets a student's educational and social needs and that will best support his or her intellectual development."[23] Criteria often conflict with one another. Just as the optimal college graduation rate is not 100 percent, there may be good reasons for choosing a college that has a selectivity level below the student's qualifications—but this should not be the norm. The Chicago study found that in many instances "mismatches" (in its terminology) were due to lack of information, inertia, and a simple lack of planning for college. These are not good reasons for mismatches (undermatches).

We believe a student should be made aware of the full range of higher educational opportunities available to someone with his or her credentials and then encouraged to reach for the most challenging opportunity that is a realistic option for the student.[24] There may be compelling reasons for choosing what may be a "safer" or "more comfortable" option (to be nearer to home, for example), but such decisions should be made deliberately, after weighing all the pros and cons. Our impression, buttressed by the Chicago public school study and other research, including research in Boston, is that the sorting process is often more haphazard, less carefully considered, and less informed than it should be.[25]

Presumptive Eligibility

The first step in analyzing matches is to decide what qualifications presumptively qualify a student for admission to a selective institution. We focus on combinations of SAT scores and high school GPA, because these are objective measures and commonly used admissions criteria. We created an eligibility frontier based on the actual admissions outcomes of the '99 cohort of North Carolina high school seniors who applied to North Carolina State University (NC State) and the University of North Carolina–Chapel Hill (UNC–Chapel Hill) (Figure 5.4).[26] If more than 90 percent of students with a particular combination of SAT scores and high school GPA who applied to NC State were admitted to either NC State or UNC–Chapel Hill, we assume that another student with the same academic qualifications would have had a very good chance of gaining acceptance to a SEL A institution in North Carolina (these two universities account for over 90 percent of all SEL A enrollments).[27] This SEL A frontier (shown with the dark shading in the bottom right-hand corner of the figure) bounds the relevant area.

Even though it is an empirical fact that some students with lower SATs and GPAs were admitted to and enrolled at SEL A universities, we do not think other students with these somewhat weaker qualifications can be assumed to have had a *strong* chance of attending a SEL A. Obviously if we had elected to adopt a less stringent test of presumptive eligibility (and had specified, for instance, that only 80 percent, rather than 90 percent,

		SAT Scores							
		Below 800	800–890	900–990	1000–1090	1100–1190	1200–1290	1300–1390	1400 and Above
High School GPA	2.0 and Below	NO 16.7		NO 11.1	NO 0.0	NO 0.0			
	2.3	NO 0.0	NO 0.0	NO 5.4	NO 12.1	NO 10.5			
	2.7	NO 6.1	NO 5.2	NO 10.8	NO 18.8	NO 33.3	NO 31.6		
	3	NO 7.1	NO 10.1	NO 15.4	NO 28.9	NO 41.2	NO 49.2	NO 68.2	
	3.3	NO 2.6	NO 20.7	NO 22.1	NO 41.9	NO 63.3	NO 73.2	YES 92.7	
	3.7	NO 14.8	NO 17.5	NO 35.1	NO 62.9	NO 86.3	YES 93.8	YES 94.4	YES 96.8
	4	NO 21.7	NO 45.9	NO 62.5	NO 85.9	YES 96.2	YES 98.1	YES 98.8	YES 100.0
	4.3			NO 83.6	YES 93.1	YES 98.7	YES 99.6	YES 100.0	YES 100.0

Figure 5.4. Grid for Estimating "Presumptive Eligibility" to Attend a SEL A
Source: North Carolina High School Seniors Database.

Notes: Each cell indicates the percentage of all NC State applicants with the indicated combination of high school GPA and SAT scores who were admitted to NC State or UNC–Chapel Hill, along with the presumptive eligibility ("NO" or "YES") for students with those GPAs and test scores. All cells with fewer than 10 students were dropped from this table. The boundary line is drawn at the threshold admit rate of 90 percent. High school GPA is a self-reported value from the SAT survey.

of the students in an SAT-GPA cell be admitted to NC State or UNC–Chapel Hill), the number of estimated undermatches would be much higher—but, to repeat, we wanted to be conservative in assuming that a student who met our presumptive eligibility criteria would have had a realistic chance of enrolling at a SEL A.

The Extent of Undermatches

How frequently did undermatches occur? We begin by looking at the population of students who took the SAT and—by our rather conservative criteria—were presumptively eligible to attend a SEL A (by dint of having had an SAT of at least 1000 and a GPA of 4.3, an SAT of at least 1100 and a GPA of 4.0, an SAT of at least 1200 and a GPA of 3.7, or an SAT of at least 1300 and a GPA of 3.3). All told, 6,217 students satisfied these criteria. A major finding is that of these highly qualified students, more than 40 percent did *not* attend a SEL A university but instead enrolled at a SEL B (30 percent), an HBCU (1 percent), a two-year college (3 percent), or no college at all (9 percent, according to the National Student Clearinghouse data).[28] Of course, some number of undermatches are to be expected; still, the fact that the overall number is this high suggests that it is worth carefully probing the characteristics of those who undermatched, which is what we do next, focusing initially only on those undermatched students who took the SAT because some key items of information are available only for this (large) sub-group.

Within this highly qualified group of seniors, undermatches appear to have been more common among black students (especially black women) than among white students—in part because a number of black students undermatched to HBCUs.[29] Unfortunately, we do not have sufficient data to look at undermatch rates among Hispanic students. Evidence from the Chicago Consortium research suggests that undermatching is a particularly serious problem within the Latino population in Chicago,[30] and if this finding applies nationally, this is grounds for serious concern, given the projected growth in the Hispanic population.

Not surprisingly, family income and parental education are both strongly correlated with college choices and drive many undermatches (Figure 5.5). Within this high-talent group of seniors, whom we regard as presumptively qualified for admission to SEL As, those from more affluent and better-educated families were appreciably more likely than their less privileged peers to attend one of the most selective universities.

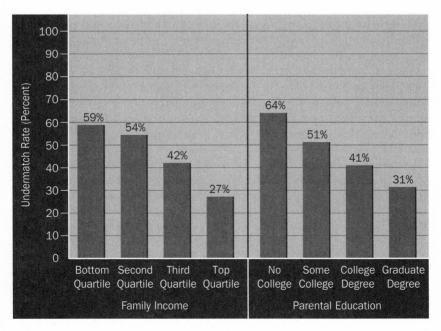

Figure 5.5. Undermatch Rates by Family Income and Parental Education
Source: North Carolina High School Seniors Database.

Nearly three-fourths of those from families in the top income quartile enrolled in a SEL A (only 27 percent undermatched), as did more than two-thirds of those from families in which one or more parent had a graduate degree. At the other end of the spectrum, it is striking—and disturbing—that *only about one-third* of all of these well-qualified seniors who came from families with no previous experience of higher education (neither parent had more than a high school diploma) attended a SEL A: 42 percent went to a SEL B, 2 percent went to an HBCU, 9 percent went to a two-year college, and 12 percent did not go to any college, giving us an overall undermatch rate of 64 percent. Similarly, the undermatch percentage for students from families in the bottom quartile of the income distribution was 59 percent—an equally troubling statistic.

To be sure, parts of these raw differences (roughly half in the case of parental education and roughly one quarter in the case of family income) are due to associated correlations with other variables. Still, regression analysis tells us that family income and parental education, though highly correlated, have strong independent effects on enrollment patterns. Although the quality (level) of the high school, high school GPAs, and SAT scores all vary with the SES of the student, controlling for these characteristics made only a modest difference on estimates of the overall impacts of parental education and family income. Both of these measures of SES have strong "net" effects on undermatches (Appendix Table 5.6). Moreover, it seems unlikely that differences in cost between SEL As and other institutions of higher education explain these patterns because in-state tuition is so low at all public institutions in North Carolina.[31]

We suspect that the primary forces leading to such high undermatch rates were a combination of inertia, lack of information, lack of forward planning for college, and lack of encouragement. These are the factors emphasized in the detailed Chicago Consortium reports, which include much qualitative analysis as well as case studies; there is every reason to assume that these same factors are operative in North Carolina—and everywhere else in the country, for that matter. There is also anecdotal evidence that some students from modest circumstances may have thought that they would be uncomfortable at a prestigious university such as UNC–Chapel Hill. However, although it is easy to accept the logic of this "lack-of-comfort" explanation, we have no way of estimating its quantitative significance.

In any case, the scale of the undermatch phenomenon among students from modest backgrounds suggests that there is a considerable opportunity to increase social mobility and augment the nation's human capital. The key is to find ever more effective ways of informing high-achieving students and their parents of the educational opportunities that are open to them—and of the benefits they can derive from taking advantage of these opportunities. Then, better ways need to be found to help these students navigate the process of gaining access to the strongest academic programs. To be sure, there is a "capacity" issue here, and we do not know how much elasticity there is in the North Carolina system (or in other state systems)—that is, we do not know whether the SELAs could in fact enroll more of these well-qualified students. But even if they could not simply add numbers, there is much to be said, we believe, for some "reshuffling" of places, which would presumably result in gains in opportunity and equity. Such a reshuffling might also lead to improvements in overall educational outcomes if the most highly qualified of these undermatched students did better than the students they displaced.

To sharpen our understanding of when in the admission and enrollment process students undermatched, we carefully examined the NC State and UNC–Chapel Hill admissions data. On the basis of these data, we are able to state categorically that the undermatch problem for students who were presumptively eligible to attend these two selective universities but failed to do so was concentrated at the application stage of the application and enrollment process.[32] Of the students who undermatched, nearly two-thirds (64 percent) were lost at the application stage; that is, only 36 percent of those who undermatched even applied.[33] Another 28 percent of those who undermatched were lost at the enrollment stage (i.e., they chose to go to a less selective institution—or no college at all—even though they were accepted at either UNC–Chapel Hill or NC State). The remaining 8 percent were lost because at least one of these universities rejected their applications.[34]

The April 2009 Chicago report offers, if anything, even stronger evidence attesting to the importance of the application stage of the process. In this study, Roderick and her colleagues found that, of all academically advanced students, "more than two-thirds . . . apply to two or fewer match colleges, and more than one-quarter of AP and selective enrollment students do not apply to a single match college."[35]

Looking next at even finer-grained differences in academic standing within this highly qualified population of seniors, we find that those who had excelled in high school—with both SATs of 1200 or better and high school GPAs of 3.5 or better—had an undermatch rate of 35 percent, whereas those who were not quite as strong academically—with either SATs of less than 1200 or GPAs of less than 3.5—had undermatch rates of 54 percent and 41 percent (left-hand side of Figure 5.6). It is encouraging that roughly two-thirds of the very ablest of the presumptively eligible students attended SELAs, but it is surprising that only about half of those with slightly weaker credentials enrolled at SELAs.

The academic level of the high school, which appears in the raw data (right-hand side of Figure 5.6) to be rather strongly related to under-

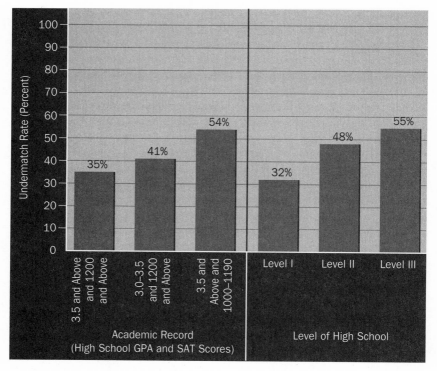

Figure 5.6. Undermatch Rates by SAT Scores, High School Grades, and Level of High School
   Source: North Carolina High School Seniors Database.

match rates, does not in fact affect these rates once we control for associated differences in family income, parental education, other high school characteristics, and test scores and grades (Appendix Table 5.7).[36] Other school characteristics such as size and location also had little effect on undermatch rates. Family income, parental education, and academic achievement are clearly more important than the characteristics of the high school in determining whether a high-achieving student attends one of the most selective universities for which he or she is presumptively qualified.[37]

Implications of Undermatching

Whether undermatching is in fact a serious problem depends to a large extent on how students who undermatched did in college as compared with comparable members of the '99 cohort who actually went to the more selective colleges for which all of the undermatched students were presumptively eligible. The North Carolina data allow us to answer this pivotal question with some precision.

Among students who were presumptively eligible to attend SEL A universities but went to SEL Bs, there were in fact substantial differences in both six-year and four-year graduation rates between those who actually went to SEL As (who "matched") and those who went to SEL Bs (who "undermatched").[38] The simple associations (Figure 5.7) reveal that, among all students who were presumptively eligible to attend SEL As, those who undermatched to SEL Bs had a six-year graduation rate that was 15 points lower than the six-year graduation rate for those who matched to SEL As (66 percent versus 81 percent). Time-to-degree was also faster for the matched students than for the undermatched group— as can be seen by comparing the four-year graduation rates. Of the matched students who graduated within six years, 73 percent graduated in four years compared to 67 percent of those who undermatched.

When we use regression analysis and include all of the standard controls, the differences in outcomes are muted somewhat, but not dramat-

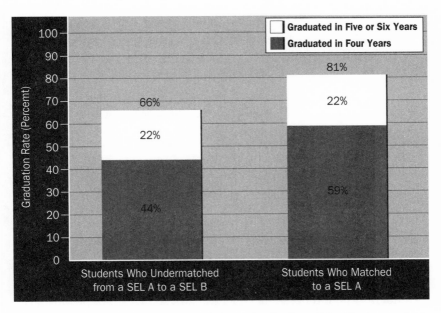

Figure 5.7. Comparison of Graduation Rates for Students Who Undermatched to a SEL B and Students Who Did Not Undermatch
Source: North Carolina High School Seniors Database.

ically (Appendix Table 5.8). The adjusted difference in four-year graduation rates is especially striking: it is 10 percentage points. Nor do transfer patterns "explain away" these differences, although they narrow them modestly.[39] In short, the undermatched students paid a considerable price in terms of the time it took them to complete their program of studies and in the reduced probability that they would finish at all.

It is also true, however, that the undermatched students at the SEL Bs— who went to less competitive institutions than their high school classmates who were in the same SAT and high school GPA categories but attended SEL As—earned higher grades than the students who matched. These patterns hold when measured both at graduation and at the time students exited from their schools, whether they had graduated or not. This result is exactly what we would expect. The undermatched students at the SEL Bs obviously had higher test scores and better high school grades relative to their classmates, whereas the matched students at the SEL As were competing with equally high-achieving peers. The adjusted differences in rank-in-class, obtained after we include standard controls in regressions, are considerable: 23 percentile points on the rank-in-class distribution among graduates and 20 points among all students at exit, whether they graduated or not. There is a clear trade-off here, between higher graduation rates and lower rank-in-class.[40] We presume that the graduation rate advantage of attending a SEL A university trumps the price paid in terms of rank-in-class, but this supposition needs to be confirmed by surveys of later-life outcomes.[41]

Undermatches to Two-Year Colleges and to No College (Including Students Who Did Not Take the SAT)

The previous analysis of North Carolina data captures the small number of students who undermatched from a SEL A to a two-year college. But many more students surely undermatched from a SEL B or an HBCU to a two-year college, and it would be highly desirable to carry out a comprehensive analysis that includes all of these students. The Chicago Consortium study argues that undermatches from four-year colleges to two-year colleges are, in fact, especially common and especially troubling; the large numbers of undermatched students in their schools include many who did not go to any four-year college. In North Carolina, we do not have either high school grades or SAT scores for most students who went to two-year colleges (or for students who did not go to college at all), so we cannot provide a rigorous assessment of this source of undermatching in this state.

The more limited data available to us on this source of undermatching are eighth-grade test scores. Consistent with our conservative approach to the definition of "presumptive eligibility," we select as presumptively eligible for a four-year institution those seniors who were in the top quartile of the distribution of eighth-grade scores. We know that 70 percent of these students went to four-year institutions, so this seems a reasonable cut-off. In the other quartiles, including the third quartile, fewer than half of the students attended four-year colleges, so we are unwilling to say that students with these scores could have been confident about their chances of going to four-year colleges (although many of them did in fact do so).

Overall, 11 percent of students in the top quartile went to two-year colleges, and another 18 percent apparently went to no college at all (according to National Student Clearinghouse data, which may well miss some college enrollments). We regard these students, who were overwhelmingly white (92 percent), as another group of definite undermatch candidates. In fact, 60 percent of these students took the SAT, and top-quartile students had an average SAT of 1098 and an average high school GPA of 3.5; being in the top quartile of eighth-grade test-takers certainly appears to be a good proxy for presumptive eligibility to attend at least a SEL B university.

Consistent with what we found earlier about the raw relationship between overall college enrollment and the kind of high school a student attended, data on the college-going behavior of seniors in the top quartile of the distribution of eighth-grade scores show that undermatch rates are related to the academic level of the high school (Appendix Table 5.9). Among students at Level I high schools, 5 percent of those in the top quartile of eighth-grade test scores went to two-year colleges and 15 percent apparently went to no college. At the other end of the spectrum, of the top-quartile students at the Level III high schools, 15 percent went to two-year colleges and 23 percent went to no college, implying a potential undermatch percentage of 38 percent. There appears to be a real opportunity to increase educational attainment by encouraging more of these students with excellent eighth-grade test scores to enroll in four-year colleges.

It would be highly desirable to know how differences in college enrollment and graduation rates translated into differences in later-life outcomes, such as earning advanced degrees, having different lifetime-earnings profiles, feeling more or less satisfied with the contribution one is making to society, and so on. To answer these questions requires either survey data or data derived from records such as those maintained by the Social Security system. We do not have such data for the North Carolina students we studied. However, data on later-life studies of somewhat similar populations suggest that there is indeed a high personal and societal cost associated with failing to take advantage of challenging educational opportunities. Graduating from college, graduating from a more selective institution, and graduating in a relatively short time confer long-lasting benefits.[42] There are certainly strong reasons for suspecting that undermatching in general—especially among those academically strong students who went to two-year colleges or to no college—has imposed a real penalty both on individual students and on society in general.[43]

In concluding this discussion of undermatching, we would re-emphasize these points:

- The high degree of undermatching among students from modest family backgrounds is noteworthy and worrying. SEL A universities were able to enroll *only 36 percent of these well-qualified seniors who came from families with no previous experience of higher education and only 41 percent of those from families in the bottom quartile of the income distribution.*

- Similarly, the numbers of students with top-quartile test scores who did not attend any four-year college are substantial, and the large number of students in academically advanced programs who undermatched in Chicago is striking. We suspect (without hard evidence) that students from low-SES backgrounds are disproportionately represented in these undermatch groups.

- The extent of undermatching is especially troubling in light of the evidence of differences in educational outcomes—lower graduation rates and longer time-to-degree—associated with failing to take full advantage of the educational opportunities for which students were presumptively qualified. Efforts need to be made nationwide to improve the process by which students are channeled (or channel themselves) into educational settings that too often fail to encourage them to realize their full potential.[44]

CONCLUSION

The evidence assembled here, from national data on high schools attended by students at flagships and other public universities in the four state systems and from more detailed data for North Carolina, is quite consistent. Some of the main findings—and some of the most surprising findings—are negative ones: contrary to what one might have expected to find, very basic characteristics of high schools, such as size, racial/ethnic mix, and location, have no clear association with either enrollment patterns or graduation rates. It may be that such relationships exist but are too "fine-grained" to reveal themselves in the large data sets under review here. *Academic* characteristics of high schools, on the other hand, are associated—albeit only modestly—with both enrollment rates and graduation rates. But attendance at academically strong high schools does seem, if anything, to be more important for high-achieving students than for students in general.

We are left with the general impression that high schools are indeed a lever that can be used to improve later educational outcomes but that care needs to be taken to avoid exaggerating their effects. Later-stage outcomes depend enormously on the qualifications that entering high school students bring with them from the eighth grade and on immutable personal attributes such as race/ethnicity, gender, and family background.

An even more powerful conclusion is that there is ample room for improvement in the imprecise and seemingly rather haphazard process by which students match themselves and are matched by others to postsecondary educational opportunities. The overall extent of "undermatching" and the prevalence of undermatching among students from low-SES groups is both disturbing and an open invitation to find ways—ideally, with high schools, colleges, and perhaps third-party entities collaborating—to improve the sorting process. Such improvements could lead to substantial gains on the equity, opportunity, and human capital fronts, conceivably at relatively modest cost.[45]

It is also clear, especially from the work of the Chicago Consortium, that high schools need to communicate another signal loudly and clearly: high school grades are tremendously important. It will not do for high school students to believe that "just getting through" is enough. The evidence presented in the next chapter is compelling, we believe, in underscoring the importance of inculcating a culture of high academic achievement in high school. High school students need to acquire both substantive knowledge and the coping skills that will enable them not just to begin college work but to finish degree programs successfully.

We turn now to a detailed examination of the predictive power of high school grades, SAT/ACT tests, and other tests that emphasize achievement. One recurring theme will be that different measures of achievement and promise have widely varying predictive power in different institutional settings and for various sub-groups. When we attempt to predict different things—college grades, college graduation rates, and time-to-degree—we must avoid a one-size-fits-all mentality.

CHAPTER 6

Test Scores and High School Grades as Predictors

THIS CHAPTER, more than any other, has its roots in the past, with branches that extend in many directions. Since at least the 1930s, back to the time of James Conant at Harvard and his close relationship with Henry Chauncey, the first director of the Educational Testing Service (ETS), there has been an ongoing debate over standardized testing and its proper role in "matching" students to suitable educational programs. Important books, including Nicholas Lemann's *The Big Test: The Secret History of the American Meritocracy*, have been written on this subject. Richard C. Atkinson, president emeritus of the University of California, has stimulated debate over how various standardized tests should be used. Eminent deans of admissions, such as William R. Fitzsimmons at Harvard, have tried to move beyond ideology by encouraging rigorous assessments of the claims of various admissions criteria in different settings.[1] Recent studies of high schools, such as the work of the Chicago Consortium, have produced valuable new evidence on the significance of high school grades. Organizations such as the College Board and ACT have had an entirely understandable interest in how the work of their organizations is received. There is an extraordinary degree of public interest in testing, a veritable industry of entities and individuals eager to help students improve their test-taking skills, and no lack of advocacy organizations opposed to testing (such as the National Center for Fair and Open Testing).

Our role is not to revisit this vast territory but rather to contribute what we regard as important new evidence based on the college records of nearly 150,000 first-time, full-time members of the 1999 entering cohorts at flagship public universities spread across the country and in four state systems. It would be wrong to fail to connect our findings to the major themes that have emerged in this ongoing debate, and we will intersperse references where they seem especially appropriate; but we must inevitably fail to do justice to this part of our task if we are to keep the length of this chapter under some semblance of control.

Our main interest is in how test scores and high school grades relate to the outcomes of most interest to us—especially graduation rates—and in how they affect disparities in outcomes that are related to socioeconomic status (SES) and to race. To anticipate one of our principal conclusions, different tests and other sources of evidence that can be used to predict academic potential and academic outcomes, such as high school grades, measure different things. A particular piece of evidence may be of great value for one purpose and of little or none for another. For example, an instrument that is useful in predicting college grades may have negligible value in predicting graduation rates. Moreover, which measures are most useful may vary depending on what population is under study; tests and other indicators that differentiate well among applicants to the most selective universities may differ from those that work best at less selective ones.

The issues discussed in this chapter can be highly contentious, and it may be helpful if we provide some context. To minimize the risk of misunderstandings, we wish to emphasize at the outset that standardized tests can be used for many purposes and that neither the SAT nor the ACT was designed to predict graduation rates. The results of the ACT, for example, "can be used to help guide students into the appropriate remedial or standard-level college courses . . . and can also help campuses identify students most in need of academic support programs."[2] Our work is limited to studying the power of these tests to predict graduation rates, time-to-degree, and college grades; we have no way of assessing their (perhaps considerable) value for placement and other purposes. As explained in Chapter 1, it is useful for our purposes to convert ACT scores to the SAT scale so that we can work with a single measure of test results regardless of which test a student took. Later in this chapter we present data showing that for the universe of students and institutions that we are studying, the two tests generate nearly identical predictions of graduation rates.[3] But of course the two tests are by no means the same, and readers interested in understanding the differences between the tests should consult the Web sites of the College Board and ACT.

THE MAIN STORY LINE: HIGH SCHOOL GRADES ARE A MUCH BETTER INCREMENTAL PREDICTOR OF GRADUATION RATES THAN ARE SAT/ACT TEST SCORES

In this book, for what we view as good reasons (see Chapter 1), the single outcome of greatest interest is graduation rates. At the same time, we recognize that other measures of success in college are also important, and near the end of this chapter we consider college grades—as we did in Chapter 4, where we examined grades, fields of study, and time-to-degree.

In the light of our focus on graduation rates, the main story line is straightforward. High school grades are a far better predictor of both four-year and six-year graduation rates than are SAT/ACT test scores—a central finding that holds within each of the six sets of public universities that we study.[4] As we will say again later in the chapter, it generally makes sense to use a combination of high school grades and test scores in predicting outcomes of all kinds, but how much weight to assign to the different predictors in various settings remains a most important question—a question to which our evidence speaks directly. The most convenient way to summarize the mass of data that underlies our conclusion concerning the primary role of high school grades is by presenting coefficients from regressions used to predict graduation rates (see Appendix Tables 6.1 and 6.2).[5]

The basic results obtained from this analysis for six-year graduation rates are summarized in Figure 6.1. We show pairs of regression coefficients, one for test scores and one for high school GPA, that predict six-year graduation rates within each of the six sets of universities in our study. Each of these coefficients shows the "net" (or "incremental") effect of the variable in question after allowing for the effects of the other predictor as well as the effects of any control variables included in the regression.[6] These coefficients are all standardized, with each unit representing a difference of one standard deviation in the measure—a convention that allows us to make direct comparisons of the sizes of coefficients for test scores and high school grades.

The findings are dramatic. As can be seen from the light gray bars in Figure 6.1, the coefficients for SAT/ACT scores are always less than 0.02, which means that an increase in test scores of one standard deviation is associated with an increase of less than 2 percentage points in six-year graduation rates; this relationship is even negative at the historically black colleges and universities (HBCUs). In sharp contrast, an increase of one standard deviation in high school GPAs is associated with increases of more than 10 percentage points in graduation rates at the less selective sets of universities (an impact that is five times greater than the impact of a comparable difference in test scores) and with differences of more than 6 percentage points at the selectivity cluster (SEL) II flagships and the SEL A state system schools. Even at the most selective public institutions (the SEL I flagships), a difference of one standard deviation in GPA has more than twice as large a net impact as a difference of one standard deviation in test scores. Results for four-year graduation rates are very similar. The main difference between the two sets of results is that both test scores and high school grades are stronger predictors of four-year graduation rates than of six-year graduation rates. The far greater relative predictive power of high school grades is again evident. (See bottom panel of Appendix Table 6.1.)

To check on the broad applicability of this key finding concerning the net effects of high school grades and SAT/ACT scores as predictors of graduation rates, we ran separate regressions for each of the 52 individual universities for which we had enough data. The consistency of the re-

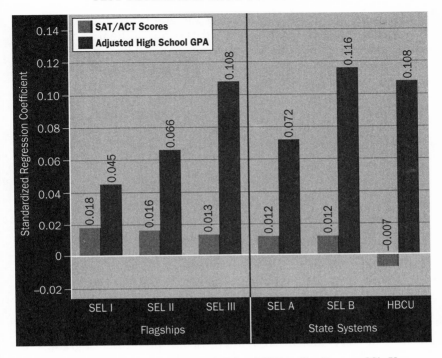

Figure 6.1. SAT/ACT Scores and High School GPA as Predictors of Six-Year Graduation Rates, Standardized Regression Coefficients, 1999 Entering Cohort
Source: Appendix Tables 6.1 and 6.2.

sults is extraordinary. *In all but one of these more than 50 public universities, high school GPA remains a highly significant predictor of six-year graduation rates after taking account of the effects of test scores.* The standardized coefficients for high school grades cluster tightly around the values shown in Figure 6.1 and, as the figure implies, tend to be larger at the less selective universities. In the SEL III and SEL B universities, as well as in the HBCUs, the standardized GPA coefficients are regularly in the range 0.9–0.12 and occasionally reach 0.16–0.17, which implies that an increase of one standard deviation in high school grades is associated with increases in graduation rates of 10–20 percentages points.[7]

Test scores, on the other hand, routinely fail to pass standard tests of statistical significance when included with high school GPA in regressions predicting graduation rates—especially once we leave the realm of the most highly selective public universities (where, as we saw in Appendix Tables 6.1 and 6.2, there is a modestly significant relationship). In the larger set of less selective public universities, there is rarely any significant relationship between SAT/ACT scores and graduation rates (the modal "net" coefficient is in the range 0.00–0.01), and in the half dozen institutions where there is a mildly significant relationship, it is as likely to be negative as positive. These institution-specific data underscore the exceedingly modest added value of test scores as predictors of graduation rates, especially when seen alongside the added value of high school grades. And, as we will see later in the chapter (Figure 6.5), the remaining incremental predictive power of the SAT/ACT scores disappears entirely when we add controls for high school attended, whereas the predictive power of high school GPA increases.[8]

Finally, we looked separately at the predictive power of the SAT and the ACT to be sure that our decision to consolidate the two test scores into a single measure was not a mistake. Looking first at the 24,000 students in the flagships who took both tests in 1999, we find that the incremental effects of an increase in scores of one standard deviation are nearly identical for the SAT and the ACT. For six-year graduation rates, the coefficients on the SAT and ACT scores are, respectively, 0.011 and 0.014. The corresponding coefficient on high school GPA is 0.07—about five or six times larger. The results for four-year graduation rates and for students in the SEL B Ohio universities who took both tests are qualitatively similar (Appendix Table 6.3). In short, there is no difference of consequence between the SAT and the ACT when used as predictors of graduation rates—and both are dominated by the predictive power of high school grades.[9]

Looking inside the Regression "Black Box"

One convenient way to provide more texture and a more intuitive sense of these results is to look at a "portfolio" of grids that show six-year graduation-rate outcomes in relation to both high school grades and SAT/ACT scores (see Appendix Tables 6.4–6.8).[10] To make it easier to recognize patterns in these data, we have highlighted selected "slices" of these tables.[11] In effect, we first hold grades constant and look at differences in graduation rates related to test scores *within a defined GPA range* (the vertical slices in the tables); then we hold SAT/ACT scores constant and look at differences in outcomes related to grades *within a defined SAT/ACT range* (the horizontal slices). In forming these slices, we have chosen the SAT/ACT and GPA ranges that include the largest number of students at each set of universities.

These grids are, we hope, easy to read, and we will comment only on the most distinctive findings. As we saw in Figure 6.1, the relative importance of test scores versus high school grades varies markedly by institutional selectivity. But even in the case of the SEL I flagships, we see from Appendix Table 6.4 that the relationship between SAT/ACT scores and graduation rates, holding GPA constant at 3.67–3.99, is quite "flat." Specifically, the graduation rate rises 6 percentage points (from 84 percent to 90 percent) as the SAT/ACT score increases from the 1000–1090 range to 1300 and above. The slope of the relationship between high school GPA and graduation rates is much steeper. When we hold the SAT/ACT score constant at 1300 and above, the graduation rate rises by 12 points (from 81 percent to 93 percent) as GPA increases from the 3.33–3.66 range to 4.2 and above.

The findings are similar at the SEL II flagships (Appendix Table 6.5), but it is worth noting that the relationship between SAT/ACT scores and graduation rates is even flatter here than it was in the case of the SEL Is.

The differences in slopes are even more pronounced at the less selective universities, and here we use figures to make it even easier to visualize the findings (Figures 6.2–6.4). Again we look at "slices" that first hold GPA constant (top panels) and then hold SAT/ACT constant (bottom panels). In the case of the SEL IIIs, the least selective of the flagship universities, what is striking is how much graduation rates rise when GPA increases from 3.0 to 4.0 and above—from 52 percent to 87 percent (Figure 6.2 and Appendix Table 6.6). The state system SEL Bs are in many ways the most interesting of all in that SAT/ACT scores had almost no power to predict graduation rates for the more than 41,000 students who attended these mid-level universities. In the "slice" of data shown in Figure 6.3 and in Appendix Table 6.7, the six-year graduation rate increases only erratically as SAT/ACT scores rise from below 900 to 1100 and above (and is actually slightly lower in the top SAT/ACT range than in the 900–990 and 1000–1090 ranges). High school GPA, on the other hand, is an extremely strong predictor of graduation rates at these universities; the six-year graduation rate increases dramatically, from 39 percent to 72 percent, as GPAs rise from below 3.0 to 3.67 and above. Finally, at the HBCUs (Figure 6.4 and Appendix Table 6.8), the graduation rate rises steadily and sharply with high school GPA and not at all with SAT/ACT scores.

Does the High School Attended (and Its Grading Standards) Matter When Assessing the Predictive Power of High School Grades and SAT/ACT Scores?

Suspicions about the reliability of high school grades are deep-rooted and grow in part out of the decentralized nature of American secondary education. Following his election as president of Harvard in 1933, James

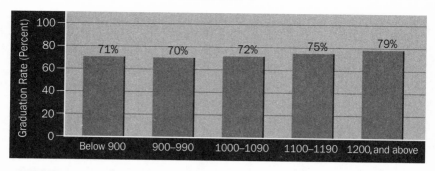

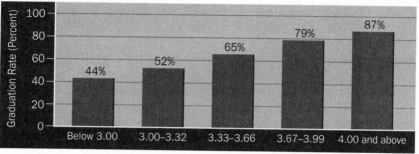

Figure 6.2. Six-Year Graduation Rates by SAT/ACT Scores (Holding High School GPA Constant at 3.67–3.99) and by High School GPA (Holding SAT/ACT Scores Constant at 1200 and Above), 1999 Entering Cohort, SEL III Flagships
Source: Appendix Table 6.6.

Conant was determined, in the words of Nicholas Lemann, "to depose the existing, undemocratic American elite and replace it with a new one made up of brainy, elaborately trained, public-spirited people drawn from every section and every background."[12] In considering how to set up a new scholarship program that would enroll students of academic excellence, initially from the Midwest, Conant and his young colleague, Henry Chauncey, had to answer the following question (again using Lemann's formulation): "How could you tell which high school seniors, in all the vastness of public education in the United States which was under the purview of 15,000 local school boards each free to set its own standards, were the most likely to perform brilliantly at Harvard?" Concerns about varying and even erratic grading standards are of course entirely understandable, and admissions officers constantly wrestle with the question of how much weight to give to an excellent academic record earned at what they regard as a poor high school.

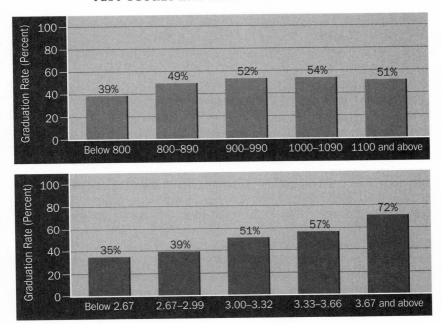

Figure 6.3. Six-Year Graduation Rates by SAT/ACT Scores (Holding High School GPA Constant at 3.00–3.32) and by High School GPA (Holding SAT/ACT Scores Constant at 1100 and Above), 1999 Entering Cohort, State System SEL Bs
Source: Appendix Table 6.7.

Thanks to the huge set of nationwide data available to us, we are able to offer a new perspective on this perennial issue. The findings already presented in this chapter certainly suggest that high school grades matter—indeed, that they matter a lot—but these initial findings do not tell us what the relationship between high school GPA and graduation rates would look like if we also controlled for the characteristics of the high school attended. The most straightforward approach is to add dummy variables identifying the student's high school to the regression equations used to predict six-year graduation rates—an approach that permits us, as it were, to "hold the high school constant" and compare the effects of high school grades on graduation rates at particular high schools on an "other-things-equal basis" (Figure 6.5 and Appendix Tables 6.9a and 6.9b).[13]

Two findings stand out. The first one, which concerns the "net" predictive power of SAT/ACT scores, initially surprised us. Adding the high school dummies deprives SAT/ACT scores of any significant incremen-

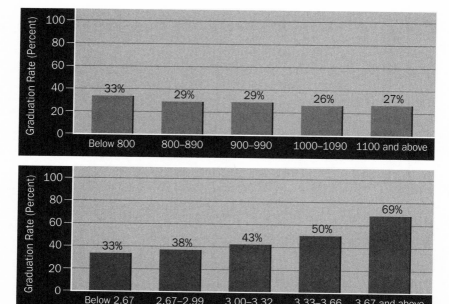

Figure 6.4. Six-Year Graduation Rates by SAT/ACT Scores (Holding High School GPA Constant at below 2.67) and by High School GPA (Holding SAT/SAT Scores Constant at below 800), 1999 Entering Cohort, State System HBCUs

Source: Appendix Table 6.8.

tal impact on graduation rates; indeed, the adjusted coefficients for SAT/ACT scores used to predict six-year graduation rates become slightly *negative* within all six sets of universities. We interpret this at first surprising reversal of the apparent direction of impact as indicating that in the previous regressions SAT/ACT scores were serving as a proxy for high school effects ("better" high schools had both higher SAT/ACT scores and students who ended up with slightly above-average college graduation rates).[14] This finding demonstrates that, where it is not possible to include high school fixed effects in the analysis, SAT/ACT scores may function as a means of adjusting at least crudely for differences in high school quality. This is an argument for using both high school grades and SAT/ACT scores in assessing the qualifications of a student, especially in the absence of reliable information about the high school attended.

The second and even more consequential finding is that, as we had expected, adding high school dummies consistently increases the sizes of the

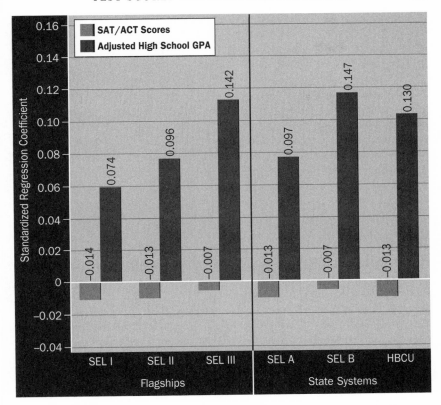

Figure 6.5. SAT/ACT Scores and High School GPA as Predictors of Six-Year Graduation Rates with High School Dummies Included, Standardized Regression Coefficients, 1999 Entering Cohort
Source: Appendix Tables 6.9a and 6.9b.

GPA coefficients—by between 2.3 and 3.1 percentage points within all six sets of universities when predicting six-year graduation rates. We believe these increases in the sizes of the GPA coefficients reflect the fact that—as Conant understood—some high schools have tougher grading standards than others. Secondary school grades, which we saw are highly consequential independent of knowledge of the high schools attended, are even stronger predictors of graduation rates when we take account of the characteristics of particular high schools. The adjusted coefficients suggest that, other things equal, an increase of one standard deviation in high school GPA is associated with an increase in the six-year graduation rate of 7.4 percentage points at the SEL Is, 9.6 points at the SEL IIs, 14.2 points at the

SEL IIIs, 9.7 points at the state system SEL As, 14.7 points at the state system SEL Bs, and 13.0 points at the HBCUs. These are *very* big coefficients by any reckoning—especially when we recognize that the overall six-year graduation rate at the state system SEL Bs, for example, is just 51 percent.

We were also able to examine the relationships among high school grades, the academic standing of the high school attended, and college graduation rates in an even more fine-grained way using the North Carolina data. Because we know so much about particular high schools in that state, we can compare outcomes for students within specified high school GPA ranges who attended high schools classified as Level I, Level II, and Level III (following the classification system described in Chapter 5). Put crudely, the questions of most interest to us can be stated as follows: Does, say, a high school GPA in the range 3.5–4.0 have the same predictive power in terms of college graduation rates if a student attended a Level I, Level II, or Level III high school? Should admissions officers take seriously a high GPA earned by a student who attended a relatively weak (Level III) high school? Conversely, should admissions officers overlook a low GPA earned by a student who attended a high school with a strong academic profile (a Level I school)?

Simple tabulations (Appendix Table 6.10) reveal, first, that across both SEL As and SEL Bs in North Carolina, six-year graduation rates *within specified GPA ranges* tend to be only modestly higher for students from Level I high schools than for students from Level II and Level III high schools— a finding consistent with our fuller discussion of the effects of the level of high school in Chapter 5. The differences by level of high school are clearest among students with high school GPAs above 4.0 who attended the most selective universities; there are only small differences at SEL Bs and none at HBCUs. More generally, most of the differences between Level II and Level III high schools are very small.

The parallel, and even more revealing, finding is that high school GPA is very positively and very consistently associated with six-year graduation rates *whatever the level of the high school that the student attended.* From the perspective of our interest in predicting the probability that a student will earn a bachelor's degree, the conclusion is straightforward: with modest qualifications, "a grade is a grade is a grade."[15] Students with very good high school grades who attended not-very-strong high schools nonetheless graduated in large numbers from whatever university they attended. On the other hand, students with relatively weak academic records in high school have much lower graduation rates than their higher-achieving high school classmates—again, whatever the academic level of the high school that they attended.

This is not to say that the academic level of the high school makes no difference when it comes to interpreting the meaning of high school grades. It does—as we saw clearly in the national data when we added high school dummies to the regressions predicting graduation rates, and as we see again in the North Carolina data.[16] There are also a number of other studies that indicate that both peer effects and grading standards in high schools affect success in college.[17]

Still, the central point to take away from this analysis is that grades earned by students in high school are extremely strong predictors of graduation rates even when we cannot (or do not) take account of the characteristics of the high school that the student attended. From our perspective, what is most striking about the high school GPA coefficients reported in Appendix Tables 6.9a and 6.9b is how large they are *before adding dummies that identify the high school attended*. It is these only-partially-adjusted coefficients (which are based on regressions that include standard controls but do not take account of high school attended) that speak most directly to the importance of a student's performance at whatever high school the student attended.

One other piece of evidence from North Carolina reinforces all of these conclusions. The richness of the North Carolina data allows us to study the power of the SAT and high school GPA to predict bachelor's degree attainment (including graduation from colleges and universities into which students transferred) for all '99 seniors who took the SAT, wherever they went to college. (This discussion pertains only to the SAT, because the ACT is not widely used in North Carolina.) We thought that this even larger data set, and this even broader investigation, might increase the predictive power of the SAT because bachelor's degree attainment reflects *both* enrollment rates and graduation rates—and SAT scores clearly influence admission decisions and enrollment patterns. But this is not what we have found (Appendix Table 6.11). Using "partial controls" (i.e., controlling for all of the standard variables but *not* controlling for high school fixed effects or university attended), the standardized regression coefficients for SAT scores and high school GPA are, respectively, 0.044 and 0.155—that is, the high school GPA coefficient is almost four times larger. When we add high school fixed effects, this difference becomes even more pronounced: the SAT coefficient falls from 0.044 to 0.017 while the high school GPA coefficient rises from 0.155 to 0.185. In short, this analysis reinforces the point that high school grades measure a student's ability to "get it done" in a more powerful way than do SAT scores—a conclusion that holds, we wish to emphasize, regardless of the high school attended but that is even stronger when we take account of high school characteristics.[18]

Our interpretation of this entire set of findings is a simple one. High school grades are such a powerful predictor of graduation rates *in part* because they reveal mastery of course content. But the "in part" formulation is critically important. In our view, high school grades reveal much more than mastery of content. They reveal qualities of motivation and perseverance—as well as the presence of good study habits and time management skills—that tell us a great deal about the chances that a student will complete a college program. They are one measure of coping skills and whether a student is likely to "stay the course." They often reflect qualities such as the ability to accept criticism and benefit from it and the capacity to take a reasonably good piece of one's work and reject it as not good enough. Getting good grades in high school, however demanding (or not) the high school, is evidence that a student consistently met a certain standard of performance. It is hardly surprising that doing well on a single standardized test is less likely to predict the myriad qualities a student needs to "cross the finish line" and graduate from college.[19]

Evidence from Chicago

Many other studies, including some conducted in California by Saul Geiser and his colleagues and a number carried out by the College Board and the ACT, have also shown that high school grades, seen alone and looked at in conjunction with various test score results, are powerful predictors of college outcomes.[20] Research carried out by the Chicago Consortium on School Research is yet another strong indicator that the findings we report, and our interpretations of them, are consistent with other evidence.

The results for students in Chicago mirror those reported here very closely. A recurring theme is that high school grades are a much stronger predictor of both college enrollment and college graduation than either test scores or the rigor of the high school curriculum. The Chicago Consortium study finds: "Students who graduated from high school with a GPA less than 3.0 were very unlikely to graduate from college. . . . On the other hand, more than 60% of students who graduated from high school with an A average (a 3.6 or higher) completed a 4-year college degree within six years. . . . To put it simply, students who were not successful in their high school courses were unlikely to succeed in college."[21] Interestingly, the data for the SEL III flagships and the SEL B state system universities in our study also show that there is a real break in the probability of graduating between students with high school GPAs above and below 3.0. At SEL IIIs, only 47 percent of students with high school GPAs below 3.0 graduated compared with 58 percent of those with high school GPAs between 3.0 and 3.3; at state system SEL Bs, only about 37 percent of matriculants with high school GPAs below 3.0 graduated compared with 51 percent of those with high school GPAs between 3.0 and 3.3 (refer back to Appendix Tables 6.6 and 6.7).[22]

The Chicago study also debunks the idea that differences in grading standards make high school grades in a city like Chicago of dubious value as predictors:

> There is a popular and compelling folktale of the urban high school student who gets straight A's, graduates at the top of her class and then, on entry to college, finds that she is not adequately prepared. There is a common perception that grades are vastly inflated in lower-performing high schools, and that students are given higher grades for doing more basic and poorer quality work than they would receive in selective enrollment or suburban high schools. . . . Data on the GPAs of CPS [Chicago Public Schools] graduates suggest that few fit the characterization of the urban folktale. In fact, many struggle throughout high school and graduate with GPAs that reflect mediocre performance in their coursework. . . . Low GPAs do not resolve the question of whether grades are inflated, [but] it appears that CPS teachers are not reluctant to give students D's or F's in core classes. (p. 41)

The report is unequivocal in stating: "The [highly positive] GPA-graduation relationship was consistent regardless of the high school that the students attended."[23]

The authors' explanation for these findings also resonates with our interpretation of the reasons that high school grades have such strong predictive value. They write: "Grades are . . . a measure of whether students have mastered the material in their classes, and *they indicate to colleges a different kind of college readiness—whether students have demonstrated the work effort and the study skills needed to meet the demands of a college environment*" (p. 37, our emphasis).

RACE AND SES

Another important question posed at the start of this chapter is do the same relationships among SAT/ACT scores, high school GPAs, and graduation rates hold for sub-groups of students defined by race/ethnicity, gender, and SES—or are there substantial differences in the predictive power of these measures across these sub-groups? The answer is easy: there are few, if any, differences of consequence when we look at these sub-groups separately (Appendix Tables 6.12–6.14). In general, the relationships are so consistent, and so much like those that we have already reported for all students, that there is little more to be said. High school GPAs are invariably stronger incremental predictors of six-year graduation rates than are SAT/ACT scores, across all categories of race/ethnicity, gender, and SES. Nor are the sizes of the coefficients among the sub-groups sufficiently different to merit extensive comment.[24] These highly consistent results are, we believe, both important in their own right and further grounds for trusting the overall findings reported in the previous sections of this chapter.

Race and SES interact with SAT scores in another, quite different, way that raises questions about the "equity" effects of relying heavily on these scores in the admissions process. The equity issue is hardly a new concern. In *The Big Test,* Lemann reports that during World War II Henry Chauncey had been disturbed to learn that aptitude test results strongly reflect social inequalities: "During the War, Chauncey had himself been quietly shocked and mystified when he saw, as the public and the test-takers had not, that overall statistics on the Army-Navy College Qualification Test showed far below average scores for southerners, Negroes, and [the] poorly-educated."[25] In the summer of 1948, two well-known educators, Davis and Havighurst, published an article in *Scientific Monthly* in which they argued that, in Lemann's words: "Intelligence tests were a fraud, a way of wrapping the fortunate children of the middle and upper-middle classes in a mantle of scientifically-demonstrated superiority. The tests, they said, measured only 'a very narrow range of mental activities,' and carried a 'strong cultural handicap for pupils of the lower socio-economic groups.'"[26]

Our data for all '99 high school seniors taking the SAT in North Carolina are consistent with the findings of other research in showing that race and SES are more highly correlated with SAT scores than with high school grades (Appendix Table 6.15).[27] In fact, race/ethnicity is quite a strong predictor of SAT scores. Other things equal—including family circumstances and high school attended—both black male and black female test-takers had SAT scores that were almost one standard deviation lower than the SAT score for a comparable white man (and just over half a standard deviation lower than the score for a comparable white woman). Hispanic females had predicted SATs that were about one-half of a standard deviation lower than the SAT scores for white males, and Hispanic males had predicted SATs that were one-third of a standard deviation lower. The coefficients for high school GPAs are all smaller (i.e., closer to zero), and, except for black males, much smaller.

Our two measures of SES (parental education and family income) also prove to be statistically significant predictors of SAT scores on an "other-things-equal" basis. Parental education is an especially consequential predictor of SAT scores and high school GPA, even after controlling for differences in family income. This important finding demonstrates again that highly educated parents have a major impact on the skills that their children take to high school, to college, and then on into life. Looking across all high schools, family income is also a stronger predictor of SAT scores than of high school GPA, but this difference largely vanishes when we look within high schools. In any case, the central point is clear: SES and race predict both high school GPA and SAT scores, but, in general, the impact on SAT scores is somewhat greater.[28]

The policy implications of these relationships between various predictors and race and SES need to be considered thoughtfully. On the one hand, it is clear that the association between SES and test scores is not spurious or an artifact but rather reflects a real "learning" advantage enjoyed by the children of high-SES families. Our own data and other studies show that, although test scores are correlated with SES, controlling for SES does not have much impact on the estimated predictive validity of the SAT/ACT.[29] However, it is also true that when test scores do not provide much additional information about likely outcomes, putting heavy weight on them has the (no doubt unintended) effect of giving an admissions boost to children from high-SES families with little commensurate gain in expected educational attainment. High school GPA is also correlated with SES, as we have seen, but less strongly. In its report on testing, the National Association for College Admission Counseling's Commission devotes a long section to "test score differences" and warns against allowing an overemphasis on SAT/ACT scores to "exacerbate existing disparities among under-represented students."[30]

PREDICTING COLLEGE GRADES

Thus far in this chapter, when reporting statistical results we have focused on predictions of graduation rates because our principal interest is in understanding factors that affect "finishing." The College Board, on the other hand, has focused on predicting first-year college grades (FYGPA) since its earliest days—in part, presumably, because Conant was interested from the first in finding tests that would identify high school students from the Midwest who not only would graduate (that was assumed) but would "perform brilliantly" at Harvard.[31] This emphasis on the ability of tests to predict FYGPA (which is how "validity" is defined) continues to this day, as can be seen by perusing the College Board's research reports.[32] Similarly, the ACT has also focused on predicting first-year college grades, as the materials at its Web site indicate.

Our data can be used to study the power of the SAT/ACT and high school GPA to predict first-year college grades, but we prefer, in most of our work, to predict cumulative GPA (or, often, rank-in-class) "on exit"— that is, when a student leaves the college or university first attended, whether by graduating, transferring, or dropping out. Rank-in-class on exit is a fuller measure of academic performance than is FYGPA, but we also make some use of FYGPA (see Chapter 3).

Our results are easily summarized. We find that SAT/ACT scores have a greater incremental power to predict college grades than to predict graduation rates. (Compare Figure 6.6 with Figure 6.1, and compare Appendix Tables 6.16 and 6.17 with Appendix Tables 6.1 and 6.2.) SAT/ACT scores clearly add "value" as predictors of college grades (as the research reports of the College Board and ACT correctly emphasize).[33] Still, here again, high school GPA is an even more powerful incremental predictor than is the SAT/ACT. This general conclusion holds for students at all six sets of universities that we study.

However, there are differences in findings depending on institutional selectivity. SAT/ACT scores are stronger predictors at the more selective universities than elsewhere (especially at the SEL Is, where they are nearly as strong as high school GPA). At the less selective flagships and state system SEL Bs, as well as at the HBCUs, a difference of one standard deviation in high school GPA has roughly double the incremental impact on predicted rank-in-class of a difference of one standard deviation in the SAT/ACT score. At both the SEL III flagships and the state system SEL Bs, a difference of one standard deviation in high school GPA predicts a difference of 12 percentile points in rank-in-class, whereas a difference

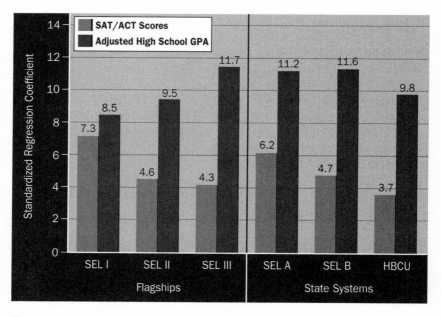

Figure 6.6. SAT/ACT Scores and High School GPA as Predictors of Rank-in-Class at Exit, Standardized Regression Coefficients, 1999 Entering Cohort
Source: Appendix Tables 6.16 and 6.17.

of one standard deviation in the SAT/ACT score predicts a difference of roughly 5 percentile points in rank-in-class.

Because our data all pertain to the '99 entering cohort of students, we have no evidence concerning the predictive power of the "new" SAT and the writing test that is part of it.[34] The College Board, however, has published the results of its assessment of the validity of the new SAT. Its report is based on results for a large sample of students who entered 110 four-year colleges and universities in the fall of 2006 and completed their first year of college in May or June of 2007. In brief, the College Board found: "The changes made to the SAT did not substantially change how predictive the test is of first-year college performance. Across all institutions, the recently added writing section is the most highly predictive of the three individual SAT sections. As expected, the best combination of predictors of FYGPA is high school GPA and SAT scores."[35]

Three economists at the University of Georgia studied the predictive power of the new SAT for 4,300 University of Georgia first-time freshmen in the 2006 freshman class. The authors found that the SAT writing test (SATW) is a better predictor of FYGPA than SAT–Verbal or SAT–Math and that the effect of the new SATW largely subsumes the effect of the SAT–Verbal. Another key finding is: "At the margin, high school GPA is a stronger predictor of first-year GPA than any individual SAT score."[36]

ACHIEVEMENT TESTS, "SIGNALING" EFFECTS, AND GENERAL CONCLUSIONS ABOUT TESTING

We had not expected to find that SAT/ACT scores are such relatively weak incremental predictors of college outcomes—as compared with high school grades—but now that the new evidence is in, we want to warn against misinterpreting its implications. We do not conclude that testing in general is to be deplored. The right way to frame this entire set of questions is not, we believe, by asking whether tests are good or bad but rather by asking in what settings different kinds of tests are particularly useful as complements to a careful examination of a student's high school record.

SAT II Tests ("Subject Tests") and Advanced Placement Test Scores

Right now an especially trenchant aspect of this discussion focuses on tests of "achievement" versus tests of "general reasoning." The SAT, certainly as it existed at the time it was taken by the '99 seniors in our study, was widely regarded primarily as a test of ability to learn rather than as a test of mastery of content (achievement). ACT has always argued that its exam is more a test of achievement, but the fact that the scores on the two tests are so highly correlated and generate such similar predictions of graduation rates and grades makes it hard to assess this difference; Atkinson and Geiser argue that the two tests have tended to converge over time.[37] Both SAT II subject tests and Advanced Placement (AP) tests, on the other hand, unquestionably measure a student's knowledge of the content of specific subjects, such as math and history.

These two sets of achievement tests have been administered by the College Board for many years, and we have data showing the scores on the SAT IIs of about 14,000 students in the '99 entering cohorts at SEL I flagships and of 11,000 at state system SEL As (Appendix Table 6.18). When we add a measure of SAT II scores to regressions predicting six-year graduation rates that already include both regular SAT/ACT scores and high school GPA, we find that the coefficient for SAT II scores is small but statistically significant at the SEL Is and that including this variable drives the value of the coefficient for the regular SAT variable to zero (while leaving the coefficient for high school GPA essentially unchanged). But in the state system SEL As, the SAT II coefficient is itself zero.[38] However, the average SAT II scores are very strongly correlated with SAT/ACT scores (0.80 at both the SEL Is and the SEL As), so coefficients from regressions that include both variables should be interpreted with caution.

Fortunately, we have AP scores for many more students across a wider range of universities—indeed, we have scores for almost 60,000 students spread more or less evenly over SEL I and SEL II flagships and state system SEL As and SEL Bs.[39] (But here too there were insufficient data to allow us to present results for students at Flagship SEL IIIs and at HBCUs.) The average AP score is a significant predictor of six-year graduation rates at three of these four sets of universities (see Appendix Table 6.19a); only at the state system SEL Bs do we fail to find a statistically significant relationship.[40] The standardized coefficients are in the 2- to 3-point range, which means that an increase of one standard deviation in average AP scores was associated with an increase of 2 to 3 percentage points in graduation rates (after controlling for associated differences in regular SAT/ACT scores, high school GPAs, and university attended). This achievement test score was a far better incremental predictor of graduation rates than were scores on the regular SAT/ACT and, as in the case of SAT IIs, including this achievement-test variable in the regression equation entirely removed any positive relationship between the regular SAT/ACT scores and graduation rates. High school GPA, in contrast, continued to be an even stronger incremental predictor of graduation rates than was the AP score when all three measures were included in the same regression—especially in the SEL IIs and the state system SEL As and SEL Bs.[41]

We conclude that scores on achievement tests of various kinds, especially AP tests, are very useful additions to the bank of information used to select and place students—particularly high-achieving students who are applying to highly selective universities. It is also important to emphasize that scores on achievement tests are better predictors of outcomes than SAT scores for all students, including minority students and students from low-SES backgrounds. It is ironic that in the 1930s President Conant opposed achievement tests because he thought that "they favored rich boys whose parents could buy them top-flight high school instruction."[42] Contrary to what Conant believed in an earlier day (and he later expressed a different viewpoint), a judicious combination of cumulative high school grades and content-based achievement tests (including tests of writing ability) seems to be both the most rigorous and the fairest way to judge applicants. If AP scores of large numbers of students are not available, standard SAT/ACT tests also have a role to play, particularly as calibrators of high school quality and high school grading standards.

We think careful consideration should be given to the possibility, over time, of making much more extensive use of the results of the AP examinations. These tests are especially good predictors of four-year graduation rates (Appendix Table 6.19b), and we agree with Gaston Caperton, president of the College Board, that timely completion of bachelor's degree programs is especially important when financial pressures on individual students and institutions are so pronounced. At present, however, the general usefulness of AP test scores is reduced somewhat because—in spite of recent progress—African American students are still much less likely to take AP tests than are other students.[43]

If there is a movement toward wider use of content-based achievement tests, as we hope there will be, one consequence could be at least some push toward development of a national curriculum—again, in our view, a potentially desirable (though also surely controversial) development. The value of content-based achievement tests clearly depends on how well such tests are aligned with curricula. It is revealing to note that where there is a close match, as in the case of the Graduate Record Examination subject tests at the graduate level, the predictive power of achievement tests is very strong.[44]

Signaling Effects

Among the many participants in the long debate over the respective merits of test scores and high school grades, Richard Atkinson, president emeritus of the University of California (and a distinguished psychologist), has been unusually persistent and thoughtful. In his "personal perspective" on these issues, presented as an invited lecture to the American Educational Research Association in 2004 and then published in 2005, President Atkinson called attention to the "signaling" effects of different kinds of tests. Atkinson recalled that when he visited his granddaughter, then in the sixth grade, he found her "already diligently preparing for the SAT by testing herself on long lists of verbal analogies." He continued: "She had a corpus of quite obscure words to memorize, and then she proceeded to construct analogies using the words. I was amazed at the amount of time and effort involved, all in anticipation of the SAT. Was this how I wanted my granddaughter to spend her study time?"[45] At the end of his talk, Atkinson observed: "One of the clear lessons of history is that colleges and universities, through their admissions requirements, strongly influence what is taught in the schools. From my viewpoint, the most important reason for changing the SAT [as it has now been changed] is to send a clear message to K–12 students, their teachers and parents, that learning to write and mastering a solid background in mathematics is of critical importance." Even though the predictive value of the "new" SAT is about the same as the predictive value of the old SAT, it can be regarded as a definite improvement over its predecessor precisely because of the clear signals it sends about the importance of writing and mathematics.[46]

Curriculum-based achievement tests, especially AP tests, would seem to have even stronger signaling effects. As Geiser has suggested, these signaling effects may be a better argument in their favor than modest statistical differences in their predictive power. They reinforce teaching and learning of a rigorous academic curriculum, and they also serve a diagnostic function: "Achievement-test scores provide feedback on the specific areas of the curriculum where students are strongest and weakest."[47]

Signaling effects can of course be negative as well as positive. If greater emphasis were to be given to both high school grades and achievement tests, it would be important to be alert to the possible presence of "general equilibrium" effects. One person has suggested that such a move might trigger the establishment of an "AP-exam-coaching" industry, much as the emphasis on the SAT has stimulated Kaplan and others to help students prepare to take these tests. Putting more weight on high school grades might also increase incentives to "game" such grades as well —for example, families might be more inclined to choose high schools with easier grading policies, and high schools might find themselves under more pressure to ease up on grading standards. We believe that putting more emphasis on content-based tests of various kinds can serve as some protection against "grade inflation" at the high school level—at the same time that the achievement tests provide valuable diagnostic information in their own right. In general, it is a judicious combination of high school grades and achievement tests (especially AP tests, including the writing component) that we regard as especially promising.[48] In many settings (especially in the case of highly selective institutions, and especially in the absence of AP scores for many applicants), standard SAT/ACT tests also have definite value—in part because of their usefulness in predicting grades and in part as a check on any tendency to "game" high school GPA measures.

––––––––––

In concluding this discussion, we want to return to the theme that the right question is not "To test or not to test?" Rather, the basic question is this: What set of tests and other measures is most useful in a particular setting? What makes sense for the small number of Harvards of this world may make little if any sense for the typical university in a state system. The case for continued use of standard SAT/ACT tests is, as we have said, strongest at the most selective colleges and universities. It is easy to understand why President Conant was interested in the creation of a test that would predict "academic brilliance." He did not have to worry about Harvard's graduation rate. But most universities do have to be concerned about how many of their entering students finish, and the evidence is compelling that high school grades and scores on achievement tests are the best predictors of whether a student will graduate.

From a national standpoint, it is unfortunate, in our view, that so much emphasis has been placed on predicting first-year grades. It is easy to understand the appeal of this metric because evidence can be obtained so early in a student's academic career and so soon after the test was administered—and predicting grades is a valuable thing to do. But it would be better, we believe, to exercise more patience. Testing organizations need to continue working to devise tests that complement high school grades, including both content-based achievement tests and tests of non-cognitive skills, in order to help students, parents, high schools, and colleges make the best possible educational matches—bearing in mind the importance of "finishing" and not just getting off to a good start. It is also important that we continue to devise tests that will not further disadvantage students who are already disadvantaged—tests that will not discourage worthy students from modest backgrounds from even applying to an appropriate college. Finally, tests should send the right signals to all parties about the need for students to master content and not just be good at test-taking, which is of course a means to an end, not an end in and of itself.

Transfer Students and the Path from Two-Year to Four-Year Colleges

OUR STUDY of educational attainment necessarily focuses on four-year in-stitutions, for it is receipt of bachelor's degrees that is of particular in-terest to us. More specifically, we focus on first-time, full-time freshmen at the 21 flagship universities and in the four state systems in our study because the "traditional" path to a bachelor's degree is to matriculate at a four-year college the fall after finishing high school, then graduate from college four years later. However, we have seen that a non-trivial number of students leave their initial four-year institution and earn degrees else-where (Chapter 3) and that even those who remain and graduate often take more than four years to do so (Chapter 4). Additionally, many stu-dents pursuing four-year degrees begin their studies at two-year institu-tions. Figure 7.1 shows that two-year institutions were a rapidly growing sector of American higher education from the mid-1960s through the mid-1970s and enrolled a majority of first-time freshmen from 1972 to 1985. The two-year enrollment share has declined only slightly since then and was 45 percent for the 1999 entering cohort (the cohort we study in-tensively) and 41 percent in 2005 (the most recent year for which data are available).[1]

Beginning at a two-year college can yield substantial financial savings. In 2006–07, the average in-state yearly tuition at four-year public univer-sities was $5,685, more than twice the $2,016 charged by two-year institu-tions.[2] The cost difference is quite a bit smaller for low-income students if differences in grant aid are taken into account. But there are also ad-ditional potential cost savings if attending a nearby community college allows the student to live at home.[3]

However, starting at a two-year college with the hope of later transfer-ring to a four-year college and earning a bachelor's degree can be risky. Using nationally representative data and controlling for differences in the characteristics of entering students, Reynolds estimates that begin-ning at a two-year college decreases bachelor's degree attainment rates by approximately 30 percentage points.[4] In recent years, several states have created programs aimed at encouraging students to enroll at two-year institutions and then transfer to four-year programs.[5] For example, the New Jersey STARS (Student Tuition Assistance Reward Scholarship)

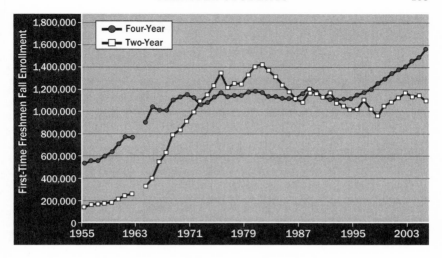

Figure 7.1. First-Time Freshmen Fall Enrollment, 1955–2005
Source: NCES *Digest of Education Statistics 2007.*

program has paid full community college tuition and fees for students
who graduate in the top 20 percent of their high school class and maintain a GPA of at least a 3.0 in college. Students who then transferred to a
participating four-year public university in New Jersey have received a
scholarship covering the full cost of tuition and fees.[6] Another state that
explicitly encourages students to start at two-year colleges is Virginia,
which recently introduced a policy that provides students who earn an associate's degree from a community college with additional financial aid
to complete their junior and senior years at a public university.[7]

This chapter approaches the study of transfer students in three ways.
First, we examine the decision to start at a two- or a four-year college from
the perspective of the student. Using data for the 1999 North Carolina
high school seniors, we find that students who began their studies at two-
year colleges were much less likely to earn bachelor's degrees than were
similar students who started at four-year institutions. As we shall see, this
large effect is observed even for the least well-prepared students, who
might be expected to benefit the most from starting at a two-year college.
This finding is consistent with Reynolds's work using national data.[8]

In the second part of the chapter, we adopt the perspective of the four-
year institution by comparing the entering characteristics and college
outcomes of the incoming transfer students and first-time freshmen at
the broad group of public universities in our study. In order to sharpen
comparisons and focus on traditional-age college students, we exclude all
students (both transfers and freshmen) aged 24 and older. As expected,

we find that transfers from two-year schools are substantially more likely to be from low-income families and to enter with weaker credentials (as measured by high school GPA and SAT/ACT scores); however, they graduate at higher rates than first-time freshmen with similar entering credentials. This pattern, which is especially pronounced at the state system selectivity cluster (SEL) B universities, suggests that many of the universities in our study might well improve both their socioeconomic diversity and their graduation rates by accepting more transfer students from two-year colleges.

Finally, in the last part of the chapter, we adopt a system-wide perspective and attempt to reconcile the seemingly conflicting policy implications of the student perspective, which suggests that more students should start at four-year schools, with the institutional perspective, which points to the desirability of having four-year institutions enroll more well-qualified transfers from two-year colleges, especially students from modest backgrounds.

THE STUDENT PERSPECTIVE: STARTING AT A
TWO- VERSUS FOUR-YEAR COLLEGE

In the first part of this chapter, we take advantage of rich data from North Carolina to examine whether students who started at a two-year college were more or less likely to ultimately earn a bachelor's degree than they would have been had they started at a four-year college. In general, it seems that the most direct route to a four-year degree is most likely to lead to success in earning a bachelor's degree. However, we might expect the least well-prepared students to be more likely to be frustrated by the difficulty of initially embarking on a four-year program and thus be more likely than their better-prepared high school classmates to benefit from starting at a two-year college. For the typical high school student in North Carolina, that does not turn out to be the case.

Students who began their studies at two-year colleges are very different from those who went directly to four-year schools, so it would be foolish to simply compare the bachelor's degree attainment rates of these two groups. In order to make a cleaner comparison, we first limit our analysis to students who took the SAT (and thus were at least thinking about going to a four-year college) and who indicated on the SAT survey that they wanted to earn at least a bachelor's degree.[9] We exclude students who attended a SEL A four-year institution (any school with an average SAT score of at least 1150), because most students who are deciding between two- and four-year colleges are likely to be considering only less selective four-year schools.

In order to adjust for the substantial remaining differences in student characteristics, we next divide students into 10 "propensity" groups based on their estimated likelihood of starting at a two-year college, which is determined by their high school grades, SAT scores, gender, family income quartile, parental education, and educational aspirations.[10] Within each of these propensity groups, students who started at two-year colleges are fairly similar to the students at four-year colleges, and thus their bachelor's degree attainment rates can be compared. We conduct this analysis separately for white and black students, because we suspect that many black students deciding whether to attend a two-year college are also considering historically black colleges and universities (HBCUs), which we wish to separate from predominantly white institutions (PWIs) in studying outcomes.

Figure 7.2 shows the bachelor's degree attainment rates of white students in each of the 10 groups separately for those who started out at two- and four-year colleges.[11] The leftmost pair of points includes students who were estimated to be the least likely (0–5 percent) to start at a two-year college, and indeed very few of them did (57 out of 1,091). The entering characteristics of two- and four-year matriculants in this category are very similar; their high school GPAs differ by only 0.03 (3.96 versus 3.99), and their average SAT scores are only 6 points apart (1204 versus 1198). Yet their bachelor's degree attainment rates are 36 points apart: 47 percent versus 83 percent. A dramatic difference!

We might have expected the difference in bachelor's degree attainment rates to be smaller among students who were more likely to start at a two-year college—in other words, those with weaker academic credentials. However, the lines in Figure 7.2 narrow only slightly as we move from lower to higher propensities. The rightmost pair of points, which represent 830 two-year and 317 four-year matriculants (with average high school GPAs of 2.60 and 2.65 and average SAT scores of 771 and 811), are 29 points apart. The attainment difference for each of the 10 groups ranges from 26 to 36 points.[12]

We repeat this analysis for black students, examining four-year PWIs and HBCUs separately, and present the results in Figures 7.3a and 7.3b. The results are noisier due to the smaller number of black students than white students, but the patterns are very similar.[13] Compared to black students who started at PWIs, those who started at two-year colleges were much less likely to ever earn a bachelor's degree. The lines converge somewhat, but the negative two-year effect is still 17 points among the two groups of students with the weakest academic credentials (and thus the highest propensity to attend a two-year college). When we replace the PWIs with the HBCUs, the pattern is largely similar—indeed there is even less convergence of bachelor's degree attainment rates as we move from lower to higher propensities to attend a two-year college.

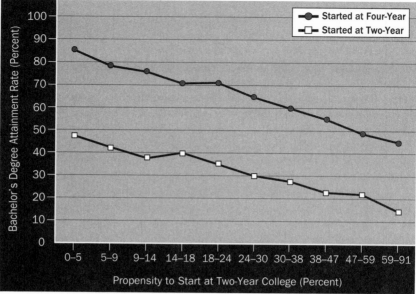

Figure 7.2. Bachelor's Degree Attainment Rates of White Students Who Started at Four-Year versus Two-Year Schools, North Carolina High School Graduating Class of 1999

Source: North Carolina High School Seniors Database.

In short, students in North Carolina who wish to earn a bachelor's degree are much more likely to do so if they begin their studies at a four-year institution rather than at a two-year college. The consistency of these results with Reynolds's analysis of national data is striking. Long and Kurlaender find a similar negative effect using data from Ohio, although it is somewhat smaller in magnitude.[14] Nonetheless, despite the negative effect of starting at a two-year college on bachelor's degree attainment, many students who aspire to earn a bachelor's degree still start at one. This is especially true of students from low-income families. These students are substantially more likely than students from high-income families to start at a two-year college (30 percent versus 18 percent), no doubt in large part because of the lower tuition and the greater possibility of saving money by living at home. Even among students with high school GPAs above 3.0, low-income students are more than twice as likely to start at a two-year college as are high-income students (23 percent versus 9 percent).[15] These results suggest that a potential way for four-year institutions to graduate more students from modest circumstances is to enroll more transfer students from two-year colleges—where large numbers of these students, including students with high school GPAs that are rea-

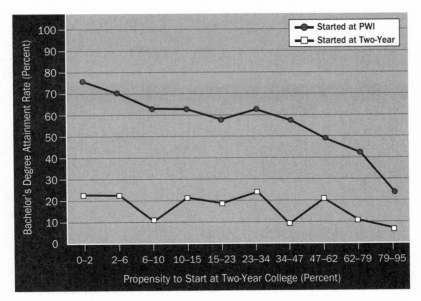

Figure 7.3a. Bachelor's Degree Attainment Rates of Black Students Who Started at a Predominantly White Four-Year School versus Any Two-Year School, North Carolina High School Graduating Class of 1999
Source: North Carolina High School Seniors Database.

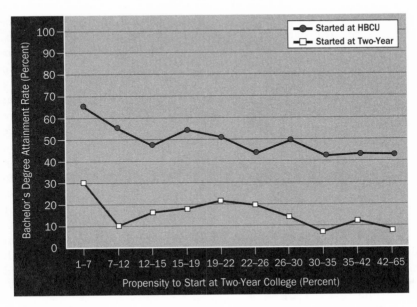

Figure 7.3b. Bachelor's Degree Attainment Rates of Black Students Who Started at a Four-Year HBCU versus Any Two-Year School, North Carolina High School Graduating Class of 1999
Source: North Carolina High School Seniors Database.

sonably high, are enrolled. But what does the evidence suggest about both the characteristics and the college outcomes of students from two-year colleges who do in fact transfer to the public universities in our study? This is the next question we address.

THE INSTITUTIONAL PERSPECTIVE: CHARACTERISTICS AND OUTCOMES OF TRANSFER STUDENTS

This part of our analysis looks well beyond North Carolina and includes data from the national set of flagship universities and state system universities in Maryland.[16] Even so, we cannot compare the outcomes of transfers by the selectivity of the institutions they attend using selectivity groupings as fine-grained as those in our analysis of freshmen because of the smaller number of incoming transfer students. In order to examine broadly similar institutions while maintaining large enough cell sizes, we split the 16 flagships and two systems of state universities for which we have the relevant data on transfer students into two groups, placing the flagships and state system SEL As in one group and the state system SEL Bs in the other. These two sets of universities, along with summary statistics, are listed in Appendix Tables 7.1a and 7.1b. The transfer admissions rate and number of transfers enrolled varies widely across these universities, as do the percentages of transfers coming from two- versus four-year colleges. Transfer policies presumably vary across these universities, and the findings presented in this chapter should be thought of as applying to the "typical" university in each grouping but not necessarily to each individual institution.

One important pattern, noted earlier, is that transfers from two-year colleges are much more likely to come from low-income families than are both first-time freshmen and transfers from four-year colleges (Figure 7.4).[17] Compared to freshmen, two-year transfers at the flagships and state system SEL As are much less likely to come from families in the top income quartile (25 percent versus 44 percent) and much more likely to come from bottom-quartile families (24 percent versus 14 percent).[18] In fact, the two-year transfers at these schools are about equally divided over the four income quartiles and in this respect can be thought of as "representative of America" in a way that no other group of matriculants in this study can be. The pattern is similar at the state system SEL Bs. At both groups of schools, the four-year transfers are only slightly less advantaged than the freshmen.

In addition to being from lower-income families, transfer students (especially those from two-year colleges) arrive with weaker academic credentials, at least as measured by high school GPA and SAT/ACT scores

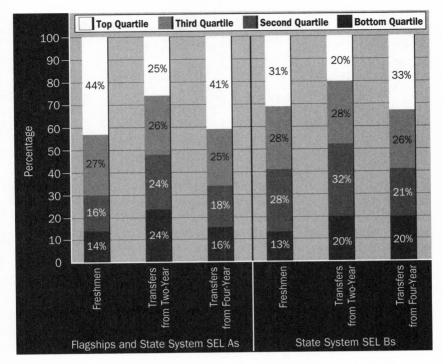

Figure 7.4. Family Income Distribution of Transfers and Freshmen, 1999
Entering Cohort
  Source: Flagships Database and State Systems Database.

(Appendix Table 7.2). At the flagships and state system SEL As, two-year
transfers scored 145 points lower on the SAT/ACT and earned high
school GPAs 0.48 points lower. The corresponding differences at the state
system SEL Bs are smaller, but still pronounced: 86 points on the SAT/
ACT and 0.38 GPA points.

Given these large differences in entering credentials, it is certainly
noteworthy that transfers graduate at the same rate (about 75 percent)
as the freshmen enrollees at the flagships and state system SEL As and at
a *higher* rate at the state system SEL Bs (65 percent versus 53 percent) (Figure 7.5). As expected, the transfers also graduate somewhat faster, because most arrived having already earned college credits toward their degrees. The transfer process, however, is not without time costs; two-year
transfers who graduated were about a year older at graduation than students who matriculated as first-time freshmen.[19] Nevertheless, given that
they chose to start out at a two-year college instead of taking the poten-

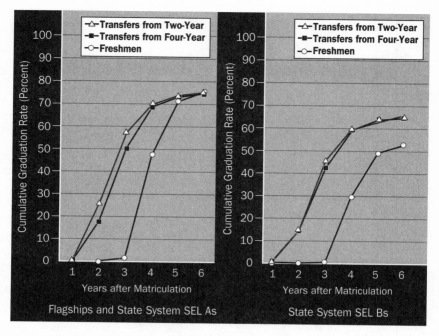

Figure 7.5. Graduation Rates of Transfers versus Freshmen, 1999 Entering Cohort
Source: Flagships Database and State Systems Database.

tially more desirable route of going directly from high school to a four-year college, they are clearly better off earning a bachelor's degree in five years than not earning one at all.

Compared to freshmen with similar high school GPAs and SAT/ACT scores, transfer students are much more likely to graduate. At the flagships and state system SEL As, transfers are 7–10 percentage points more likely to graduate than are comparable freshmen (Figure 7.6a). At the state system SEL Bs, the unadjusted difference of 13 points grows to an adjusted difference of 15–18 points (Figure 7.6b). If bachelor's degrees earned by the non-graduates at institutions subsequently attended (reported in the National Student Clearinghouse data) are counted, these differences decrease only modestly (Appendix Table 7.3). In other words, although freshmen enrollees are somewhat more likely to transfer than transfer students are to transfer again, this difference is not nearly great enough to explain the differences in graduation rates between the two groups.

Another important finding is that the graduation rate differences between transfers and freshmen enrollees are most pronounced among students from low-income families as well as among those with weaker high school grades and test scores. At the flagships and state system SEL As, two-year transfers from families in the bottom income quartile are 8 percentage points more likely to graduate than are low-income freshmen enrollees. The difference, at 15 points, is even larger at the state system SEL Bs (Appendix Table 7.4a).[20] Among students with high school GPAs between 2.50 and 2.99, two-year transfers are 21–24 points more likely to graduate than are freshmen enrollees (Appendix Table 7.4b). Four-year transfers in this high school GPA category also post markedly higher graduation rates than do those enrolled as freshmen but rates that are not as high as those achieved by the two-year transfers. The differences between transfers and freshmen enrollees are smaller but still substantial among students with higher high school GPAs.[21]

We believe that these superior graduation rates among transfers (after adjusting for differences in observable credentials and background characteristics) reflect strong selection effects. That is, students who come to four-year institutions from two-year colleges have already successfully managed the transition from high school to one kind of college experience. We strongly suspect that their subsequent success at four-year institutions, compared with the outcomes of first-time freshmen, reflects differences in aspirations, maturity, social capital, and coping skills (including a demonstrated ability to "stay the course"). The two-year colleges, in short, are a "sorting mechanism" that works to the benefit of the four-year institutions to which their students transfer.[22]

If we compare transfers to "homegrown" juniors—first-time freshmen who survived the sorting process of the first two years of college at the four-year institution at which they initially enrolled—we find that the homegrown juniors are slightly more likely to graduate. Controlling for high school GPA and SAT/ACT scores, the difference between juniors and transfers is 5 points at the flagships and state system SEL As and 3 points at the state system SEL Bs.[23] The same selection effects that increase the graduation rates of the transfers from two-year colleges to four-year colleges help the graduation rates of homegrown juniors at four-year colleges vis-à-vis the entire group of entering freshmen.

In addition to graduating at rates similar to or higher than the entire group of first-time freshmen, transfers in large part majored in the same fields and earned comparable grades as the freshmen. At the flagships and state system SEL As, transfer graduates were less likely to major in engineering and more likely to major in the social sciences, but these differences are modest and are not found at the state system SEL Bs (Appendix Table 7.5). Transfer graduates earned modestly lower grades than the graduates who enrolled as freshmen, but these differences are reversed once high school grades and test scores are taken into account (Appendix Table 7.6). As in the case of graduation rates, the difference

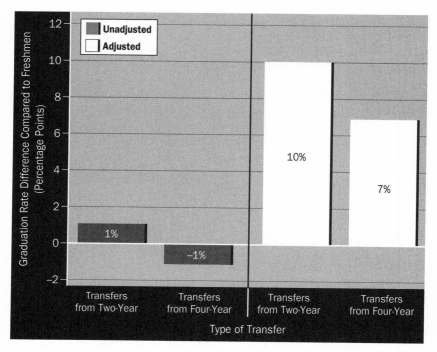

Figure 7.6a. Differences between Transfers and Freshmen in Six-Year Graduation Rates, 1999 Entering Cohort, Flagships and State System SEL As, Unadjusted and Adjusted

Source: Flagships Database and State Systems Database.

Note: Adjusted differences control for SAT/ACT scores, high school GPA, and university attended.

in college grades between transfers and freshmen enrollees is especially pronounced among students with weaker high school GPAs and SAT/ACT scores (Appendix Tables 7.7a and 7.7b). However, the differences in rank-in-class are not nearly as large as those in graduation rates.

Comparing freshmen and transfers with similar high school grades and SAT/ACT scores might be thought to allow us to observe whether transfers do better in college than we would expect them to do had they come directly from high school with those same credentials—as indeed they do. But, as we argued earlier, there are selection effects operating, for transfer students who demonstrated both the ability to finish an associate's degree and the commitment needed to go on to a four-year institution are presumably different from students with similar high school grades who followed a different path. Thus, a better measure of transfers' academic preparedness is the GPA they earned at their previous college. At the

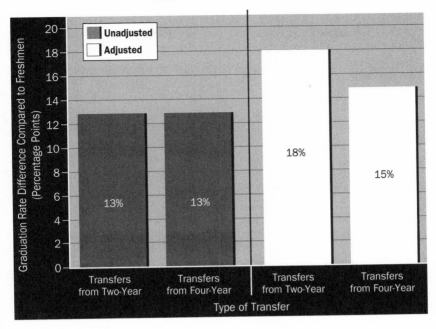

Figure 7.6b. Differences between Transfers and Freshmen in Six-Year Graduation Rates, 1999 Entering Cohort, State System SEL Bs, Unadjusted and Adjusted

Source: State Systems Database.

Note: Adjusted differences control for SAT/ACT scores, high school GPA, and university attended.

eight flagships for which transfer GPA data are available, transfer GPA is a much stronger predictor of both graduation rates and rank-in-class than is either high school GPA or SAT/ACT scores (Appendix Table 7.8).[24] Additionally, as we might expect, high school GPA and SAT/ACT scores are better predictors of college outcomes among those who entered as first-time freshmen than among transfer students (Appendix Table 7.9).

We are not able to analyze race/ethnicity and gender in this chapter because of the relatively small number of transfer students. The number of non-white transfer students, when classified by gender, university grouping, and other student characteristics, is simply too small to yield reliable results. However, we did find that transfer students at the HBCUs in the Maryland and North Carolina state systems graduated at substantially higher rates than did freshmen enrollees (Appendix Table 7.10). Although the number of transfer students at these institutions is quite small, the large graduation rate difference of 12–13 points between transfers and freshmen enrollees suggests that HBCUs, as well as the state system SEL Bs, might improve their overall graduation rates by enrolling more transfers if they have this option.

The patterns we have just described certainly suggest that many of the institutions in our study could enroll and graduate more low-SES students—and at the same time increase their overall graduation rates—by enrolling more transfers, especially those from two-year colleges. The value of this practice is clearest at the state system SEL Bs and HBCUs, where the average transfer does better than the average freshman enrollee, but most of these schools are relatively small and many are already admitting almost all of their transfer applicants (Appendix Table 7.1b). The flagships and state system SEL As, on the other hand, might achieve a similar result by admitting more transfers and fewer freshmen with weak high school credentials. For example, at these schools, only half of freshmen with high school GPAs below 3.0 graduate. Among two-year transfers in this same high school GPA category, 69 percent graduate. These transfers also come from modestly less advantaged families than do freshmen (Appendix Table 7.11).[25] Thus, even if the "next available" rejected transfer applicants have lower expected graduation rates than the transfers who are admitted under the current system, they would most likely outperform freshmen enrollees with similar high school grades. Additionally, it is likely that more of the "next available" transfers will be from low-SES backgrounds than will the freshmen they would replace. There is clearly an argument to be made that even some modest substitution of this kind, where pools of applicants allow it, would be one way of helping these leading public universities continue to serve their historical missions as "engines of opportunity."

A SYSTEM-WIDE VIEW

The previous two sections of this chapter examined the student and institutional perspectives more or less in isolation from each other. In the first section we found that, other things more or less equal, the typical high school senior is more likely to earn a bachelor's degree if he or she starts at a four-year school rather than at a two-year college. The analysis in the second section suggested that, other things more or less equal, the typical four-year institution in our study could increase its socioeconomic diversity without decreasing its graduation rate (and perhaps increasing it) by enrolling more transfers from two-year colleges.

But if we are to consider the full implications of possible shifts in enrollment patterns and policies affecting large numbers of students and institutions, such as encouraging the former to enroll directly at four-year schools and the latter to take more transfers, the behavior of all other students and institutions can no longer be treated as a given. For example, if many institutions start taking more transfers and fewer freshmen, this could encourage (or even force) more high school graduates to start at two-year colleges, which would decrease their chances of attaining a bachelor's degree. However, such a shift could also somewhat mitigate the negative effect of starting at a two-year college, especially if a large part of that negative effect is the result of there not being enough places at four-year schools for transfers from two-year colleges.

Any large-scale policy changes thus need to be considered very carefully. For example, we suspect that many students who start at two-year colleges, especially those from low-SES backgrounds, do so even though they could have started at a four-year school. (This is certainly what our analysis of "undermatches" in North Carolina suggests; see Chapter 5.) If these patterns of initial choice of institutions by students cannot be changed, creating more places at four-year schools for two-year transfers is an attractive option for helping such students earn bachelor's degrees. But any institution or system pursuing such a policy would need to be careful not to discourage high school seniors from starting at a four-year school, which would be a particularly salient concern if the policy were to decrease the number of places available for first-time freshmen.

The system of public higher education in California, while lauded by some for the large number of two-year transfers who enroll at the state's four-year campuses (including the elite University of California [UC] system), has been criticized by others for encouraging too many students to start at community colleges. A former president of UC, Richard C. Atkinson, and Saul Geiser argue that California's strict limitations on applicants' eligibility to enroll at a public four-year institution have led it to rank almost last among states in the percentage of high school seniors who matriculate directly at a four-year school.[26] They point out that fewer than a third of college students in California are enrolled in four-year institutions compared to 49 percent in states such as New York and Michigan. And they argue that these patterns, coupled with the negative effect on degree attainment of starting at a two-year college, have led to a disappointing overall bachelor's degree attainment rate in California.[27] Census data show that California ranks 28th among states in terms of its overall bachelor's degree attainment rate (26 percent) and does not have a large number of students with associate's degrees (7 percent) (Appendix Table 7.12). Florida, which also has a reputation for facilitating transfers between two- and four-year colleges, ranks 34th, with a bachelor's degree attainment rate of 23 percent.

At the three flagships in California and Florida that are in our study— UC–Berkeley, UCLA, and the University of Florida—transfers from two-year schools have a graduation rate of 92 percent, 6 points higher than that of freshmen.[28] Perhaps these data, rather than being viewed simply as evidence of these states' success in graduating transfer students, should be interpreted as an indication that many other graduates of two-year colleges in these states might well have benefited from increased opportunities to transfer to a four-year institution. This conjecture is supported by data indicating that the number of transfer applicants rejected by the average four-year public university was 1,719 in California, 1,092 in Florida, and an average of 405 in each of the other 48 states and the District of Columbia.[29]

It is clear that more research is needed on this crucial set of issues, including examination of facets that are outside the scope of our study. For example, there are potential resource cost savings (at least per enrolled student) in encouraging more high school seniors to spend their first two years at a community college. But, as the experience of California suggests, such a policy runs the risk of decreasing overall attainment. We cannot estimate the "net" effect on resource outlays of such policy shifts or their effectiveness (counting the costs of attrition). Additionally, there may be equity concerns if an increasingly limited number of places for freshmen at four-year colleges go disproportionately to particular groups of students. Atkinson and Geiser write: "It has long been recognized that UC's eligibility requirements pose a major obstacle to expanded admissions of underrepresented minorities. . . . The most recent statewide survey . . . found that 31.4 percent of Asian and 16.2 percent of White high-school graduates met UC's eligibility requirements, while just 6.5 percent of Latino and 6.2 percent of African American graduates were UC-eligible."

The somewhat conflicting student and institutional perspectives on the effects of encouraging transfers from two-year to four-year institutions, combined with the need to take a system-wide view, suggest that an essential goal of future research should be to determine how best to balance incentives here. On the one hand, it seems desirable to encourage more talented high school seniors to start at four-year institutions (and to make such an option viable for them); at the same time, it is also desirable to ensure that students who choose, for whatever reasons, to begin their studies at two-year colleges, and who do well there, have opportunities to earn bachelor's degrees by transferring to four-year institutions.[30] This option seems to us especially important for students from low-SES backgrounds who begin at two-year colleges.

CHAPTER 8

Financial Aid and Pricing on a National Level

In Chapter 2 we provided an overview of national evidence on college enrollment and completion before plunging into the analysis of data from our study. Here we perform the same task for the topics of financial aid and college pricing before reporting new findings from our own data in Chapter 9.

The process of determining the actual bottom-line cost a family will face in sending a family member to a particular university or college is surprisingly—and for many families discouragingly—complicated. For the majority of American students, the financial package that they will ultimately confront includes contributions from a variety of actors—federal and state governments, colleges and universities drawing on their own funds, parents and other relatives (especially for younger students), and the students themselves. Some expenses are financed "out of pocket," while others are financed over time through debt. Here we attempt to describe in a broad way the elements that make up these financing packages, how they have evolved over time, and how they vary among types of colleges and universities.

It makes good sense to link concerns about the cost of college to the generally lower college matriculation and completion rates observed among lower-income families. Even though we know that students from lower-income families differ in ways other than financial capacity that affect college-going—most obviously in weaker academic preparation on average than is seen for other students—a number of empirical studies conclude that, just as one would expect, the college-going behavior of lower-income families is indeed responsive to variations in price—and more responsive than that of higher-income families. Financial aid policies designed to offset the effects of rising tuition are surely one potentially important tool that can be used by governments and universities to combat the lower graduation rates we observe among disadvantaged populations, both low-income students and students of color. Indeed, there is growing awareness that the proper role of financial aid lies in enabling students not simply to attend school but to finish their degrees. In making the case for effective federal funding of education initiatives, Bill and Melinda Gates note: "It is our view that we have emphasized for too long access to college rather than completion of a degree. . . . The greatest economic benefits accrue to individuals and the greater economy upon credential attainment."[1] In this chapter we describe the national trends in aid and pricing and what can be learned from existing studies about the effects of pricing and aid on student behavior, both enrollment in college and persistence to degrees. The next chapter builds on this evidence through the analysis of data from the group of institutions we have studied in depth.

OVERVIEW OF NATIONAL TRENDS

Figure 8.1 shows the year-to-year changes in inflation-adjusted tuition and fees at public and private four-year institutions over the past 30 years.[2] Prices have clearly risen in real terms, sometimes dramatically: of particular note is the nearly 10 percent increase in public university tuition in the 2003–04 academic year. Even though prices at public four-year institutions remain substantially below those at their private counterparts (Appendix Table 8.1 shows tuition levels during this period, weighted by student enrollment), it is striking that in recent years prices at four-year public institutions have risen much more rapidly than prices at private institutions —with a pause, unlikely to be repeated, in the most recent year. This pattern reflects the increasing squeeze on state government budgets as they cope with pressures to limit taxes and to meet growing demands for the funding of other parts of state budgets, notably health care costs.[3] Most observers anticipate that the economic downturn the nation entered in 2008 will add to the upward pressure on public university prices.

Responding to the pressures of rising prices, both governments and colleges and universities have expanded their own student aid programs. Grant aid, which does not have to be repaid, directly reduces the prices families face. (Since 1998, some families have also qualified for tuition tax credits and deductions, which also reduce the costs they have to cover. These tax credit receipts are not reflected in the data we present here.[4]) Figures 8.2a and 8.2b show, separately for public and private four-year institutions, how student aid "discounts" alter the affordability of college— that is, how the year-to-year real growth in the "net price" of tuition, defined as tuition minus grant aid, compares to the growth in published tuition rates, or the "sticker price" of tuition, over the period from 1994–95 to 2008–09. One striking feature of this pair of graphs is the relative discontinuity between movements in the sticker price and net price at public universities—a pattern not seen in the private sector. Although any given price increase in dollar terms will disproportionately affect public institutions in percentage terms because of their lower starting tuition, we might still expect the sticker price and the net price to move gener-

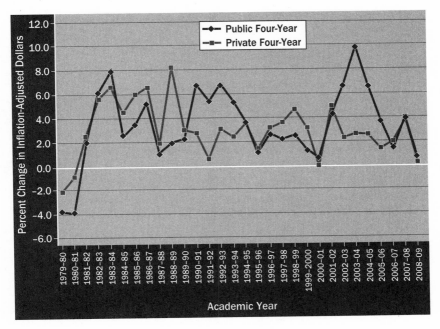

Figure 8.1. Year-to-Year Change in Published (In-State) Tuition and Fees at Public and Private Four-Year Institutions, 1979–80 to 2008–09
  Source: Trends in College Pricing (College Board 1999, 2008a) and authors' calculations.

ally in the same direction. The observed divergence reflects in part the complex and often political decisions that determine public university tuition and grant aid.[5]

The cumulative changes tell an important story as well. Over the decade from 1998–99 to 2008–09, the net price at public four-year institutions grew by about 32 percent compared to a 50 percent growth in sticker price (Appendix Table 8.2 shows published tuition and net tuition levels as well as year-to-year changes, adjusted for inflation and weighted by student enrollment). At private four-year institutions, the comparable growth was 22 percent net compared with 27 percent gross. Indeed, because family incomes have grown so slowly since the beginning of the 1990s, it is also the case that college costs consume a larger share of family income than was the case in earlier times.[6]

With the net costs of college to families continuing to rise, it is not surprising that borrowing has come to play a larger role in financing college for both students and families. Since 1965 the federal government has encouraged banks to lend to students by taking on a large share of the

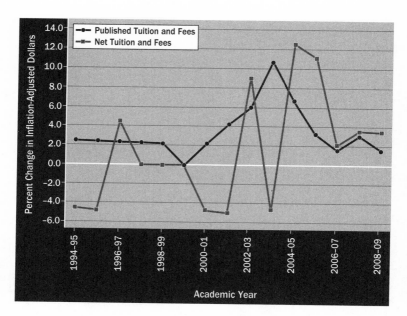

Figure 8.2a. Year-to-Year Change in Published and Net In-State Tuition and Fees at Public Four-Year Colleges and Universities, 1994–95 to 2008–09
Source: Trends in College Pricing (College Board 1999, 2008a) and authors' calculations.

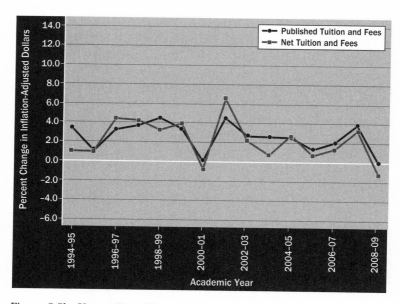

Figure 8.2b. Year-to-Year Change in Published and Net Tuition and Fees at Private Four-Year Colleges and Universities, 1994–95 to 2008–09
Source: Trends in College Pricing (College Board 1999, 2008a) and authors' calculations.

risk of default through a guarantee program.[7] The federal government has also subsidized these loans by capping the interest rate and paying interest during the student's enrollment.[8] In 1994 the government complemented this guarantee program with a direct federal lending program for students, and through its budget proposal for FY 2010 the Obama administration has signaled that it favors phasing out the guarantee program entirely in favor of direct lending.[9] These two programs are jointly referred to as "Stafford loans." The percentage of all students who take advantage of these programs has grown over time. As Figure 8.3 shows, the number of borrowers grew steadily between 1997–98 and 2007–08, by slightly more than 50 percent, in a decade during which enrollments grew at about half that rate.[10] Interestingly, the average annual borrowing per student borrower in the Stafford programs has not grown—in fact it shrank by about 10 percent in real terms between 1997–98 and 2007–08, as shown in Figure 8.4. This decline is explained in part by the fact that for most of this period the maximum amount students could borrow under the Stafford programs was fixed in nominal terms. (It has recently been raised.) Parental borrowing is much less common than student borrowing, but participation in parental programs has grown, and

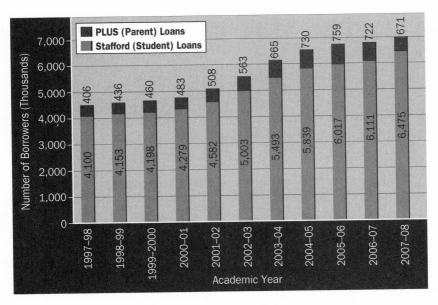

Figure 8.3. Number of Borrowers in Stafford and PLUS Loan Programs, 1997–98 to 2007–08

Source: Trends in Student Aid. Copyright © 2008, The College Board.

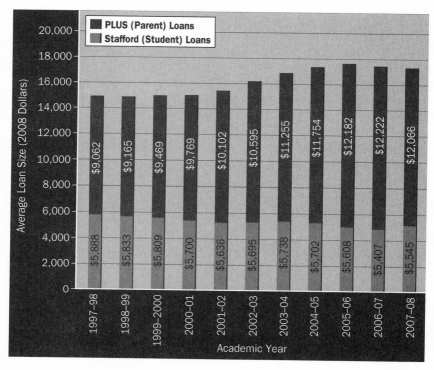

Figure 8.4. Average Loan Size in Stafford and PLUS Loan Programs, 1997–98 to 2007–08

Source: Trends in Student Aid. Copyright © 2008, The College Board.

the size of parental loans both is much larger than the size of the typical student loan and has grown in real terms.

A big part of the difference in loan size between students and parents lies in the amount of borrowing that is permitted. Parents can borrow all they want (with credit approval) up to the cost of attendance (including room and board and other expenses) net of any other aid the student receives. Students can borrow only up to a maximum loan limit, regardless of need or remaining cost. With college prices continuing to rise, these limits have caused more students to turn to the private loan market, where loans have been available to credit-worthy borrowers or those who have a co-signer, usually on less favorable terms than federally guaranteed loans. This market grew rapidly in the current decade, with borrowing at $5.5 billion (in constant 2007 dollars) in 2000–2001 and rising to $19 billion in 2007–08.[11]

The discussion so far has focused on averages and aggregates, but it is also true that students' background characteristics—including their own and their family's financial resources and their academic promise—substantially influence the kinds and amounts of student aid they receive. In the next chapter we will report on these matters in some detail for the universities that are the focus of our study; here we will simply present some basic points.

Over the period from the late 1950s to the early 1970s, a basic framework for awarding financial aid to "needy" students developed in the United States. In 1973, the federal government for the first time introduced a formula-based program of grant awards to individual college students; awards depended on students' ability to pay and the cost of the college they attended.[12] These "Pell Grants," as they came to be called, have provided a kind of floor of support for qualified low-income students in the United States. Over the same period, governments in a number of states began to develop "need-based" aid programs of their own, which awarded grants on a formula basis keyed to ability to pay and to college costs. These programs came to be a second "layer" of support for students attending college. The colleges and universities themselves, which collaborated through an arm of the College Board to agree to a formula to determine their own students' need for assistance, provided the third layer. Putting aside a bewildering array of details and qualifications, this approach to creating a package of grant aid to help students with their college costs is now the predominant framework for awarding aid to students with limited ability to pay for college.

For many students, the combination of grant support and the amount that their families are estimated to be able to contribute (through parental resources, student savings, and student work) leaves a gap. The main way in which this gap is usually closed is through the inclusion of a recommended loan in the financial aid package. Ideally, this arrangement will allow families to finance their children's education (or, in the case of independent students, students' ability to finance their own education) through reasonable levels of work and borrowing. Sometimes, however, aid packages include recommended loan amounts that many would consider unreasonable, and sometimes colleges simply recommend packages of aid that add up to less than the amount of financing the family is calculated to need (a practice referred to as "gapping").[13] In these circumstances families may turn to other credit sources (including credit card debt) to finance education, or they may simply decide against investing more money in their children's college education.

This system may strike the reader as complicated enough, but a few further complexities require highlighting. First, many colleges and some state governments weigh students' academic merit (or other desirable traits) as well as financial need in determining the size of grant awards.[14] Second, a byproduct of this way of determining aid is that students and families face considerable uncertainty about how much college will really cost. A student's aid package is generally determined only after the student has been admitted, and the student is generally informed of the aid offer less than six months before the beginning of school. This is a significant impediment to planning from the standpoint of deciding both whether and where to attend college. Third, most colleges perform these calculations and determine aid awards one year at a time. Usually the calculations take a similar form from year to year, but for a variety of reasons, students often face progressively higher net prices as they proceed through school. What looked like a reasonable plan starting out may seem less so as time goes on, and students are hampered in developing in advance a strategy for getting through their undergraduate career. Despite its complexities and qualifications, this system does succeed in targeting a large amount of grant resources at needy students.

As we have already seen, prices in inflation-adjusted dollars have been rising steadily, even after allowing for increases in financial aid grants. However, families in different parts of the income distribution have fared differently over time. Federal student aid grants, the bulk of which take the form of formula-based Pell Grants, are heavily focused on low-income students.[15] Traditionally, most state government student grant programs have also been income-sensitive, although generally providing benefits that extend to students with higher family incomes than Pell Grants do.[16] Both public and private institutions supplement these funds with grant aid from their own resources. Private institutions, with higher prices, invest more in "discounts" and direct the majority, though by no means all, of their funds to need-based aid. Public four-year colleges split their institutionally controlled grant funding more evenly between need-based and merit-based funding. Figures 8.5a and 8.5b show the combined effect of these different sources of grant programs on average net prices for full-time dependent students at public and private four-year colleges and universities in 1992–93 and 2003–04 by family income quartile. Net tuition and fees at public institutions actually declined in real terms for the bottom income quartile, reflecting in good part the relatively rapid increase in federal student aid grants just before and after the year 2000. For low-income students at private four-year colleges and universities, net prices increased only very slightly. Other income groups at both public and private institutions experienced increases in net price.

The amount of grant aid that a particular student receives is generally determined by those who provide the funds, but the amount of loans received by a student is generally determined by the student and the student's family, within limits set by lenders' rules. The broad distribution of these loan funds, first by income and then by type of institution, is shown in Figures 8.6 and 8.7; both figures include student and parent loans (averaged across borrowers and non-borrowers) from federal and private

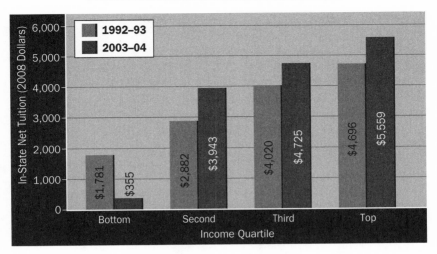

Figure 8.5a. In-State Net Tuition and Fees at Four-Year Public Colleges by
Family Income Quartile, 1992–93 and 2003–04
  Source: National Postsecondary Student Aid Study (NPSAS) and authors' calculations.

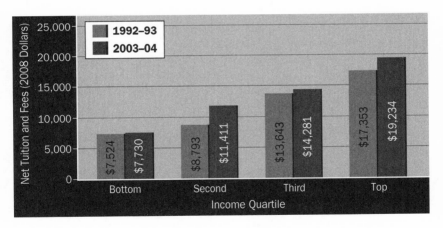

Figure 8.5b. Net Tuition and Fees at Four-Year Private Colleges by Family
Income Quartile, 1992–93 and 2003–04
  Source: NPSAS and authors' calculations.

sources, adjusted for inflation. The pattern in terms of family incomes,
shown in Figure 8.6, shows a regressive initial distribution, with students
in the lowest income quartile in 1992–93 borrowing almost three times
as much as those in the top income quartile. Although this pattern evens
out over time, students with the highest family income consistently bor-

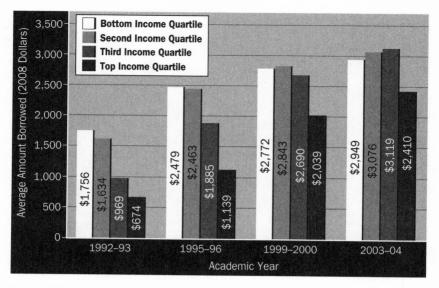

Figure 8.6. Average Amount Borrowed from Federal and Private Sources
(Including Non-borrowers), by Family Income Quartile, 1992–93 to 2003–04
Source: *Trends in College Pricing* (College Board 1999, 2008a) and authors' calculations.

row less than everyone else. Appendix Table 8.3 displays average loan amounts among borrowers only, as well as the percentage borrowing, showing that higher-income students borrow less frequently, but when they do, they borrow larger amounts. This reflects in part the fact that students from higher-income families attend more expensive institutions and in part the fact that they tend to receive fewer grants and therefore have a larger net tuition bill to cover.

Figure 8.7 indicates that families of students at colleges in different sectors use loan finance in differing degrees, in a pattern fairly consistent through time. In particular, students at public two-year colleges borrow relatively little ($589 in 2003–04, the latest year for which these data are available), while students at for-profit institutions borrow the most ($5,446 in the same year). Students at public and private (non-profit) four-year institutions, the focus of this chapter, borrow at rates falling between these extremes: $2,759 and $5,025, respectively, in 2003–04. Appendix Table 8.4 shows average loan amounts among borrowers only and the percentage of students borrowing. Low rates of borrowing and smaller loan amounts among those who do borrow at public two-year institutions reflect the generally low prices in this sector. In other sectors, borrowing is much more prevalent. In 2003–04, well over half of the stu-

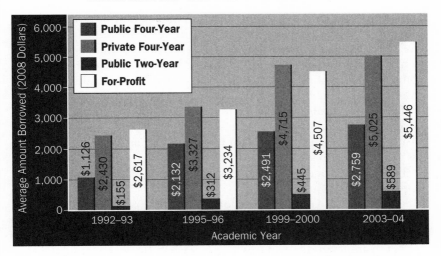

Figure 8.7. Average Size of Student Loan from Federal and Private Sources (Including Non-borrowers), by Sector, 1992–93 to 2003–04
Source: *Trends in College Pricing* (College Board 1999, 2008a) and authors' calculations.

dents at private institutions borrowed, and average loans were nearly $8,000. In public four-year institutions, in the same year, nearly half of the families of all dependent undergraduates borrowed, and those who borrowed had an average loan level of nearly $6,000.

BEHAVIORAL EFFECTS OF STUDENT AID GRANTS AND TUITION PRICE CHANGES

Does all this money (over $100 billion in grant and loan aid in 2007–08) make any difference in what students do? In particular, does it make them more likely to attend college and to finish their programs after they get there?

Increases in student aid grants or reductions in college tuition directly lower the amount that families have to pay for college. Loans do not reduce the total amount that must be paid but instead spread the cost over time. In this section we discuss the evidence on the effects of grants and tuition changes; then, in the last section, we report on the significance of loans in college finance.

The seemingly obvious question of what difference is made by grants and prices turns out to be surprisingly difficult to answer convincingly. In particular, it has turned out to be very difficult to establish any clear causal link between the introduction of the Pell Grant program and enrollment in college. Even though the awards were substantially larger relative to tuition in the early days than they are now, economists have not been able to detect any important change in student enrollment trends around the time of the program's introduction.[17] One plausible explanation for the lack of visible effect of this large program is in fact its complexity and the resulting difficulty for families in understanding how Pell awards change their opportunities. As we have seen, these awards are only one component of aid packages for most students, and students and families get clear feedback about how those components fit together only after they have decided to apply to college and complete a rather onerous financial aid application.

If complexity and inadequate information are explanations for the failure to observe an effect of the principal federal student aid grant program, we should be able to detect effects of programs that are simpler and better understood. And this is in fact what the evidence shows. In a set of highly regarded studies, Susan Dynarski has examined several major aid programs that are marked by their simplicity. In one line of analysis, she has examined the Georgia HOPE scholarship program, which commits the state to pay the full tuition and fees at any public college or university in Georgia for any student with a high school GPA of 3.0 or higher, along with a similar program in the state of Arkansas. (In its first year, the Georgia program had a family income limit, but that has since been eliminated; Arkansas still has a limit.) These programs can be criticized for providing generous benefits for families who can well afford college, but they have the important virtue of great simplicity. In fact, there is good evidence that students and parents in Georgia and Arkansas know how the programs work. And Dynarski's work comparing enrollment trends in Georgia and Arkansas with those in other states shows substantial effects of the programs not only in keeping students in their home states for college but in increasing the total number of state residents who enter college.

More recently, Dynarski has taken advantage of data released in the 2000 census to look at college completion rates for citizens of these states and has found that the programs have had a significant positive effect. Although she is not able to determine precisely how much of the programs' effect on college completion results from greater persistence and how much from enrollment of a larger number of first-year students, she is able to infer that the offer of free tuition increased persistence to a bachelor's degree by between 5 and 10 percent.[18]

Dynarski offers an important caution about the implications of her findings. Her results, she says, "clearly indicate scholarships *alone* will not keep the bulk of dropouts from leaving college. The programs studied in this paper drove to zero the direct costs of schooling for many entering students, yet even with this offer of free tuition a large share of students continued to drop out of college." She goes on to observe that her results "suggest that the direct costs of college are not the only (or even the central) impediment to degree completion. Policymakers and researchers will need to explore additional avenues in order to substantially increase the stock of college educated labor."[19]

The other program Dynarski has examined was a comparably simple one. Until 1982, the Social Security system extended the "survivor" benefit for young people who had lost a parent, a benefit that normally ended at age 18, to age 22, provided they attended college. This benefit was worth a substantial sum (on average about $7,800 in 2007 dollars), and the program was certainly well understood by those affected. As the federal government moved into the business of providing need-based aid on a formula basis to high-need students, the "survivor" program was ended. As a result, there was a sharp discontinuity in the cost of college for families who qualified for the program, and by comparing college entry rates before and after the cutoff, Dynarski was able to estimate the program's effect, which she found to be substantial. Moreover, by comparing college completion rates before and after the cutoff, she was able to see if the cutoff affected college attainment as well as entry. Although she was able to measure only additional years of schooling completed and not degree completion, she did find evidence that the survivor benefit had a substantial effect on college persistence as well as initial entry.

Dynarski's studies provide some of the best evidence currently available about the effect of grant aid on college entry and persistence. Their reliability stems from Dynarski's use of "natural experiments" in which the effects of clear, policy-induced price differentials presented to otherwise similar students can be compared.[20] They thereby avoid a major worry in many studies that the effects of uncontrolled differences among students are confounded with the effects of student aid. The limited number of studies of initial entry to college that do convincingly control for differences among students consistently find that lower prices or greater aid induce more students to enter college—when the offer is easy for families to understand.[21]

Convincing studies providing evidence on the effect of aid on persistence are even rarer than studies of the effects on initial entry. One carefully designed study by Eric Bettinger makes a good case that year-to-year changes in the federal formula for calculating Pell Grants result in differential rates of persistence between those who benefit from the changes and those who do not.[22] Two other studies report experimental evidence on the effect not only of financial aid but of other support services on students' persistence. Angrist and his colleagues conducted a randomized controlled trial of programs that offered scholarships as a reward for good performance, support services, or both, and found that the combination of monetary incentives for achievement and support services was most effective at increasing persistence in college.[23] In a second study, researchers at MDRC introduced randomized controls on interventions that combined scholarships, counseling, and other support services at a set of community colleges. The general conclusion of these studies is that such programs have positive effects on persistence and that they work best when enhanced aid is combined with support services.[24]

Perhaps the two biggest lessons from the literature on the effects of pricing and aid on student behavior are, first (a conclusion highly congenial to economists), that money does indeed matter when it comes to both college entry and persistence and, second (a conclusion economists may have been slow to come to), that it is not only the amount of aid that matters; how simply and clearly aid is delivered makes a big difference in whether and how students respond. In a sign that these lessons are finally reaching the policy sphere, the Obama administration has proposed changes to the Pell Grant program that would make its funding consistent and index the maximum award to inflation, thus achieving greater predictability for families.[25]

THE ROLE OF CREDIT IN STUDENT FINANCE

In the absence of governmental assistance, financially needy students have a difficult time borrowing money for college because, unlike when borrowing for investment in physical assets, there is no way to offer a lender collateral in the form of a claim on the assets being purchased. The introduction of federally guaranteed student loans in 1965 gave banks backing when students defaulted on their loans and thus relieved the "credit constraints" facing many needy students.

Nearly all observers agree that the introduction of these loan guarantees had much to do with the rapid expansion of college enrollment in the ensuing decades, especially among low- and middle-income students, although quantifying the effect is quite difficult. (Measuring the effect would require answering the question of how the market for higher education would have evolved in the absence of widespread borrowing for college.) Beyond agreement on the broad point that the availability of lending facilitates college attendance, there are a number of questions on which evidence is much murkier.

One important question is whether the loan limits—the amounts students can borrow with a federal guarantee—are high enough to relieve credit constraints. Loan limits have been raised from time to time but have lagged inflation in college expenses. Carneiro and Heckman introduced a helpful distinction between short-term borrowing constraints that reflect families' cash flow problems in financing college and long-term borrowing constraints that reflect the fact that wealthier families invest more in their children, from an early age, than do low-income families. They present indirect evidence suggesting that, although long-term constraints are undoubtedly important, relatively few families are seriously constrained in terms of short-term cash flow—given that there is already a set of financial aid programs aimed at helping with that problem.[26] Stinebrickner and Stinebrickner find, in a richly detailed study of students at Berea College (which has free tuition, leaving families to finance only living costs), that borrowing constraints are a real but limited factor in causing dropouts.[27] Kane reviewed the evidence provided by scholars with differing views and concluded that there is no decisive test of the importance of these short-term constraints at this time.[28]

A very important consideration only recently addressed in the literature is that, as noted earlier, loan limits in the federal programs have not kept pace with rises in college expenses over time. Most strikingly, the limits were held constant in nominal dollars from 1993–94 to 2006–07, a period when public college prices (in nominal terms) more than doubled. It is thus entirely plausible that the answer to the question of the significance of credit constraints is different at different times. Lochner and Monge-Naranjo argue that the growth of the private loan market since the turn of the century suggests that the federal programs were becoming increasingly inadequate over time.[29] A reasonable policy conclusion is that the federal government should adopt a policy of automatically raising the loan limits in proportion to some suitable cost index, such as the Consumer Price Index.

Another vexing question is whether students make good choices about how they balance decisions about consumption, work, and debt in negotiating their college experience. Investing in college involves trading present costs in money and time for future benefits. In making those decisions, students'—and families'—attitudes toward risk, their willingness to defer gratification, and their understanding of financial concepts all come into play.[30] Thus, some students may display a psychological tendency called "loan aversion"—a reluctance to borrow even for reasonably safe and profitable investments.[31] Such students may decide not to go to college at all, or alternatively they may be determined to finance their education by working long hours while attending school. There is evidence that excessive work while in college reduces students' GPAs and increases their likelihood of dropping out.[32]

Other students' approach to borrowing and to work may be shaped by a reluctance to defer gratification—to reduce consumption levels while in college in order to make the investments that will permit a higher living standard later. Administrators at campuses we visited often spoke of the tendency among their students to want "stuff" (such as flat-screen televisions) now. This impatience could lead to excessive borrowing to finance their college education or—more worrisome in terms of their success in completing college—if they are unwilling or unable to borrow, they may instead undertake excessive term-time work to get the stuff they are not willing to wait for. The fact that they may also "borrow" from study time to enjoy their stuff only compounds this problem. Leonhardt argues: "The norms of the last two decades or so—consume before invest; worry about the short term not the long term—have been more than just a reflection of the economy. They have also *affected* the economy."[33] We suspect that such norms have had a noticable impact on persistence in college and time-to-degree.

The extent of such behavior is very difficult to quantify, but in a recent paper Judith Scott-Clayton offers a perspective that may have value.[34] She introduces the idea of "fuzzy" borrowing constraints, to be contrasted with "strict" constraints. Students face a strict credit constraint if they cannot meet tuition and a subsistence living standard without either external funding or excessive work. They face a fuzzy constraint if either (a) they cannot match the living standard they would have if they worked full time or (b) owing to loan aversion, they are unwilling to borrow enough to meet the strict standard (even though loan funds are available). Scott-Clayton presents a circumstantial case that this "behavioral" conception of credit constraints is better able to account for growing hours of student work over time than are other potential explanations. Although (as she acknowledges) the idea needs much further development, this outlook seems to capture rather well what we heard in conversations with people at several of our participating universities.

A final consideration regarding student borrowing is the problem of information. In the field of economics there is a growing awareness that choices people make about complex financial matters are very much influenced by incomplete information.[35] Many of the people whom the federal loan programs aim to benefit are not sophisticated about finance. The existing federal loan programs present an unduly complicated picture to families, with two different types of Stafford loans (subsidized and unsubsidized) that have subtle and complex distinctions between them, as well as a variety of repayment options. On top of this complexity, for-profit suppliers of loans that lack a federal guarantee are also offering alternatives and providing information of varied quality and reliability. A vast simplification of this menu, coupled with better provision of straightforward information about families' options, would certainly increase the odds that students and parents would make reasonable choices among college financing options.

CONCLUSION

The state of the evidence on the effects of grants and loans on college entrance and completion is less developed than we would want it to be. Yet some points stand out clearly. First, there is a widespread consensus that in the absence of federal and state subsidies, many fewer people would begin and complete college than do now. This is an obvious point but one worth remembering. Second, studies that have looked at college completion as well as college entrance consistently find that policies that encourage attendance also independently promote college completion. This too is not surprising, given that the decision to attend the second and subsequent years of college is very much like the decision to attend the first year and should be influenced by the same factors. Third, there is quite consistent evidence that bigger grants or lower tuition promotes college attendance and completion—provided that the terms of the grant programs are simple enough and well enough known to inspire action. Estimating the effect of loan eligibility or of decisions about how much to borrow is a much more difficult challenge statistically, and there are few clear-cut results. Nonetheless, it is reasonable to conclude, fourth, that the existence of a system of federally guaranteed loans has had a positive effect on college attendance and completion and, further, that simplifying that system and making it more reliable would magnify its effects. In its budget proposals, the Obama administration has called for the creation of a $2.5 billion fund to provide support for states that propose to test in a rigorous way the effect of innovative programs to encourage college completion. It is likely that innovations in the provision of student aid will be one mechanism that states will consider in developing new programs.[36]

In the next chapter, we turn from this examination of national data and past studies to describe what can be added to existing knowledge through a close examination of the universities and students in our data set.

CHAPTER 9

Financial Aid at Public Universities

IN THE PREVIOUS CHAPTER we reviewed information on pricing and student aid for American higher education as a whole as well as the statistical evidence that the net cost to students of attending college has a measurable impact on students' initial enrollment and likelihood of graduation. Here we examine the circumstances of the students at the flagship universities and state systems in our study—and the circumstances of the institutions themselves—looking both at how students pay for college and whether the net costs they face affect their behavior.

OVERVIEW OF PRICING AND AID

We focus most of our attention on those students who attend college full-time in their home state, are classified as "dependent" on their parents for purposes of determining their financial aid status, and entered one of the colleges in our study as freshmen. Out-of-state, transfer, part-time, and adult students all face quite different pricing-aid questions than do the students we focus on, and putting their situations to one side allows us to keep our analysis tolerably simple.[1]

As we explained in the preceding chapter, at American colleges and universities much student aid has been based on the principle of meeting students' need for financial assistance, with students generally having more need if their families have lower incomes or, for any given income level, if they enroll at higher-priced institutions. Some aid, however, is also awarded for reasons other than financial need. Such "non-need-based aid" generally goes to students who are seen as more desirable for one or another reason, such as demonstrating academic merit or athletic prowess.

The importance of need-based aid for student finances is evident in our data. Lower-income students receive significantly more grants than do higher-income students. Figures 9.1a and 9.1b are based on a data set that combines information for 16 of our state flagship universities with data for the four more selective ("SEL A") universities in the Virginia state system (we will refer to this group as flagship/SEL A institutions).[2] These figures show how the likelihood of receiving grants and the average amount of grant aid per recipient vary by income quartile among freshmen at flagship/SEL A institutions. Figure 9.1b and succeeding figures also show the average value of grant aid among all students, including non-recipients of grants. Nearly all students from the lowest income quartile (92 percent) receive grants, with an average award of $6,539 and an average of $6,027 if we include non-recipients. This amount is considerably higher than the average in-state tuition ($3,548) facing low-income students, so most of these students are receiving some help toward meeting their living expenses in addition to covering tuition. Both the fraction of students receiving grants and the average amount received fall steadily with income, so in the top quartile only 35 percent of students receive grants, which average $2,783, yielding an average grant aid of $977 among all students in the top income quartile. Figure 9.2 shows how "net price"—tuition less total grants—varies with income for these students. (Note that the average net price figures include those students who receive no grant money.[3]) Low-income students receive, on average, $2,769 toward living costs or other college expenses beyond what is needed to pay tuition, while those in the top income quartile pay a net charge of $2,124.

Figures 9.3a, 9.3b, and 9.4 present the same kind of data for 15 of the state system SEL B institutions in Virginia and North Carolina. The patterns are quite similar, with the percentage of students receiving grants and the average grant award generally declining with income. But while the patterns are similar, there is one interesting difference. The net price facing freshmen at these two groups of institutions is quite similar for students in the top two income quartiles, but for students in the bottom half, especially students in the bottom income quartile, net prices are actually *higher* at the less selective institutions. This is true even though tuition is lower by approximately $750 at the SEL B institutions (see Appendix Tables 9.1a and 9.1b).[4] The difference is explained by the fact that grant recipients in the bottom income quartile at flagship/SEL A universities receive on average $1,428 more in grant aid than do those at SEL B institutions.

As Appendix Tables 9.1a and 9.1b show, this difference in grant aid for bottom-quartile students is primarily a result of differential grant award levels for black and Hispanic students. Black grant recipients at flagship/SEL A institutions from the bottom income quartile receive on average $1,955 more in grant aid than do whites in that income quartile, whereas for Hispanics compared to whites the difference is about $2,096. We believe that this difference reflects the strong efforts made by these more selective institutions to increase their representation of students from underrepresented groups. Thus the difference in net price for white students between the flagship/SEL As and the SEL Bs is $83, whereas for blacks and Hispanics the differences in net price are $1,438 and $2,367, respectively.[5]

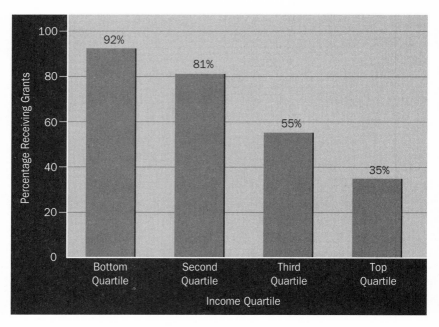

Figure 9.1a. Percentage of Full-Time, Dependent, In-State Freshmen Receiving Grants by Family Income, 1999 Entering Cohort, Flagships and State System SEL As
Source: Flagships Database and State Systems Database.

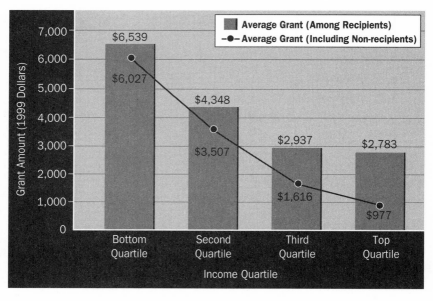

Figure 9.1b. Average Grant Amount Awarded to Full-Time, Dependent, In-State Freshmen by Family Income, 1999 Entering Cohort, Flagships and State System SEL As
Source: Flagships Database and State Systems Database.

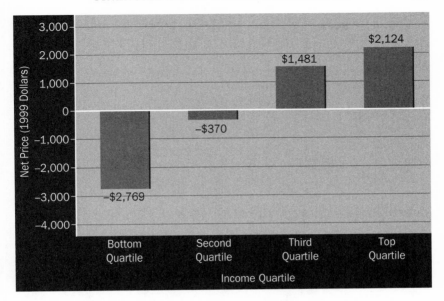

Figure 9.2. Average Net Price of Tuition for Full-Time, Dependent, In-State Freshmen by Family Income, 1999 Entering Cohort, Flagships and State System SEL As

Source: Flagships Database and State Systems Database.

Many families rely on borrowing to help meet costs of college that are not covered by grants. Most of this money is provided either through direct federal lending or through a bank loan that is backed with a federal guarantee.[6] We refer to both these types of loans as "Stafford loans," the name of the program under which they are authorized. Regrettably, with only a few exceptions, the data available in our study do not let us distinguish between loans to parents (through the federal Parent Loan for Undergraduate Students [PLUS] program described in the previous chapter) and loans to students, nor, for the most part, can we distinguish between loans incurred under the "subsidized" versus the "unsubsidized" components of the Stafford student loan program. Figures 9.5a and 9.5b show that 60 percent of families from the bottom income quartile with students at our 20 flagship/SEL A institutions borrow an average of $3,302 for their students' freshman year of college. The frequency of borrowing falls off for families in the top two income quartiles, to a low of 23 percent among those with the highest incomes, but the average amount borrowed by those who do borrow is higher. The higher amounts of borrowing among those with higher incomes who do borrow may reflect a

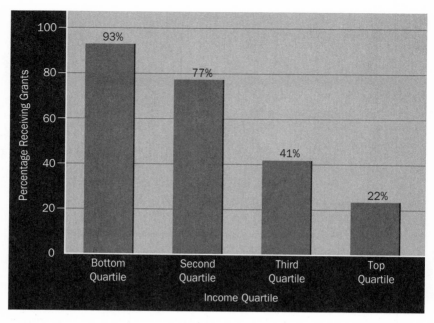

Figure 9.3a. Percentage of Full-Time, Dependent, In-State Freshmen Receiving Grants by Family Income, 1999 Entering Cohort, State System SEL Bs
Source: State Systems Database.

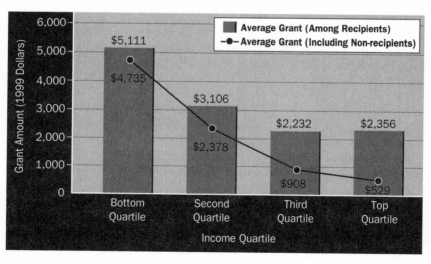

Figure 9.3b. Average Grant Amount Awarded to Full-Time, Dependent, In-State Freshmen by Family Income, 1999 Entering Cohort, State System SEL Bs
Source: State Systems Database.

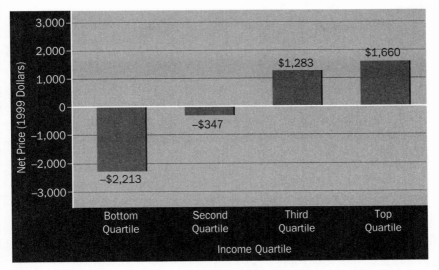

Figure 9.4. Average Net Price of Tuition for Full-Time, Dependent, In-State Freshmen by Family Income, 1999 Entering Cohort, State System SEL Bs
Source: State Systems Database.

recognition that these loans are a relatively cheap source of credit, as well as (perhaps) a judgment among some families that it is not worth the trouble to borrow relatively small amounts.[7]

Figures 9.6a and 9.6b report comparable data for the eight less selective public institutions in Virginia (SEL B institutions).[8] The patterns across income quartiles are very similar to those for the flagship/SEL A institutions, with somewhat higher rates of borrowing and somewhat smaller amounts borrowed among loan recipients.

Figure 9.7 puts together grants, loans, and prices at the 20 flagship/ SEL A institutions in a single chart, showing for each of the income quartiles how the total cost of attendance is financed. Notice that for each income group part of the cost of attendance at college is met by funding sources about which we lack information. Thus for low-income families, grants and loans together meet on average (combining results for recipients and non-recipients) $8,539 of a total $12,204, leaving a "gap" of $3,665 to be filled in other ways.[9] Top-quartile families fill a gap of (on average) $8,506.

How do families meet these gaps? We do not have data that allow us to answer that question. Most obviously, some parents, especially in higher-income groups, simply write checks, drawing either on current income or on savings.[10] Parents may also borrow through vehicles that are not

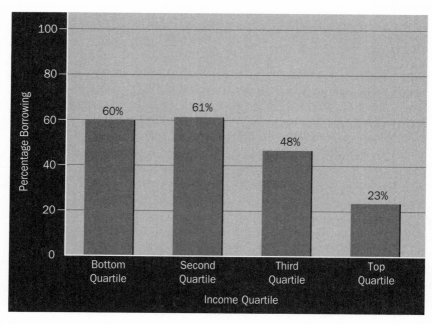

Figure 9.5a. Percentage of Full-Time, Dependent, In-State Freshmen Borrowing by Family Income, 1999 Entering Cohort, Flagships and State System SEL As
Source: Flagships Database and State Systems Database.

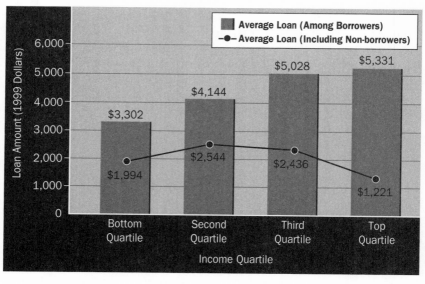

Figure 9.5b. Average Loan Amounts among Full-Time, Dependent, In-State Freshmen by Family Income, 1999 Entering Cohort, Flagships and State System SEL As
Source: Flagships Database and State Systems Database.

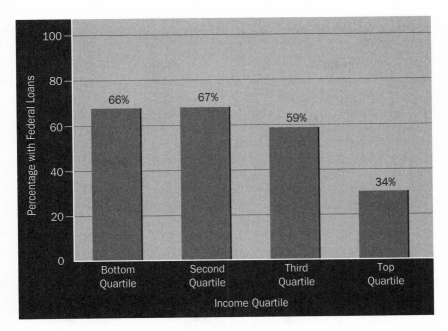

Figure 9.6a. Percentage of Full-Time, Dependent, In-State Freshmen with Federal Loans by Family Income, 1999 Entering Cohort, State System SEL Bs in Virginia

Source: State Systems Database.

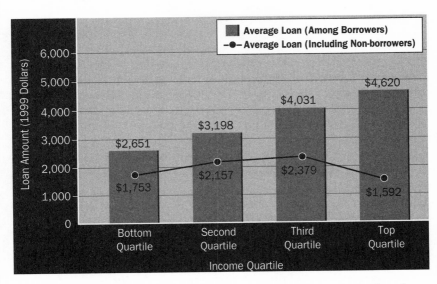

Figure 9.6b. Average Federal Loan Amounts among Full-Time, Dependent, In-State Freshmen by Family Income, 1999 Entering Cohort, State System SEL Bs in Virginia

Source: State Systems Database.

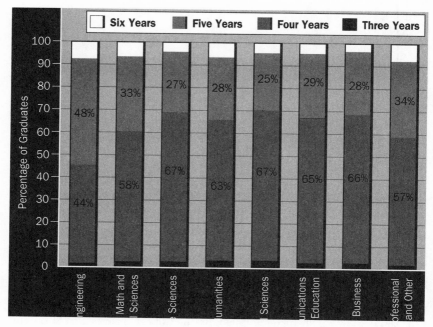

Figure 9.7. Cost of Attendance and Amount of Financial Aid for Full-Time, Dependent, In-State Freshmen by Family Income, 1999 Entering Cohort, Flagships and State System SEL As
Source: Flagships Database and State Systems Database.

labeled "college loans"—home equity loans, loans from relatives, and so on. Of course, grandparents or others may also chip in to help meet costs.

A particularly significant form of "gap-filling" is student term-time work. Hours of work and employment rates among traditional students, who are the main focus in this chapter, have been growing, and work is no doubt a more important source of funding for students from less affluent families.[11] There is also evidence that working long hours while in school is associated with less study time, lower grades, and lower college completion rates—and probably has a negative influence on other parts of the college experience as well.[12] Regrettably, our data provide no evidence on the number of hours students work; this is a generic void, and there would be great value in developing data sets that included total hours of student work.[13] We think it is highly plausible that excessive term-time work is one of the factors that make lower-income students less likely to graduate, other things equal, but we cannot document the extent of any such effect using our data.

SOURCES OF AID

The "packages" of aid we have been describing have a variety of sources, and their roles differ across income groups. Seven institutions in our study provided us with detailed information about funding sources, and we focus on that limited set of flagship institutions here.[14] (Because we are working with a more limited sample, the numbers we report do not correspond in detail with those discussed earlier in the chapter, but patterns are similar.)

Figures 9.8a and 9.8b show the percentages of students receiving grant aid from particular sources and the average amount received per recipient. Federal grants, from the Pell and Supplemental Educational Opportunity Grant (SEOG) programs, are heavily targeted at students from the bottom half of the income distribution as the law intends. Only a few students from the top two income quartiles, with unusual financial circumstances, receive any federal grant aid. State grant aid is much more widely distributed, with 44 percent of students from the top half of the distribution receiving support from this source. Part of the explanation is that some states award all or part of their aid on the basis of academic merit as well as (or instead of) financial need. Even many states that award aid on the basis of need conceive their programs as supplements to the federal Pell and SEOG programs and use formulas that distribute more of the aid to middle- and sometimes upper-middle-income students.

Institutional grants are also widespread across income quartiles, as are "private" grants from outside sources. As we note later, these private grants often provide support only for the first year of attendance—a policy that, unless counteracted by adjustments in other aid, may lead to financing problems down the line for recipients and their families. Interestingly, more than half of all freshmen at this set of flagship universities receive at least some grant money to help in paying for college—a fact that reminds us of the complexity of the financing picture and of how misleading the "sticker price" can be in assessing college affordability. Figure 9.8b shows that, even though the share of students receiving various forms of grants generally declines with income, the average amount of grant aid for those who receive any grants is roughly similar among the top three income quartiles (with students in the bottom quartile receiving considerably more).

Figures 9.9a and 9.9b show sources of loan funds at these seven flagship universities. The most important source is the Stafford loan program, relied on by almost 50 percent of students in the bottom half of the income distribution. As we noted in the previous chapter, at the time our cohort of students matriculated, freshmen taking subsidized loans were limited to borrowing the lesser of $2,625 or their "remaining need" after

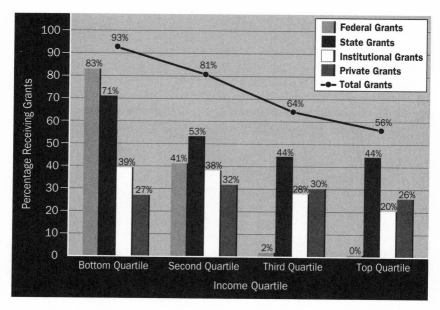

Figure 9.8a. Percentage of Full-Time, Dependent, In-State Freshmen Receiving Grants by Grant Source and Family Income, 1999 Entering Cohort, Flagships
Source: Flagships Database.

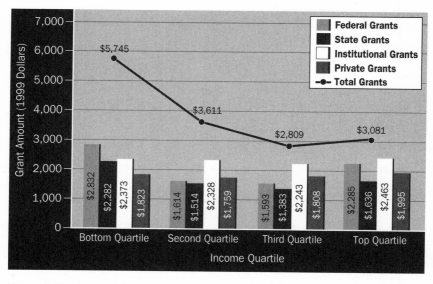

Figure 9.8b. Average Grant Amount Awarded to Full-Time, Dependent, In-State Freshmen by Grant Source and Family Income, 1999 Entering Cohort, Flagships
Source: Flagships Database.

taking into account grant aid they had received. Roughly half of all students from the bottom two income quartiles took out subsidized loans compared to 26 percent in the third quartile and only 4 percent in the top quartile, reflecting the fact that relatively few high-income students met the financial need requirement to qualify for a loan subsidy. Students do not have to have financial need to take unsubsidized Stafford loans, but the sum of the total amount they could borrow from the subsidized and unsubsidized Stafford programs as freshmen faced the same limit of $2,625 at the time of our study. Few students from the bottom income quartile took unsubsidized loans, presumably because they instead took subsidized loans that came close to their federal loan limit. As we move up the income scale, we see more students taking unsubsidized loans, 23 percent and 17 percent in the top two income quartiles, reflecting the fact that subsidized loans were not available to most of these more affluent students.

The PLUS program's loans to parents, used by relatively small numbers of families, are similarly unconstrained by need.[15] In these data for 1999, other sources of loans, notably private commercial loans, were used by relatively few students. This pattern has changed markedly in more recent

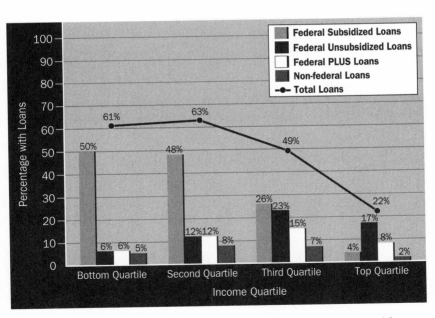

Figure 9.9a. Percentage of Full-Time, Dependent, In-State Freshmen with Loans by Type of Loan and Family Income, 1999 Entering Cohort, Flagships
Source: Flagships Database.

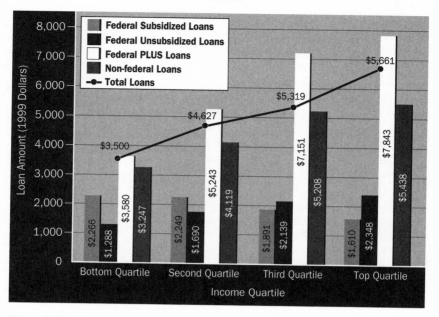

Figure 9.9b. Average Loan Amount among Full-Time, Dependent, In-State Freshmen Who Borrow by Type of Loan and Family Income, 1999 Entering Cohort, Flagships
Source: Flagships Database.

years, with private loans now accounting for nearly a quarter of the volume of total lending, although only about 10 percent of undergraduates take them.[16] (The financial crisis that began in 2008 appears to have substantially reduced the availability of these private loans.) These loans are often more expensive than other borrowing options. A problem that has persisted to the present day is that students turn to these programs (and parents sometimes encourage them to do so) even before exhausting their options for loans with better terms. There is reason to worry that lending institutions have sometimes steered students in this direction and away from less costly alternatives.

FINANCING OVER A COLLEGE CAREER

Our analysis thus far has focused mainly on pricing and aid for students in their first year. However, an important factor influencing staying in college is how the financing picture changes as students move through their college years. This point is particularly salient when the universities themselves are living through tumultuous times like the present. Public universities, despite diversifying their sources of funding in recent years, continue to rely heavily on state appropriations, especially to finance undergraduate education, and state tax revenues are highly cyclically sensitive. Reductions in funding for state universities pose worries not just for students planning to attend college but also for those already enrolled.

The students in our study were enrolled in college during a period that spanned the terrorist attacks of September 2001 as well as the "dotcom" boom and bust, which were roughly coincident. The resulting, relatively mild, recession of 2002 put stress on state revenues and resulted in sharp increases in tuition at state colleges and universities. During the time between our students' freshman and senior years, tuition and fees at public four-year colleges rose nationally by 12.8 percent after inflation. The following year—which is relevant to the many students who did not graduate in four years—tuition and fees rose another 9.9 percent in real terms.[17]

How did the students in our study, attending schools where price increases actually outpaced these national averages, fare under these changing circumstances? We need to approach this question carefully, because the composition of the enrolled student body changed over these years, as a result of the fact that the students who dropped out were different in various ways from those who persisted. We also lack detailed financial information on many students for some years of their college careers. To address these issues and to achieve consistency in data and student characteristics, we have created a panel of students drawn from our pool of in-state, dependent students at 11 flagship universities[18] who share two characteristics: first, they attended the same institution full-time for four years in a row, and second, they applied for financial aid—completing the federal financial aid form—each year.[19] This latter restriction is very important, because many students from the top income quartile do not apply for aid.[20] We underscore that this panel is *not* representative of the student bodies at these universities: it is made up not only of students who persisted but also in large part of students whose families believed that they had a good chance of receiving need-based financial aid. In particular, the borrowing rate among students in this sub-set is much higher than that among the full flagship/SEL A sample, especially when comparing higher-income students. These panel data cannot, therefore, tell us what level of aid all students from a particular income group typically received, but they are useful in showing how consistent the treatment of this sub-set of students was over these years.

Figure 9.10 summarizes the changes in financing patterns that occurred over time among this selected group of students. Each column shows the cost of attendance (which includes tuition and non-tuition expenses including the cost of room and board, travel, books, and other costs) and the portion of that cost that was covered by grants, loans, and other sources of funding (including perhaps living more cheaply than the calculation assumes). All values are adjusted for inflation to their 2002 levels. The cost of attendance actually fell slightly relative to inflation in the relatively prosperous year of 2000 before rising in real terms thereafter. In the bottom quartile, grant aid remained reasonably stable over the four years in real terms but was lower by a little over $100 in the fourth than in the first year. However, with the cost of attendance rising, students and parents combined to increase their annual borrowing over the four years by almost half, from $2,493 to $3,651 (after inflation). This was more than enough to cover the rising tuition costs these families were facing, so students who were willing to borrow (or whose parents were willing to borrow) did not have to increase their work hours or reduce their consumption levels.[21] Students in the three higher-income quartiles also increased their borrowing sufficiently to avoid increasing their requirement for financing from other sources. We need to remind ourselves once again that this is a selected group: these are students who persisted for four years, and we do not know if their colleagues who dropped out or transferred would have been equally willing or able to increase family borrowing. (Much of the additional borrowing among the more affluent families, we believe, represents borrowing by parents; the average amounts borrowed exceed the amounts students could borrow in the federal programs, and private loans were not an important source of financing at that time.) It is also important to remember that these are all families that completed the Free Application for Federal Student Aid (FAFSA) form. The FAFSA is required for all federal grant aid and for both subsidized and unsubsidized Stafford loans, so this sample of students is heavily biased toward those who expected to take out Stafford loans.

In all but the bottom quartile, there was a significant drop in average grant aid after the first year. It turns out that this drop can be traced mainly to "third-party" grants and scholarships awarded to students by outside sources (see Appendix Table 9.2a). Between 27 percent and 35 percent of the students in each of the quartiles received such awards in their first year, and the amounts were not small—the average award among recipients was over $1,500 per year. But few students had awards that were renewed after the first year, with the share of students receiving these awards dropping by well over half at that time.[22] Unless families an-

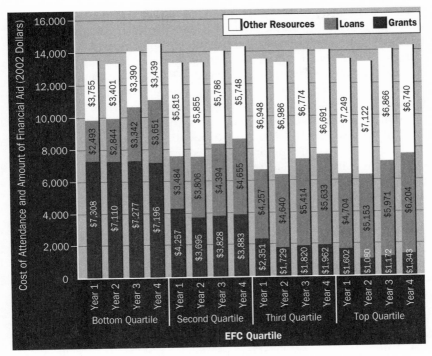

Figure 9.10. Changes in the Financial Aid Packages of Full-Time, Dependent, In-State FAFSA-Filers by Type of Aid and EFC, 1999 Entering Cohort, Flagships
Source: Flagships Database.

ticipated this drop, they may have been left with an unexpected shortfall in their financing plans for later years.

It is hard to know what implications to draw from these data about how the affordability of college changed for these students over their four years (Appendix Table 9.2c details the broader context of changes in family income, EFC, and tuition). In the face of a rising real cost of attendance, students in all four income quartiles (including non-recipients) received on average smaller real amounts of grant assistance as seniors than as freshmen. We do not know all the factors that went into producing this result, but it certainly suggests that the universities did not (or could not) move strongly to offset the rising cost of attendance with expanded grant aid to those with demonstrated need. To meet the rising net cost of attendance, these students and their parents increased their borrowing year by year, incurring over four years indebtedness (in 2002 dollars) that ranged from $12,330 in the bottom income quartile to

$22,032 in the top income quartile—averages that include non-borrowers (see Appendix Table 9.2b). These are students who in fact managed to get through four years of rising net prices through increased borrowing, but such a prospect may have discouraged other students from completing their degrees. Indications are that the 2008–09 economic downturn may produce substantially more severe pressure on state budgets and higher education appropriations than did the downturn in 2001–03, and it is quite possible that the pressures on student budgets will be substantially more severe.[23] Indeed, as of this writing in June of 2009, all segments of the California public higher education system—including the community colleges, which are normally open-access—were actively planning to restrict enrollments to help with managing their budgets. At the same time, the governor of California has suggested that it may be necessary to suspend the state's large program of state-funded student aid, the CalGrant system.

HOW PRICING AND AID POLICIES
AFFECT COLLEGE COMPLETION

We now turn to the question of what our data can tell us about the responsiveness of students' college completion rates to the net prices they face. Tuition levels and policies toward student aid vary substantially among the universities in our sample, with the result that students with similar socioeconomic backgrounds and qualifications will face very different net prices at their in-state flagship public university depending on the state in which they reside. This situation comes about partly because of variations in sticker price (from over $4,000 at Ohio State University and the University of Michigan, for example, to under $1,500 at the University of Florida in 1999). State grant policies also differ widely in levels of award and in distribution, with at least one state that has a university in our study awarding on average less than $10 per student, whereas the average is over $2,000 per student in another state. Some states distribute their aid widely across students from different economic backgrounds, while others focus aid heavily on students from low- and moderate-income families. Finally, both individual universities and private donors in different states vary in the policies they follow in making scholarship awards.

The variations we see across universities in the net prices facing students from similar income backgrounds are big enough that we might expect observable impacts on their graduation rates. In the lowest income quartile, for example, the least expensive flagship in our group has a net price of about –$5,000, while the most expensive provides grants that exceed tuition by less than $1,000. In the next income quartile, net price ranges from roughly –$2,500 to nearly +$2,500. Studies reported in the previous chapter suggest that net price differences of this magnitude should yield substantial differences in graduation rates, other things equal.

To see if we can observe such differences in outcomes in our data, we need to control for differences among students at our flagship institutions that may affect their graduation rates other than the net prices that they face. We do this by generating "adjusted graduation rates" between institutions for students in each income quartile to control for the effect on graduation rates of differences in students' background characteristics such as test scores and high school grades (but not net price). We then see if the differences in net price by income quartile are related to differences in the adjusted graduation rates for students in that income quartile.

It is important to stress that this approach makes the most sense in studying the state flagship institutions rather than the state system institutions. The reason is that students who live in different states face substantially different price and aid policies at their home-state flagship institution. This fact creates a kind of natural experiment that allows us to examine the effect of pricing and aid on graduation probabilities.

Thus, the accident of being raised in, say, Minnesota rather than Florida has a significant effect on what net price will be faced by those who attend the home-state flagship institution. And because there is generally a large gap between the in-state and out-of-state net price, each flagship is isolated to some degree from its neighbors.[24] Hence a high-income student (who is unlikely to receive financial aid) will face a considerably higher price in a state like Ohio than will a similar student who lives in a relatively low-tuition state like North Carolina. And the Ohio student cannot take advantage of the better "deal" offered in North Carolina because if he or she enrolls in North Carolina the out-of-state tuition rate applies. In the same way, a low-income student will receive a better deal if he or she happens to live in a state with very generous need-based aid rather than in a state with a more limited aid program (assuming that the tuition levels are similar). In short, there is not a "level playing field" in college-shopping across state borders, as there is within a single state like North Carolina.

What we are after is not the specific price-and-aid combination offered to a particular student, because that offer is influenced by characteristics of that individual that may also affect his or her likelihood of graduation independent of the effect of price and aid. Rather we are focused on the fact that the pricing-and-aid *policy* is different from one state (and therefore one flagship university) to another. We approximate these policy differences by measuring the average levels of net price—tuition price less grant aid—received by freshmen in different income quartiles.

We then relate these differences in prices and grant aid across flagship institutions to differences in the adjusted graduation probabilities of students attending these institutions. Our expectation is that institutions with lower net prices will have higher graduation rates, other things equal.[25] We expect to see this effect particularly for lower-income students, for whom financial considerations matter more. We also expect a bigger effect on four-year than on six-year graduation rates, because financial exigencies are likely to interfere with continuous progress toward a four-year degree more than they interfere with eventual degree attainment.

These are precisely the patterns that we find. Figures 9.11a and 9.11b are scatter-plots displaying these relationships between adjusted graduation probabilities and net price among students in the bottom income quartile for our set of 18 flagship universities.[26] Figure 9.11a shows four-year graduation probabilities, and Figure 9.11b shows six-year graduation probabilities. The downward-sloping lines in the two figures show that higher net prices are associated with lower adjusted graduation rates at both the four-year and the six-year graduation levels. (Appendix Tables 9.3a and 9.3b report the regression coefficients and standard errors of these estimates.) This is what we would expect if more grant aid (or a lower price) makes it easier for financially needy students to stay in college and graduate. Moreover, the relationship between net price and graduation probability is much stronger (about 50 percent stronger) for the four-year than for the six-year graduation rate. Figures 9.12a and 9.12b show the same relationships for students in the second income quartile, and again we see that higher prices are associated with lower graduation probabilities, although the relationships are weaker (as we expected them to be).

Our estimates imply that an increase in annual net price of $1,000 is associated with a decline of 3 percentage points in the six-year graduation rate and a decline of 4.5 percentage points in the four-year graduation rate for students in the lowest income group. (Of course this difference in net price cumulates to about $4,000 over a four-year college career.) Although we put little stock in our specific estimate of the size of this effect, it appears to be of roughly the same magnitude as that found in the work reviewed in the preceding chapter. These differences are certainly large enough to indicate that policy choices about pricing and aid can make a material difference in students' likelihood of completing college. Pricing and aid have an even greater impact on time-to-degree, a finding of importance for policy and one that makes a great deal of sense, because even temporary financial disruptions are likely to prove real setbacks for students seeking to graduate in four years who are struggling to make ends meet. As we have noted, the differences are smaller in magnitude but the same in direction for the second income quartile.

Among students in the third and top income quartiles, on the other hand (Figures 9.13a–9.14b), we find essentially no relationship between net price and graduation probability. The overall picture that

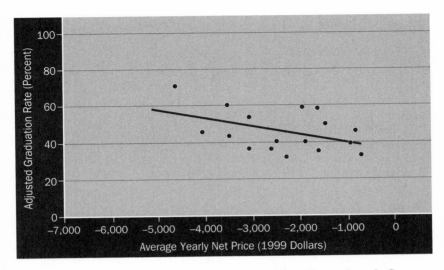

Figure 9.11a. Four-Year Graduation Rate for Full-Time, Dependent, In-State Freshmen in the Bottom Income Quartile by Net Price of Tuition, 1999 Entering Cohort, Flagships
Source: Flagships Database.

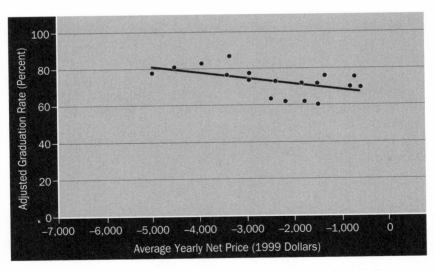

Figure 9.11b. Six-year Graduation Rate for Full-Time, Dependent, In-State Freshmen in the Bottom Income Quartile by Net Price of Tuition, 1999 Entering Cohort, Flagships
Source: Flagships Database.

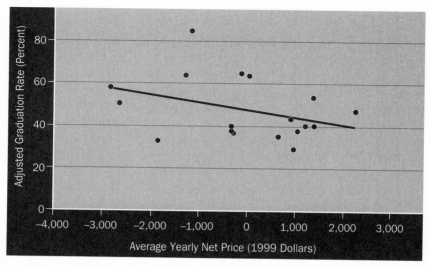

Figure 9.12a. Four-Year Graduation Rate for Full-Time, Dependent, In-State Freshmen in the Second Income Quartile by Net Price of Tuition, 1999 Entering Cohort, Flagships
Source: Flagships Database.

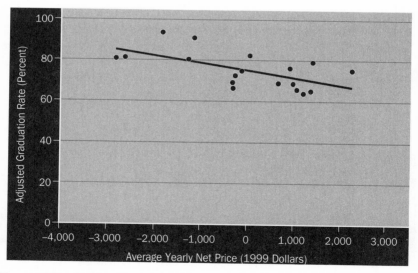

Figure 9.12b. Six-Year Graduation Rate for Full-Time, Dependent, In-State Freshmen in the Second Income Quartile by Net Price of Tuition, 1999 Entering Cohort, Flagships
Source: Flagships Database.

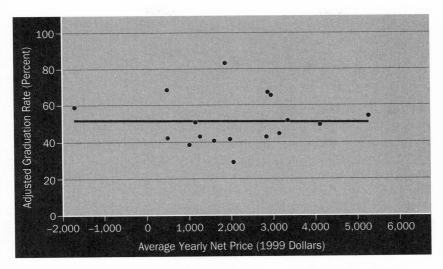

Figure 9.13a. Four-Year Graduation Rate for Full-Time, Dependent, In-State Freshmen in the Third Income Quartile by Net Price of Tuition, 1999 Entering Cohort, Flagships

Source: Flagships Database.

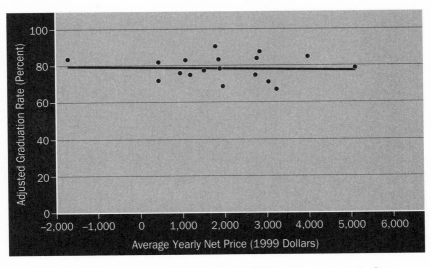

Figure 9.13b. Six-Year Graduation Rate for Full-Time, Dependent, In-State Freshmen in the Third Income Quartile by Net Price of Tuition, 1999 Entering Cohort, Flagships

Source: Flagships Database.

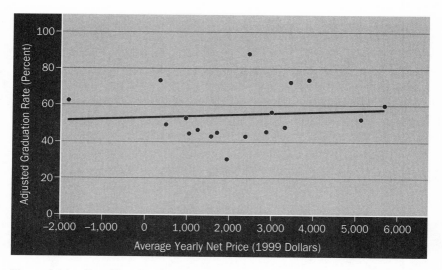

Figure 9.14a. Four-Year Graduation Rate for Full-Time, Dependent, In-State Freshmen in the Top Income Quartile by Net Price of Tuition, 1999 Entering Cohort, Flagships

Source: Flagships Database.

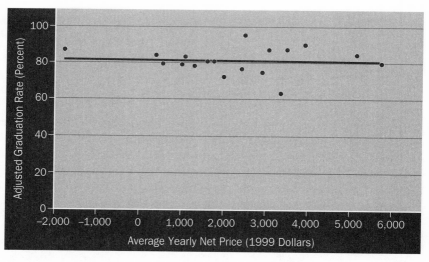

Figure 9.14b. Six-Year Graduation Rate for Full-Time, Dependent, In-State Freshmen in the Top Income Quartile by Net Price of Tuition, 1999 Entering Cohort, Flagships

Source: Flagships Database.

emerges from this analysis is consistent with what has been found in earlier work on this subject: price and aid matter to student success in completing college and in shortening time-to-degree, and they matter much more for lower-income students than for others.

CONCLUSION

Readers who have made their way to the end of this analysis will have acquired a lively awareness of the complexity of pricing and aid at public colleges and universities (a story that is no less and in some ways more complicated at private institutions). There is every reason to think that this complexity, in and of itself, poses problems for students and families as well as for those studying this subject.

The "typical" student at one of our institutions finances his or her education through a combination of grants and loans from various sources as well as earnings, savings, and contributions from the student's family. Moreover, even when students understand first-year financing, they generally have little information about how they will solve their financing problems in the years to come. Although the evidence is that, over the period we study, those who were willing to increase their indebtedness appeared able to get through college in a reasonable way, they had little reason to know that that would be the case when they started out—and no doubt some of the students who did not make it through were discouraged by some combination of uncertainty and reluctance to add to their debt.

One conclusion, then, which has become close to a consensus among analysts of higher education policy, is that reliable, simple, and predictable provision of financial aid is important not just to initial access to college but to success in graduating.[27] An important factor interfering with the simplicity and predictability of pricing and aid for public higher education is the tremendous cyclical volatility of state appropriations for higher education. The irony is that public universities lose funding at just the time when families become less able to pay. Universities generally respond to these cuts in appropriations by raising tuitions and sometimes by cutting back on aid at just the wrong time in terms of families' ability to pay. Finding ways to buffer public university budgets (and arguably state budgets more generally) against the vagaries of the business cycle has to be an important priority for those seeking to stabilize the financial picture facing families with children in college.[28]

Recently, the flagship institutions in a number of states have begun to develop policies aimed at making their financial aid offers to their lowest-income students easy to understand. In North Carolina, for example, the Carolina Covenant guarantees that all admitted students whose income is less than 200 percent of the poverty line will be able to afford to attend the University of North Carolina–Chapel Hill (UNC–CH) for a full four years without any loans through a combination of financial aid grants and moderate student work-study requirements.[29] The Carolina Covenant and a similar program at the University of Virginia are accompanied by aggressive communication and outreach efforts to raise student and parent awareness of the opportunity. A number of public universities have implemented analogous programs or have them in development.[30]

These programs have two serious limitations. First, of course, they may be quite vulnerable to economic downturns that threaten their funding. Particularly in light of the aim of these programs to build relationships with population sub-groups and particular high schools that have not traditionally had much connection to the flagship public institutions, a temporary interruption in the funding of such a program may have long-lasting negative effects. Second, a key condition for being able to offer such a promise is having high enough admissions standards that relatively few low-income students enroll—a paradoxical proposition, given the objectives of these programs, but a very real one nonetheless. In North Carolina, for example, UNC–CH is probably the only public institution that could even contemplate committing itself to financing such a policy without a wholesale revision of other priorities.

A more general point, established in the studies discussed in Chapter 8 and confirmed by the work reported here, is that money matters. Low- and moderate-income students who reside in a state where the flagship university is more expensive (taking account of both tuition level and provision of student aid grants) are less likely to graduate than are comparable students from states where they face a lower net price—and considerably less likely to graduate in four years. Financial aid policy must be a consideration in any concerted effort to raise graduation rates.

It is not easy for public universities that face severe fiscal pressures to find ways to deliver lower net prices to students, but our findings do suggest some important points. An obvious but important first proposition, demonstrated again in this study, is that lower net prices matter much more to students from low- and moderate-income backgrounds than to others. For institutions that enroll large numbers of more affluent students, keeping the price low across the board is an expensive way to lower the price to those whose behavior will be affected by it. As economists have argued for a number of years, it is far better from this point of view to charge a higher price and use some of the revenue to discount the price more heavily to needy students through need-based grants.

Second, many of the universities in our study provide substantial amounts of grant aid to students whose family incomes place them in the top half of the income distribution. Although some of these families qualify for need-based aid, many of them receive "no-need" grants, usually based on test scores and high school grades. In fact, the College Board reports that in 2006–07 only 44 percent of student aid grant dollars at public four-year institutions went to students who had financial need. Nearly 40 percent went to non-need students, and 18 percent went to recruited athletes (including a number, of course, who have need).[31] There is no evidence in our data that grants to more affluent students actually influence the likelihood that these students will graduate—nor is it easy to find such evidence in other studies. It is true, of course, that many of these families struggle to meet college costs, but the tuitions they pay at public institutions are already subsidized considerably through the appropriations state governments provide to their universities.

Universities offer awards to students who do not have financial need (according to established standards) partly because they may judge that those standards are too severe but largely in order to attract high-quality students to their campuses.[32] Enrolling such students no doubt adds to a university's prestige and reputation, and improving the quality of the entering class may also improve the education of students in general by raising expectations and improving the academic atmosphere on campus. Nonetheless, the policy of using non-need-based aid is problematic; to the extent that competing institutions offer merit awards to the same students, these offers may simply offset each other and have no effect on students' choice of institution. Moreover, investing in a merit-aid strategy leaves fewer dollars available for the alternative strategy of providing better grant support to lower-income students, for whom it does improve graduation probabilities.

There is one more point we want to stress. The focus in this chapter has been on generally applicable aid and price policies and their effects on students. Most aid is, and no doubt should be, delivered according to general policies and rules. But there is good reason to think that providing key actors in a university with a meaningful amount of discretionary funds can make a real difference to the effectiveness of aid. Students from low- and moderate-income families have few additional resources to draw on when a short-term emergency arises, and in fact sometimes they have to provide emergency resources to other family members. Shirley Ort of UNC–CH has spoken and written eloquently about the difference it can make for an officer of the university to be able to respond quickly and without excessive bureaucracy with a short-term interest-free loan or supplemental grant to help a student and family over a rough spot.[33] Making sure that key officials are equipped to present this human face of the university to those in need is effective, we think, and certainly the right thing to do.

CHAPTER 10

Institutional Selectivity and Institutional Effects

THROUGHOUT OUR STUDY, we have examined groups of universities separately by selectivity groupings in order to compare outcomes at broadly similar institutions while still maintaining adequate cell sizes and protecting the confidentiality of results for individual institutions. Although many findings—such as the disparity in graduation rates between students from families of high and low socioeconomic status (SES)—are consistent across these selectivity groupings, overall graduation rates vary widely. The six-year graduation rate ranges from 86 percent at the selectivity cluster (SEL) I flagships to 51 percent at the state system SEL Bs (refer back to Figure 3.1a). These pronounced differences by selectivity cluster often eclipse other disparities. For example, black men at state system SEL As are 10 percentage points *more* likely to graduate than are white men at state system SEL Bs (Figure 3.12c).

In this chapter we examine in detail differences by institutional selectivity and also touch on other institutional differences, such as those between public and private institutions and between historically black colleges and universities (HBCUs) and predominantly white institutions (PWIs). Of course, we would expect that a large part of the differences by selectivity can be attributed to differences in students' entering characteristics. More selective universities, by definition, enroll students with stronger entering credentials who are more likely to graduate regardless of where they go to college. We find, however (somewhat to our surprise), that controlling for students' high school GPAs, SAT/ACT scores, and demographic characteristics reduces the differences in graduation rates across institutions only modestly. Substantial differences remain, and although these differences are strongly correlated with institutional selectivity, there are clearly other forces at work.

Later in the chapter, we also examine whether students benefit from certain types of within-institution experiences, such as living in on-campus residence halls and enrolling in honors colleges at public universities.

INSTITUTIONAL EFFECTS AMONG PUBLIC UNIVERSITIES

The strong positive relationship between graduation rates and institutional selectivity that we found when comparing clusters of universities is

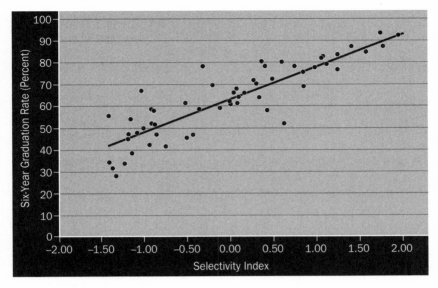

Figure 10.1. Six-Year Graduation Rates versus Selectivity, 1999 Entering Cohort
Source: Flagships Database and State Systems Database.

even more striking when we look at individual institutions in Figure 10.1, which plots six-year graduation rates against institutional selectivity.[1] To measure selectivity we have constructed a selectivity index that places equal weight on the average SAT/ACT scores and high school GPAs of students at each institution.[2]

The correlation between graduation rates and selectivity is extremely high (the correlation coefficient between raw graduation rates and the selectivity index is 0.88). As already noted, part of this strong association reflects the fact that students who attend universities whose students have earned higher average SAT/ACT scores and high school GPAs themselves rank higher on these measures and thus are more likely to graduate no matter which college they attend. The key question is how strong an association there is between graduation rates and institutional selectivity—if there is any association at all—after we adjust for differences in both students' entering characteristics (SAT/ACT scores and high school GPA) and demographic variables (race/ethnicity, gender, state residency status, and family income quartile). As one would expect, the relationships between institutional selectivity and these adjusted graduation rates are flatter than the relationships based on unadjusted graduation rates, but they are still strongly positive and statistically significant (Figures 10.2a and 10.2b).

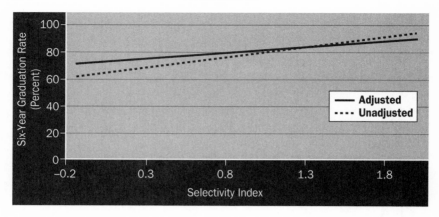

Figure 10.2a. Six-Year Graduation Rates versus Selectivity, 1999 Entering
Cohort, Flagships and State System SEL As
Source: Flagships Database and State Systems Database.

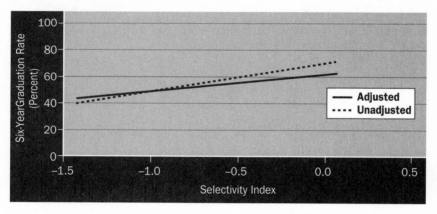

Figure 10.2b. Six-Year Graduation Rates versus Selectivity, 1999 Entering
Cohort, State System SEL Bs
Source: State Systems Database.

We plot the adjusted graduation rate for each university in Figure 10.3a
for the flagships and state system SEL As and in Figure 10.3b for the
state system SEL Bs. The inter-institutional differences in these adjusted
graduation rates indicate the predicted difference in graduation rates between a student at institution "X" and an observationally equivalent student at institution "Y."[3] For example, if two universities have adjusted
graduation rates of 60 percent and 70 percent, this would indicate that
students at the former institution are 10 percentage points less likely to

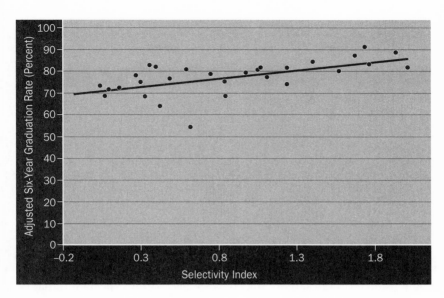

Figure 10.3a. Adjusted Six-Year Graduation Rates versus Selectivity, 1999
Entering Cohort, Flagships and State System SEL As
  Source: Flagships Database and State Systems Database.

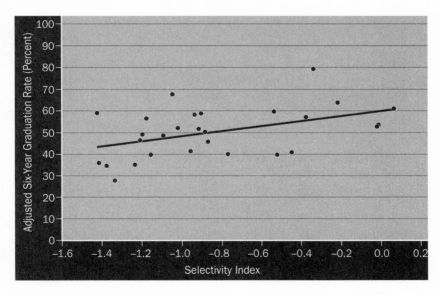

Figure 10.3b. Adjusted Six-Year Graduation Rates versus Selectivity, 1999
Entering Cohort, State System SEL Bs
  Source: State Systems Database.

graduate, on average, than are students with similar characteristics at the latter institution.

If the inter-institutional differences in graduation rates shown in Figure 10.1 were explained entirely by differences in students' academic preparation and demographic characteristics, all of the points in Figures 10.3a and 10.3b would be clustered around a horizontal line (i.e., all of the adjusted graduation rates would be the same). However, that is not what we find. Substantial differences in graduation rates remain, and these adjusted differences are positively correlated with institutional selectivity at both groups of universities; however, they are especially pronounced at the flagships and state system SEL As. The correlation coefficients are +0.61 at the flagships and state system SEL As and +0.44 at the state system SEL Bs.[4] Later in the chapter we will return to factors that may explain these distinctly positive relationships. To anticipate, we suspect that they are due at least in part to peer effects (going to college with students more likely to graduate makes a student more likely to graduate) and the role of norms or expectations (at highly selective institutions with generally high graduation rates, there may be a widely shared expectation that essentially everyone will graduate).[5]

The consistently positive relationship between adjusted graduation rates and institutional selectivity is far from the only story line, however. Comparing universities with similar selectivity indexes, we still find quite a bit of variation in adjusted graduation rates, which suggests that there are other factors at play. The plotted points do not fall perfectly along the regression lines shown in either of these figures, and there is even more variation around the regression lines for the state system SEL Bs (Figure 10.3b) than for the flagships and state system SEL As (Figure 10.3a).

THE "DIPPING-TOO-LOW" HYPOTHESIS

The fact that substantial institutional differences in graduation rates remain even after we control for students' academic preparation rebuts the idea that colleges and universities could increase their graduation rates substantially by simply rejecting all applicants with marginal credentials. F. King Alexander, president of California State University–Long Beach, has been critical of the emphasis people place on achieving high graduation rates. Here is his proposition: "Everyone knows that to get your graduation rate up, the best way to do that is turn away all the academically challenged students and there is evidence of this all over the United States."[6]

To test this assertion at the universities in our study, we did as Alexander suggested and retrospectively rejected all students who had high school GPAs below 3.0 and then recalculated the six-year graduation rate. The results of this experiment (shown in Figure 10.4) decisively rebut the proposition that low overall graduation rates are caused by admissions officers' "dipping too low." (We chose the 3.0 GPA cut-off because the Chicago Consortium study found that students with high school GPAs below 3.0 were unlikely to graduate from college. Substituting an SAT/ACT threshold, such as 1000, for the high school GPA cut-off of 3.0 produces nearly identical results.)

Retrospectively rejecting students with high school GPAs below 3.0 changes the graduation rate barely at all at the two most selective sets of flagships—which is hardly surprising, because they take very few students with such low grades (only 2–3 percent of all their students fall into this category). But there is also only a tiny gain in the overall graduation rate at the SEL III flagships, which admit appreciably more students (about 13 percent of all their students) with high school grades below 3.0. And even at the state system SEL Bs, where 30 percent of all students had a high school GPA of less than 3.0, excluding these lower-performing students raises the graduation rate by just 6 percentage points. There is, to be sure, a larger jump at the HBCUs, but this is because fully 60 percent of their students were in the below-3.0 category—and surely no one would suggest that the HBCUs should have refused to admit all these students.

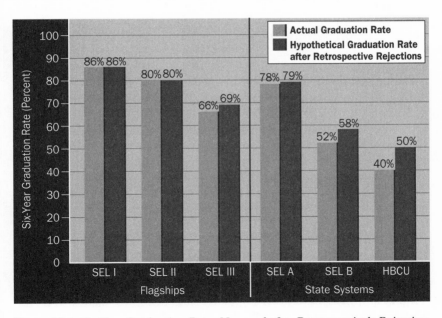

Figure 10.4. Six-Year Graduation Rates Now and after Retrospectively Rejecting Students with High School GPAs below 3.0, 1999 Entering Cohort
Source: Flagships Database and State Systems Database.

The real story line, however, is not that the universities in our study insist on a high level of baseline qualifications (though most do) but that *failures to graduate occur throughout the high school GPA and SAT/ACT scales.* This is especially true at the less selective state system universities. For example, at the state system SEL Bs, the graduation rate among students who had high school GPAs of 3.33–3.66 was just 57 percent (refer back to Appendix Table 6.7). The reality is that graduation rates vary dramatically across universities even when we look at students with good high school grades and impressive test scores.[7] Students who are reasonably well prepared academically and come from mid- to high-SES backgrounds, yet do not graduate, are a "target population" (a group of students who might be worth special attention as part of an effort to improve overall levels of educational attainment) that we consider in the next chapter.

THE "OVERMATCH" HYPOTHESIS
AND OTHER FACTORS TO CONSIDER

Although there is in general a positive relationship between selectivity and institutional effects, it could still be the case that students with weak credentials would be better off at a less selective institution. In other words, perhaps students with weak preparation find highly selective universities too demanding. Such an "overmatching" problem would be exactly the opposite of the "undermatching" phenomenon that we discussed in Chapter 5.

To look at this question in the context of this chapter (we return to the question as it applies specifically to minority students in the next chapter), we examined three groups of students defined by their high school GPA. For each group, we looked at how their graduation probability (adjusted, as described earlier, for their background characteristics) varied with the selectivity of the university they attended. We found that attending a more selective institution *increases* students' graduation probabilities regardless of the high school GPA group to which they belong. In fact, students with low high school GPAs actually appear to benefit more from attending a more selective institution (among the flagships and state system SEL As) than do students with higher high school GPAs. This pattern is illustrated in Figure 10.5a by the fact that the line showing the relationship between adjusted graduation rate and selectivity index is steeper for low-GPA students than for high-GPA students. At the state system SEL Bs, there are essentially no differences by high school GPA, but there is also no evidence that students with low high school GPAs would have been better off attending less selective universities (Figure 10.5b).

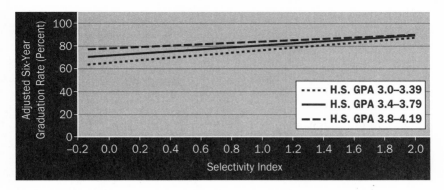

Figure 10.5a. Adjusted Graduation Rates versus Selectivity by High School GPA, 1999 Entering Cohort, Flagships and State System SEL As
Source: Flagships Database and State Systems Database.

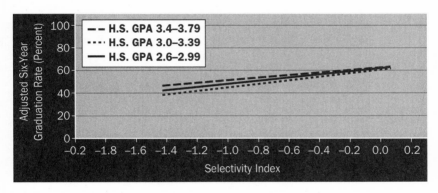

Figure 10.5b. Adjusted Graduation Rates versus Selectivity by High School GPA, 1999 Entering Cohort, State System SEL Bs
Source: State Systems Database.

We also used multiple regressions to examine the relationships between the institutional coefficients and measures of scale (number of students), resources (expenditures per student), and "campus community" (percentage of freshmen who live on campus). Only the selectivity and on-campus residence variables were statistically or substantively significant (Appendix Table 10.1a and 10.1b).[8] The result for the on-campus housing variable suggests that "campus-like" institutions are more successful at graduating their students. This appears to be the result of both an individual-student effect and an overall institutional effect. Students who lived in a university residence hall during their first semester (at one of the 33 colleges and universities[9] for which these data were available)

were 7 to 8 percentage points more likely to graduate than were students
who lived off campus—a result we obtain after controlling for (relatively
modest) differences in entering credentials and background characteristics, including family income (Appendix Table 10.1c).[10] When we
re-run the institution-level analysis with adjusted graduation rates that
control for the individual-living-on-campus variable, the results are qualitatively similar to those reported in Appendix Table 10.1b.[11] We interpret
this pair of findings as suggestive evidence that individual students benefit from living on campus *and* that all students benefit from attending an
institution where more students live on campus.[12]

These findings could reflect both the general educational benefit of
being part of a reasonably close-knit residential community and associated job effects—that is, students who do not live on campus may be more
inclined than on-campus students to take jobs away from campus that reduce the likelihood of finishing their degree in a timely fashion. Unfortunately, the lack of good data on jobs makes it impossible to test this
proposition.

There may be no evidence of a scale effect because it is not overall scale
that matters but rather the size of the institutional sub-unit that the student is part of. For example, many large flagship universities are divided
into smaller colleges, programs defined by major field of study, and so
on. Later in this chapter we examine the outcomes of students who were
enrolled in the honors college at 11 of the flagship universities in our
study. A final point to note is that our failure to find an institutional resource effect could be due to the lack of measures of resources that are
truly comparable across universities.

As is explained in Appendix A, the tensions between the pursuit of excellence in research and graduate education, on one hand, and mass
teaching of undergraduates on the other have clearly become much
more pronounced since World War II. As the most selective public universities have come to compete with the great private universities, the
public universities have had to provide better research opportunities to
recruit faculty. Although this trend might lead us to expect lower graduation rates at the more selective flagships, the existence of the opposite
relationship could mean that increased emphasis on research at these
highly selective universities also produces learning environments that are
better for at least some highly talented undergraduates. These students
may find stimulating faculty mentors, take some graduate courses, and
benefit from having more able graduate students as their teaching assistants. Less selective public universities, in contrast, may have lower graduation rates partly because they are less able to attract highly talented faculty and outstanding graduate students. The limitations of our data and
the absence of other research on this question mean that we can only

speculate as to whether faculty and graduate students who are better at research are also better at teaching, and possibly better at inspiring students with their own enthusiasm for their subject, which is enhanced by their research.[13] The larger point is that we have to be careful to not be too "mechanical" in how we think about the connections between institutional selectivity and undergraduate teaching quality. There can be dynamic interactions present in which some aspects of life at the more selective research universities benefit the ablest undergraduates.

PUBLIC-PRIVATE COMPARISONS

Our study focuses on public universities for the many reasons discussed in the preface to this book and in Chapter 1. It is nonetheless instructive to compare the graduation rates of public universities with those at private colleges and universities. For this purpose, we use data for the 1995 entering cohort at a group of Ivy League universities and private liberal arts colleges collected as part of an earlier study, *Equity and Excellence in American Higher Education* (2005).[14] Also, we have good data for the 1999 entering cohort at private colleges and universities in the state of Virginia. Needless to say, there are many differences between private and public institutions of higher education besides their official "control." For example, the private institutions are generally smaller and often wealthier, and many of them are therefore able to offer more generous financial aid as well as other forms of support. Another big difference is that generally only public institutions receive substantial operating subsidies from state governments and thus are able to charge lower tuition, especially for in-state students. Private-public comparisons reflect all of these (and other) differences.

We first compare the graduation rates of the 1999 entering cohort at six SEL I flagships to those of the 1995 entering cohort at six Ivy League universities and 17 liberal arts colleges.[15] The most selective flagships had six-year graduation rates that were similar to those of the liberal arts colleges (86 percent versus 85 percent) and modestly lower than those of the Ivies (93 percent) (Figure 10.6). However, four-year graduation rates at these flagships were 20 and 14 points lower than those at the Ivies and the liberal arts colleges, respectively. These "raw" differences are reduced only slightly by controlling for students' SAT/ACT scores, race/ethnicity, and gender (Appendix Table 10.2).[16] In particular, large differences in four-year graduation rates remain.

We find strikingly similar patterns using data on the 1999 entering cohort at a much broader range of public and private universities in Virginia. Looking within selectivity clusters, the public and private institutions have

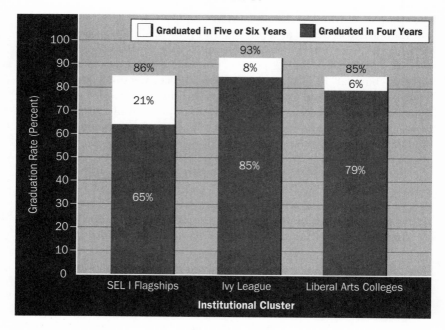

Figure 10.6. Graduation Rates, Public and Private Colleges and Universities, 1999 Entering Cohort (Publics) and 1995 Entering Cohort (Privates)
    Source: Flagships Database and Expanded College and Beyond Database.

nearly identical six-year graduation rates but very different four-year graduation rates (Figure 10.7).[17] At public and private SEL As, the six-year graduation rates are 84 percent and 85 percent, respectively. At SEL Bs, the corresponding rates are 56 percent and 55 percent. However, the four-year graduation rate is 15 points higher at the private than at the public institutions among SEL A universities, with a corresponding difference of 13 points at the SEL Bs. Controlling for student characteristics reduces the differences between SEL As and Bs by about half but leaves the public-private comparisons essentially unchanged (Appendix Table 10.3).

Such simple descriptive statistics cannot provide definitive evidence on the causes of these large differences, but one plausible hypothesis is that the higher tuition charged by private institutions is a strong incentive for students to finish more quickly. For the 1999–2000 school year, the average tuition charged by the universities in our study was $3,899 at public SEL As ($12,969 for out-of-state students), $18,483 at private SEL A, $3,776 at public SEL Bs ($11,057 out-of-state), and $14,843 at private SEL Bs.[18]

A crude way to test this hypothesis is to compare time-to-degree for in-state and out-of-state students at the public institutions, because these two

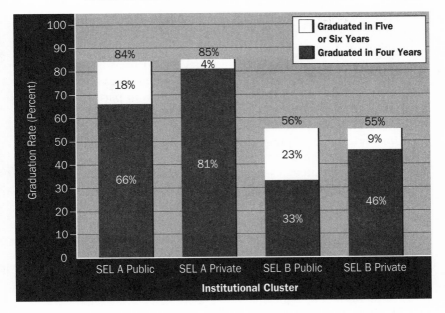

Figure 10.7. Graduation Rates, 1999 Entering Cohort, Public and Private
Colleges and Universities in Virginia
   Source: State Systems Database.

groups face vastly different tuition prices.[19] Looking only within institutional clusters, the six-year graduation rates of out-of-state students are
slightly lower than those of in-state students.[20] However, this pattern is reversed when we examine four-year graduation rates, with out-of-state students 1 or 2 percentage points more likely to graduate than are in-state
students in all clusters except the public SEL Bs, where they are 7 points
more likely to graduate. Consequently, 72 percent of out-of-state students
who graduate from public SEL Bs do so in four years compared to only
55 percent of in-state students. Although the corresponding difference
at the public SEL As is muted (81 percent versus 76 percent), these comparisons support the hypothesis that higher tuition encourages students
to finish their degrees in less time. However, there are clearly other factors —correlated both with public versus private institutional control and
with in-state versus out-of-state status—that could be driving this result.
   Other potential reasons for finding small public-private differences in
six-year graduation rates but large differences in four-year graduation
rates, while purely speculative, include the hypothesis that the more generous financial aid available to low-income students at private universities
allows these students to finish in less time by reducing the pressure to

work. Another hypothesis is that the concept of a graduating *class* (e.g., thinking of the 1995 entering cohort as "the class of 1999") is generally stronger at the private institutions.

A final hypothesis is that private colleges and universities provide a smaller, more intimate, learning environment than does the typical public university. We can test this hypothesis, at least in part, by examining data for the honors colleges that are found at many flagship universities —because the honors colleges are specifically designed to provide settings for study that encourage close contact among students and between students and faculty members. At 11 of the flagships in our study, we can look separately at outcomes for students in general and for students who were enrolled in the university's honors college each semester.[21] We estimated the impact on graduation rates of students' being enrolled in the honors college by controlling for their observable characteristics using propensity score analysis. We classified students into 10 different groups based on their estimated likelihood of enrolling in the honors colleges (their "propensity score"), which we found to be strongly related to their high school GPAs and SAT/ACT scores. (In this analysis, we also took into account race/ethnicity, gender, state residency status, family income quartile, and university attended.) We then compared the graduation rates of students who did or did not enroll in an honors college within each of these 10 groups (Figure 10.8).

Ignoring the three bottom groups on the left side of Figure 10.8 (which include hardly any students who actually enrolled in an honors college), there appears to be a consistent honors-college-graduation-rate advantage of about 10 points. Although this estimate is likely biased by selection of students into honors colleges based on unobservable characteristics (such as motivation to apply), we interpret this finding as suggestive evidence that honors colleges do make some difference—even if the difference is not as large as 10 percentage points on top of what are already fairly high graduation rates. Many private liberal arts colleges and private universities with relatively small undergraduate classes function de facto as "honors colleges," which is why we think this examination of honors college students at the public universities is relevant to the private-public difference in graduation rates. What we observe here is almost certainly more than simply a size effect. Like liberal arts colleges, honors colleges rely less on teaching assistants and have fewer large lectures. In other words, they are not just a smaller version of a large institution but actually use a rather different educational "technology."

A related finding is that there are essentially no differences in graduation rates by family income quartile among students who started in an honors college, whereas family income has quite a strong effect on graduation rates of non-honors-college students at these universities (Appendix Table 10.4). Although this pattern could be the result of a selection

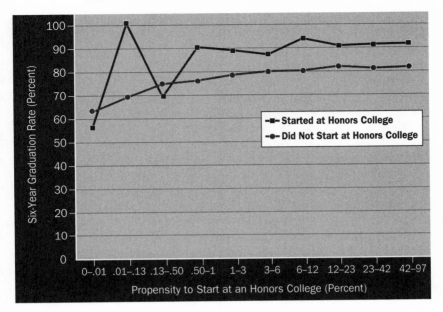

Figure 10.8. Graduation Rates and Honors Colleges, 1999 Entering Cohort, Flagships
  Source: Flagships Database.

effect, it is also consistent with the notion that the characteristics of honors colleges may themselves narrow disparities in outcomes by socio-economic status. This proposition is supported by the finding that adjusted differences in graduation rates by income quartile are also essentially nil at the Ivies and the liberal arts colleges (Appendix Table 10.5). Taken together, this evidence suggests that having additional family resources matters more in a somewhat amorphous setting—such as a large public university—and less in an intimate setting, such as a private college or a public honors college within a large university. In the more intimate settings, the institutions themselves may be providing more of the support for students from all backgrounds that family resources help to buy for the more affluent students in the less intimate settings.

HISTORICALLY BLACK COLLEGES AND UNIVERSITIES

An institutional effect highly relevant to the educational attainment of black students is the availability of enrollment opportunities at HBCUs. Using data from North Carolina, we compared the bachelor's degree attainment rates of black students who started at an HBCU to the gradua-

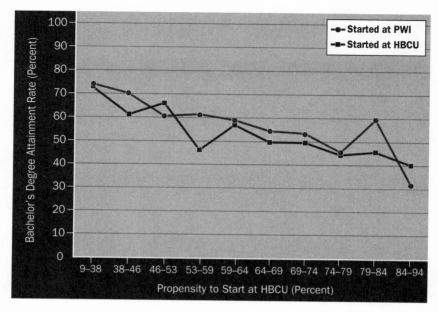

Figure 10.9. Bachelor's Degree Attainment Rates of Black Students Who Started at HBCUs versus PWIs, North Carolina High School Graduating Class of 1999
Source: North Carolina High School Seniors Database.

tion rates of comparable black students who started at a PWI with an average SAT score below 1150. The "comparability" of students was defined by their likelihood of attending an HBCU, based on a propensity score analysis that grouped students into one of 10 groups.[22] Within each of the propensity groupings, attainment rates are generally slightly higher at the PWIs, but the differences are not large (Figure 10.9). Given that students with weaker entering credentials were more likely to attend an HBCU, a modest amount of selection on unobservable characteristics that goes in the same direction could easily explain this small difference. Finally, it should be noted that the HBCU effect does not vary systematically with students' characteristics (as measured by their propensity to attend an HBCU).

"Institutional effects" are of course only one of many sets of factors that affect the graduation rates of black students versus other students. In the next chapter, which is devoted to a more detailed analysis of "target populations," we consider a variety of explanations for the pronounced disparities in graduation rates related to race/ethnicity and gender. Particularly puzzling are the relatively low graduation rate and the relatively long time-to-degree of black men compared both with black women and white men.

CHAPTER 11

Target Populations

THIS PENULTIMATE CHAPTER has two connected themes. The first is the need to reduce the gross disparities in graduation rates that exist today among groups classified by race and socioeconomic status (SES)—an objective that is important in its own right given this country's long-standing belief in promoting social mobility and a widely (though by no means universally) shared commitment to continuing to redress the legacy of this country's "unlovely" racial history. The second is the need to improve the overall level of educational attainment in the United States—an objective that can be advanced, we believe, by focusing on targeted populations that badly need increases in graduation rates and are able to contribute mightily to our overall stock of human capital if more of their members cross the finish line. Reducing disparities in outcomes and improving national levels of educational attainment are mutually reinforcing goals.

The first target populations discussed in this chapter are defined by race/ethnicity and gender, with special attention paid to black men and to the Hispanic population. Next we consider students from low-SES backgrounds. Race/ethnicity and social class are both risk factors for college achievement, but they confer different vulnerabilities.[1] The last target group includes an array of students who are neither black nor Hispanic, who are not from low-SES backgrounds, but who nonetheless have surprisingly modest graduation rates.

BLACK MEN

The disappointing levels of educational attainment among black men are so glaring and so well known that it will suffice to recall just a few summary facts. Nationally, only about 15 percent of black men in the 25–29 age group have earned bachelor's degrees. This statistic is the product of a low high school graduation rate, a low college enrollment rate, and a low college graduation rate among those who do enroll. Of those black men who enrolled in one of our flagship universities in the 1999 entering cohort, 59 percent graduated within six years (compared with 75 percent of white men and 72 percent of black women). Only 26 percent of the black men attending these leading public universities graduated within four years, and slow time-to-degree among those who did graduate is a particularly serious problem for this group. The same pattern of a low six-year graduation rate and then a much lower four-year graduation rate was found among the black men at the least selective institutions we studied, the state system schools in selectivity cluster (SEL) B: 38 percent graduated within six years and just 12 percent in four years.[2]

These low graduation rates are explained in considerable part by the well-known fact that black students enter college with weaker academic credentials than those presented by many of their college classmates. Also, black students are more likely to come from family backgrounds that are associated with below-average graduation rates (with "family backgrounds" in this context thought about primarily in terms of a lower level of parental education and lower family income). However, even after accounting for differences in both academic credentials of entering students and family backgrounds, the six-year graduation rate for black men at the flagship universities is 6 percentage points lower than the graduation rate for similarly situated white men (refer back to Figure 3.13a).

In his extensive study "Black Male Students at Public Flagship Universities in the U.S.," prepared for the Joint Center for Political and Economic Studies in Washington, Shaun R. Harper follows the presentation of data similar to those just summarized with this simple statement: "Unarguably, attention and resources must be devoted to reversing the plight of the black male collegian." The factors Harper cites as contributing to this problem at the flagships include "missing mentors," small numbers of black students in many large classes, a lack of institutional accountability, and the need to devote more resources to programs and student organizations that engage and retain black male students.[3]

Everyone recognizes that "the plight of the black male collegian" has its origins in family structures and pre-collegiate lifestyles and experiences. The underlying issues (and puzzles) are anything but new. As Michael Fletcher has observed: "Over the past 100 years, perhaps no slice of the US population has been more studied, analyzed and dissected than black males. . . . [They] have been the subject of at least 400 books."[4] This vast body of literature defies ready summarization, and that is not our task in any event. Suffice it to note that family structure (especially the presence of so many single mothers) and neighborhood and high school effects are widely agreed to be very important, though there is little agreement by scholars as to precisely how the various factors interact to affect the educational outcomes of black men.[5]

Mismatches ("Overmatches") or Undermatches?

Although we cannot contribute to this discussion of circumstances that fundamentally condition what happens to black men before and after they graduate from high school, we do have evidence that is directly relevant to a central question at the collegiate level—namely, whether black students, especially black men, have been encouraged to attend colleges and universities that are too difficult for them academically, resulting in discouragement and failure. This argument is sometimes referred to as the "mismatch" hypothesis, though it might more accurately be called the "overmatch" hypothesis. It is often made by opponents of affirmative action who claim that race-sensitive admissions policies harm the very minority students they purport to help by stigmatizing them and forcing them into harmful competition with white classmates of greater ability. In an earlier analysis of this hypothesis based on an extensive study of outcomes among members of the 1989 entering cohort at 28 mostly private colleges and universities (*The Shape of the River*), Bowen and Bok concluded that there was absolutely no support for it.[6]

In this study we have data for a more recent cohort of students (those who entered in 1999 rather than 1989) at a large set of public universities, and because we have so much data, we can separate black men from black women (which could not be done in *The Shape of the River* because of data limitations). The conclusion is the same; if anything, it is even stronger. One intuitively appealing way of testing the "overmatch" hypothesis is to group black men by their high school GPAs and then see if those with relatively low GPAs who enrolled in the more selective public universities graduated at lower rates than those with the same GPAs who went to less selective schools (where more of their classmates would have had similar GPAs). The left-most panel of Figure 11.1 demonstrates convincingly that precisely the *opposite* pattern prevails. Of black male students with high school GPAs below 3.0, those who went to the most selective universities (the SEL Is) had a 46 percent graduation rate, those who went to the SEL IIs had a 40 percent graduation rate, those who went to the SEL IIIs had a 38 percent graduation rate, and those who went to the state system SEL Bs had a 29 percent graduation rate.[7]

In other groupings by high school GPA, the pattern is essentially the same—black male students who went to more selective institutions graduated at *higher*, not lower, rates than black students in the same GPA interval who went to less selective institutions. *Moreover, contrary to what the overmatch or mismatch hypothesis would lead us to expect, the relative graduation rate advantage associated with going to a more selective university was even more pronounced for black men at the lower end of the high school grade distribution than it was for students with better high school records.*[8]

As a further check on the validity of these findings, we used regression analysis to control for other variables, including SAT/ACT scores, state residency status, and income quartile, as well as high school GPA, and we obtained essentially the same results. Perhaps the most apt comparison is between the graduation rates of black men who attended a state system

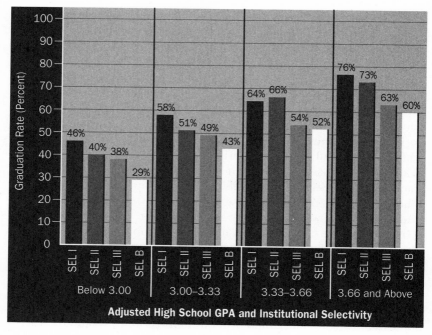

Figure 11.1. Graduation Rates of Black Men by Adjusted High School GPA and Institutional Selectivity, 1999 Entering Cohort
Source: Flagships Database and State Systems Database.

SEL B university and students with comparable characteristics who attended a SEL I public university. Those who attended the state system SEL Bs had a predicted graduation rate that was approximately 10 points *lower* than the predicted graduation rate for comparable students who went to a SEL I—a finding that holds both for black students with high school GPAs below 3.0 and for all black students, controlling for GPAs (Appendix Table 11.1). There is certainly no evidence that black men were "harmed" by going to the more selective universities that chose to admit them. In fact, *the evidence available strongly suggests that students in general, including black students, are generally well advised to enroll at the most challenging university that will accept them.*[9]

This last observation leads directly to a proposition that is the obverse of the overmatch hypothesis: the disappointing outcomes for black men can be attributed in part to the fact that a number of them were "undermatched"—that is, as explained in Chapter 5, some black men enrolled in either two-year colleges or four-year colleges that were less demanding than the colleges for which they were presumptively qualified, and some enrolled in no college at all. The Chicago public schools study found that 28 percent of black high school graduates "enrolled in a college that was far below a match."[10] In our data for state system universities in Ohio, we find that 66 black men with high school GPAs of 3.33 and above enrolled at SEL Bs compared with 69 at the two SEL As in that state. These numbers, however, serve only to illustrate the likely presence of undermatches, because we do not have the kinds of admissions data for Ohio that we used in North Carolina to estimate presumptive eligibility frontiers (and thus the number of undermatches). Also, the presence in North Carolina of a large number of historically black colleges and universities means that we cannot simply extrapolate results from that state to other states that have a different mix of educational institutions.

The conclusion of this section is straightforward: the way to improve graduation rates and other outcomes for black men is *not* to discourage them from enrolling in academically strong programs that choose to admit them. On the contrary, more presumptively well-qualified black men should be encouraged to "aim high" when deciding whether and where to pursue educational opportunities beyond high school.

Interventions

Once students are enrolled in a particular college or university, their success depends not only on their own efforts (surely the most important factor) but also on how well their college or university is able to support them. As many studies and articles remind us, there have been a great many interventions in individual universities intended to improve outcomes for black students. Noteworthy are the Meyerhoff Scholarship Program at the University of Maryland–Baltimore County, the CARE (Center for Academic Retention and Enhancement) program at Florida State University, the University System of Georgia's African American Male Initiative, and City University of New York's Black Male Initiative.[11] Towson University in Maryland has closed its once-large black-white graduation gap entirely, and this result is said to have been achieved largely by "giving more weight to high school grades and less to SAT scores in deciding who to admit"— an approach entirely consistent with our findings in Chapter 6.[12]

More generally, the Association of American Colleges and Universities (AAC&U) has documented a number of "high impact" educational practices (such as "learning communities," "writing intensive courses," "undergraduate research programs," and "capstone courses and projects") that have been found to benefit students from many backgrounds. This study, directed by George D. Kuh, also found: "Some groups of historically underserved students are less likely to participate in high-impact activities—

those first in their family to attend college and African American students in particular." It continues: "While engagement and persistence are positively correlated for all students, engagement has a compensatory effect for African American students relative to white students in that as the African American students become more engaged, they also become more likely to surpass white students in the likelihood that they will persist."[13]

Freeman Hrabowski's Meyerhoff Scholars Program at the University of Maryland–Baltimore County (UM–BC) is perhaps the most ambitious and best-known effort to enhance the success of minority students and, in particular, the success of black men in earning degrees in science and engineering.[14] The program employs a highly competitive application process with rigorous standards, provides generous financial support, and utilizes a variety of pedagogical techniques to encourage students to work collaboratively, to stay engaged with their work, and to have high expectations. The Meyerhoff Program has clearly achieved its objectives. As of May 2008, 87 percent of its participating students had graduated from UM–BC in the Meyerhoff Program, and 91 percent went on to graduate and professional programs—mostly in math and science, consistent with the program's objectives.[15] It is also clear that the success of the program should be attributed to both "selection" and "treatment" effects.[16]

Thanks to detailed data for both UM–BC and the University of Maryland–College Park made available to us for this study (and analyzed by our former colleague, Murrayl C. Berner), we were also able to ask a more complicated question: to what extent did the presence of the Meyerhoff Program on the UM–BC campus have "spill-over" effects on the graduation rates of other black students? In the case of the '99 entering cohort, the adjusted graduation rates for all black men at College Park and for black men at UM–BC who were *not* part of the Meyeroff Program were essentially the same (relative to the respective graduation rates for white men). Thus, it is difficult to claim the existence of strong spill-over effects. We interpret this finding not as evidence of any failure at UM–BC but as evidence of how hard it is to change deep-seated forces driving the educational attainment of black men in the absence of very explicit, targeted features, such as those incorporated in the Meyerhoff Program.[17]

It is hard to know what to say about the replicability of the Meyerhoff Program. In principle, its features could certainly be copied in other institutional settings. But the program is expensive, and the outlays required may preclude other institutions' introduction of similar programs. Also, it is clear that the leadership qualities of Freeman Hrabowski have had a major impact on the success of the program at UM–BC. We believe that the leadership Hrabowski has demonstrated in guiding this program would be hard to replicate on a large scale. There are just not that many Freeman Hrabowskis!

A very different kind of intervention that seems especially important in the case of black men is the relatively recent use of a number of efforts to counter what Claude Steele identified as "stereotype vulnerability," which refers to "being at risk of confirming, as self-characteristic, a negative stereotype about one's group." In several experiments, Steele and Aronson showed that black students performed less well than white students on standardized tests when their race was emphasized.[18] Scholars have now demonstrated in field experiments that exercises in "self-affirmation," "ability reframing," and "forewarning" can have quite dramatic effects on the academic performance of black students—having led, for example, to a 40 percent reduction in the racial achievement gap among seventh-graders in one study.[19] Thomas Dee at Swarthmore has pointed out (in personal correspondence, August 2008) that one attraction of this class of interventions is that they seem affordable and capable of being taken to scale.

HISPANIC STUDENTS

Nationally, Hispanics have a lower overall level of educational attainment (defined in this context as the percentage of students 25–29 years of age who completed four or more years of college) than do African Americans and whites: 10.8 percent in 2006 compared with 16.6 percent for African Americans and 31.9 percent for whites.[20] The Hispanic population is an especially important target group because of both its low absolute level of educational attainment and the extraordinarily rapid increase in the number of Hispanic graduates of U.S. public high schools—a group projected to increase by 54 percent between 2004–2005 and 2014–2015 (see Chapter 1). Increasing the educational attainment of this target group has to be our number-one priority if we are to improve the overall educational attainment level in the United States—and to reduce disparities related to race/ethnicity.[21]

A number of scholars have studied the factors associated with attainment rates for Hispanics, and this literature suggests that, in general, the same variables affecting attainment for other groups (academic preparation in secondary school, aspirations, integration into the college environment, and so on) apply here as well. One factor specific to Hispanics is the high proportion of this group that enrolls initially in two-year colleges. In the fall of 2000 (the last decennial census year for which detailed data are available), 58 percent of Hispanics enrolled in college were attending two-year institutions compared to 42 percent of African Americans and 36 percent of white students. And peer effects—measured here by the odds that a student's high school classmates were going to attend a four-year college—have been found to be a critically important determinant of college-going plans of Hispanic high school students.[22] As in the case of black men, some of the reasons for the low attainment rates of Hispanic students can be traced back to overall family conditions. The Chicago Consortium study points out that "Latino students are particularly disadvantaged because so few of their parents have any college experience. . . . Fully 60 percent of Latino seniors state that their mother has no schooling beyond high school, and 18 percent reported that they did not know their mother's level of education."[23]

Hispanic students who did enroll in one of the public universities in our study had lower college graduation rates than white students but slightly higher graduation rates than blacks (Figure 3.12a)—which does not contradict the pattern summarized earlier because it is deficits in four-year college *enrollment* rates, not graduation rates, that are mainly responsible for the lower overall levels of educational attainment of Hispanics (refer back to Figure 2.5). In their "Portrait of Latina/o Freshmen at 4-Year Institutions, 1975–2006," Hurtado and her colleagues at the Higher Education Research Institute at the University of California–Los Angeles emphasize that although Hispanic students now come from more educated families than they did in the 1970s, "they remain the racial/ethnic group with the lowest parental education attainment levels."[24]

The main substantive contribution we can make to understanding the low graduation rate of Hispanics (relative to white and Asian students) is to repeat for this target population the "mismatch" or "overmatch" analysis that we performed for black men. The findings are strikingly similar. As in the case of black men, there is absolutely no evidence of any "mismatch" or "overmatch" problem for Hispanics. Within each grouping by high school GPA, including the below-3.0 category, Hispanic students graduated at higher rates the more selective the institution they attended (Figure 11.2). *In fact, the positive "other-things-equal" association between graduation rates and institutional selectivity is even stronger for Hispanics than it is for blacks* (Appendix Table 11.2). Holding constant test scores, high school GPA, gender, and family income, Hispanic students who attended a state system SEL B institution were 20 points less likely to graduate than were observationally equivalent students who attended a SEL I university. Among Hispanics with the lowest high school GPAs (for whom overmatch would be most likely to occur if it occurred anywhere), the corresponding graduation rate advantage is 16 percentage points—an even larger relative difference.

Thus, there is no evidence whatsoever of a chronic "overmatch" problem with the Hispanic population—but there is a massive "undermatch" problem, we believe. Unfortunately, the only state in which our data allow us to study undermatches properly and in full detail is North Carolina (because it is only there that we have admissions data). But the rapid growth of the Hispanic student population in that state is so recent that

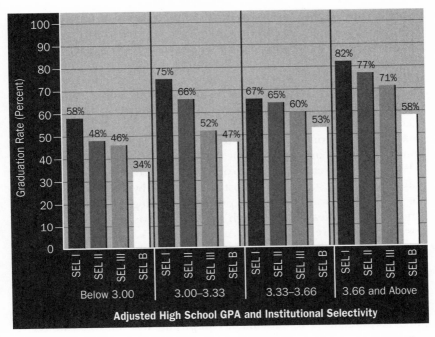

Figure 11.2. Graduation Rates of Hispanic Students by Adjusted High School GPA and Institutional Selectivity, 1999 Entering Cohort
Source: Flagships Database and State Systems Database.

data for the '99 entering cohort include too few Hispanic students to allow us to study the extent of undermatches. However, the Chicago public schools "Potholes" study has an enormous amount of relevant data. In Chicago, "Latino students were significantly less likely than any other racial/ethnic group to enroll in a college with selectivity levels that matched or exceeded their levels of qualifications." Almost half of Latino students (44 percent) enrolled in colleges with selectivity levels "far below match, as compared with 28 percent of African-American high school graduates." The study report continues: "Even among students who had worked hard throughout high school and earned the GPAs and ACT scores that give them access to very selective colleges, fewer than 30 percent of Latino graduates enrolled in [such a college] compared to 40 percent of African-American and other White/Other Ethnic graduates with similarly high qualifications."[25]

The Chicago report then examines in great detail the factors that lead to so much undermatching among Hispanic students. Financial concerns are part of the problem, compounded by difficulty in completing complicated Free Application for Federal Student Aid (FAFSA) forms. But many of the Chicago case studies also point to problems in the application process, including lack of information and proper guidance, failure to understand the importance of applying to more than one "match" school, and lack of a "college-going culture" at the student's high school. The authors conclude that high schools must both increase their capacity to facilitate the matching process and help students understand that " 'college' does not mean just any college."[26] Working hard to improve "match" is surely one of the interventions most likely to improve educational attainment among Hispanics (even more so than among blacks).

We also want to call attention to one national program, the Posse Foundation program established almost 20 years ago by Deborah Bial, which has an enviable track record in promoting college graduation among inner-city graduates of public high schools. Approximately 39 percent of Posse Scholars have been African American/Black, 31 percent Hispanic/Latino, and 21 percent Asian/Pacific Islander or Biracial/Multiracial. The high percentages of black and Hispanic students in the program make it directly relevant to this discussion of ways of improving educational outcomes for both black men and Hispanics. Overall, the Posse program has consistently achieved six-year graduation rates in the range of 85–95 percent—a remarkable accomplishment even when we recognize that many of these students are attending selective private colleges with very high graduation rates for all students and graduation rates for underrepresented minorities that are distinctly above average. Still, with almost no exceptions, Posse Scholars graduate from partner colleges and universities at higher rates than do underrepresented minority students in general.[27]

One of the main features of the Posse program is a rigorous selection process that both focuses on academic achievement and places a distinctive emphasis on non-cognitive predictors of success such as leadership skills and ambition to succeed. Full-tuition scholarships are provided by the partner colleges that enroll the Posse Scholars. A third, very important, feature of the program is its emphasis on sending "posses" of students to participating colleges. Students are grouped into cohorts after they are selected, are given pre-collegiate training together, and are made aware that they are expected to help each other once they arrive, as a "posse," on a campus. The on-campus program includes a structured mentoring component, and the philosophy of the entire program is "strength-based"—that is, the conversation is not about correcting deficits but rather about shared expectations of high achievement. The Posse program resembles the Meyerhoff Program in many ways, and it, too, clearly works.

With regard to replicability, the Posse program has demonstrated its ability to expand into new cities (for recruitment of students) and new campuses (where the recruited students matriculate). But, like the Meyerhoff Program, it is expensive, and it is unclear to what extent the costs involved, both scholarships offered and programmatic expenses, will limit its growth within the public university sector. (At present, the University of Wisconsin–Madison, the University of Michigan, and the University of Illinois are the only public universities hosting Posse Scholars.) At the minimum, both the Meyerhoff and the Posse programs demonstrate that graduation rates for target populations can be increased substantially if enough resources—and creativity—are put to work. An intriguing question that we would like to investigate in a follow-on study, if there is support for the idea, is whether the cohort/posse concept itself could be utilized more aggressively by public universities in recruiting both underrepresented minority students and students from low-SES backgrounds.[28]

LOW-SES STUDENTS WHO ARE NOT
UNDERREPRESENTED MINORITIES

A third target group of special interest is students from modest backgrounds who are neither black nor Hispanic. At the universities for which we have the requisite SES data, 12 percent of students are low-SES but neither black nor Hispanic. The percentages of low-SES students are appreciably higher at some universities (such as the University of California–Berkeley, the University of California–Los Angeles, and Stony Brook University) and in some state systems (in our set of states, Maryland stands out) than elsewhere. As we are led to expect by our earlier discussion (Chapter 3) of the effects on graduation rates of SES and its components (parental education and family income), low-SES students graduate at appreciably lower rates than do high-SES students—and the relative gap is larger at the SEL III flagships and the state system SEL Bs than it is at the more selective flagships (Figure 11.3).[29]

In considering what might be done to increase the number of low-SES students who earn bachelor's degrees, it is important to recall that low-SES students do much better, relative to high-SES students, at highly selective private colleges and universities, where there are essentially no differences in graduation rates between the groups.[30] It was this finding, combined with evidence showing little or no difference in outcomes of other kinds, such as grades and earnings in later life, that led to the recommendation in *Equity and Excellence* that these selective institutions admit more students from modest backgrounds by putting a "thumb on the scale." This now seems to be happening at a number of institutions, and the result should be at least some reduction in disparities in outcomes

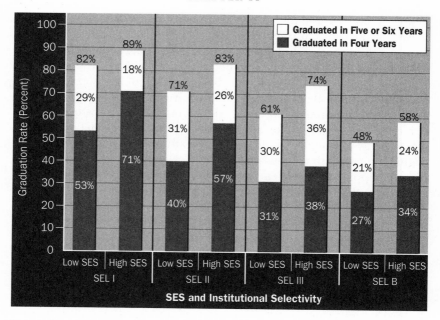

Figure 11.3. Graduation Rates of Non-Black, Non-Hispanic Students by SES
and Institutional Selectivity, 1999 Entering Cohort
Source: Flagships Database and State Systems Database.

related to SES. But the overall impact will be modest given the small
fraction of the college-going population that attends these colleges and
universities.

The graduation rate pattern is plainly different, however, at the public
universities in this study—as, indeed, it was at the small number of public universities included in the *Equity and Excellence* database (where, consistent with the findings reported here, graduation rates were lower for
low-SES students than for high-SES students).[31] It is not clear why the patterns are as different at the private and public institutions as they appear
to be. It may be that the greater wealth of many of the private colleges
and universities allows them to provide more financial assistance for students from modest backgrounds, which in turn reduces the pressure to
work too many hours or otherwise worry about how to make ends meet.[32]
Our analysis in Chapter 9 certainly suggests that a lower net price increases graduation rates among students from families in the bottom half
of the income distribution. It is entirely possible that the most effective
way of reducing the disparities in outcomes related to SES at the public
universities would be to make more aid available to their needy students.

But this approach is much easier to contemplate than to adopt given the intense, and intensifying, fiscal pressures on state systems. The necessary resources may not be available.

One other clue to the puzzling private-public differences in graduation rate outcomes related to SES may lie in the finding reported in Chapter 10 that family income bears very little relationship to graduation rates among students at public universities *who were enrolled from the start in an honors college.* In that discussion of institutional effects, we speculate that the amount of family resources available to a student may matter less in a relatively intimate setting in which the institution itself provides more support for low-SES students. Stanley Ikenberry, former president of the University of Illinois, has suggested that students from poorer families, and from families with less experience of higher education, may simply need more help and more nurturing in large university settings than do their classmates from families that are more experienced in dealing with the cultural, social, and academic challenges of college. One implication of the strong finding for honors colleges is that creating "learning communities" of one kind or another may be especially helpful for low-SES students attending large public universities.

NON-MINORITY STUDENTS FROM
MIDDLE- TO HIGH-SES BACKGROUNDS

As noted in Chapter 2, a surprising finding is the far from trivial number of students from middle- to high-SES backgrounds who enroll in four-year colleges but then fail to graduate. Nationally, just over two-thirds of students from the highest SES category earn bachelor's degrees (Figure 2.2), and close inspection of what happens at various stages of the educational process reveals that it is at the college *completion* stage (not the enrollment stage) that the most slippage occurs (Figure 2.4a).

The far more detailed data available to us for students in the three state systems we are studying in which parental education data are available (Maryland, North Carolina, and Virginia) show that this problem of non-graduation exists even among students from middle- to high-SES backgrounds with reasonably good academic qualifications. It is instructive to exclude from this target group not only students who were black, Hispanic, or from low-SES backgrounds but also those who had SAT/ACT scores below 1000 and/or high school GPAs below 3.0—who may well have had low graduation rates simply because of their relatively weak academic credentials. Within the remaining group of reasonably well-qualified students from middle- to high-SES backgrounds, we find that just 72 percent graduated within six years from the college they had first entered.[33] If we look only at the students who entered the SEL B universities in these three states, the same-school graduation rate drops to 62 percent. We recognize that the right target rate is certainly not 100 percent; presumably some number of students should not graduate for whatever reasons, personal or academic. Still, it seems to us that these graduation rates are low enough that they must surely represent a not inconsiderable amount of wasted opportunity—for individuals and for the country.

We regard this group of non-minority students from middle- to high-SES backgrounds as one that deserves to be targeted not because improving their graduation rate will do anything to address disparities in outcomes by SES (plainly it will not, by definition) but because this group seems to offer a ready pool of potential graduates who could, if they received degrees, significantly improve overall educational attainment. We estimate that there were nearly 15,000 students in this target population in the '99 entering cohorts in Maryland, North Carolina, and Virginia and that roughly 4,200 of these students failed to graduate from the institution that they first entered. We would expect that many of these students, and their parents, would see the value to them (in terms of pure self-interest) of finishing their college programs.

If—and it is a big "if"—parents provide their expected financial contributions, financial constraints should not be an over-riding problem for most of these students because they are attending relatively low-cost institutions and come from families with above-average resources and access to capital markets. As already noted, the analysis in Chapter 9 of the effects on graduation rates of "net price" suggests that, as we would have expected, it is low-income students, not students from these higher SES categories, who are most at risk of having to leave school for financial reasons. But we have to bear in mind that some (unknown) number of these students from middle- to high-SES backgrounds come from families that are simply not willing to contribute to their children's education, even though the FAFSA forms say that they should be able to do so. Financial aid officers worry a lot about these young people, who do not qualify for financial aid but lack the resources they need to complete their educational programs. These cases present a real conundrum for a system that presumes that part of a student's college bill should be paid by parents if they can afford it but that has no realistic way of enforcing this expectation. Of course, changing to a system in which parents were released from the expectation that they would pay, according to their financial means, would dramatically increase the demands on other sources of funds—principally governments—to replace lost parental contributions.[34]

Still, recognizing that financial support is not always what is seems to be, we suspect that a combination of weak motivation or interest on the part of students and institutional impediments such as poor advising or lack of access to gateway courses may be more consequential in causing a number of these students not to graduate. Surely the first step in working to improve graduation rates among this group is simply to recognize the need to do so and to shine a bright light on candidates whom we might expect to do better than they are doing. Kevin Carey is convinced that a big source of the problem of "too-low" graduation rates is "lack of attention" on the part of university faculty and staff. In his words, "The key issue is not whether universities say they're committed to helping all students succeed. It's whether they really mean it. Too often they don't."[35] Also, some kind of "Hawthorne effect" (making students aware that their institution expects them to do better and is taking what steps it can to help them) might itself improve graduation rates.[36]

In considering specific program interventions, individual universities will know best what might work in their own settings. The 2008 menu of "high impact" educational practices identified by the AAC&U (and George Kuh) should definitely have applicability in this context. In a 131-page report published just two days after President Obama's speech to Congress stressing the need to raise graduation rates, the Lumina Foundation describes detailed steps that institutions and federal and state governments can take to increase the proportion of Americans with "high quality" degrees and credentials.[37]

More generally, an older treatise by Vincent Tinto still has considerable value in explaining the complexity of the longitudinal process that causes students to stay in school or to leave. Tinto summarized a mass of research results assembled over some years, and his work is especially valuable, we think, in emphasizing the interactions between classroom experiences and those other aspects of student life that are so important in determining the student's degree of engagement with his or her college setting. The crude dichotomy between "required withdrawals" and "voluntary withdrawals" misses the subtleties of such interactions. Tinto's analysis focuses on "how events within the institution come to shape the process of departure" and thus complements the "macro/empirical" approach of this book. As Tinto recognizes, individual departures have many roots, which he categorizes as "intention, commitment, adjustment, difficulty, congruence, isolation, obligations, and finances."[38]

Finding the most effective institutional policies is no simple process, but there are, in Tinto's terminology, basic "principles of effective retention" and "of effective implementation" from which institutions can learn. A key "implementation principle" is: "Institutions should place ownership for institutional change in the hands of those across the campus who have to implement the change."[39] This simple-sounding proposition is in fact profound in its implications and reminds us of the importance, in the affirmative action context, of expecting all members of the campus community, not just those specially chosen to be affirmative action "officers," to assume responsibility for the success of efforts to make minority students feel fully included in the life of the college. Embedding an emphasis on retention in the fabric of the institution is essential.

Tinto's principles—which, we recognize, are much easier to state than to act on—apply to all four of the target groups discussed in this chapter. But some of the steps that might be taken to improve graduation rates have more applicability to certain of our target groups than to others. "Undermatch," for example, is an especially serious issue for minority students—and, within this group, particularly for Hispanics. Financial aid is of primary concern to low-SES students in all racial/ethnic groups. Other institutional interventions—and simply focusing on the importance of program completion—should help all students, including those who in some sense "should" graduate but have simply been lost from view.

CHAPTER 12

Looking Ahead

Pervasive, persistent, but not intractable. That is how we view the disparities in educational attainment that we have documented in this book. Similarly, the failure of the overall level of educational attainment in this country to increase in recent years, as it did so steadily for most of our nation's history, does not have to be accepted as an immutable fact of life in 21st-century America.[1] In this concluding chapter we will use the findings reported in previous chapters to look ahead—to define the challenges before us and to identify ways of addressing them.

CHALLENGES TO OVERCOME

We have identified five principal challenges.

- *First, the overall level of educational attainment in the United States today is both too low and stagnant.* The apparent inability of today's traditional college-age population to earn more bachelor's degrees is unacceptable. And it is *finishing* programs of study—earning degrees, not just starting out in college—that is the metric to be emphasized. The new Gates initiative in education clearly reflects a recognition of this central point, as do the statements and early initiatives of the Obama administration.[2]

  The current level of educational attainment in this country is particularly troubling when seen alongside the dramatic progress that is evident all around the world—in overall levels of educational attainment and especially in degrees awarded in science and engineering (refer back to Chapter 1).

  Nor can the United States expect to continue to benefit to the extent it has in the past from its success in importing educated talent. Countries on many continents now work hard to keep their own educated citizens at home and, for that matter, to attract talented young people from abroad. To recall just one telling vignette from Chapter 1, China now imports more students than it exports.

  Over several decades, leading economists have done a great deal of work in documenting the large contribution to economic growth of investments in education, both in the United States and globally.

Goldin and Katz (see Chapter 1) have shown in persuasive fashion how America's success in expanding educational attainment in the 20th century proved decisive in driving this country's remarkable growth during that century and how the slowdown in growth of educational attainment evident in recent decades poses a serious risk to our nation's economic leadership.

- *Second, the U.S. educational system harbors huge disparities in outcomes— especially as measured by graduation rates—that are systematically related to race/ethnicity and gender, as well as to socioeconomic status (SES).* Moreover, these disparities appear to be growing rather than narrowing. This pattern is unacceptable because of its implications for social mobility and access to opportunity, as well as because of what it says about our collective failure to take full advantage of pools of latent talent.

- *Third, these two problems are linked: the only way to substantially improve overall levels of educational attainment is by improving graduation rates for the rapidly growing Hispanic population, for underrepresented minority students in general (with black men requiring special attention), and for students from low-SES backgrounds.* To be sure, we can and should graduate higher proportions of white students from middle- and upper-SES backgrounds. But this group already has above-average graduation rates, and it will decline in absolute numbers in the coming decades; it would be a mistake to count on progress with this group to solve the country's need for a higher overall level of educational attainment.

- *Fourth, time-to-degree matters as well as ultimate graduation rates.* A long (and increasing) time-to-degree among underrepresented minorities and students from poor families harms access to later educational and career opportunities. Moreover, a long time-to-degree for students from all backgrounds carries high costs for the system as well as for individuals. Reductions in time-to-degree would allow universities to educate more students without adding proportionately to institutional outlays—a point of special consequence at a time when resources are so strained. Some legislators are again calling for colleges to offer three-year bachelor's degree programs, but we think it is more practical to focus on reducing the number of undergraduates who take more than four years to earn their degrees. Colleges could be more proactive in encouraging students to take less time to graduate. For example, West Virginia's PROMISE (Providing Real Opportunities for Maximizing In-State Student Excellence) Scholarship Program has introduced the idea of rewarding steady progress toward degree completion, not just maintaining a high GPA.[3]

- *Fifth and last, it is essential to recognize that public universities have to be the principal engines of progress in addressing these challenges.* Important as it is, the private sector is not large enough, nor does its mission focus as strongly on social mobility as does that of the public sector. It is the public sector that has the historical commitment to educational attainment for all, as well as the scale, the cost-pricing structure, and the greatest extant opportunities to do better (given present graduation rates). As Eugene M. Tobin writes in Appendix A of this book: "America's flagship universities were created to meet the social and economic needs of the states that chartered them, to serve as a great equalizer and preserver of an open, upwardly mobile society, and to provide 'an uncommon education for the common man.' Any citizen, regardless of socioeconomic status, who fulfilled a standard set of academic requirements, would, in theory, be admitted to one of the state's public higher education institutions." Douglass and Thomson also see the unique purpose of public institutions: "It is not an exaggeration to say that the health of America's economy and the character of social stratification will remain dependent on the vibrancy of its public higher education institutions. . . . For middle- and lower-income students, public institutions will remain the primary entry point."[4]

SORTING OF STUDENTS I:
TEST SCORES AND HIGH SCHOOL GRADES

Outcomes, especially graduation rates, depend greatly on achieving an optimal match between students and institutions. We are dealing here with a double selection process—one in which colleges select students and students select colleges—that does not always work as well as it should. That is the theme of this section and the next.

In selecting students, colleges rely on a variety of criteria that often vary, as they should, from institution to institution. It is clear to us that different types of tests and other sources of evidence that can be used to predict academic potential and academic outcomes, such as high school grades, measure different things. The right question is not "Should we, or should we not, use tests?" Rather the question is "In what settings can we expect various kinds of tests, and other measures, to be especially helpful?" A particular piece of evidence may be of great value for one purpose and of little or none for another. An instrument that is useful in predicting grades may have far less value as a predictor of graduation rates. Moreover, which measures are most useful depends on the relevant population of students; tests and other indicators that differentiate reasonably well among applicants to the most selective universities may be of marginal value, at best, in the context of less selective colleges and universities. *A "one-size-fits-all" mentality is to be avoided.*

Still, several main story lines are straightforward. The mass of new evidence we have assembled on the predictive power of high school grades and standardized test scores is, we believe, nothing less than compelling (see Chapter 6). Here are the main take-aways.

- *High school grades are a far better incremental predictor of graduation rates than are standard SAT/ACT test scores—a central finding that holds within each of the six sets of public universities that we study.* The additional predictive power of high school GPA is especially strong—really overwhelming—in the setting of the less selective flagships, which we call selectivity cluster (SEL) IIIs, and the less selective state system public universities, which we call SEL Bs. Scores on general reasoning or aptitude tests add little if anything in these contexts once we have taken account of high school GPA. SAT/ACT scores have more value in predicting graduation rates at more selective institutions (and somewhat greater value yet in predicting college grades, again especially at the more selective institutions), but here too high school GPA is a stronger incremental predictor.
- *Overly heavy reliance on SAT/ACT scores in admitting students can have adverse effects on the diversity of the student bodies enrolled by universities.* The correlation between family background and aptitude tests is consistently stronger than the correlation between family background and high school GPA.
- *The strong predictive power of high school GPA holds even when we know little or nothing about the quality of the high school attended.* In general, students with high grades from a weak school are appreciably more likely to graduate than are students with weak grades from an academically demanding high school. We believe that the consistently strong performance of high school GPA as a predictor of graduation rates derives in large part from its value as a measure of motivation, perseverance, work habits, and coping skills, as well as cognitive achievements. This is not to say that the quality of the high school is of no consequence. The quality of the high school matters too, and high school GPA has even greater predictive power when combined with knowledge about the high school attended. But whatever the high school, the in-school performance of the student dominates the effect of the high school itself in predicting graduation rates.
- *Scores on achievement tests, especially Advanced Placement tests, are better predictors of graduation rates than are scores on the standard SAT/ACT tests. As a general rule, colleges and universities selecting students are well advised to use a judicious combination of information about high school GPA, achievement test results (including the results of tests of writing skills), and the quality of the high school looked at in conjunction with standard SAT/*

ACT scores. "Triangulating" the selection process in this way is a strong protection against tendencies to "game" the system, which could be encouraged by focusing on only one predictor.

• *Putting more emphasis on content-based achievement tests has the further advantage of sending clear signals to high schools that they should concentrate on teaching content, including basic skills such as writing and the ability to use mathematics.* High schools should not be encouraged to "teach to the test" when the test allegedly measures reasoning skills and general aptitude; instead, more weight should be given to content-based tests that measure how well students learn what high school classes aim to teach.

Finally, testing organizations and others interested in testing should be encouraged to continue developing new tests and techniques of assessment that will facilitate matching processes of all kinds. Recent efforts by scholars at the Berkeley Law School to develop instruments that will predict "successful lawyering" are one example of this approach, and there also appears to be renewed interest at the undergraduate level in developing broadly gauged tests of "college readiness."[5] A further example is the effort by the eminent psychologist and now dean of the faculty at Tufts University, Robert Sternberg, to base admission to that university partly on "assessing students' creative and practical abilities."[6]

SORTING OF STUDENTS II:
"OVERMATCHING" AND "UNDERMATCHING"

Broadly speaking, educational attainment suffers, and students (and higher education in general) are harmed, whenever two types of sorting errors occur: (a) students are "overmatched" by enrolling in programs for which they are not qualified or (b) students are "undermatched" by failing to attend colleges and universities at which they will be appropriately challenged. The findings reported in this study fail to provide any evidence of overmatching but demonstrate that undermatching is a massive problem.

The Overmatch Hypothesis

As we noted in the previous chapter, opponents of affirmative action have often claimed that race-sensitive admissions policies harm the very minority students they purport to help by inducing them to attend colleges that are too demanding, thrusting them into harmful competition with white classmates of greater ability and demoralizing them as they fail to meet applicable standards. The data for the 1999 entering cohorts at the public universities we study offer no support whatsoever for this hypothesis (see Chapter 11).

In fact, our research indicates that black male students who went to more selective institutions graduated at *higher,* not lower, rates than did similarly prepared black students who went to less selective institutions. There is no evidence that black men were "harmed" by going to the more selective universities that chose to admit them.

- *Students from all backgrounds, including black students, are generally well advised to enroll at one of the most challenging universities that will accept them.*

Undermatching

An obverse proposition deserves much more attention than it has received.

- *The frequently disappointing graduation rate outcomes for students from underrepresented minority groups and for students from low-SES backgrounds are due in no small part to the fact that a number of them were "undermatched"—that is, appreciable numbers of these students enrolled in either two-year colleges or four-year colleges that were less demanding than the colleges for which they were presumptively qualified, and some enrolled in no college at all.*

Among all high school graduates in North Carolina (the state with the richest data connecting experiences in high school to later collegiate outcomes) whom we classified as presumptively eligible to attend one of the most selective public universities in that state, over 40 percent failed to do so—that is, they undermatched (Chapter 5). Not surprisingly, disproportionate numbers of these students came from families with low incomes and low levels of parental education. Many highly qualified students from low-SES backgrounds went to a community college or to no college at all. Supporting evidence comes from impressive studies of Chicago high school students that found that 28 percent of black high school graduates in that city "enrolled in a college that was far below a match," that Hispanic students were even more likely than black students to undermatch, and that less than half of the students in the most academically demanding programs ended up enrolling at colleges that match their qualifications.[7]

- *The scale of the undermatch phenomenon among students from modest backgrounds suggests that addressing this problem offers a real opportunity to increase social mobility and simultaneously to increase overall levels of educational attainment.*

Undermatching occurs primarily at the application stage of the admission process; in the main, it is not a result of students applying and being turned down or of failing to accept an admission offer. The key is to find ever more effective ways of informing high-achieving high school students and their parents of the educational opportunities that are open to them—and of the benefits they can derive from taking advantage of these opportunities. Then, better ways need to be found to help these students navigate the process of gaining access to strong academic programs. We were surprised to learn how powerfully eighth-grade test scores that are content-based predict later college outcomes, and there is much to be said for identifying high-performing students from disadvantaged backgrounds early and tracking them carefully to reduce risks of undermatching. At the same time, we also recognize that the undermatch problem is by no means confined to either low-SES students or students with off-the-scale high school records. Students in general would benefit greatly from improved advising and counseling—functions that are too often under-resourced and uninformed. Finding ways to improve the matching process should be a high priority. Consideration should be given to ways of improving the use of digital technologies and online resources, and to the possibility of assigning special "coaches" the task of helping high-achieving students from modest backgrounds complete their applications and financial aid forms.

TRANSFER PATTERNS

A major advantage of the new public university databases that we have built is that they include students who transferred into these public universities as well as first-time freshmen. We also studied "transfer-out patterns." Some students who withdrew from the university at which they first enrolled ultimately graduated from another four-year institution, but taking these students into account raises overall graduation rates by only about 5 percentage points on average at the flagship universities and 10 percentage points at the state system universities. Taking account of transfer-out patterns does not change any of the main findings based on analysis of graduation rates at the institution first attended.

It is the transfer-in population that is of greatest interest, and there are three main empirical findings from this part of our research that deserve to be highlighted.

- *High school seniors who wanted to earn a bachelor's degree eventually, but who began at two-year colleges, were much less likely to earn a bachelor's degree than were comparable students who went directly from high school to a four-year program.*

- *Overall, transfer-in students did well. Those attending the more selective universities in our study graduated at about the same rate as first-time freshmen in spite of entering with weaker pre-collegiate credentials; transfer students at the less-selective four-year universities in our study graduated at higher rates than did first-time freshmen even though they entered with weaker pre-collegiate credentials.*
- *Transfer students from two-year colleges were substantially more likely to be from low-income families than were first-time freshmen.*

It is not easy to draw policy conclusions from these findings at a system-wide level because, as we explain in detail in the last section of Chapter 7, there may be some conflict between incentives for students and incentives for institutions—and there are also complex issues of resource allocation to be considered. But it does seem clear that a number of the universities in our study might improve both their socioeconomic diversity and their graduation rates by accepting more transfer students—who have, after all, demonstrated both motivation and accomplishment by completing a two-year course of study and seeking admission to a bachelor's degree program.[8] It also seems clear that states should not encourage students with bachelor's degree aspirations and the necessary qualifications to enroll in a two-year program when they could have enrolled in a four-year college directly out of high school (the undermatch problem yet again). Nor should the existence of transfer opportunities justify underinvestment in creating places at four-year institutions.

MONEY MATTERS

Our research confirms an obvious proposition: the net cost of going to college and a family's resources together significantly affect both the probability that a student will graduate and the probability that the student will graduate in four years (Chapters 8 and 9).

- *At every point in our analysis we find that students from high-income families are significantly more likely to graduate from college, and to graduate "on time," than are students with comparable qualifications from low-income families.*
- *Need-based grant aid was available to students attending all groups of public universities in our study, and there is clear evidence that such aid boosts both the numbers who attend such institutions and their graduation rates. Nonetheless, despite the presence of need-based aid, the graduation rate for students from low-SES families at these public universities was lower than the graduation rate for other students. In contrast, at highly selective private colleges and universities, graduation rates were essentially the same among students who differed in SES.[9]*

- *Comparisons across states between "net price" (tuition less grant aid) and adjusted graduation rates demonstrate that low- and moderate-income students who reside in states where attendance at the flagship university involves a higher net price are less likely to graduate than are comparable students from states where they face a lower net price—and they are considerably less likely to graduate in four years. Thus, we conclude that making college less expensive for students from modest backgrounds has to be a key consideration in any concerted effort to raise graduation rates and shorten time-to-degree.*

- *The data also clearly show that there is no such relationship between net price and graduation rates among students from families in the top half of the income distribution—a less obvious and potentially more consequential conclusion.*

- *Finding more resources for need-based student aid, while obviously difficult at all times, especially when fiscal constraints are so tight, is demonstrably less expensive than keeping the net price low by reducing tuition across the board— a policy that provides further subsidies to well-off families without improving their graduation rates.*

During the period of our study, undergraduates faced severe limits on the amount of money they could borrow under the federal loan programs, limits that had not risen since 1992. Students who needed to borrow more than the limit had to find other lenders outside the federally supported system and generally faced higher interest rates, if indeed credit was available to them at all. In the face of these constraints, some students no doubt sought to fill financial gaps by working in off-campus jobs—which of course can slow progress toward a degree. A complicating factor, alluded to by many campus commentators, is that a significant number of students are unwilling to defer their desire for "stuff" like flat-screen televisions until they have reaped the rewards of graduation. As a result, they may perform less well in college and even drop out altogether as they seek to satisfy their consumption preferences through long hours of work. To go beyond these anecdotal speculations requires more information than is available even in our rich data set—including, crucially, information on off-campus work patterns.

A particularly sensitive aspect of financial aid discussions is the role played by merit aid. According to a College Board study, only 44 percent of grant aid dollars at public four-year institutions went to students who had financial need. Nearly 40 percent went to non-need students, and 18 percent went to recruited athletes (including, of course, a number with need). As already noted, there is no evidence in our data that grants to more affluent students actually influence the likelihood that these students will graduate.

- *Although it is easy to understand an institution's wish to attract better students, the "cost" of using scarce grant aid dollars to pursue such a policy (which may or may not be effective if peer institutions match offers) can be too high. Reallocating some amount of money from merit-based aid to need-based awards could make a real difference.*

There is broader agreement on another proposition: that the complexity and uncertainty surrounding the financial aid process is itself a serious problem. There is a growing consensus (reflected, for example, in the "Rethinking Student Aid" study sponsored by the College Board and in statements made by the Obama administration) in favor of restructuring the provision of student aid.

- *Reliable, simple, and predictable provision of financial aid is important not just to initial access to college but to success in graduating.*

In this day of increasing transparency and greater accountability, it is surely desirable that most financial aid be delivered according to well-understood general policies and rules. However, financial aid programs, like programs of all kinds, can become too rigid and too bureaucratic. There is considerable anecdotal evidence that students from low-income families, in particular, are forced to leave college, perhaps never to return, because of unanticipated emergencies or family crises of one kind or another. One major advantage of coming from a family with the financial capacity simply to "write a check" is that such crises can usually be buffered and prevented from changing one's life course.

- *We are increasingly persuaded that providing key campus actors (presumably deans in most instances) with a meaningful amount of truly discretionary money that can be quickly deployed to relieve distress could make a real difference to completion rates and time-to-degree.*

We regret our inability to say more about the effects of loan programs of various kinds on completion rates. The data are hard to assemble and, when assembled, hard to interpret. In any case, it is clear that there is a continuing role for borrowing, and perhaps an increasingly important role for well-conceived contingent repayment loan programs. Here again, more evidence is needed—especially from careful analysis of loan aversion tendencies on the part of low-income students and their families. We agree that students in general, and low-income students in particular, should not be asked to assume such large debt obligations that their future is compromised. But it is equally clear that students can be too reluctant to borrow. Unwillingness to take on reasonable amounts of debt can itself exact a high "price" if the consequence is a longer and more tortuous path to a degree or no degree at all.

Finally, money matters in terms of the effects of economy-wide woes on state funding of both two-year and four-year public institutions. Anticipated budget cuts (in 2009) are causing many state systems to consider capping or even cutting enrollment. In addition, reductions in faculty can cause key courses to be closed, with obvious implications for time-to-degree and, in some cases, for the ability of students to complete degree programs. The perverse effects of cyclical funding on higher education are all too apparent—and unresolved.[10] In the fiscal environment of the United States in late 2008 and 2009, there has been much talk of providing fiscal stimulus by investing in the nation's "infrastructure" of roads, bridges, and the like. There is much to be said for viewing expenditures on education as investments in "human infrastructure" that may well be equally productive in the near term and arguably more durable than investments in bridges and tunnels.

INSTITUTIONAL SELECTIVITY AND GRADUATION RATES

One of the most relentlessly consistent findings in this study is the powerful association between graduation rates and institutional selectivity as measured by a combination of the test scores and high school grades of entering undergraduates. To be sure, more selective universities, by definition, enroll students with stronger entering credentials who are more likely to graduate regardless of where they go to college.

- *We find, however, that controlling for students' high school GPAs, SAT/ACT scores, and demographic characteristics fails to remove anything like all of the pronounced differences in graduation rates related to institutional selectivity. Substantial differences remain (see Chapter 10).*

These persistent differences are, we believe, driven principally by five broad sets of factors:

1. *Peer effects.* Students learn from each other. Being surrounded by highly capable classmates improves the learning environment and promotes good educational outcomes of all kinds, including timely graduation.
2. *Expectations.* The high overall graduation rates at the most selective public universities unquestionably create a climate in which graduating, and graduating with one's class, are compelling norms. Students feel real pressure to keep pace with their classmates.
3. *Access to excellent educational resources.* In the main, highly selective universities also have superior faculty and distinctly above-average library and laboratory resources. It seems reasonable to suppose that these factors improve learning environments for at least some highly talented undergraduates, who may succeed in identifying stimulat-

ing faculty mentors, take some graduate courses, and benefit from
having exceptionally able graduate students as teaching assistants.

4. *Financial aid and student work opportunities.* In general, students at
highly selective universities—especially those who are members of
ethnic and racial minorities—are, as our data indicate, likely to have
access to more generous financial aid than other students. Also, research grants and contracts obtained by faculty members can provide attractive on-campus work opportunities, especially in the sciences and engineering, that foster engagement with the academic
process and facilitate degree completion.

5. *Unobservable selection effects.* Finally, we suspect that there is some
modest association between enrollment at the most selective flagship universities and unobservable characteristics of entering students, such as ambition and drive.

Universities that lack the established pulling power of a Berkeley, a
Michigan, or a Chapel Hill cannot instantly and easily acquire their ad-
vantages. But they can strive to create "sub-environments" such as honors
colleges and structured learning communities that can be used to set
high expectations and create peer effects that reinforce these expectations. There is evidence in our data that honors colleges improve graduation rates, even after controlling for differences in student characteristics
—but it should also be noted that honors colleges generally enroll disproportionate numbers of high-SES students and so may accentuate
rather than diminish disparities in outcomes related to SES.

There has been debate for years over whether a heavy emphasis on
cutting-edge research by faculty and on building top-ranked graduate
programs helps or hurts undergraduate instruction (see Appendix A and
the references there to concerns expressed by Clark Kerr back in the early
1960s). Some undergraduates thrive in such settings, while at the same
time others suffer from what can be impersonal, uncaring, and even in-
timidating environments. It is hard to generalize. But it is possible that
the strong positive association between institutional selectivity and graduation rates reflects to some degree the impact of stimulating research
environments at truly excellent universities.

Pressures to focus on research and to build up graduate programs may
be every bit as strong, perhaps even stronger, at mid-level universities. The
quest for excellence—and for prestige—is entirely understandable, but
we suspect that, unless managed with great skill, it can have unintended
consequences for undergraduate education. An example is the amount of
support universities below the top tier often provide for less-than-out-
standing graduate programs. Seeking to improve such programs, while

obviously desirable, can siphon off resources that might be better invested, at least in some settings, in strengthening undergraduate education.

One fact stands out: flagship public universities as a group have become much more selective since the 1960s, as measured by the percentages of incoming students with A or A+ high school grades rather than Bs or Cs (see the data in Chapter 1 and the general discussion of this trend in Appendix A). These universities face a difficult challenge in remaining true to their historical "access" missions while at the same time competing for faculty and students with ambitious and well-resourced universities in the private as well as public sector. Because selectivity per se is associated with higher graduation rates, there is no inevitable conflict between attracting larger and larger numbers of outstanding students and the desirability of graduating ever-higher fractions of entering undergraduate classes. But because undergraduate qualifications are so strongly correlated with family background, there can be a quite direct conflict with the desire to serve egalitarian ends by reducing disparities in outcomes.

- *This tension between "egalitarian" and "elitist" goals is an important reason for thinking carefully about how admissions criteria, transfer policies, and decisions about pricing and financial aid can be used to find the most appropriate balance.*

These are difficult issues, and each university and university system has to decide for itself, in conjunction with the state government that oversees it and provides support, what priority to give to different aspects of its mission and how to allocate resources that are often much too limited. A temptation to avoid is for all public universities to seek to "be Berkeley"; after all, there are many ways to excel, and many worthwhile missions to serve. We would not want all universities to look alike.

PROMOTING PERSISTENCE IN INDIVIDUAL INSTITUTIONS

There is no substitute, at the end of the day, for addressing completion rate and time-to-degree issues at the level of the individual institution. This approach requires a type of micro-analysis that is beyond the scope of this study, which focuses mainly on macro relationships. Our detailed data on semester-by-semester patterns of persistence across large numbers of institutions are, however, directly relevant to the question of how institutions should think about this set of issues.

- *In contrast to transfers, which are heavily concentrated in the first two years of college attendance, we find that withdrawals continue to occur, quite regularly, all along the path to graduation. There are modest "spikes" in withdrawals at the end of the second and fourth semesters, but nearly half of all withdrawals occur after the second year (Chapter 3). This finding is an important reminder that, although some "front-loading" of efforts to increase persistence makes good sense, it would be a big mistake to believe that addressing the "early-days" problems of students is all that is needed to improve graduation rates.*

The detailed data on the power of institutional effects documented in Chapter 10 and referenced in the previous section of this chapter contain an important insight relevant to efforts that individual institutions can make to improve outcomes. In fact, at given levels of selectivity there is considerable variation in adjusted graduation rates (adjusted to take account of differences among institutions in entering student characteristics and demographic factors); thus, it is possible to measure the extent to which some universities have done better at graduating students than have others that operate at the same level of institutional selectivity.

Careful examination of the characteristics of universities that do better or worse in this regard than their students' characteristics predict fails to reveal broad patterns related either to scale or to educational expenditures per student. But the data do indicate that residential patterns matter (Chapter 10).

- *Other things more or less equal, "campus-like" institutions have somewhat higher graduation rates and shorter time-to-degree. Students who lived in a university residence hall during their first semester were more likely to graduate than were off-campus students after controlling for differences in entering credentials and background characteristics, including family income. There is also evidence of institution-wide effects. All students appear to benefit from attending an institution where more students live on campus.*

The implication cannot be that all universities need to become more residential, a proposition that makes no sense in many contexts (urban universities confront very different choice sets than do those in more rural settings) and would often be too costly. It would be totally unrealistic to expect public universities in general to create residential arrangements like those at a William and Mary or a Penn State. What may be more realistic, and what in fact many universities are already doing, is to provide surrogates for on-campus living experiences in, for example, university-owned apartments reasonably close to campus. For those students who do commute, it may be valuable to provide a safe, easy, and attractive environment on or around campus for their use between or after classes. The general point is simply that on-campus or near-campus living and learning options can increase the engagement of students with their university, which in turn should encourage higher graduation rates and shorter time-to-degree.

One frequently cited impediment to raising graduation rates for minority students and students from low-SES families is the discomfort such students often feel on campuses very different from anything they have experienced before. Such problems are compounded when there are very few students "like them" on their campus and in their classes. We have become intrigued by an approach to this problem pioneered by Deborah Bial through her national "Posse" program, which recruits inner-city students and sends them to colleges in "posses" so that they can support one another. We do not know whether such a cohort-based recruitment effort would prove to be workable and cost-effective if applied in more large-scale public university settings, but we think there is merit in experimenting with pilot programs.

Of course, there are innumerable interventions that have proved successful in particular college and university settings, and we will not repeat here the references provided earlier to summaries of "high-impact" approaches provided by the Association of American Colleges and Universities, the Lumina Foundation, and a number of scholars, including Vincent Tinto (Chapter 11). One broader thesis persuasively advanced by Kevin Carey of Education Sector is that "just paying attention" can make a tremendous difference. That is, universities are beset fore and aft by pressures of all kinds, and it is easy to allow a concern for student completion rates to fall "between the cracks." Carey's point is simply that a top-down commitment demonstrated by deeds and not just by words can galvanize efforts of many different kinds to keep students on track.

Also, we suspect that too little attention is paid to timely completion of programs. One recent graduate of a highly selective flagship university said that at his university graduating in four years was like "leaving the party at 10:30 p.m." In light of the costs to the system and the need for more student places at many flagship universities (in part to deal with the undermatch problem), it should not be made too easy for students simply to "hang around." Shining a bright light on the dropout problem, on the need to monitor time-to-degree, and on specific steps designed to help students complete their programs of study—such as careful organization of learning communities and relentless tracking of students with at-risk characteristics—can have a surprisingly large impact. There is much to be said for self-conscious efforts to inculcate the right "norms," including timely completion of degree programs.[11]

The "accountability" movement, which is here to stay (see Chapter 1), can stimulate efforts to monitor progress in, for example, raising graduation rates for subsets of students. It is noteworthy that groups of colleges and universities, such as the Association of Public and Land-Grant Universities, the American Association of State Colleges and Universities, and the National Association of Independent Colleges and Universities, have taken the initiative to create Web sites that make available data on outcomes of many kinds. And we find it even more encouraging that there is a growing interest at all levels of education in evidence-based research on results that matter. There is certainly much to learn—and much to accomplish.

———————

In concluding this book we want to thank again the individuals at the universities we have studied for their commitment to studying these issues and for using what they learn to improve educational outcomes. Their openness to evidence, and their lack of defensiveness in confronting data suggesting the need to do better, are highly encouraging. Now it is up to policy makers at state and national levels to provide both the moral support and the tangible assistance that will allow many of these institutions to improve overall levels of educational attainment and reduce the stark disparities in outcomes related to race/ethnicity and SES that are so problematic.

The Modern Evolution of America's Flagship Universities

EUGENE M. TOBIN

MARTIN TROW, the distinguished sociologist of education, once observed that American higher education differs from the educational systems of other advanced nations in terms of its responsiveness to market forces, institutional and structural diversity, and absence of central authority, as well as the pervasive role of general education in first-degree courses and the rapidity of its evolution from an elite system to a mass system and then to a universal system.[1] To call American higher education a "system" may sound like a term of art or an oxymoron, something that exists by default and whose sole purpose is to serve as a stark contrast with other nations' more structured systems. But of course there is a system, however unplanned, incremental, and haphazard its character and early development. This essay provides an historical analysis of U.S. public higher education in the second half of the 20th century, with special attention given to the undergraduate teaching mission at flagship state universities.

The centerpiece of William G. Bowen, Matthew M. Chingos, and Michael S. McPherson's *Crossing the Finish Line* is an extensive statistical analysis of educational attainment that draws on data from 21 flagship institutions and on more complete data from the public higher education systems in Maryland, North Carolina, Ohio, and Virginia. Rather than attempt a similarly comprehensive historical treatment, this complementary essay uses the experiences of several state universities as case studies and relies on contemporary presidential and national commission reports as markers of shifting public interest in *undergraduate* public higher education since 1945. One of this essay's most important take-aways is

Eugene M. Tobin is program officer for higher education and the liberal arts colleges at The Andrew W. Mellon Foundation. He thanks Bill Bowen, Mike McPherson, and Matt Chingos for their close and generous reading of this essay and gratefully acknowledges the contributions and support of current and former colleagues including Philip Lewis, Harriet Zuckerman, Don Randel, Joseph Meisel, James Shulman, Dyuti Bhattacharya, Pat McPherson, Jo Ellen Parker, Susanne Pichler, Ellen Nasto, Lisa Bonifacic, and Jonathan Veitch.

that since the end of World War II, undergraduate education at flagship universities has become a smaller part of the increasingly variegated missions of these complex institutions and the statewide systems to which they belong. Without passing judgment on other parts of public universities' operations and responsibilities, this essay records the inexorable movement toward what Clark Kerr famously called the "multiversity" and the attendant changes in the way education is delivered at the undergraduate level. Although the story is too complex to be reduced to shorthand observations about the shift of time, resources, and rewards to graduate and professional education, the gradual withdrawal of senior faculty from undergraduate teaching, and their replacement by graduate teaching assistants, such trends raise the question of whether the flagships (and other public institutions) have given a high enough priority to the issue of successful degree completion for the undergraduate students they enroll. At the same time, the trend toward greater division of labor and growing specialization reflects the unusually wide range of responsibilities that a modern state higher education system is expected to assume. It is difficult to imagine that all these tasks could be addressed without considerable differentiation among types of public institutions as well as within them. This chronicle focuses on the post-war era but begins with a brief look back at the era of institution-building in the early 20th century.

America's flagship universities were created to meet the social and economic needs of the states that chartered them, to serve as a great equalizer and preserver of an open, upwardly mobile society, and to provide "an uncommon education for the common man."[2] Any resident, regardless of socioeconomic status, who fulfilled a standard set of academic requirements would, in theory, be admitted to one of the state's public higher education institutions.[3] In principle, the flagship university of the late 19th and early 20th century was an institution that served everybody, but in an era when few people completed high school (and many who did pursued non-college preparatory curricula), the notion of the "people's university" was more symbol than reality. In 1900, as Claudia Goldin and Lawrence Katz note, when the primary reason to attend high school was to gain college admission, barely 20 percent of high school–age students enrolled in high school and only 10 percent graduated.[4] A decade later, only six universities had enrollments of more than 5,000 students—five private institutions (Columbia, Cornell, Harvard, and the Universities of Chicago and Pennsylvania) and the University of Michigan, which was the only state university to rank in the top six.[5] These enrollments pale in comparison with the later mid-century growth of public universities, but as Laurence Veysey observes, a university with 5,000 students is much more similar to one with 50,000 than it is to one with

500. Moreover, contemporary accounts in which undergraduates in large lecture courses (with 200 or more students) were "left adrift unaided . . . in an extremely impersonal environment" suggest that students' impressions of the quality of teaching at some early 20th-century state universities bore a striking similarity to the complaints and laments of later generations of students and faculty.[6]

The relatively steady growth of public higher education during the 1920s owed a great deal to the consistently rising secondary school enrollments spurred by compulsory attendance laws, recognition of the growing value of a high school diploma, and structural changes in the economy that increased the demand for educated workers. The percentage of high school graduates of college age who entered higher education in the 1920s remained fairly constant at just above 30 percent, but the number of high school graduates increased from 231,000 in 1920 to 596,000 in 1930, which helps explain why college and university enrollments doubled during this period. Even with a robust pipeline of high school graduates, the college-going rate among 18- to 24-year-olds increased very modestly, from 5.2 percent in 1921 to 7.4 percent by 1931 and to 8.4 percent on the eve of America's entry into World War II.[7]

In the 15 years between 1909 and 1924, public research universities doubled in size and then grew another 50 percent over the next 15 years. Although the Great Depression took its toll with respect to lost tuition revenue and declining state support, the employment programs created during Franklin Roosevelt's administration helped keep students in school and out of the regular employment markets, and the New Deal's work-relief and public works projects doubled the value of state universities' physical plants.[8] In 1939 the average size of the nation's leading public universities was 14,000 full-time students. Leading the way was the University of California–Berkeley (17,744), followed by the Universities of Minnesota (15,301), Illinois (13,510), Michigan (12,098), and Wisconsin (11,268). These figures almost doubled the average size of such private research universities as the University of Chicago (6,011), Harvard (8,209), Columbia (8,008), the University of Pennsylvania (7,347), and Cornell (6,949).[9]

In 1940, the nation's heterogeneous, decentralized, market-driven, and minimally regulated higher education system encompassed approximately 1,750 colleges and universities that educated 8.4 percent of the college-age population, a figure that compared favorably to the European average of 4 percent. Fifty-three percent of the nation's students attended public universities, a trend that would accelerate swiftly in the post-war decades.[10] On the eve of war, there was every reason to believe that public universities would continue to make important contributions in advancing knowledge and in serving their respective states, but the major post-war issues involving higher education—the broadening and sharing of educational opportunity, the transition from an elite to a mass education system, the removal of racial and economic barriers, and the roles of state and federal government—would be notably different and far more challenging than those encountered earlier.

HIGHER EDUCATION'S POST-WAR POLICY AGENDAS

> Sometimes the remark is heard, 'too many people are going to college.'
> Those who so speak are always thinking of the children of someone else, never their own.
> James Lewis Morrill, 1945[11]

The evolution of the country's leading public universities since World War II represents an important chapter in the history of American higher education. Although private colleges and universities have made seminal contributions to the nation's intellectual, cultural, and political life, public universities, because of their scale, have fueled the country's economic development and social mobility. The major post-war questions—Who should go to college? Who would go? Who should pay? Who benefits?—reflected serious concerns within the public sector about broadening educational opportunity, balancing "elite" and "mass" functions, removing racial and economic barriers, and determining the proper roles of federal and state government.[12]

In the summer of 1946, with Americans increasingly frustrated by coal and rail strikes, inflation, and deteriorating confidence in price controls and with the nation's colleges mobilizing to meet the needs of returning veterans eager to use the G.I. Bill, the Truman administration cast about for a domestic issue with potentially broad political appeal.[13] On the strong urging of George F. Zook,[14] president of the American Council on Education (ACE), President Harry Truman created a presidential commission (with Zook as chair) and charged it with examining the "functions of higher education in our democracy," particularly the "ways and means of expanding educational opportunities for all able young people."[15]

The Zook Commission's surprisingly ambitious six-volume report, *Higher Education for American Democracy,* was released between December 1947 and February 1948.[16] The commissioners proposed a significant expansion of educational opportunity, including legislation that would remove all racial, religious, geographic, and economic barriers.[17] Among a number of controversial proposals, including calls for government-funded undergraduate scholarships and expansion of public, tuition-free, two-year community colleges, it was the commission's "education-for-all" recommendation that catalyzed the public debate.[18] Specifically, the commission recommended an expansion of government expenditures for public higher education that would double the undergraduate enrollment to 4 million by 1960.[19] This number represented almost three and a half times as many students as enrolled at the pre-war peak in 1940, when less than 10 percent of the college-age population had received an education beyond high school. Acknowledging the economic barriers that had limited college enrollment before the war, the Zook Commission dismissed the notion that "any boy can get a college education who has it in him"; the commissioners proposed the elimination of all fees at public institutions for students through the first two years of college.[20]

The ensuing public debate took place on two levels: a relatively brief discussion led by major national opinion makers curious to see if the Truman administration would send any of the commission's recommendations to Capitol Hill—none were ever sent—and a second, much more substantive, contentious discussion within the higher education community that revealed the diverging priorities of the public and private sectors. Because this debate represented the first time a presidential commission had been convened to consider the federal government's role in higher education, the commission's proposals accentuated the higher education system's deep-seated and growing divisions. The prominent national educational associations and their college and university members lined up along a continuum of philosophical and operational differences: public versus private, elite versus non-elite, religious versus secular, centralized versus decentralized, research versus teaching, general education versus specialized knowledge.[21] Critics predicted that the combination of a significant expansion of enrollment with a more prominent role for the federal government would lower standards, sacrifice liberal for general and vocational education, favor public over private institutions, lead to the loss of political control, and create a dangerous oversupply of frustrated college graduates for whom there would be an insufficient number of well-paying jobs.[22]

The principle of educational opportunity was never in doubt, but there was no consensus about some fundamental issues. How much opportunity was appropriate? What percentage of college-age students needed an education beyond high school? Who should pay for that training?[23] The answers to these questions were so profound in their implications—for the nation in terms of social mobility and equity and for colleges and universities in terms of private versus public control, market competition, and the future of federal support—that the debate transcended the pettiness of academic politics.[24]

THE GOLDEN AGE OF PUBLIC UNIVERSITIES

During the 1950s, the nation's private and public research universities faced a number of common challenges, including how to take resources dedicated to instruction and channel them into core support for faculty, graduate education, and research. As Roger Geiger notes in *Research and Relevant Knowledge,* his seminal study of research universities of the middle to late 20th century, the immediate post-war American university was still organized as a teaching institution whose primary funding sources were student fees, state appropriations, and, in the case of private institutions, income from endowments. Attracting and retaining world-class scholars requires above-market salaries, reduced teaching loads, and high-ability graduate students, who claim the vast majority of the faculty's time and, in some cases, assume a significant portion of the undergraduate teaching. Research universities also depend on a costly infrastructure and an expanding intellectual curiosity among the faculty that encourages exploration into emerging areas of scholarly interest. The emergence of the federal research economy and what Clark Kerr called the "federal grant university" would soon enable research universities to build up the quality, prestige, and scale of their graduate faculties, doctoral programs, and facilities.[25] One key component of the flagships' rise to prominence, the economies of scale created by soaring undergraduate enrollments, was less than a decade away.

This was not an easy time for college and university enrollment planners. World War II veterans disappeared from the nation's campuses almost as quickly as they had appeared. Though there was some uncertainty about future enrollment trends, few demographers doubted that an "impending tidal wave of students" was fast approaching.[26] "The veteran's impact upon our institutions . . . was an emergency situation involving only temporary adjustments," observed Francis Brown of ACE in 1955. He continued: "The present and future demands will be continuous and of a positively accelerating character."[27] Experts projected that there would be 2.3 million 18-year-olds in 1955, 2.8 million in 1960, 3.7 million in 1970, and 4 million in 1975. When the post-war birth rate rose to 3.6 per woman of child-bearing age (reaching a post-war high of 3.8 in 1957), what one contemporary still called the "unanticipated population bulge" finally captured national attention.[28]

The Soviet Union's launch of the Sputnik I satellite in October 1957 and the American public's panicked reaction to an alleged educational crisis guaranteed that there would be federal intervention in higher education. Although post-Sputnik analyses focused on the deficiencies of the nation's elementary and secondary schools, "the only widespread complaints about higher education were that Americans needed more of it."[29] Sputnik may have "had the size and lethal potential of a beach ball," but doubts about the nation's scientific and military capacity and an emerging public awareness of the relationship between educational attainment and national security accelerated the federal government's direct assistance to colleges and universities.[30] Rapid passage of the National Defense Education Act (NDEA) in September 1958 provided loans for college students (with partial forgiveness for those entering elementary and secondary school teaching), graduate fellowships, and aid for programs supporting science, mathematics, modern foreign languages, and area studies.

Like the G.I. Bill, whose legislative intent had more to do with the postwar economy and recognition of past service than with expanding educational opportunity, the NDEA was primarily a national security initiative and only indirectly an acknowledgment of higher education's role in promoting social mobility. As a U.S. Department of Health, Education, and Welfare official noted, "The rationale behind the [NDEA] . . . was not that the nation owed a special group an opportunity for education but that the nation needed a special group—the talented—whose education could help in scientific and technological competition with the Soviet Union."[31] By the 1960s, however, the unprecedented volume of students moving through the nation's secondary school pipeline guaranteed that the questions of "who should go to college" and "who should pay" would become a prominent part of the public policy debate.

In 15 years the number of 18- to 24-year-olds grew 60 percent, from 15 million in 1955 to 24 million in 1970. The number of high school graduates doubled from 1.4 million to 2.8 million, high school graduation rates rose from 63 percent of the 17-year-old population in 1955 to 77 percent in 1968, and college enrollment rates increased nearly 10 percent, reaching a peak of 55 percent at the end of the 1960s.[32] During these years the federal government's commitment to higher education became more nuanced and multifaceted, particularly in the areas of research and student aid.[33]

The breakthrough came in 1965 with passage of the Higher Education Act, the first need-based federal program of student scholarships and loans, and in a separate amendment to the Social Security Act that allowed the children of deceased, disabled, or retired parents to receive benefits while in college. In symbolically signing the Higher Education Act into law on the campus of his alma mater, Southwest Texas State College, President Lyndon B. Johnson declared that "a high school senior anywhere in this great land of ours can [now] apply to any college or any university in any of the 50 states and not be turned away because his family is poor." Speaking at the apex of the "Great Society's" legislative achievements, the president encouraged his audience to "tell your children and . . . your grandchildren . . . that we have opened the road and we have pulled the gates down and the way is open, and we expect them to travel it."[34] National service and security interests had underlain government support of the G.I. Bill and the NDEA, but the Higher Education Act represented a fundamental shift in government policy. As Elizabeth Duffy and Idana Goldberg have observed, "The focus of the 1965 legislation turned to ensuring that the benefits of economic growth generally, and education more specifically, be fairly and equitably distributed to all members of society."[35] Access to higher education was well on its way toward becoming more of a right than a reward.

As late as 1950, the private and public sectors had enjoyed a 50-50 split of higher education enrollment. By 1980, 78 percent of the nation's students would be attending public colleges and universities—42 percent at four-year institutions, 36 percent at two-year colleges—and the distribution within the public sector would undergo its own significant change.[36] In 1960, 50 percent of public enrollments were concentrated in flagship universities and other graduate-level institutions. Within 20 years, 75 percent of public-sector enrollments were based in open-admission community colleges and in less selective comprehensive institutions. The former, which had been zealously championed by the Zook Commission, experienced a phenomenal growth, from fewer than 400,000 students in 1960 to over 4 million in 1980.[37] Similarly, the explosion of enrollment activity among comprehensive colleges and universities—the former state teachers colleges, which had expanded to offer master's-level and, in some cases, doctoral-level programs in many professional fields, including engineering and business administration—drove their enrollments from 500,000 students in 1960 to almost 3 million by 1980.[38]

This remarkable expansion reflected a broad post-Sputnik consensus that higher education was a public good, integrally connected to the nation's economic growth, national security, and commitment to opportunity. The federal government's support for basic university research increased seven-fold between 1958 and 1968, rising from $178 million to $1.251 billion. The budgets of statewide higher education systems also increased, from $492 million in 1950 to $5.8 billion by 1970.[39] In addition to meeting the expansive needs and research university ambitions of flagship campuses, these funds were used to meet the growing demand for public higher education. Branch campuses were created, teachers colleges were expanded into comprehensive institutions, and statewide systems of community colleges were introduced.[40] However, the differences among the states, in terms of both funding and the precedents and constraints imposed by historical and political arrangements, were telling. As in so many things, California was both a leader and an outlier.

THE CALIFORNIA MASTER PLAN

In his memoir *The Gold and the Blue*, Clark Kerr, the first chancellor of the University of California–Berkeley (1952–58) and later president of the University of California (UC) System (1958–67), describes an evolving goal at Berkeley, which was to compete for students, faculty, and federal research support on an equal footing with the nation's most distinguished private universities. Beginning in the mid-1950s, traditional comparisons with its public university peers, Michigan, Wisconsin, Illinois, and Texas were re-oriented to include Harvard, Stanford, Princeton, MIT, Yale, and Chicago. "We were moving ourselves out of the 'public university' category," Kerr observed, "to that of 'all research universities,' whether public or private."[41] Achieving such an objective would have profound enrollment and resource allocation implications for the entire University, and presumably for all public colleges in California.

Internal competition within the state's higher education community and the rising costs of educational expansion threatened the tripartite agreement that had linked the University, state teachers colleges, and public junior colleges since the early 20th century.[42] Within the UC System, Berkeley and UCLA looked warily at their rival sister campuses; outside the University, champions of the burgeoning state and junior colleges chafed at UC's efforts to limit their growth, prompting disagreements and perceived affronts. The most immediate and urgent challenge, as all of the state's higher education leaders recognized, was to devise an approach before one was imposed by the legislature.

The elegance of the resulting *Master Plan for Higher Education in California, 1960–1975*, lay in its vision that a statewide system could fuse "world-class research institutions and mass higher education."[43] The University would select its freshman class from the top one-eighth (12.5 percent) of the state's high school graduates, and the soon-to-be California State University system (representing 15 state colleges) would select its freshman classes from the top one-third. All other students seeking a four-year degree would take lower-division courses at one of the state's community colleges and, if successful, transfer to the University or to one of the state colleges under the tripartite understanding.[44]

In retrospect, the extraordinary acclaim lavished on the Master Plan has proven far more enduring than its early promise and accomplishments warranted. In 1960 enrollments in the UC and California State University systems represented about 20 percent and 30 percent, respectively, of all enrollments in public higher education in the state, while enrollments in the community colleges accounted for the other half. Almost 50 years later, the two systems' shares had fallen to approximately 11 percent and 20 percent, respectively, and community college enrollment had grown to include 70 percent of all public higher education students. In 2000, California ranked first among the states in the number and proportion of college enrollments in two-year colleges, but fewer than one-third of its students were enrolled in four-year institutions— compared with almost 50 percent in Michigan and New York.[45]

Two recent UCLA studies found that California ranked below all states except Mississippi in sending high school seniors directly to four-year colleges. In public higher education systems like those of California, which limit direct access to four-year institutions and where most students begin their post-secondary studies at two-year colleges, the bachelor's degree completion rates are much lower than in states where students directly enter four-year colleges and universities. As the authors of *Crossing the Finish Line* demonstrate in Chapter 7, the coupling of strict admission criteria for enrollment at California's public four-year institutions and the negative effect on attainment of starting at a community college have combined to produce a bachelor's degree completion rate that ranks 28th among the states. The rate of educational attainment is also much lower for African American and Latino students, who are disproportionately concentrated in two-year colleges.[46] A review of the Master Plan in the early 1970s, which was reaffirmed in later studies, documented the steady decline in transfer rates and provided clear evidence of the correlation between family income, race/ethnicity, and the segment of the higher education system that students first enter.[47]

The Master Plan was written at a time when California's population was on the verge of a major demographic transformation. In 1960, approximately 85 percent of the state's population was composed of Euro-Americans; by 1990, the percentage had fallen to 58 percent, and projections indicate that it will decline to 46 percent by 2010.[48] "California, a state that has exuded enthusiasm for public education," writes John Aubrey Douglass, "has perhaps reached a mid-life crisis."[49] Today California ranks near the bottom of all higher education systems in bachelor's degree attainment per college enrollment among underrepresented minority students. The educational leaders who wrote the *Master Plan for Higher Education in California 1960–1975* would be mortified by recent references to the "Mississippification" of public education in California because they were convinced that they had created a standard against which all state systems would be judged.[50]

THE STATE UNIVERSITY OF NEW YORK AND THE POLITICS OF DECENTRALIZATION

During its heyday, the California Master Plan became an illusive model for many states (and nations) whose citizenry lacked the same fervent commitment to public higher education and whose systems failed to differentiate the missions and responsibilities of their flagship universities, state colleges, and community colleges. Although much depended on the states' different political landscapes and special circumstances, California's early success stimulated calls for greater coordination among college and university leaders, elected officials, and the governing boards created to oversee the rapid expansion of public higher education. New York State represents an interesting contrast to the California model.

In 1948, when New York became the last of the then-48 states to establish a university system, it ranked near the bottom rung in terms of support for higher education.[51] Though it was home to many distinguished private institutions, there was no identifiable public university, and, with the exception of the municipal colleges in New York City (Brooklyn, City, Hunter, and Queens Colleges) and the statutory colleges at Cornell, there was no coordinated statewide system.[52] The planning, creation, and formative start-up of the State University of New York (SUNY) represented a complicated political calculus and intricate compromises over resources, enrollment, student aid, degree programs, governance, and the prerogatives of the private sector. During its earliest years, it was as if the Board of Regents had forced SUNY to sign non-competition agreements with the state's private institutions. As long as SUNY was seen as "supplementing and not supplanting or competing," the fledgling university system could function at a minimal level, but the constraints were debilitating. In reporting on their progress in 1951, the trustees offered this blunt assessment: "As a new university in an old State, [SUNY] has not been granted by and large the consideration, the freedom of operation, the professional autonomy, enjoyed by almost every other state university in the country." Six years later a consultant described the University as "an academic animal without a head."[53]

Within a decade, almost everything had changed. The combined impact of the post-war baby boom, the occupational and educational demands generated by the Cold War, passage of the National Defense Education Act, and, most important, Nelson Rockefeller's election as governor (1958) created a heightened sense of urgency and optimism. Mounting deficits, rising faculty costs, and a move toward greater admission selectivity on the part of the elite private institutions meant that the public sector would have to play the leading role in educating the citizens of the state. Rockefeller wanted to create a first-class, low-cost, decentralized state university—comparable in quality and prestige to the flagships and their sister institutions in California, Michigan, Wisconsin, and Illinois—that would serve as an engine of economic growth and slow the out-of-state exodus of New York students.[54] In December 1959, he asked Ford Foundation president Henry Heald to chair a three-person Committee on Higher Education and charged it with making recommendations to address how the state might provide access and opportunity, strengthen quality from the community college level through graduate and professional school levels, and meet the manpower and technical needs of the state.[55]

The Heald Committee's recommendations, supplemented by later task force reports and SUNY's own master plan, served as the blueprint and foundation for the major higher education policy initiatives undertaken in New York State during the 1960s and early 1970s. The committee's ambitious, politically savvy recommendations reflected two critical assumptions: first, that the SUNY system would provide a wide, diverse range of educational opportunities to students with various intellectual capabilities from all socioeconomic classes, and second, that a successful public university system would strengthen and complement a vibrant, financially healthy private sector, presumably through some form of state assistance. The committee made it clear that, if higher education in New York was to "cease to be a limping and apologetic enterprise and . . . achieve the spirit and style which characterizes the nation's great public universities," a commitment to "high goals" and excellence was necessary.[56]

During the 1960s, four new university centers with a full range of undergraduate, graduate, and professional programs would be created on Long Island (at Stony Brook), in Buffalo (through the takeover and merger of SUNY with the private University of Buffalo), and at Albany and Binghamton by building on the foundation of existing institutions. The colleges of education were transformed into multipurpose liberal arts institutions capable of accepting community college graduates, and new community colleges were built in the New York City metropolitan area and near the major upstate urban centers of Albany, Syracuse, Rochester, and Buffalo. Financially, control of SUNY's budget shifted from the regents to the governor's office, a state university construction fund was established to manage SUNY's expansion, tuition and fees were introduced at all public colleges, and a program of tuition assistance grants was also created.

The need for bipartisan political support predetermined that SUNY would be a decentralized system reflecting New York's upstate, downstate, and suburban political interests.[57] In December 1973, at the time of Governor Rockefeller's resignation, the 25-year-old SUNY system was the nation's largest multi-campus university. Higher education had emerged as a political and economic behemoth, and decentralization had proven to be a powerful political weapon for expansion but a flawed strategy in other critical ways. As one scholar notes, "Public attention on any single institution was localized and minimized."[58] As a result, SUNY campuses, including the four university centers, found themselves reacting to the expansion and democratization of public higher education that had begun a decade earlier but without the clear understandings so well established in California. In 1973 a Stony Brook University faculty committee observed: "We are . . . in the midst of another profound change, the attempt to provide higher education to masses of people, who for the most part would not have been admitted to college had they decided to go . . . or had they applied in the mid-sixties or before."[59] "What remained unclear," Hugh Graham and Nancy Diamond have observed, "was whether the post-war explosion of federal funding . . . when combined with investments by states and local governments and private institutions, was building a new group of first-class universities to enliven the competition so long dominated by traditional elites."[60]

PUBLIC UNIVERSITY EXPANSION, 1960–1985

In the late 1940s, planning studies had indiated that few significant economies of scale would be achieved in capital or operating costs when campus enrollments exceeded 25,000, and it was assumed that the educational experience and sense of community between faculty and students would suffer with substantially larger enrollments.[61] Still, many flagship campuses, such as Ohio State and the Universities of Texas (Austin) and Wisconsin (Madison), did not limit enrollment. It was not unusual for some campuses to have enrollments of between 25,000 and 40,000 students, reflecting both their statutory obligations as broadly accessible public institutions and the important financial role played by undergraduate education in subsidizing graduate study.

From the early 1950s through the late 1960s, efforts to integrate the South's predominantly all-white flagship campuses met with varying degrees of hostility, intransigence, and tokenism.[62] In Maryland, the university campus at College Park witnessed an enrollment increase, from 9,000 students at the time of the *Brown v. Board of Education* decision to 14,000 in 1960, 26,500 in 1965, and approximately 35,000 by 1970. In spite of the intensity of civil rights issues on campus, African American students represented only 2 percent of the undergraduate student body in 1968 and just 4 percent three years later.[63]

In neighboring Virginia, the government's 1958 decision to close the commonwealth's public schools in defiance of the *Brown* decision rather than desegregate represented the single most powerful act in limiting the expansion of educational opportunity. Though the undergraduate enrollment of the University of Virginia (UVa) doubled during the 1960s, reaching 6,576 by 1969, high tuition rates reinforced the elitist stereotypes of a student body with "an appalling sameness . . . of party school, playboy, gentleman . . . stuffiness and snobbery."[64] The number of out-of-state students reached 1,580 in 1964 and 2,472 in 1970. A few years

earlier, the Committee on the Future of the University had warned that
if UVa wanted to compete with the nation's most distinguished public
universities, maintaining high-quality research programs would require
a combined undergraduate and graduate student enrollment of between
15,000 and 18,000 students. The University first had to embrace co-
education (1969) and then overcome the persistent stain of racial segre-
gation, steps that it began to pursue aggressively in the early 1970s. By the
late 1970s, UVa's undergraduate enrollment had reached 10,000.[65]

The virulent strains of anti-Communism and racial politics also challenged the efforts of the University of North Carolina (UNC) to modern-
ize the state's business, agricultural, and high-technology sectors. Conservative legislators and commentators such as Jesse Helms associated
UNC–Chapel Hill with "godless Communism," New Deal liberalism, and
racial tolerance—even facetiously threatening to build a wall around the
campus to avoid "infecting" the rest of the state. In 1956, when the University's 36-year-old secretary, William C. ("Bill") Friday, became acting
president, UNC consisted of three state-supported institutions: the campus at Chapel Hill, North Carolina State College (now North Carolina
State University at Raleigh), and the Woman's College of the University of
North Carolina (now the University of North Carolina at Greensboro).

In 1961, North Carolina's new governor, Terry Sanford, appointed a
Commission on Education beyond the High School, also known as the Carlyle Commission, and charged it with recommending ways in which a
greater number of citizens might gain access to higher education. Together
with Friday, now firmly installed as UNC's president, Sanford sought "to
open a door of opportunity" for all North Carolinians, but the challenges
were immense. Only half of the state's students completed high school,
one-fifth sought education at the college level, and one-tenth earned a college degree. Moreover, little planning had been done to address the lack
of facilities or the impending arrival of baby boom students.[66]

Taking a page out of the California Master Plan, the Carlyle Commission recommended a tripartite division: a comprehensive system of community colleges and industrial education centers would provide job training, literacy, and adult education; the state's public senior colleges, the
former teachers colleges, would have primary responsibility for less selective undergraduate education; and the University of North Carolina,
after expansion into Charlotte and later into Wilmington and Asheville,
would remain the focus of academic excellence and serve as the primary
center for graduate and professional programs and research.[67] By 1969,
UNC consisted of six university campuses, and by 1972, the system had
expanded to include 16 formerly separate four-year regional, comprehensive, and historically black universities, all of which were under the
control of a consolidated board of governors.[68]

In the Midwest, where the flagship campuses had traditionally occupied a respected and honored place, educators and elected leaders struggled to find the most appropriate means to balance opportunity and excellence. In the quarter century after 1950, competition between Wisconsin's two public higher education systems, the University of Wisconsin system and the Wisconsin State University system, became a source of public concern, especially after the campus protests and unrest of the late 1960s and early 1970s. The student and faculty populations at the University of Wisconsin–Madison, the state's original land-grant university, tripled in size between 1950 and 1975, reaching 34,365 students (including 10,000 graduate and professional school students) and approximately 2,100 faculty members by 1974. Statewide, however, the expanding University of Wisconsin (UW) system had a total enrollment of over 73,000 students and encompassed a growing urban campus in Milwaukee, 2 four-year comprehensive institutions at Green Bay and Parkside (Kenosha), and 10 two-year freshman–sophomore centers devoted primarily to academic preparation that were integrated into the UW. The state also had a separate set of vocational schools that provided postsecondary training.[69]

In 1971, the legislature approved the merger of the UW system and that of Wisconsin State University, a nine-campus system with approximately 64,000 students, whose institutions had evolved from normal schools to state teachers colleges to regional universities. As Roger Geiger observes, whatever administrative and fiscal efficiencies may have been achieved through the creation of a homogenized "supersystem" were offset by the combination of two fundamentally different kinds of institutions. The net result was less influence within the system for the flagship campus at Madison, which was forced to compete with disgruntled sister institutions that were not its peers and resented the research university's monopoly of the most talented students and better-paid faculty.[70]

In the late 1980s, faced with growing demand and inadequate resources, the UW system capped enrollment at its most popular campuses and redistributed students to the under-utilized comprehensive, regional universities and to the two-year academic centers. The objective was to optimize the use of available resources, downsize the student population, lower the student-faculty ratio, and increase tuition and fees. Students were assigned to campuses that were not their first choices, and the effects were felt up and down the system. Candidates seeking admission to the flagship campus at Madison were placed at one of the regional universities; students denied admission to the comprehensive universities were admitted to one of the two-year academic centers, and students denied admission to the centers were given the limited opportunity of attending the technical and vocational schools. Under this tightly enforced

enrollment management strategy, admission to the Madison campus became highly selective, five of the regional universities introduced competitive admissions, and the two-year centers found themselves admitting
most of their students from the second and third quartiles of the state's
high school graduates rather than from the bottom quartile. In essence,
access to public higher education became more restrictive and less accessible in Wisconsin.[71]

Ohio's experience provides a variation on the same theme. In 1963,
Ohio created a Board of Regents that oversaw the expansion of state-
assisted campuses from 6 to 67, fulfilling a commitment to locate a public institution of higher education—community college, technical institute, branch campus of the state university, or comprehensive university
—within 30 miles of every resident.[72] When Novice Fawcett assumed
the presidency of The Ohio State University in 1956, the enrollment at the
flagship campus in Columbus was approximately 22,500; by 1968, more
than 41,000 students were enrolled there and another 3,870 attended
classes at various branch campuses. At the time of his retirement in 1972,
Fawcett had overseen the greatest expansion in the University's history.
Close to 50,000 students were enrolled at Columbus and at the University's four branch campuses at Lima, Mansfield, Marion, and Newark.
During these years, the faculty and administration worked to protect and
strengthen admission standards at the Columbus campus, but it was a
constant struggle.

Like many flagship universities, Ohio State was required by law to admit all graduates of the state's first-class high schools. As a University historian delicately put it, "To some extent, students found by the grades
which they received and the lack of academic interest which they experienced that continuing at the University would not be . . . a profitable experience."[73] The psychological cost of using attrition, the harshest of the
"cooling-out" functions that public institutions use to mediate between
cultural aspiration and individual achievement, as an instrument of enrollment management often had more to do with promoting equal opportunity than with addressing students' educational success.[74] Moreover, as John Thelin insightfully observes, when underprepared freshmen
dropped or failed courses, their re-enrollments did not generate a second state subsidy; rather, universities had to dig deeper into existing resources to create additional course slots and classroom space for students
who often did not persist to finish their degrees.[75]

Still, Ohio State's experience during the 1980s and 1990s demonstrates
how the introduction of stronger admissions criteria, beginning with a
required college preparatory curriculum, could minimize the disap-
pointment of underprepared students, more effectively utilize university
resources, attract stronger applicants, and serve as a bridge from an open-

access system to a more selective one. Better-prepared students meant fewer remedial courses, a higher retention rate, the opportunity to reduce the number of first-year students, and the flexibility to admit more upper-level and graduate students.[76] Despite this progress, at the end of the 1980s, top students in Ohio still viewed the University as "too big, too impersonal, and non-academic."[77] A faculty committee reviewing the undergraduate curriculum decried faculty overspecialization, overreliance on graduate teaching assistants, a reward system that did not value undergraduate instruction, and "an unstructured program . . . which provides no coherence . . . and no sense of what a liberal education is."[78] The introduction of a new, more rigorous curriculum contributed to the University's emergence by the late 1990s as the most selective flagship in the state.

THE ACADEMIC REVOLUTION

Growth, as Clark Kerr understood, was not neutral in its impact: "Colleges got more public money and more public control. Flagship campuses, like most research universities, became larger and more impersonal in nature."[79] Average class size increased, faculty members were frequently on leave or, if on campus, were far removed from undergraduates. Academic departments grew in size, and faculty devoted most of their working hours to their highly specialized research interests.[80] Such developments unintentionally contributed to the gradual denigration of undergraduate education. There appears to be a "point of no return," Kerr observed, "after which research, consulting, and graduate instruction become so absorbing that faculty efforts can no longer be concentrated on undergraduate instruction as they once were." Though himself concerned about the neglect of undergraduate education, Kerr had already begun to think about the consequences of such "inferior concern" by others.[81] In presenting the Godkin lectures at Harvard in 1963, he called undergraduate education at the nation's major public universities "the greatest disaster area of the multiversity—the poverty of the lower-division environment."[82]

The older, pre-war Berkeley from which Kerr had received his doctorate in economics had been a teaching-centered university. Faculty typically taught nine hours per week, and their reputations in the classroom greatly influenced promotion decisions. Professors kept regular office hours, the strongest instructors taught the department's introductory courses, and the faculty stars were the University's great teachers. Tenured and tenure-track faculty did their research on weekends, during vacations, and while on sabbatical.[83] A good deal of the lower-level undergraduate instruction was handled by continuing, non-tenure-track instructors and career assistant professors who were not expected to publish. After the war, the new stars were the Nobel laureates whose research made Berkeley one of the nation's pre-eminent research universities.

Across the nation, faculty members at flagship universities negotiated teaching loads of six hours or less per week. Responsibility for undergraduate teaching shifted from a disappearing cohort of permanent assistant professors to graduate teaching assistants who handled recitation sections, supervised science labs, read examinations, corrected papers and problem sets, listened to students' complaints, and generally "protect[ed] the professors from overexposure to the ignorant."[84] In retrospect, this trend was not the result of a conspiracy or conscious neglect, as student protesters later claimed; instead, it was a direct outcome of the broad forces of differentiation of functions among different types of public institutions with multiple missions and responsibilities. Nonetheless, one inescapable conclusion is that attending to undergraduate education, particularly at flagship campuses, had become one of many missions in the constellation of university activities.[85]

At the end of the 1950s, the sociologists Christopher Jencks and David Riesman began research on what proved to be an exceedingly provocative and influential study of post-war American higher education. In 1968, when their book *The Academic Revolution* was published, its readers assumed that they would find answers to, or at least gain a better understanding of, the student unrest that had engulfed the nation's colleges and universities. But the authors were interested in a very different "revolution," one that chronicled the rise of the academic profession, the changes that had occurred in undergraduate education, and the influence of mass higher education on social mobility and equality in America. As Jencks and Riesman observed, "Whether education makes people more or less equal is, in some ways, the central political question posed by the academic revolution."[86] They concluded that universal higher education would only modestly diminish the economic and social differences between classes. Higher education's essential role was "to spread what have traditionally been thought of as upper-middle-class customs and concerns to people whose rank in the economic and occupational spectrum will remain lower-middle."[87] Post-war prosperity may have improved Americans' standard of living; it had not significantly changed "the relative prestige of a family or individual in the social hierarchy." For Jencks and Riesman, "going to college had relatively little to do with teaching and learning" and much more to do with certification and socialization.[88] Even here, the rise of an academic meritocracy appeared to have triumphed at the expense of undergraduate education, particularly the relationships between students and faculty members.

The social history of American higher education is filled with colorful examples of student protest, subversive behavior, and defiance directed toward faculty and administrators. Rarely, however, did the generational conflicts of the 19th and early 20th centuries challenge the legitimacy of institutional authority as would the campus rebellions and student radicalism on flagship campuses during the 1960s.[89] The 1964–65 Free Speech Movement (FSM) at Berkeley grew out of students' anger over the abrogation of time-honored rights of political advocacy; a long-simmering frustration with the heavy-handed, anachronistic culture of *in loco parentis;* and a growing identification with the tactics of the civil rights movement.[90] FSM gave concrete form to what ultimately became an almost decade-long series of student protests across the country. Initially fueled by mounting opposition to the Vietnam War and by the growing strength of the civil rights and later the black power movements, student activists identified their universities not only as hypocritical, complicit agents of the establishment but as the latter's full-throated embodiment. In practice, this led protesters at private institutions (Columbia, Cornell, and Harvard), flagship public institutions (the Universities of California, Michigan, Washington, and Wisconsin and Rutgers), and regional public universities (Kent State, Jackson State, and San Francisco State Universities) to direct their upset both at the universities where they studied and at totemic institutions like the Department of Defense, the Selective Service System, Dow Chemical Company, the National Guard, and the White House. As Geiger insightfully observes, "The combination of national and local concerns imparted a powerful dynamic to events. The intense passions and moral fervor of the antiwar and civil rights movements were transferred to relatively mundane university matters."[91]

Although teaching and curricular concerns were only occasionally the driving force behind student protest, many faculty members and administrators nevertheless devoted themselves to improving pedagogy, introducing course evaluations, advancing curricular reform, and providing better training and working conditions for teaching assistants. But improving the undergraduate experience at flagship universities required a multi-faceted approach that was not always attuned to the universities' scale, reward system, or institutional priorities or to the faculty's willingness to "invest more time and attention and emotion."[92] Indeed, the curricular "reforms" of this era, such as the elimination of general education courses and the dropping or dilution of foreign language requirements, were most notable for their permissiveness and lack of rigor.[93] Nonetheless, there were some significant innovations. As universities actively recruited women, blacks, Hispanics, Asians, and other ethnic minorities, faculties responded with the introduction of multi-disciplinary courses in

African American, women's, and ethnic studies. Institutions responded to the growth of undergraduate enrollments with support services to address the needs of first-generation college-goers and students from disadvantaged backgrounds. Following congressional authorization of the 1965 Higher Education Act's funding for educational opportunity grants and guaranteed student loans, many colleges and universities established their first academic support programs of any type. Over time, these retention-focused programs would evolve into important university-wide systems encompassing admissions, financial aid, counseling, tutoring, and advising.[94]

The student revolts of the late 1960s produced a number of residual effects. Campus unrest left deep emotional scars among faculty and administrators. The confidence of colleges and universities was shaken; doubts were raised outside the academy about higher education's values, especially the dysfunctional relationship between academic learning and life experience, which would influence state support in the troubled economy of the 1970s. Jencks and Riesman had warned that academic professionalism encouraged elitism and a parochial disregard for life beyond the academy. When flagship campuses assigned teaching assistants substantial responsibility for undergraduate instruction, when they shifted resources to the graduate faculty, and when universities continued to serve as centers for government-sponsored military research, they also contributed to the impersonal, alienating, and deeply cynical environment their students decried. In many respects, flagship universities came to resemble vertically and horizontally integrated corporations in their management of undergraduate, graduate, and professional education; in their ownership and operation of hospitals, publishing companies, airports, hotels, stadiums, athletic complexes, television stations, farms, and research centers; and, in some cases, in their financing or subsidizing of low-cost housing projects. To be fair, there are notable exceptions in which the specialization of function and division of labor, so often the objects of student derision and contempt, have also had their benefits. For example, the advising of undergraduates and their socialization into a university community is a highly specialized skill that many faculty members do not possess. The delegation of that critically important academic function to professionals has, in many instances, improved the quality of undergraduates' experience. On the whole, however, campus turmoil also exposed the physical and psychological limitations of mass higher education and the unresponsiveness of an exceedingly complex public system whose physical development appeared to have outgrown its organizational and governance structure. Perhaps most remarkable to the entire higher education community was the embarrassing lack of standardized, systematically collected data and information about the finances, governance, enrollment, student composition, and types of degrees conferred among the nation's more than 2,500 institutions. There was an obvious knowledge gap in the "knowledge industry."[95]

THE NEWMAN REPORT AND THE CARNEGIE COMMISSION

"I don't expect to be unemployed very long," Clark Kerr candidly told a reporter following his dismissal as president of the University of California. Ronald Reagan had pledged to "clean up that mess at Berkeley," and in one of his first acts as governor, he pressured the regents to end Kerr's presidency.[96] Within days of his firing, Kerr accepted an invitation to lead a new Carnegie Commission on Higher Education with the unusually open-ended and unprecedented charge of investigating and providing recommendations on the "most vital issues facing American higher education in the latter part of the twentieth century."[97] Under Kerr's leadership, the Carnegie Commission focused its attention on the question of universal access to higher education and, by necessity, the future of federal financial aid.[98] By the early 1970s, public higher education was operating on a mass participation model with the expectation that educational opportunity would be extended to every American of college age. As one scholar writes, "Running through the commission reports" was "a real but cautious egalitarianism."[99] Providing equal access to higher education for minority and disadvantaged students would require active federal involvement, but this did not mean that every individual would take advantage of the opportunity. Thus, as the commission memorably observed, "We favor universal access but not universal attendance."[100]

Although most experts and elected officials focused their attention on the popular, high-reward issues of access and opportunity, an independent task force report on higher education took an aggressively contrarian position that reflected the student unrest of the past decade. Named for its chairman, Frank Newman, the report was commissioned (1969) by Robert Finch, then secretary of Health, Education, and Welfare; presented to his successor Elliot Richardson (1971); and privately funded by the Ford Foundation.[101] The Newman Report decried the expansion, homogenization, and bureaucratization of the nation's higher education system and was especially critical of low graduation rates among the traditional college-age population. "Access alone," the authors presciently observed, "does not lead to a successful education. It means only the exposure of a particular age group to whatever educational institutions there are and not the equality of the experience they are likely to find there."[102] The panel portrayed the expanding public multi-campus university systems as rigid, dysfunctional, and potentially alienating and isolating for students and faculty, much as Jencks and Riesman had done in *The Academic Revolution*.[103] Colleges and universities were strongly encouraged to integrate their students' academic and life experiences; develop "second-chance" opportunities; provide new forms of off-campus education, including that offered by means of technology; accelerate the diversification of their faculties; improve prospects for women and minorities; and accept accountability for making higher education a national enterprise. Students were urged to go to college at the age when "it would most benefit them," to stop-out or attend part-time.[104]

The Newman Report's radical, blunt, iconoclastic recommendations were greeted with disdain and public indifference by most higher education leaders. Privately, the major education associations, such as ACE and the Association of American Universities (AAU), recognized that the sector needed reform but dismissed the "unprofessional" lack of scholarly examination by a panel of "little-known academicians and college administrators."[105] Innovation and self-reform might have been more warmly received had the Newman Report not categorically rejected the "academic lockstep" of the existing system by which students moved progressively from high school to college to graduate and professional school. Instead, the panel proposed a "fresh look at what 'going to college' means" and called for education that was "less academic and more integrated with experience."[106] Worried about the reaction to such public criticism, the education associations sought to refocus the discussion. "What is needed is not more exposure of weaknesses, but more explication of specific programs based on sound perception of needs."[107] The innovative recommendations of a second Newman Report—a "G.I. Bill" for students' community service, federal scholarships to legitimize interrupted study, development of external degree programs through instructional technology-assisted "open universities," and a proposed public-private nonprofit corporation invested in educational innovation— symbolized the panel's dissatisfaction with existing orthodoxy but failed to generate support within the higher education establishment.[108] By comparison, the Carnegie Commission reports, with one notable exception involving student aid, seemed more attuned to higher education leaders' concerns and sense of direction.

The commission's first report, *Quality and Equality* (1968), recommended "an immediate doubling of federal support and a tripling of federal funding by 1980."[109] Federal assistance was especially attractive in the 1970s, when a combination of rising fuel costs, slower economic growth, double-digit inflation, unsteady enrollments, and budget deficits cast a pall over what one scholar called *The New Depression in Higher Education*.[110] As the financial situation deteriorated and competition for federal resources intensified, higher education leaders turned their eyes to Washington. The great prize was the federal government's apparent willingness to accommodate the millions of new students seeking a college education. A fundamental division had emerged, however, between the advocates of direct block grants to institutions and those who championed portable student financial aid.[111] Direct institutional funding was the holy grail of private and public colleges and universities and had been since the G.I. Bill empowered returning veterans with the ability to make their own choices. Every major higher education association, including the elite public and private research institutions in AAU and the all-inclusive sector-wide lobbying leader, ACE, supported a program of lump-sum block grants, arguing that unless the federal government adopted a formula-based program of basic institutional support, the higher education system would be at great risk.[112]

Never one to shy away from "challenges to accepted faith," Clark Kerr placed the Carnegie Commission's stake in the ground and took on the higher education establishment.[113] Kerr argued that block funding would politicize student aid and create a zero-sum game by forcing states and institutions to fight among themselves rather than make colleges and universities more responsive to market forces. "Funding students, and not institutions," as one scholar has written, "avoided or mitigated this possibility, while empowering students to choose what institution best met their perceived needs."[114] The commission argued that the federal government would be unable to sustain institutional support (fellowships and equipment) along with research and aid to individual students. Kerr and his associates also worried that a stronger federal presence would reduce the incentives for state involvement and limit institutional autonomy through unnecessary federal regulation. Faced with a choice between local and state control on the one hand and national control on the other, the commission believed that state stewardship would better reflect regional differences and that 50 competitive states constituted a much more congenial home for higher education than did the federal government. Finally, as Kerr noted, "We thought it was better, and more in keeping with federal obligations, to aid low- and lower-middle-income students to attend college, thus increasing the equality of opportunity, which was an historic national promise."[115]

In the end, the decisive voices belonged to an informal coalition of student lobbying groups who understood that members of Congress (and the voters they represented) would find a need-based, portable student financial aid program more politically palatable than approving block grants to institutions whose reputations had been tarnished by campus protests. The 1972 amendments to the Higher Education Act of 1965 greatly expanded the federal government's commitment to educational opportunity. Between 1970 and 1975, federal support for student aid grew from $1.6 billion to $3.1 billion. Most important, the government had created a program (the Pell Grant program) that accommodated all qualified students across a wide socioeconomic landscape.[116] Twenty-five years after the President's Commission on Higher Education had recommended a federal program of national grants-in-aid and scholarships, the promise was finally fulfilled. Unfortunately, the promise would be short-lived, for the major trend in the quarter century after the introduction of Pell Grants was a noticeable shift in student aid from need-based grants to loans. While loans were attractive to banks and families from more comfortable economic circumstances, this change placed an unusually heavy burden on students from lower-income backgrounds, as the authors of *Crossing the Finish Line* show in Chapter 9.[117]

THE EVOLUTION OF AMERICA'S FLAGSHIP UNIVERSITIES

Over the past 50 years, America's flagship universities have been one of the principal drivers of social mobility in the United States. Today, 17 percent of all four-year students are enrolled in these institutions; 26 percent of all bachelor's degrees and close to one-half (48 percent) of all doctoral degrees are awarded by flagship state universities.[118] The public universities' long-standing commitment to broaden access remains a key element of their social contract, and the flagship institution's historical role as an agent of social change remains a vital part of its core identity. Unfortunately, as Bowen, Chingos, and McPherson demonstrate in Chapters 3–6, disparities in the educational attainment of students from different racial/ethnic, socioeconomic, and gender groups and family backgrounds remain quite pronounced, even as some flagships are pursuing greater autonomy from public control.

The long-standing populist policy of low tuition and low aid has fallen victim to a growing reluctance of citizens to pay the taxes necessary to subsidize the substantial tuition costs of a burgeoning college-going population. Universities make up some of the funding gap with higher tuition. But higher tuition, unless offset by generous and transparent financial aid, can contribute to a growing privatization and gentrification that has led one scholar to decry the "unmaking" of the public university.[119] Although still state-owned and respected as "crown jewels" of their university systems, flagships increasingly rely on tuition and fees, private gifts, endowment growth, research grants, and other sources of non-public support.[120] In situations in which state funds represent an ever smaller proportion of university budgets, flagships have been exploring ways to become more autonomous from state control by trading legislative appropriations for the ability to set tuition at higher levels.[121] This trend poses the second major change in the social contract between the flagships and the citizens of their states.

In recent years, as competition for admission to selective colleges and universities has become the source of intense public interest and media attention, flagship campuses have been criticized for abdicating their responsibility with respect to providing access to the "people's university." Instead of providing an opportunity for *all* of the state's high school graduates to develop their talents and abilities, critics contend that the leading state universities have shifted their attention and resources to students with the strongest academic credentials.[122] Although admission to "the local public university is no longer a birthright,"[123] focusing primarily on the increasing competition for admission ignores the long-term nature of this trend and overlooks state higher education systems' creation of a differentiated grouping of technical institutes, community colleges, and comprehensive universities that were specifically designed to meet different levels of students' academic goals and capacities.

As flagships have become more selective and the number of high school graduates has continued to increase, high-achieving, affluent, and middle-income students who in earlier years might have attended first- and second-tier private colleges and universities have been attracted by the academic quality, prestige (in the case of honors colleges), broad range of programs, and comparatively lower cost of their states' public universities. Entering classes that once were filled by high school graduates with B averages have been replaced by students with A averages. At most flagships, the percentage of students whose fathers and mothers have college degrees is on the rise, as is the share of students whose parents hold graduate degrees. Of course, the fraction of all Americans with college degrees has grown, especially in the age group of the parents of recent college students, so some of this change would have occurred as a matter of course.

As a result, the percentage of students from families in the top income quartile attending the nation's top public universities increased from 21 percent in 1982 to 35 percent in 1989.[124] Between 1980 and 1994, the proportion of families with incomes exceeding $200,000 (which corresponded to a constant-dollar equivalent of $100,000 in 1980) that sent their sons and daughters to flagship campuses rose from 19.6 percent to 24.6 percent.[125] More recently, data indicate that the percentage of students at these institutions whose families earn more than $100,000 per year increased from 16 percent in 1995 to 28 percent in 2003. Concomitantly, the percentage of students at state flagships whose families earn less than $20,000 per year declined from 14 percent in 1995 to 9 percent in 2003. The data for Pell Grant recipients are equally telling. The absolute number and proportion of Pell Grant recipients at *all* U.S. institutions increased from 29 percent in 1992 to 35 percent in 2003, but the percentage of Pell Grant recipients at state flagships declined from 24 percent in 1992 to 22 percent in 2003.[126]

At a time when the United States is trying to regain its competitive position in the global economy, flagship universities do not want to be known as "engines of inequality." Recently there has been a noticeable shift among elite public institutions, a change that parallels significant efforts among private colleges and universities, to redress these imbalances by increasing the representation of students from low-income and disadvantaged backgrounds. Programs such as Access UVa, the Carolina Covenant (UNC), Illinois Promise, M-Pact (Michigan), and Husky Promise (University of Washington), among others, use a variety of financial and information strategies to "ensure that students from low-income backgrounds gain access to, and graduate from, colleges and universities at approximately the same rates as their more affluent peers."[127] Making significant progress in access for students from low-income and minority backgrounds must remain a critical priority, but the most important outcome is educational attainment.[128]

On October 17, 1960, *Time* magazine's cover featured Clark Kerr, the 49-year-old president of the UC and architect of the *California Master Plan for Higher Education*. Dressed in a dark suit and wearing rimless glasses, he looks confidently ahead, his expression giving no hint of what is figuratively taking place in the background. Behind him, thousands of students, with barely a body width between them, stream through Berkeley's Sather Gate and enter a gigantic academic mortar board, complete with gold tassel.

Although the editors used the familiar symbol of the gate as a metaphor for the promise of educational opportunity, there is no hint of what will happen to these students after they enter the university. Will they finish? What do we know about their likely educational outcomes and graduation patterns? Will there be disparities among them in rates of attainment with respect to race/ethnicity, gender, or socioeconomic status? For much of the past half-century, as the nation has moved from mass to nearly universal access, our public higher education system has focused on expanding educational opportunity—on getting students in and getting them started in college. Today, with our global competitiveness in question and our educational attainment levels ominously stagnant, we realize that the real promise of opportunity depends on completing, not just pursuing, a bachelor's degree.

Notes

Preface

1. Professor Robert Solow, Nobel Prize–winning economist at the Massachusetts Institute of Technology, deserves credit for having encouraged us, right from the start, to broaden our earlier work in building the College and Beyond database and its successor (which focused primarily on highly selective private colleges and universities and led to the publication of *The Shape of the River* and *Equity and Excellence in American Higher Education*) to include much more data on major public universities. We are very glad that we took his advice.

2. Mark G. Yudof, quoted by Josh Keller, "U. of California Report Offers New Push and Gauges for Accountability," *Chronicle of Higher Education*, September 22, 2008, online edition.

3. However, there is always the risk that governmental entities or other external funders will seize on such measures as benchmarks that just have to be met, no matter what, and will seek to tie funding to meeting what can be arbitrary goals that should be thought about in a more flexible, nuanced way. This is how we interpret the comments of the vice-chancellor of the University of Cambridge, Alison Richard, when she warned against making universities "handmaidens of industry, implementers of the skills agenda, or indeed engines for promoting social progress" ("Quality, Talent and Diversity in the UK University System," speech delivered at the Universities UK annual conference, Cambridge, September 10, 2008, available at http://www.admin.cam.ac.uk/offices/v-c/speeches/20080910.html). As other parts of her remarks indicate, the vice-chancellor is not against having the universities play a role in efforts to "promote social progress" (and the University of Cambridge has made real progress in this regard), but she does worry, properly, about overly intrusive efforts to dictate admissions standards. We are reminded of the early days of affirmative action in this country, when well-intentioned people tried to get universities to set goals and timetables that sometimes made no sense.

4. The quotations are from George Prochnik, "Hail to the Analysland," *New York Times*, May 6, 2007, online edition.

5. Prepared remarks delivered November 11, 2008. See Gates Foundation Web site.

6. See U.S. Department of Education, "35 CFR Part 99 Family Educational Rights and Privacy: Final Rule," *Federal Register* 73, no. 237 (December 9, 2008). It is heartening to see this progress, especially because so many researchers have been pessimistic about the prospects for improving these regulations. One of us (McPherson) attended a conference of data specialists at which one presenter offered mock forecasts, including one that FERPA (the Family Educational Rights and Privacy Act) would be repealed and replaced by a new law called NEVER, whose sole provision would ensure that there would be "no release of education data EVER." This comment illustrates the discomfort that there has been over the

handling of the need to balance sensible concerns over privacy and concerns that good outcomes research be done. The Gates Foundation may be able to help make this case. At their November 2008 Forum on Education, Bill Gates announced that the Gates Foundation will be helping states and districts build data systems that provide teachers feedback about student learning. He then added: "We have seen people oppose this kind of data system on behalf of privacy; I don't think that argument holds. I'm optimistic that very advanced data systems can be built that provide indispensable information on student progress while preserving legitimate privacy concerns." (The full text of his prepared remarks, delivered on November 11, 2008, is available at the Gates Foundation Web site.)

Chapter 1   Educational Attainment: Overall Trends, Disparities, and the Public Universities We Study

1. Claudia Goldin and Lawrence F. Katz, *The Race between Education and Technology* (Cambridge, Mass.: Belknap Press of Harvard University Press, 2008).

2. Ben S. Bernanke, "Remarks on Class Day 2008 at Harvard University, June 4, 2008," Board of Governors of the Federal Reserve System, Washington, D.C., p. 5, available at http://www.federalreserve.gov/newsevents/speech/bernanke 20080604a.htm.

3. David Brooks, "The Biggest Issue," *New York Times,* July 29, 2008, p. A19.

4. David Leonhardt, "The Big Fix," *New York Times Magazine,* February 1, 2009, online edition. In commenting subsequently on the sequences of the recession, Leonhardt pointed out that one positive effect could be increasing college enrollment, especially on the part of displaced workers (or potential workers) from low-SES backgrounds. Any such "surge" could, in Leonhardt's words, "make the pie larger and divide it more evenly" (David Leonhardt, "Casualties of the Recession," *New York Times,* March 4, 2009, p. B4).

5. There are powerful a priori arguments in favor of expecting degree completion to confer on the individual (and the society) benefits that are greater than those associated with simply having finished an equivalent number of years of study. Completing an organized program of study presumably entails the acquisition of skills and an integrated body of knowledge that may or may not occur simply as a result of having been enrolled for the same period of time. Acquiring a bachelor's degree also opens up opportunities for further study and for the returns (which are more than just monetary) associated with earning an advanced degree. A student is highly unlikely to be a credible candidate for a reputable law school or business school (never mind a medical school) without a bachelor's degree. This is sometimes referred to as the "option value" of a bachelor's degree. There are also "signaling" benefits in that prospective employers will know that the person with a bachelor's degree is capable of finishing what he or she starts; for this reason, degree completion reduces a prospective employer's search costs—which is a real gain for both the individuals concerned and society. Given these considerations, it would be astonishing if evidence contradicted the presumptive benefits of finishing a degree program—and, to the best of our knowledge, there is no contradictory evidence. On the contrary, several economists have found what are often called "sheepskin" effects (returns to earning a degree

above and beyond the returns associated with the number of years of schooling required to obtain the degree). Jaeger and Page, for example, found evidence of such effects by matching individuals who reported their education in terms of the highest degree earned on the 1992 *Current Population Survey* with the same individuals who reported their education in terms of the number of years of schooling completed on the 1991 survey. They found that the earnings of individuals with 16 years of schooling and a bachelor's degree substantially exceeded those of individuals with the same amount of schooling but no degree (David A. Jaeger and Marianne E. Page, "Degrees Matter: New Evidence on Sheepskin Effects in the Returns to Education," *Review of Economics and Statistics*, 78, no. 4: 733–40). It is true that the Jaeger-Page study, like others, does not deal with unobservable differences in ability between individuals, which could well bias results. Also, estimates of sheepskin effects may be upward-biased because of greater measurement error in reporting years of schooling than in reporting earned degrees (see Thomas J. Kane, Cecilia Elena Rouse, and Douglas Staiger, "Estimating Returns to Schooling When Schooling Is Misreported," NBER Working Paper 7235, National Bureau of Economic Research, Cambridge, Mass., July 1999). Still, the inability to pin down precise estimates of sheepskin effects does not mean that they are absent—or unimportant.

6. Barack Obama, "Remarks of President Barack Obama—Address to Joint Session of Congress," text of a speech released by the White House Press Office, February 24, 2009, p. 5 (italics ours). For President Obama's budget message, see Barack Obama, "Restoring American Leadership in Higher Education," from President Obama's Fiscal 2010 Budget Overview, text released by the Office of Management and Budget, Washington, D.C., February 2009, available at http://www.aacrao.org/federal_relations/2010budget4.pdf. It is also of interest that in another speech the president noted the importance of maintaining data systems like those in Florida in order to track "a student's education from childhood through college" (Barack Obama, "Remarks by the President to the Hispanic Chamber of Commerce on a Complete and Competitive American Education," text of a speech released by the White House Press Office, March 10, 2009, online edition).

7. Obama (2009a), p. 5.

8. Leonhardt (2009a), p. 48.

9. Sandy Baum and Jennifer Ma, *Education Pays: The Benefits of Higher Education for Individuals and Society* (New York: College Board, 2007); Thomas S. Dee, "Are There Civic Returns to Education?" *Journal of Public Economics* 88, no.9 (August 2004): 1697–720.

10. Reproduced here courtesy of Claudia Goldin and Lawrence F. Katz; see pp. 19–20 of their *The Race Between Technology and Education*, where they present and discuss their figure 1.4. They write: "After the 1951 birth cohort . . . a great slowdown ensued. Educational attainment barely changed for cohorts born between 1951 and 1965 (24 years old between 1975 and 1989), and for cohorts born from 1965 to 1975 (24 years old between 1989 and 1999), educational attainment started rising again but increased by just 6 months overall" (p. 19).

11. See John Bound, Michael Lovenheim, and Sarah Turner, "Understanding the Increased Time to the Baccalaureate Degree," SIEPR Discussion Paper 06-43, Stanford Institute for Economic Policy Research, Stanford, Calif., August 23, 2007.

12. See Organisation for Economic Co-operation and Development, *Education at a Glance 2008: OECD Indicators* (Paris: Organization for Economic Co-Operation and Development, 2008), table A1.3a, Population That Has Attained Tertiary Education (2006), available at http://dx.doi.org/10.1787/40147 4646362, and chart A4.2, Completion Rates in Tertiary-Type A Education (2005), available at http://dx.doi.org/10.1787/401536355051. See also Organisation for Economic Co-operation and Development, *Education at a Glance 2003: OECD Indicators* (Paris: OECD, 2003), table A2.4, Trends in Educational Attainment at Tertiary Level (1991–2001), available at http://www.oecd.org/dataoecd/0/60/14158944.xls. The OECD data have been subject to criticisms of various kinds, and it would be a mistake to invest too much importance in specific numbers (see Doug Lederman, "A Dent in the Data," *Inside Higher Education*, December 22, 2008, online edition, available at http://www.insidehighered.com/news/2008/12/22/oecd). But the overall pattern is unmistakable.

13. Obama (2009a), p. 5.

14. Adapted from National Science Board, *Science and Engineering Indicators 2004* (Arlington, Va.: National Science Foundation), figure 2-34; data from Organisation for Economic Co-operation and Development, *Education at a Glance 2002: OECD Indicators* (Paris: Organisation for Economic Co-operation and Development, 2002) and national sources, as reported in Bowen, Kurzweil, and Tobin, pp. 48–49.

15. Goldin and Katz, figure 8.1, p. 290, and text on pp. 290–91.

16. Ibid., pp. 291–92 and 293–303.

17. Goldin and Katz observe: "Standard measures of rates of return to education, particularly to college completion and to graduate and professional training, are exceptionally high today. They have increased substantially since 1980 and are currently at historically high levels. Our estimates from Chapter 2 and 8 imply about a 13–14 percent rate of return to a year of college in 2005. The true economic return would remain high even after adjusting for the direct resource costs of providing a college education" (p. 336).

18. A few people have tried to mount the claim that the price of college is now so high that the college earnings advantage no longer outweighs the costs. But these claims are readily shown to rest on miscalculation and confusion (for an exchange on this subject see *Chronicle of Higher Education, News Blog*, April 5, 2008, available at http://chronicle.com/news/article/4258/college-board-responds-to-charles-miller). A more plausible worry is that these earnings differences are not really caused by college but come about because college attendees are more capable than other people and would do nearly as well in the labor market even without attending college (Charles Murray, "Down with the Four-Year College Degree!" *Cato Unbound*, October 6, 2008, available at http://www.cato-unbound.org/2008/10/06/charles-murray/down-with-the-four-year-college-degree/). Another skeptical claim is that, even if college pays off on average for those who attend, expanding enrollment would not yield good economic returns because the students who are added are either not talented enough or not well enough prepared to benefit from the experience. A key strategy in testing these skeptical views has been to study cases in which external circumstances make one group of students more likely to go to college than another. An excellent review of such

studies appears in David E. Card, "Estimating the Return to Schooling: Progress on Some Persistent Econometric Problems," *Econometrica* 69, no. 5 (September 2001): 1127–60. One set of studies compares students who happen to live close to a college with others who live farther away. The first group of students is more likely to attend, not because they are smarter or better trained but simply because college enrollment is more convenient for them. Not only do studies of this kind show that college pays off for these students who are added at the margin, but it turns out that their returns are even higher than the average for all students. This high return suggests that these marginal students who fail to enroll do so not because they will not benefit but for other reasons, such as a lack of information about their opportunities, the absence of adequate funds to finance their investment on reasonable terms, or simply personal preference. Another kind of evidence is provided by the "natural experiment" conducted by City University of New York (CUNY) in the 1970s when it began a program of open admission to its campuses. Abruptly, many students who would never have been admitted to CUNY now entered, and close study of the lives of these added students reveals that they earned very strong economic returns for their efforts (Paul Attewell and David E. Lavin, *Passing the Torch: Does Higher Education for the Disadvantaged Pay Off across Generations?* (New York: Russell Sage Foundation, 2007); see also Paul Osterman, "College for All? The Labor Market for College-Educated Workers," Center for American Progress, Washington, D.C., August 2008).

19. Goldin and Katz, p. 325.

20. See John Wirt, Patrick Rooney, Susan Choy, et al., *The Condition of Education 2004*, NCES 2004-077 (Washington, D.C.: National Center for Education Statistics, Institute of Education Sciences, 2004), pp. 60–61. New data gathered as part of our research show similar patterns. Among high school seniors in 1999 in North Carolina who took the SAT, 75 percent indicated that their degree goal was at least a bachelor's degree. A 2009 survey conducted by Public Agenda and the National Center for Public Policy and Higher Education found that 55 percent of the adults surveyed said that college is "necessary," up from 31 percent of the respondents to the same question in 2000 (see Sara Hebel, "Americans Increasingly See College as Essential and Worry More about Access, Poll Finds," *Chronicle of Higher Education*, February 4, 2009, online edition).

21. See Bowen, Kurzweil, and Tobin, especially pp. 69–72 and 77–91, for an elaboration of some of these propositions and citations to relevant literature.

22. See Bowen, Kurzweil, and Tobin, especially pp. 44–56, for an extended discussion of this topic that includes references to many of the underlying data, including the statistic cited in the text.

23. Richard B. Freeman, Emily Jin, and Chia-Yu Shen, "Where Do U.S.-trained Science and Engineering PhDs Come From?" NBER Working Paper 10554, National Bureau of Economic Research, Cambridge, Mass., June 2004.

24. See Eugene McCormack, "Growth Rate Lags Again in Graduate Schools' International Admissions," *Chronicle of Higher Education*, August 21, 2008, online edition, and Council of Graduate Schools, *Findings from the 2008 CGS International Graduate Admissions Survey, Phase III: Final Offers of Admission and Enrollment*, Research report, Council of Graduate Schools, Washington, D.C., November 2008, available at http://www.cgsnet.org/portals/0/pdf/R_IntlEnrl08_III.pdf.

25. Aisha Labi, "As World Economies Struggle, Competition Heats Up for Students from Abroad," *Chronicle of Higher Education,* November 21, 2008, p. A22.

26. See Maria Hvistendahl, "China Moves Up to Fifth as Importer of Students," *Chronicle of Higher Education,* September 19, 2008, online edition, and other articles in the *Chronicle of Higher Education.*

27. Obama (2009b), p. 1.

28. These data are taken from the NELS longitudinal study of students who were eighth-graders in 1988 and thus putative members of a 1992 high school graduating class. See Chapter 2, Figures 2.2 and 2.5.

29. These projections of graduates of public high schools have been prepared by the Western Interstate Commission for Higher Education (WICHE) and are reported in a major publication titled "Knocking at the College Door: Projections of High School Graduates by State and Race/Ethnicity, 1992 to 2022," WICHE, Boulder, Colo., March 2008, p. xiv. We combined these projections with current completion rates for students in the NELS database to obtain the numbers presented in the text. WICHE's 2008 report does not attempt to project differences related to family income, but if recent trends toward greater inequality persist, the implication for educational attainment rates is clearly unfavorable. For additional information concerning the under-representation of Hispanic students in colleges and universities, see Michael Planty, William Hussar, Thomas Snyder, et al., *The Condition of Education 2008,* NCES 2008-031, National Center for Education Statistics, Institute of Education Sciences, Washington, D.C., 2008, which comments on issues related to language skills and attendance at high schools in low-income areas.

30. See Sam Roberts, "A Generation Away, Minorities May Become the Majority in U.S.," *New York Times,* August 14, 2008, p. A1. The other census data cited in this paragraph are also from the *New York Times* story.

31. Planty, Hussar, Snyder, et al., p. 30.

32. See Roger Lowenstein, "The Inequality Conundrum," *New York Times Magazine,* June 10, 2007, pp. 11–14.

33. See Elizabeth Gudrais, "Unequal America," *Harvard Magazine* 110, no. 6 (July–August 2008): 22–29, especially pp. 22–23. This survey article is an excellent summary of research in many disciplines (with references to the basic studies) that links inequality to societal problems of many kinds. Anxieties related to insecurity are also rising because of fundamental changes in where risk resides. See Jacob S. Hacker, *The Great Risk Shift: The Assault on American Jobs, Families, Health Care, and Retirement and How You Can Fight Back* (New York: Oxford University Press, 2006). For other references to the literature linking inequality to outcomes of various kinds, see Goldin and Katz, p. 337, note 31.

34. *Grutter v. Bollinger et al.,* 539 U.S. 306 (2003).

35. Ibid. at 331.

36. Considerable data on students attending selective private colleges and universities are available in Bowen, Kurzweil, and Tobin.

37. By "1999 entering cohort" we mean all full-time students, both first-time freshmen and transfers, who began their studies at one of the universities in our set of institutions in the fall or summer of 1999. In general, however, we study first-time freshmen and transfers separately, and we often begin by presenting

data for the first-time freshmen, where we use the number of full-time, first-time freshmen as the measure of the size of the incoming student group at each university. The total number of full-time, first-time freshmen in our flagship university data set is just over 94,000.

38. See Appendix Table 1.1 for more detail. In most of the empirical work reported in this study, we consolidate SAT/ACT scores into a single measure for analytical and expositional convenience. As explained in detail in Chapter 6, this approach works because of the high level of correlation between the scores earned by students on these tests and the nearly identical predictive powers of the two tests; however, we recognize that the SAT and ACT are different in important respects. We write "SAT/ACT" rather than "ACT/SAT" because we have roughly two and a half times more SAT scores than ACT scores in our data sets. For the same reason, we have converted ACT scores to the SAT scale rather than the other way around. Rescaling ACT scores to the SAT scale does not introduce significant measurement error; the conversion preserves the rank ordering of students, and the correlation between ACT scores and ACT-converted-to-SAT scores is 0.999. These expositional decisions are all purely pragmatic; we do not "favor" one test over the other.

39. Each of these four states also has a flagship university included in our study of flagships, and in the study we often combine the four flagships with the state system SELAs in presenting data. All told, there are a total of 21 + 47 universities (68 in all) in the study. Including the 47 state system universities gives us an additional 78,000 full-time, first-time freshmen to study. We dropped a few schools from the state systems because they were very small. Thus, the list of state system universities does not include every public university in these four states.

40. These data were assembled from information submitted by individual institutions to the College Board as part of the College Board's annual survey. We have done our best to present data for the '99 entering cohorts (or nearby cohorts, when necessary). The coverage of these data is limited to full-time first-year students, and we excluded institutions with entering cohorts of fewer than 15 students (mostly very small private colleges). We also dropped a very small number of institutions because of what were obviously data errors—for example, reported graduation rates of 100 percent. Our purpose, of course, is not to provide a definitive profile of American institutions of higher education but to provide "big picture" comparisons that will allow readers to locate the public universities we study within the far broader landscape of American four-year colleges and universities. We also complemented the College Board data by examining the total enrollment figures available from the Department of Education (IPEDS) as of 2006. This "check" on the reliability of the College Board data was very reassuring. Although there are some differences—caused mainly by the failure of a small number of institutions to send data to the College Board and by the differences between data for first-time freshmen in 1999 and total enrollment in 2006—the overall patterns are very much the same. (The six-year graduation rates we present are from the 2006 IPEDS data, because the '99 cohort of entering students would have had just over six years in which to graduate by the time the 2006 IPEDS data were assembled.) One interesting difference between the College Board and the IPEDS data is that the percentage of white non-Hispanic students is modestly

lower for all groups of universities in the 2006 IPEDS data than in the data on the '99 entering cohort from the College Board. We believe this difference reflects the rapid growth in the enrollment of Hispanic students in recent years. We should also emphasize that all data in Tables 1.3 and Appendix Tables 1.1 and 1.2 are from published sources. The data in the body of this study, on the other hand, were built up from records of individual students supplied to us on a confidential basis by the participating universities.

41. To be sure, some part of the increase in the grades of entering students at both of these sets of universities could be due to general grade inflation; it seems wildly implausible, however, to think that grade inflation explains anything like all of the huge changes in grade distributions shown in Figures 1.5 and 1.6. We are indebted to William Korn at the Higher Education Research Institute (HERI) at UCLA for the special tabulations that allowed our colleague, Dyuti Bhattacharya, to construct Figures 1.5 and 1.6 and also to generate the data on the changing parental education of students attending these universities discussed later.

42. For an extended discussion of evidence on increases in family income, see the last part of Appendix A.

Chapter 2   Bachelor's Degree Attainment on a National Level

1. The NELS surveyed a sample of the cohort of students who were in the eighth grade in 1988, most of whom graduated from high school in 1992. These students form the basis for the majority of the statistics in this chapter. Although more current information would be ideal, the NELS is the most recent nationally representative data set that includes information on the socioeconomic status (family income and parents' education) of students' families. More recent information on educational attainment overall (and broken down by race and gender) is available in the *Current Population Survey*, or *CPS* (Washington, D.C.: U.S. Census Bureau and U.S. Bureau of Labor Statistics, 2008), available at http://www .census.gov/cps/. Figure 2.6 shows statistics based on the *CPS* data (including data from 2007), but Figure 2.5 (which shows attainment patterns by race/ ethnicity and gender) uses the NELS data so that it will be comparable to Figures 2.3a and 2.3b (which show attainment patterns by parents' income and education). The following section on race and gender discusses possible reasons for the differences observed between the NELS and *CPS* data, particularly concerning the attainment gap between black males and black females.

2. The true national high school graduation rate may be significantly lower. Greene and Winters argue: "The NELS and *CPS* surveys both overstate graduation rates because they have difficulty finding and following marginalized and disadvantaged people, such as [high school] dropouts." Using publicly available data on school enrollment and number of diplomas awarded, Greene and Winters calculate a national high school graduation rate of 70 percent for the high school class of 2003 (Jay P. Greene and Marcus A. Winters, "Leaving Boys Behind: Public High School Graduation Rates," Civic Report 48, Manhattan Institute, New York, April 2006, available at http://www.manhattan-institute.org/pdf/ cr_48.pdf). Using a different method, Swanson comes to a similar conclusion

(Christopher B. Swanson, "Cities in Crisis: A Special Analytic Report on High School Graduation," Editorial Projects in Education Research Center, Bethesda, Md., April 1, 2008).

3. Very few people earn bachelor's degrees after age 26. If they did, we would expect to see a rising attainment rate over time for a given birth cohort in the CPS (with some noise due to sampling error, since the CPS data are random samples taken yearly). That is not what we find. For example, CPS data on the 1974 birth cohort exhibit a pattern that suggests sampling error around a consistent mean, not an upward trend: 31 percent had earned a bachelor's degree by age 26, 31 percent by age 27, 30 percent by age 28, 32 percent by age 29, 33 percent by age 30, and 30 percent by age 31.

4. See the discussion of international comparisons in Chapter 1. As we say there, whatever the problems of arriving at precisely comparable rates, the overall picture is clear.

5. The cut-offs for family income quartiles, in 2008 dollars, are as follows: less than $31,545; $31,545–$55,204; $55,204–$78,863; and more than $78,863.

6. It is important to note that the high school graduation rates in these figures count only recipients of high school diplomas as high school graduates. Recipients of general equivalency diplomas (GEDs) are counted as nongraduates. This is reasonable in our context, because although GED recipients are technically eligible to enroll at four-year post-secondary institutions, only 2 percent of those in the NELS data actually did so.

7. One limitation of the graduation rate statistics based on the NELS data is that they assume that all students who enroll at a four-year institution (or at least the same percentage of students of high and low socioeconomic status [SES] who enroll at a four-year institution) are pursuing a bachelor's degree. Data from the 2001–2002 Integrated Postsecondary Education Data System (IPEDS) shows that 55 percent of all post-secondary institutions that offer bachelor's degrees also offer degrees or certificates that take less than four years to complete. However, in 2001–2002, the schools that offered both types of degrees awarded far more bachelor's degrees than less-than-four-year degrees (83 percent versus 17 percent; calculations by the authors). Although it is likely that the students who enroll at four-year schools but pursue less-than-four-year degrees are disproportionately low-SES, this statistic will most likely overstate the completion rate gap only slightly.

8. A student is counted as having graduated within four years if he or she earned a bachelor's degree by the end of August 1996. A student is counted as having graduated in more than four years if he or she earned a bachelor's degree between September 1996 and the time that the NELS survey was administered in 2000.

9. Test administered as part of the NELS survey. The test was actually administered four years after the students were in the 8th grade, which was when most but not all of the survey respondents were in the 12th grade.

10. We also observe large disparities in SAT scores (including SAT scores predicted by ACT scores) among students who took the SAT or ACT. Among students who matriculated at a four-year college, those from the bottom income quartile had an average SAT/ACT score of 846, compared to 978 for those from the top

income quartile. First-generation college students had an average score of 885, compared to 986 for non-first-generation students.

11. We are indebted to Dean Nancy Weiss Malkiel at Princeton University for calling attention to the importance of this aspect of the analysis.

12. Additionally, first-generation college students are excluded.

13. See Sarah Turner, "Going to College and Finishing College: Explaining Different Educational Outcomes," in *College Choices: The Economics of Where to Go, When to Go, and How to Pay for It,* ed. Caroline M. Hoxby, 13–56 (Chicago: University of Chicago Press, 2004).

14. The data in Tables 2.2–2.4 should be interpreted with some caution because the definition of the income quartiles changes over time. This is because in the NELS data income is reported in discrete categories that do not fall perfectly into quartiles. For example, in 1992 only 20 percent (instead of 25 percent) of students were classified into the third quartile, while 32 percent were in the top quartile. Thus, students in the third quartile in the NELS data had a lower average income than those in the "true" third quartile because the nature of the data forced us to code some of the NELS students who were in the true third quartile in 1992 as being in the top quartile. The percentages of students classified into each income quartile (from bottom to top) in each year were as follows: 26 percent, 22 percent, 26 percent, and 25 percent in 1972; 23 percent, 28 percent, 31 percent, and 19 percent in 1982; and 24 percent, 24 percent, 20 percent, and 32 percent in 1992.

15. Ellwood and Kane calculate enrollment at a four-year institution within 20 months of high school graduation by income quartile. We calculate enrollment at a four-year institution by age 26 (the end of the NELS) by income quartile. Allowing the students more time to enroll in a four-year institution enables us to capture those who initially matriculated at a two-year institution and then transferred to a four-year institution. Finally, we restrict the HS&B sample to the 1980 sophomores (Ellwood and Kane also include the 1980 seniors) in order to make cleaner 1982/1992 comparisons (David T. Ellwood and Thomas J. Kane, "Who Is Getting a College Education? Family Background and the Growing Gaps in Enrollment," in *Securing the Future: Investing in Children from Birth to College,* ed. Sheldon Danziger and Jane Waldfogel, 283–324 [New York: Russell Sage Foundation, 2000]).

16. Ellwood and Kane, p. 307.

17. Another explanatory factory is the increase in income inequality that occurred during this period. For example, the top income quartile in 1992 was richer on average than the top income quartile in 1982. Ideally we would also want to calculate attainment rates for students with similar real incomes in each year (e.g., compare students with incomes between $50,000 and $60,000 in real dollars rather than students in a given quartile of the income distribution). Unfortunately, the income bands used in the 1982 HS&B and the 1992 NELS surveys do not line up well enough with each other (in terms of real dollars) to allow such an analysis.

18. It is important to note that these statistics are meant to paint a general, descriptive picture of how enrollment, completion, and attainment rates have changed between 1982 and 1992. They do not attempt to take into account

changes in the myriad factors that influence enrollment and completion, including academic preparation, the cost of college, and financial aid policies, among others. Hoxby calculates enrollment rates using the 1972 NLS and 1992 NELS data broken down by family income and college preparedness and finds that college became substantially more accessible to low-income students over this 30-year period. However, her analysis does not consider completion or attainment rates (Caroline M. Hoxby, "Testimony Prepared for U.S. Senate, Committee on Governmental Affairs, Hearing on 'The Rising Cost of College Tuition and the Effectiveness of Government Financial Aid,'" in Senate Committee on Governmental Affairs, *Rising Cost of College Tuition and the Effectiveness of Government Financial Aid: Hearings*, 120–28 [106th Cong., 2d sess., S. Hrg. 106-515, February 9, 2000]).

19. Once again, the high school graduation rates calculated from the NELS data likely overstate the actual rates. Greene and Winters calculate high school graduation rates for the class of 2003 of 78 percent for white students, 55 percent for African American students, and 53 percent for Hispanic students. Swanson calculates similar rates using data from the 2003–2004 school year.

20. The statistics on completion rates and overall attainment rates for black males and black females in the NELS data have quite large standard errors and thus are imprecise (as are any statistics based on small numbers of observations in the NELS). The 95 percent confidence interval for the black male graduation rate is (11 percent, 44 percent); for black females it is (42 percent, 64 percent). The confidence interval for the black male bachelor's degree attainment rate is (6 percent, 15 percent); for black females it is (16 percent, 27 percent).

21. The Hispanic population is excluded from Figure 2.6 because its composition has varied substantially over time due to changing immigration patterns. Thus, it would not be appropriate to compare the U.S. Hispanic population at different points in time over the past 50 years.

Chapter 3   Finishing College at Public Universities

1. See Tables 1.1, 1.2, and 1.3 for a list of these institutions and some of their characteristics—seen in the context of comparable data for all public and private four-year institutions. As we point out in Chapter 1, a large sub-set of our state system universities (those we call the SEL Bs) is surprisingly similar in characteristics to all four-year colleges and universities in the United States.

2. We present an analysis of incoming transfer students in Chapter 7. Although the main part of our study focuses on the educational outcomes of students who had already enrolled in college, we also have very rich data on all 1999 high school seniors in North Carolina and present an analysis of their college enrollment patterns in Chapter 5.

3. Thus, this analysis counts as non-graduates students who transferred to another school. However, as we point out in a note later in the chapter, taking account of transfer-out patterns does not alter the findings presented here; in fact, it strengthens some of them.

4. Throughout our study, when we present results separately for SEL A institutions, we include the four flagship universities in the state systems.

5. The analysis of the timing of dropouts and transfers presented in this chapter was done by our colleague Christopher L. Griffin Jr. This part of the analysis excludes the five flagships and one state system with insufficient parental education data. The universities excluded are the University of Illinois at Urbana-Champaign; the University of Iowa; the University of Minnesota–Twin Cities; the University of Nebraska–Lincoln; the University of Wisconsin–Madison; and the universities in the Ohio system.

6. See Vincent Tinto, *Leaving College: Rethinking the Causes and Cures of Student Attrition,* 2nd edition (Chicago: University of Chicago Press, 1993), p. 152.

7. Looking separately at each institution, there are no real outliers in this regard. At each flagship and state system SEL B, the cumulative withdrawal rate increases each semester—it does not level off.

8. As explained in Appendix B, we estimate income quartiles for students for whom we do not have a direct measure of income using self-reported information from the SAT and ACT questionnaires and the socioeconomic characteristics of the neighborhood where the student lived during high school (obtained from U.S. Census block group data). The parental education data are drawn primarily from the relevant questions on the SAT Student Descriptive Questionnaire, which are not asked on the ACT questionnaire. We exclude from all analyses that include parental education the five flagship universities for which parental education data are missing for most students. They are the same universities listed in note 5.

9. To clarify, the "some college" category indicates that at least one parent attended college, and the "college degree" category indicates that at least one parent graduated from a four-year college. The category is assigned based on the parent with the highest level of education, so the student would be included in the "college degree" group if one parent graduated from college but the other did not.

10. Specifically, we estimate probit regressions with graduation status as the dependent variable. We then report the marginal effects (predicted differences in probability of graduation) between the listed group and the reference group, holding all control variables at their means.

11. Figures 3.7–3.9 show results for the flagships only, but, as we discuss later and show in the appendix tables, the results for the state systems are remarkably similar.

12. The reason that the adjusted difference at the SEL Bs is larger than the unadjusted difference is that low-SES students have higher high school grade point averages, or GPAs (by 0.07, on average), than do the high-SES students. At the flagships, high-SES students have high school GPAs that are 0.10 higher, on average, than those of low-SES students.

13. We also examined differences that adjust for sub-sets of our control variables (Appendix Table 3.4) to see which variables appear most important (with particular attention paid to academic credentials, as measured by SAT/ACT scores and high school GPAs, and to sorting across universities, as captured using university dummies). At the flagships, academic preparation and sorting across institutions appear to be of similar importance in explaining differences in graduation rates by SES. In the state systems, sorting across universities by SES within

each of the three states appears to be more important than differences in entering credentials in explaining differences in outcomes. This result is consistent with the analysis of "undermatching" that we present in Chapter 5.

14. In order to keep the sample of students consistent, we restrict this part of the analysis to the 16 flagship universities and the three state systems for which data on parental education are available (even though some results do not take parental education into account).

15. The only clear pattern that emerges from these appendix tables is found in North Carolina and Virginia, where the adjusted differences by parental education are noticeably larger at the SEL Bs than at the SEL As. However, the same does not hold for family income, where adjusted disparities are somewhat larger at the SEL As than at the SEL Bs in these two state systems. Family income appears to matter the most in Ohio, although we are unable to separate out the role that parental education plays there due to data limitations. In general, the Maryland results are too noisy to be interpreted (note the large standard errors).

16. Because of sampling error, the range of estimated coefficients likely overstates the variability of the true coefficients.

17. We also examined withdrawal over time separately by parental education and family income and found patterns largely similar to those reported here for our combined measure of SES.

18. These adjusted differences are calculated using discrete-time hazard analysis, which applies the basic tools of logistic regression to a multiple-outcome scenario (multinomial logistic regression). For each semester, we regress the set of possible outcomes (withdrawal, four-year transfer, and graduation) on a variable of interest and our standard set of covariates. The resulting coefficients are transformed into hazard estimates for each outcome and for each of two values for the variable of interest. For example, calculating the difference in adjusted withdrawal hazards in a given semester by SES requires a multinomial logistic regression of the three outcomes on an indicator for low SES, an indicator for high SES, and the set of control variables. We then compute the predicted difference in the probability of withdrawal occurring that semester between the high- and low-SES categories, holding all control variables constant at their respective means (with the means calculated based only on students still enrolled each semester).

19. Native American and "other race" students are omitted from this analysis because they number so few in this data set.

20. Results that control for sub-sets of our control variables are presented in Appendix Table 3.5. Focusing on black and Hispanic males and controlling for income and state residency attenuates the differences (compared to white males) somewhat at both flagships and state system universities. In both settings, high school GPAs and SAT/ACT scores explain much more of these differences than do the university dummies; this is especially true in the case of black males.

21. It is important to bear in mind that these results compare a given group to white males, who do not make up the highest- or lowest-performing group (as was the case with the reference categories for family income and parents' education). If the reference group were either the lowest- or highest-performing in terms of graduation rates, the estimated gaps would be much larger. In order to compare

two groups if one of the groups is not white males, one needs to take the difference of reported statistics. For example, the adjusted gap between Hispanic males and Asian females at the flagships (Figure 3.13a) is $7 - (-7) = 14$ percentage points. We found that controlling for parental education (using data from the sub-set of 16 universities) had only a negligible impact on the adjusted graduation gaps by race/ethnicity and gender, and therefore we do not present those results here.

22. It is also worth noting that the *unadjusted* difference in graduation rates between white and black men is close to zero at the SEL Bs in North Carolina and Virginia.

23. We do not examine the timing of black-white differences among females because we found that these differences are usually entirely explained by differences in entering credentials.

24. However, there is an adjusted difference of almost 1 point in the second semester (Figure 3.15a).

25. The difference is somewhat larger in the first semester, when black men are about 2.2 percentage points *less* likely to withdraw than are comparable white men (Figure 3.15b).

26. An important remaining question is to what extent the disparities reported earlier are mitigated by transfer patterns. For example, perhaps low-SES students are less likely to graduate from their initial institution but are more likely to transfer and receive a degree elsewhere. This would cause us to overstate the bachelor's degree attainment gap between low- and high-SES students. We have data from the National Student Clearinghouse on degrees received by the students in our database from any institution that reports such data to the Clearinghouse. Although these data are not comprehensive (they cover only about half of post-secondary enrollment in the United States), they provide a rough sense of whether transferring and graduating are changing the observed disparities in bachelor's degree attainment. In order for the limited nature of the Clearinghouse degree data to bias our results, students from different groups would have to disproportionately transfer to schools that do (or do not) report degree data to the Clearinghouse. We do not think this is likely. As a check on our results, we also looked separately at North Carolina, where most receiving institutions (including all in-state public universities) report degree data to the Clearinghouse. The patterns are similar to those reported for all state system SEL A and SEL B schools in Appendix Tables 3.7a and 3.7b, with North Carolina transfer graduation rates only 1 or 2 percentage points higher than those for all three state systems.

Appendix Tables 3.7a and 3.7b show the percentage of students who earned a degree from a university other than the one where they started in fall 1999. These numbers can be added to the original-institution graduation rates to calculate approximate total bachelor's degree attainment rates. For example, Figure 3.4 shows graduation rates of 68 percent for low-SES students and 83 percent for high-SES students at the flagships. Adding the transfer graduation rate of 4 percent in Appendix Table 3.7a (which, once rounded, is the same for both groups) yields total bachelor's degree attainment rates of 72 percent and 87 percent—a "correction" that leaves the difference between high- and low-SES students unchanged.

We find that high-SES students are generally at least as likely to earn a degree elsewhere as are low-SES students. White students are generally slightly more likely to transfer and graduate than are black students of the same gender. Thus, if anything, transfer patterns appear to exacerbate the disparities we have documented in this chapter. However, the differences in transfer graduation rates are generally small, so the real take-away is that the results we have reported do not need to be modified in light of the transfer-out data.

The transfer graduation rates warrant a final comment: although they do not vary substantially in absolute terms by SES, race/ethnicity, or gender, if they are calculated as a fraction of non-graduates rather than as a percentage of all matriculants in each sub-group, substantial differences become apparent. For example, among low-SES students at flagships who do not graduate from their initial institution, 12 percent eventually earn a degree somewhere else. For high-SES students, the corresponding figure is 22 percent. In other words, among students who leave their original institution without graduating, those from high-SES families are substantially more likely to earn a bachelor's degree elsewhere than are those from low-SES families.

27. See, for example, Krista D. Mattern et al., "Differential Validity and Prediction of the SAT," College Board Research Report 2008-4, College Board, New York, October 2008, and Jennifer L. Kobrin et al., "Validity of the SAT for Predicting First-Year College Grade Point Average," College Board Research Report 2008-5, College Board, New York, October 2008. For research on the predictive power of the ACT of first Year GPA, see Julie Noble and Richard Sawyer, "Predicting Different Levels of Academic Success in College Using High School GPA and ACT Composite Score," ACT Research Report 2002-4, ACT, Iowa City, Iowa.

28. The correlation coefficient between adjusted high school GPA and first-year college GPA is 0.34 at SEL Is, 0.43 at SEL IIs, 0.46 at SEL IIIs, 0.41 at SEL As, and 0.38 at SEL Bs.

Chapter 4 Fields of Study, Time-to-Degree, and College Grades

1. The analysis of choice of major excludes the following five universities, which did not have at least one graduate major in each of the seven categories of major fields of study and thus could not be included in the adjusted analysis: Stony Brook University, University of Mary Washington, University of North Carolina–Asheville, University of Virginia's College at Wise, and the Virginia Military Institute.

2. The "Professional and Other" category includes primarily students from four groups of fields: agriculture, agriculture operations, and related sciences; health professions and related clinical sciences; family and consumer sciences and human sciences; and parks, recreation, leisure, and fitness studies. Business is counted as a separate category due to the large number of students it attracts.

3. We combine the results for the flagships and state system SEL As because they are very similar.

4. The difference between the unadjusted and adjusted results for engineering, math, and physical science majors is explained mostly by academic preparation, particularly SAT/ACT scores. At the flagships, controlling for income quar-

tile, state residency status, and university attended reduces the white-black difference among men from 11.4 to 11.1 points. Adding SAT/ACT scores changes it to a reverse gap of 4.5 points. Replacing SAT/ACT scores with high school GPA yields a (non-reverse) gap of 3.5 points. Adding both SAT/ACT scores and high school GPA yields an adjusted reverse gap of 7.0 points. This general pattern is similar for the white-black difference among women.

5. David Leonhardt, "The Big Fix," *New York Times Magazine,* February 1, 2009, pp. 22–29, 48–51; quote on p. 50.

6. For the fall 1999 entering cohort, three-year graduates are defined as those who finished their degrees on or before September 6, 2002. Four-year graduates received their degrees between September 7, 2002, and September 6, 2003; five-year graduates between September 7, 2003, and September 6, 2004; and six-year graduates between September 7, 2004, and September 6, 2005. The September 6 cut-off is chosen based on our data, which suggest that September 6 is the latest that any of the universities in our study award degrees completed during the summer term.

7. This calculation is made by classifying students by the semester in which they graduated (classifying students with graduation dates between September 7 and January 31 as fall graduates and those with graduation dates between February 1 and September 6 as spring graduates). Students who took 9 semesters to graduate were enrolled for 0.7 semesters more than the 8-semester (i.e., four-year) graduates on average; thus we estimate that they spent 70 percent of the additional time enrolled. The corresponding differences for 10-, 11-, and 12-semester graduates (still relative to 8-semester graduates) are, respectively, 1.5, 2.0, and 2.7 semesters, which correspond to shares of additional time spent enrolled of 75 percent, 67 percent, and 68 percent. All of these differences are regression adjusted for institution attended and choice of major (because different universities and majors require different numbers of credits to graduate).

8. A full load is approximately 12 to 15 credits per semester. Differences in semesters enrolled, credits earned, and credits attempted are calculated from data for 19 of the 21 flagship universities in our study (the University of Texas–Austin and the University of Washington are omitted due to missing data on credits attempted and earned). These differences are regression adjusted for institution attended and choice of major (because different universities and majors require different numbers of credits to graduate).

9. Recall that at state system SEL B universities, low-SES students entered with *higher* high school GPAs than did their high-SES classmates.

10. Disaggregated results can be found in Appendix Tables 4.6a and 4.6b.

11. We used a stepwise regression analysis to identify which variables were most responsible for the difference between the unadjusted and adjusted results but found that our conclusions were very sensitive to the order in which the control variables were added.

12. The state system results follow a somewhat erratic pattern, with significant adjusted differences between high- and low-SES students at SEL As and Bs in Maryland, at SEL As in North Carolina, but not at SEL Bs in North Carolina or SEL As and Bs in Virginia. (Lack of data on parental education prevents us from presenting similar results for Ohio.)

13. The rightmost panel of Figure 4.10a removes any effect of parental education on finishing on time through the effect of parental education on family income.

14. Unadjusted and adjusted differences by parental education and family income for all selectivity clusters (not just SEL Is, IIs, and As) are shown in Appendix Tables 4.7a through 4.8b. At the SEL III flagships, both the unadjusted and adjusted differences are small. However, as in the case of SES, the results in the state systems do not follow a consistent pattern by selectivity.

15. Results by state system (Appendix Table 4.9b) vary considerably but show that black-white adjusted differences are consistently larger at SEL As than at SEL Bs, and for women they sometimes go in the reverse direction at SEL Bs.

16. The academic performance analysis excludes the University of Texas–Austin and the University of Washington, for which data on college grades are not available. All measurements of college grades use rank-in-class, which compares the cumulative GPAs of students within each institution. Thus we are measuring not absolute academic performance but rather relative academic performance within one's college cohort (defined here as the 1999 entering cohort of first-time, full-time freshmen at each university).

17. Because rank-in-class is a measure that is standardized within universities, the absolute numbers do not vary and so are not presented in the figures or tables. A difference of 10 percentile points in rank-in-class has basically the same meaning everywhere, unlike graduation rates, which vary widely with institutional selectivity.

18. Because the results are so similar at the flagships and the state system SEL As, we combine them in Figures 4.13–4.15.

19. When we exclude major at graduation as a control variable in the adjusted differences presented in Figures 4.13–4.16b, we obtain qualitatively similar results.

20. We also find some evidence that failing to control for high school GPA (and using only SAT/ACT scores as a predictor of college grades, as much of the literature on this subject does) will overstate the extent of minority underperformance at more selective universities. Appendix Tables 4.14a and 4.14b show that adding high school GPA as a control has a sizable impact on the estimated white-black difference among men. The SAT/ACT-adjusted coefficient (in the third column of each panel) drops by 36 percent, 64 percent, and 42 percent (at SEL Is, IIs, and As, respectively) when high school GPA is added as a control (in the fifth column of each panel). At the less selective institutions (SEL IIIs and Bs), adding high school GPA as a control has only a small or trivial effect on the white-black difference among men. Adding high school GPA as a control also decreases the adjusted female-male difference among white students in nearly all settings.

21. The summary analysis excludes the University of Texas–Austin and the University of Washington, for which college grades data are not available.

22. At the state system SEL Bs (Appendix Table 4.15b), differences in outcomes by SES are largely unaffected by adjusting for test scores and high school grades. The reason is that low-SES students at these universities enter with lower test scores but higher high school GPAs than do their high-SES classmates.

23. There is one exception, which is that differences by race at the state system SEL Bs are very small once student characteristics are taken into account (Ap-

pendix Table 4.16b). However, our analysis of individual outcomes showed that there are remaining disparities by race in some but not all of the state systems.

24. In the case of the North Carolina seniors, Hispanic men and women fared less well than black students, largely because of the appeal of historically black colleges and universities (HBCUs) to many black students in North Carolina.

Chapter 5   High Schools and "Undermatching"

1. See Clifford Adelman, *Answers in the Tool Box: Academic Intensity, Attendance Patterns, and Bachelor's Degree Attainment* (Washington, D.C.: Department of Education, Office of Educational Research and Improvement, 1999), and the many references cited therein.

2. Melissa Roderick, Jenny Nagaoka, Elaine Allensworth, with Vanessa Coca, Marena Correa, and Ginger Stoker, "From High School to the Future: A First Look at Chicago Public School Graduates' College Enrollment, College Preparation, and Graduation from Four-Year Colleges," Consortium on Chicago School Research, Chicago, April 2006.

3. See Melissa Roderick, Jenny Nagaoka, Vanessa Coca, Eliza Moeller, with Karen Roddie, Jamiliyah Gillian, and Desmond Patton, "From High School to the Future: Potholes on the Road to College," Consortium on Chicago School Research, Chicago, March 2008, and Melissa Roderick, Jenny Nagaoka, Vanessa Coca, and Eliza Moeller, "From High School to the Future: Making Hard Work Pay Off," Consortium on Chicago School Research, Chicago, April 2009. The Chicago Consortium studies also cite the work of many other authors and thus are an excellent starting point for anyone interested in studying high schools, especially those in urban systems. Of course there is also a considerable body of other literature on this subject, some of it predating the work of the Chicago Consortium.

4. For ACT, see the studies listed at their informative Web site and referenced in ACT publications. Many of these studies (such as Richard Sawyer, "Benefits of Additional High School Course Work and Improved Course Performance in Preparing Students for College," ACT Research Report 2008-1, ACT, Iowa City, Iowa) emphasize the critical importance of the connection between test scores and curricular patterns and course content. The College Board and ETS Web sites likewise provide links to their research and programmatic efforts on high school success and college readiness.

5. See Goldin and Katz, especially pp. 129–62, for an excellent discussion of this feature of American education at the pre-college level.

6. We recognize that these data may be of independent interest to some scholars, but permission of the College Board and the ACT would be required to obtain access to the full database.

7. The greater apparent impact of the quality of the high school among students who attended flagship and SEL A universities is consistent, once again, with what we have come to call the "Hoxby hypothesis," namely that the quality of both entering students and the high schools from which they come matter at least slightly more if the student attends a more selective university—but the difference is not great.

8. See Appendix C for a full discussion of the North Carolina database and Appendix Table 5.10 for summary statistics describing North Carolina high schools. The good news about the North Carolina data is that they are so rich; the "bad" news is that the richness of these data tempts us to go into more detail on some topics than will interest most readers. The generic problem confronting scholars interested in studying the effects of the high school experience on the full range of later educational outcomes is that, in general, record-keeping systems at the high school and college levels do not connect. The data available to Roderick and her colleagues at the Consortium on Chicago School Research and reported in "From High School to the Future" (2006) are a noteworthy exception to this generalization. Other states, including Florida, Ohio, Massachusetts, and Texas, have also been working hard to make these connections, and even more states, including New York, are at earlier stages of work designed to close this data gap. In Texas, Marta Tienda and others have done substantial work linking high school records to college enrollment; see Sunny Xinchun Niu, Marta Tienda, and Kalena Cortes, "College Selectivity and the Texas Top 10% Law," *Economics of Education Review* 25, no. 3 (June 2006): 259–72, and Jason M. Fletcher and Marta Tienda, "High School Peer Networks and College Success: Lessons from Texas," paper presented at the National Bureau of Economic Research Higher Education Working Group Meeting, Cambridge, Mass., May 2, 2008. Jesse Rothstein at Princeton has also worked extensively with California data to examine the links between high school and college and has written (among other papers) "SAT Scores, High School, and Collegiate Performance Predictions," working paper, Princeton University, Princeton, N.J., June 2005, available at http://www.princeton.edu/~jrothst/workingpapers/rothstein_CBvolume.pdf. Using the same California data, Saul Geiser and Maria Veronica Santelices have published a paper titled "Validity of High-School Grades in Predicting Student Success beyond the Freshmen Year: High-School Record vs. Standardized Tests as Indicators of Four-Year College Outcomes," Research and Occasional Paper Series CSHE.6.07, Center for Studies in Higher Education, University of California–Berkeley, June 2007, available at http://cshe.berkeley.edu/publications/docs/ROPS.GEISER._SAT_6.13.07.pdf.

9. It is necessary, however, to interpret this result cautiously. Differences in eighth-grade scores capture both differences in academic achievement observed before students entered high school and differences in family backgrounds. If it were somehow possible to wave a wand and give all black students the same eighth-grade scores as white students, we would still not expect them to exhibit the same college-going behavior as their white peers *unless* we could also give the black students the same family backgrounds (and resources) that undoubtedly played such a large role in helping the white students do well on the eighth-grade tests.

10. See, for example, the longitudinal study by Hart and Risley, which shows large differences in verbal production (words spoken) by parents and extremely large correlates with children's IQ (Betty Hart and Todd R. Risley, *Meaningful Differences in the Everyday Experience of Young American Children* [Baltimore: Brookes, 1995]). We are indebted to Professor Nathan Kuncel for this reference. Carneiro and Heckman also stress the importance of family resources in a child's forma-

tive years (Pedro Carneiro and James J. Heckman, "The Evidence on Credit Constraints in Post-Secondary Schooling," *Economic Journal* 112, no. 482 [October 2002]: 705–34).

11. The ACT has reached a very similar conclusion based on data drawn from many more states. In the words of an ACT memo prepared for us, "Our research shows that high schools . . . are important, but are considerably less important than students' achievement prior to high school in impacting college readiness at the time of high school graduation" (see "The Forgotten Middle: Ensuring That All Students Are on Target for College and Career Readiness before High School," ACT Policy Report Series, ACT, Iowa City, Iowa [2009]).

12. We refer here to SAT scores alone, not to "SAT/ACT" scores, because North Carolina is "an SAT state"; the ACT is not widely used in North Carolina.

13. These academic levels reflect both the curricular offerings of the schools (as measured crudely by the number of Advanced Placement [AP] courses taken, which also serves as a proxy for other curricular characteristics) and the overall academic standing of the senior class, including college aspirations as reflected in test-taking behavior. Thus, peer group effects as well as the richness of academic offerings should be captured through analysis of these levels. For some purposes, it would have been desirable to create a measure of the academic standing of a high school that is independent of the quality or aspirations of the students attending the school, but we were unable to find an entirely satisfactory way to do this. However, following the suggestion of one reviewer of an early draft of this discussion, we "worked backward" and predicted the relationship between each individual high school and an outcome of interest, such as enrollment at a four-year college (controlling for eighth-grade test scores and for race/ethnicity and gender). We then created a new variable that assigns the coefficient generated by this regression to each high school. As a next step we correlated these coefficients with the variables we used to assign schools to Level I, Level II, and Level III. The correlation with actual and adjusted average SAT scores is very low, as we would expect because eighth-grade scores (which are strong predictors of SAT scores) were included as controls in the underlying regression equation. But the correlations with the percentage of students taking the SAT and with AP courses offered were 0.62 and 0.54, respectively, which suggests that these two variables chosen to classify high schools into levels were reasonably good choices. As a further check on whether our classification system is reasonable, we grouped high schools into terciles on the basis of (a) their coefficients on college enrollment and (b) one of our classification variables, such as number of AP courses offered. Again, the results were at least mildly reassuring in that the lowest-ranked schools offered the fewest AP courses and had the lowest percentages of students taking the SAT.

14. These are of course the actual ("raw") differences that do not take account of associated differences in other variables (as we do later in this discussion). The 34 percent eventual graduation rate for those from Level I schools is the product of a 54 percent matriculation rate and a 63 percent graduation rate among those who matriculated; the 14 percent eventual graduation rate for those from Level III schools is the product of a 27 percent matriculation rate and a 51 percent graduation rate among those who matriculated. Disadvantages (disparities) accumulate.

15. When we divided North Carolina universities into selectivity clusters (as explained in Chapters 1 and 3), we found that the academic level of the high school has no "net" effect on enrollment at the SEL As, but it does have an effect on enrollment at the SEL Bs. This rather surprising result may reflect, at least in part, admissions practices at SEL As in North Carolina. We are told by people familiar with these practices that SEL As are under some pressure "to make their entering classes as representative of the state as possible"—not to take too many students from "elite" high schools and to enroll some number of students from the less prestigious high schools. This constraint is analogous to pressures in Michigan for the leading universities to take some number of students from the Upper Peninsula. On the basis of admissions data, we know that the University of North Carolina–Chapel Hill (UNC–Chapel Hill) is more likely to admit students from Level III high schools than from Level I high schools on an "other-things-equal" basis.

16. Unfortunately, it is very hard to estimate the effect on graduation rates (which vary by the selectivity of the university) of having attended a Level I high school versus a Level III high school. One problem is that fewer than 500 students from Level III high schools in North Carolina attended one of the most selective (SEL A) universities. Another problem is that high school level potentially affects whether and where students go to college, further complicating the estimation of the effect of high school level on graduation rates.

17. See Caroline M. Hoxby, "The Effects of Geographic Integration and Increasing Competition in the Market for College Education," revision of NBER Working Paper 6323, May 2000. This same "Hoxby hypothesis" may help explain another pattern we found when we examined the relationships among eighth-grade scores, level of high school attended, and enrollment patterns. Much stronger, and highly positive, effects on enrollment at four-year colleges are associated with being at a Level I school among students in the top two quartiles of eighth-grade scores. There is no real relationship between attendance at a Level I high school and enrollment in a four-year college for students in the bottom two quartiles. However, we did find that students who entered a Level I high school with relatively low eighth-grade scores were more likely to enroll at a two-year college than were students with comparable entering credentials who attended Level II or Level III high schools—where such students may have been less likely to consider any college option at all.

18. See Roderick et al. (2006), p. 42 (our emphasis).

19. We do not understand why the Chicago Consortium finds much larger high school effects than we do. Part of the explanation may be that we are able to control more fully for family background characteristics than the Chicago researchers can do. It may also be that the more "aggregative" nature of our analysis leads to an "averaging out" of differences that can be identified by more detailed examinations of individual schools.

20. See Roderick et al. (2009), p. 52 and figure 16.

21. Of course, students can also "mismatch" by going to schools that are too demanding (they can, as it were, "overmatch" as well as "undermatch"). In principle, we would hope that admissions offices would guard against this danger by not admitting students who are ill equipped to do the work, and the research un-

derlying Bowen and Bok's *The Shape of the River* suggests that, in the main, admissions offices have met this responsibility (William G. Bowen and Derek C. Bok, *The Shape of the River: Long-Term Consequences of Considering Race in College and University Admissions* [Princeton, N.J.: Princeton University Press, 1998]). We will also report findings of our own on this subject in Chapter 6 when we focus on college admissions.

22. These issues are reflected in two recent reports highlighting "match" problems. The first concern is that "many young people who could succeed at [four-year colleges] are not being encouraged by their families or schools to apply" (Peter Schmidt, "Mismatches Found between Student Achievement and Parents' College Expectations in Federal Survey," *Chronicle of Higher Education*, April 23, 2008, online edition, an article describing a new report by the U.S. Department of Education titled "Parent Expectations and Planning for College"). The second concern is that "black students are two-and-a-half times more likely to enroll at a college where they have a 70 percent chance of not graduating than at a college where they have a 70 percent chance of graduating" (see Scott Jaschik, "The Graduation Rate Gap," *Inside Higher Education*, April 21, 2008, online edition, an article describing a new report by Education Sector titled "Graduation Rate Watch: Making Minority Student Success a Priority"). It should be noted, however, that the latter report does not take account of differences among students in qualifications, which we believe need to be factored into any study of mismatches.

23. Roderick et al. (2008), p. 71.

24. In Bowen and Bok's book (1998, pp. 59–68), the authors find that the belief that minority students should not "overreach"—that is, should not go to schools where the average SAT is much higher than their own SAT—is false. Instead, they find that black and white students at the middle to the low end of the SAT spectrum graduated at higher rates if they attended a more selective institution and that they had lower graduation rates at institutions where they were surrounded by peers with similar SAT scores. They found this to be true for students in all of the SAT ranges. In Chapter 11 we report similar findings for the minority students in this study.

25. Thomas Kane and Christopher Avery at Harvard University have determined that in public high schools there is very little guidance and advising in the college admissions and financial aid process. They found that at most Boston public schools, a guidance counselor was in charge of 250 students or more. To address the vast difference between public and private school guidance, they created a program called College Opportunity and Career Help (COACH) that trained Harvard graduate and undergraduate students to advise seniors at high schools in Boston. A main finding was that better advising improves "matching" more than it affects college-going in general (see Ken Gerwertz, "COACHing the High-Jump to Higher Education," *Harvard Gazette*, September 30, 1999, online edition).

26. We also made analogous calculations for both white and black students based on each race's own enrollment patterns. As one would expect because of the existence of affirmative action, black students were more likely to be admitted by SEL As than were students in general who had similar test scores and grades. Thus, even more black students would have had reason to expect to be able to enroll at SEL As than the "all students" analysis suggests. However, the pat-

terns were not sufficiently different to warrant separate presentation, and again, we wanted to be conservative and to avoid exaggerating the number of potential undermatches.

27. For students that applied only to North Carolina State University (NC State), the admissions outcome is simply whether they were admitted to NC State. For those that applied to both NC State and UNC–Chapel Hill, the admissions outcome is whether they were admitted to either school (although in practice, very few students who were admitted at UNC–Chapel Hill failed to gain admission at NC State). Students who applied only to UNC–Chapel Hill do not factor into the presumptive eligibility calculation.

28. These data measure attendance at colleges in and outside of North Carolina. The Clearinghouse data cover 91 percent of the post-secondary enrollment in the United States, and because the coverage is less than 100 percent, a small number of students who actually went to college show up as "no college" in our data. This finding is amazingly consistent with the results of the study by Roderick et al. at the Chicago Consortium (2008, p. 5), which found that "among the most highly qualified students in CPS [Chicago Public Schools], only 38 percent enroll in a match college."

29. This is one instance in which the data from North Carolina are not very helpful in understanding broader patterns. The reason is that the unusual prominence of HBCUs in North Carolina creates complicated interactions that are peculiar to states like North Carolina. For this reason, we do not present data on under-matching by race/ethnicity and gender here.

30. Roderick et al. (2008), especially pp. 74–75.

31. In 2008, the average in-state tuition at the SEL As in North Carolina was just over $3,000 compared with an average of almost $2,200 at the SEL Bs, roughly $1,800 at the HBCUs, and under $1,300 at the two-year community colleges. Such small differences pale in comparison with the differences in graduation rates, earning power, and access to advanced degree programs by type of institution. We should acknowledge, however, that for some families, who see college costs as "expenses" rather than as "investments," even this level of outlay may have some effect on decision making.

32. This conclusion is consistent with the survey findings for Virginia of Christopher Avery and Sarah E. Turner (see their "Playing the College Application Game: Critical Moves and the Link to Socio-Economic Circumstances," preliminary draft, December 29, 2008).

33. Before we had the actual admissions data for UNC–Chapel Hill and NC State, we thought it might be possible to use SAT score–sending behavior as a proxy for applications. We determined that more than 70 percent of those undermatched students presumptively qualified to attend a SEL A had in fact sent their scores to one of the three SEL As in North Carolina (NC State, UNC–Asheville, and UNC–Chapel Hill). But, as the actual data on applications cited in the text illustrate, many of these students did not end up applying. Apparently score-sending behavior does not proxy for actual applications as well as we thought that it would.

34. A detailed regression analysis of factors associated with patterns at each stage of the admissions and enrollment process (where we looked only at students pre-

sumptively eligible to enroll at a SEL A) provides a little more information on the stages at which SES, in particular, appears to have determined whether students undermatched. Higher levels of parental education and higher family income were both strongly associated, on an other-things-equal basis, with the probability that a student applied to a SEL A in North Carolina. These family background factors were also associated with decisions to accept offers of admission and to enroll. On the other hand, they were not correlated at all with the judgments reached by the universities as to whether to accept one of these undermatched students; therefore, fear of rejection need not have influenced students' application decisions (had they understood the admission probabilities, which they may not have).

35. Roderick et al. (2009), p. 51 and figure 14.

36. This finding differs from the emphasis in the study by Roderick et al. (2008) at the Chicago Consortium on the importance of a "high school college-going culture" in determining undermatches (p. 45). The Chicago study did not, however, control for differences in family characteristics.

37. It is necessary to remember that we are looking at undermatches only among students who took the SATs. Attending a Level I high school may induce more students to take the SAT, and if these "extra" students undermatch differently than do other students, focusing on this subpopulation may lead us to understate the effect of school level. But we doubt that this is a major source of bias.

38. In this part of the analysis, we can look only at the undermatched students who went to a four-year college (and to a SEL B in this discussion). Of course, those who went to a two-year college or to no college have no four-year graduation rates to examine.

39. Of the students at SEL Bs who were presumptively eligible to attend SEL As, 15 percent earned a bachelor's degree from a university other than the one at which they initially matriculated. The corresponding figure for presumptively eligible students who attended SEL As was 7 percent.

40. These differences in rank-in-class are not simply the product of different raw college GPA distributions at SEL As versus SEL Bs. The adjusted differences in raw cumulative GPA between matched and undermatched students were 0.25 among graduates and 0.19 among all students.

41. A similar trade-off was evident among the minority students included in the research for *The Shape of the River*. Subsequent survey data showed that attendance at a more selective university paid off for students, even though they incurred a rank-in-class cost by competing for grades with exceptionally talented classmates (see especially chapters 2, 3, 4, and 5).

42. See Bowen and Bok (1998), chapters 5 and 6, for a detailed discussion of how attending highly selective colleges and universities, and graduating from them on time, positively affects future prospects. In these chapters the authors used the College and Beyond database to look at the long-run outcomes of students who matriculated at 28 academically selective colleges and universities in 1976. The outcomes under consideration were employment, earnings, and civic participation, as well as satisfaction in life and at the workplace. See also Caroline M. Hoxby, "The Return to Attending a More Selective College: 1960 to the Present," mimeo, Harvard University, for more discussion on the subject.

43. In Chapter 7 we examine the question of the cost of starting out at a two-year college to the student who hopes ultimately to earn a bachelor's degree.

44. It is encouraging that both the College Board and ACT are actively involved in efforts to address the undermatching problem, including contributing data to a promising project being led by President John Hennessy and Caroline Hoxby at Stanford and by Sarah Turner at the University of Virginia (currently titled "Expanding College Opportunities").

45. This conclusion is buttressed by evidence assembled by Caroline Hoxby and Chris Avery (unpublished paper, 2008) from a snapshot of SAT test-takers, which the authors then adjust for ACT test-takers. Hoxby and Avery found that there are very substantial numbers of "high-merit" and "elevated-merit" students who do not even submit their scores to colleges and universities for which they are presumptively eligible (a result similar to the one we report in this chapter). A careful study of matriculation patterns in the United Kingdom carried out by Claire Crawford, Stephen Machin, and Anna Vignoles ("Closing the Gap in University Participation: Reaching Out to High Achieving Disadvantaged Pupils," unpublished paper, September 2008) comes to similar conclusions. These authors identify "sizeable target groups of low SES students who have had high achievement in the past (e.g., at GCSE [a set of subject-specific exams in the United Kingdom]) who do not then go on to university" (p. 2). Both of these studies, as well as other research, are summarized in an unpublished paper by Caroline Hoxby and Sarah Turner ("Improving Outcomes for High-Achieving Low-Income Students through Collective Action") prepared for the Windsor Group conference held in Charlottesville, Virginia, on October 28, 2008.

Chapter 6   Test Scores and High School Grades as Predictors

1. In September 2008, the National Association for College Admission Counseling (NACAC) released a report by a commission chaired by Dean Fitzsimmons ("Report of the Commission on the Use of Standardized Tests in Undergraduate Admissions," National Association for College Admission Counseling, Alexandria, Virginia, September 2008, hereafter NACAC [2008]) proposing that colleges and universities give less emphasis to the SAT and ACT and that the entire standardized testing process, including the uses of tests, be reformed (along with the tests themselves). Overall, the conclusions of the Fitzsimmons Commission closely mirror the broad thrust of the arguments presented in this chapter.

2. The quotation is from p. 15 of a summary research report prepared for us by Ranjit Sidhu, senior vice-president of ACT, titled "Comparing the Validity of ACT Scores and High School Grades as Predictors of Success in College," ACT, Iowa City, Iowa, April 3, 2009. See also the extensive materials at the ACT Web site, including "Issues in College Success: What We Know about College Success: Using ACT Data to Inform Educational Issues," ACT, Iowa City, Iowa, 2008. The College Board has of course also been concerned with placement issues and with efforts to improve the high school curriculum. Reports on their work can be found at the College Board's Web site.

3. See Chapter 1, note 38. As we point out there, we have converted ACT scores to the SAT scale (using the concordance tables published by the College Board) rather than the other way around because our data sets contain roughly two and a half times more SAT scores than ACT scores. (We write "SAT/ACT" rather than "ACT/SAT" for the same reason.) Rescaling ACT scores to the SAT

scale introduces no significant measurement error; the conversion preserves the rank ordering of students, and the correlation between ACT scores and ACT-converted-to-SAT scores is 0.999. The use of a single measure of test score results works for our purposes because of the high correlation between the scores earned by students on these tests. (See Thomas R. Coyle and David R. Pillow, "SAT and ACT Predict College GPA after Removing *g*," *Intelligence* 36 [2008]: 719–29, and Neil J. Dorans, "Correspondences between ACT and SAT I Scores," College Board Report 99-1, ETS RR 99-2, College Entrance Examination Board, New York, 1999. Within our more limited universe, we have found similarly high correlations.) Although our data sets contain many more SAT scores than ACT scores, we have both scores for more than 30,000 students and it is this sub-universe of overlapping test-takers that we use to compare the coefficients of the two tests in regressions used to predict graduation rates.

4. Some of our universities rely mainly on SAT scores, some mainly on ACT scores, and some on a mix of SAT and ACT scores. For an informative history of the ACT and how it was created to challenge the Educational Testing Service (ETS) and the SAT, see Nicholas Lemann, *The Big Test: The Secret History of the American Meritocracy* (New York: Farrar, Straus and Giroux, 1999), pp. 95, 102–4. The National Association for College Admission Counseling's Commission Report (2008) and studies cited in it also discuss the evolution of selective admission and testing (pp. 16 ff). See also Richard C. Atkinson and Saul Geiser, "Reflections on a Century of College Admission Tests," Research and Occasional Paper CSHE.4.09, Center for Studies in Higher Education, University of California–Berkeley, April 2009.

5. In these regressions, we first use only university dummies as controls; then we include additional controls for state residency status, race/ethnicity, gender, family income, and parental education (when the availability of data permits). Adding these controls has only a negligible effect, however, on our estimates of how graduation rates vary with test scores and high school grades. Our data also show that limiting the set of universities studied to those for which we have data on parental education has a minimal effect on the results. Thus, we are able to adopt the simple approach of focusing on the regressions containing only SAT/ACT scores, high school grades, and institutional dummies as independent variables. We should also note that in these regressions we use "adjusted high school grades," which is a measure of high school performance we are able to calculate on a consistent basis across groups of students and groups of universities. Our calculation, which is explained in detail in Appendix B, begins with self-reported grades and takes into account other self-reported data including the number of years every subject was studied, the number of honors courses taken, and the number of AP courses taken. This measure is slightly less precise than the grades that can be obtained from institutional data, but institutions do not always use the same scales, and thus it is hard to compare grades across institutions. Fortunately, the adjusted GPAs turn out to have a predictive value that is very similar to the predictive value of the institutionally reported data when the two measures can be compared (see Appendix Table 6.9c). Finally, although we show results for both six-year and four-year graduation rates in most appendix tables, the patterns are quite similar, and we generally focus on six-year graduation rates in the text for ease of exposition.

6. As the "grid" data shown later in this chapter (in Appendix Tables 6.4–6.8) indicate, there are positive "raw" or "bi-variate" relationships between graduation rates and both SAT/ACT scores and high school GPA, and these grids also illustrate the simple correlation between test scores and high school GPA. But it is the "incremental" or "net" effects of different predictors that are most relevant to our analysis (and to admissions offices choosing among candidates). A key question, which the coefficients shown here answer, is how much *additional* information is provided by both test scores and high school GPA after taking account of the information provided by the other variable. We are indebted to Professor Paul Sackett at the University of Minnesota for emphasizing the importance of distinguishing between incremental ("net") effects and bi-variate relationships.

7. Promises of institutional confidentiality preclude our showing the actual results for individual institutions, but we can report that the GPA coefficients are somewhat larger, both in absolute terms and in relation to their standard errors, when we use students' actual high school grades as recorded by the universities (which we can do when working with the data for individual universities) rather than the adjusted measure of grades that we use to achieve consistency across universities.

8. An op-ed column in the *New York Times* by Peter D. Salins ("The Test Passes, Colleges Fail," November 18, 2008, p. A27) illustrates how easy it is to confuse discussions of the predictive power of test scores versus grades by conducting the "wrong experiment"—or, more generally, by failing to invoke normal standards of evidence. Salins reports that State University of New York campuses that raised SAT admission standards while leaving high school GPA the same observed higher graduation rates than did campuses that left both measures alone. This "finding" is hardly surprising, because *any* increase in selectivity is going to raise graduation rates. Salins fails to ask this key question: what would have happened to graduation rates had campuses raised the high school GPA standard and left SAT scores alone? Based on the massive amount of evidence assembled for this study, it is highly likely that graduation rates would have risen even more. As a number of letters to the editor (e.g., "Just Name, Rank and SAT Number," *New York Times,* November 24, 2008, p. A24) point out, naïve interpretations of the kinds of comparisons Salins uses can lead to serious confusion about effects of admissions policies.

9. Regressions that control for (in addition to university attended) race/ethnicity, gender, state residency status, and family income quartile (Appendix Table 6.3) yield very similar results.

10. Before discussing the tabular data presented next, we wish to make four general comments about the regression analysis: First, these regressions predict graduation rates at the institution initially attended and do not give institutions "credit" for students who transfer and then earn a degree elsewhere. But we have determined that treating transfer-out students as non-graduates has no effect on the conclusions pertaining to the predictive power of test scores and GPAs. Second, a commentator on an early draft of this chapter warned that multi-collinearity between SAT/ACT scores and high school GPAs might make it hard to interpret the regression results. We know that SAT/ACT scores and high school GPAs are correlated and failing to take account of such correlations can

obscure the real relationships. However, the simple correlations between SAT/ACT scores and high school GPAs in these data are not as strong as one might have expected them to be. They are 0.40 at SEL Is, 0.39 at SEL IIs, 0.49 at SEL IIIs, 0.42 at state system SEL As, 0.42 at state system SEL Bs, and 0.35 at HBCUs. Moreover, the tabular comparisons of graduation rates by both SAT/ACT scores and high school GPAs discussed next in the text and reported in Appendix Tables 6.4–6.8 convincingly demonstrate that the regression results mirror the underlying data. Third, another commentator thought that we might have misspecified our regression equations by failing to recognize that the relationships between SAT/ACT scores and graduation rates, and between high school GPAs and graduation rates, may be non-linear. This is an important question, and we performed an extensive analysis of it (using local polynomials) that shows very little evidence of non-linearity over the relevant ranges. Fourth, it is true that we are looking at students who matriculated when what we would really like to know is predictive power among applicants. There is some evidence, however, that this is not likely to be a significant problem. As we understand the concern, as expressed by another commentator, it is that if colleges are putting more weight on test scores than on high school GPA in the admissions process, the range of test scores among the admitted students will be smaller than among the applicants (and to a greater extent than the same is true for high school GPA). As a result, the predictive power of test scores among the enrolled students will be smaller than the predictive power would have been among all applicants (and the test score versus high school GPA comparison will be biased). However, the admissions data we have for two public universities in our 1999 data (Chapel Hill and NC State) and three public universities in our 1995 data (Penn State, UCLA, and UVa) indicate that the opposite pattern prevails—more weight was put on high school GPA in the admissions process than was put on SAT scores. At all of these universities, the standard deviation of both test scores and high school GPA is, as one would expect, smaller among admits than among all applicants, but this is true to a much greater extent for high school GPA than for test scores. In other words, if this pattern holds more generally, our results likely *understate* the predictive power of high school GPA relative to test scores because of the greater selection on high school GPA than on test scores in the admissions process.

11. The bottom panels of these appendix tables show results for four-year graduation rates, which again mirror closely the results for six-year rates and thus require no separate discussion.

12. Lemann, p. 5. This splendid book contains a full account of the evolution of the SAT (and other standardized tests, including especially the ACT) over the years and documents the ways in which reality often overtook the idealistic aspirations of people like Conant. The next quotation is also from Lemann, p. 28.

13. The notes to these tables specify the other control variables, which include family income quartile, race/ethnicity, gender, and university dummies. The data set is restricted to students with non-missing data on all the control variables and to students from high schools that sent at least two students to the universities in the study and whose students did not all either graduate or fail to graduate.

14. This finding is qualitatively the same as the finding of Jesse Rothstein in his work with data from California, already cited. In studying the power of SAT scores to predict first-year GPA in college, he found that when he added high school

fixed effects, "the SAT coefficient falls by nearly half." As the bottom panels of Appendix Tables 6.9a and 6.9b show, the SAT/ACT net regression coefficients are essentially zero when we include high school fixed effects and predict four-year graduation rates. One commentator raised the question of whether using high school fixed effects deprives test scores of their "rightful" predictive power, given the correlation between SAT/ACT scores and high school attended. This could be true to some degree, but note that including the high school dummies simply drives what are already exceedingly small test-score coefficients (refer back to Appendix Tables 6.1 and 6.2) to zero. Also, and more fundamentally, it seems relevant to ask what information is added by the SAT scores on top of that provided by high school GPA and the characteristics of the high school attended.

15. One commentator reminded us that, as explained in Appendix B, we adjust raw self-reported grades to take account of aspects of coursework, and therefore it is a mild exaggeration to say that "a grade is a grade is a grade." But the adjusting process makes very little difference. We get essentially the same results when we use actual university-reported high school GPAs, which also take rigor into account to some degree by weighting honors courses more heavily (see Appendix Table 6.9c); in fact, the actual high school GPA results presented in this appendix table show even stronger effects of grades per se on graduation rates, presumably because the adjusted high school GPAs are measured with error.

16. A more rigorous way of answering the same basic question is (using the North Carolina data) to take account of interactions between high school grades and the academic level of the high school when predicting graduation rates. For both SEL As and SEL Bs in North Carolina, this approach yields results that are essentially the same as those shown by the more intuitive tabulations reported in Appendix Table 6.10 and described in the text. At the more selective SEL As, the slope of the relationship between high school grades and graduation rates is steeper for students from Level I high schools than for students from Level III high schools. This is not true, however, in the case of SEL Bs, where the slope is steeper among students from Level III high schools.

17. See, for example, D. J. Woodruff and R. L. Ziomek, "Differential Grading Standards among High Schools," ACT Research Report 2004-2, ACT, Iowa City, Iowa, 2004, and D. Bassiri and E. M. Schulz, "Constructing a Universal Scale of High School Course Difficulty," ACT Research Report 2003-4, ACT, Iowa City, Iowa, 2003.

18. Although the North Carolina data cover a broader population than just those students who attended the universities in our study, they do not include all high school seniors in the state because not all seniors take the SAT. An important question is whether we would obtain the same results if we looked at an unselected population of students. The state of Illinois requires that all high school graduates take the ACT, and Jesse Rothstein and his colleagues have rigorously looked at selection bias using these data. They find that there is indeed, as one would expect, positive selection bias in test participation both within and across schools. Despite this, they conclude that "school-level averages of observed scores are extremely highly correlated with average latent scores. . . . As a result, in most contexts the use of observed school mean test scores in place of latent means understates the degree of between-school variation in achievement but is otherwise unlikely to lead to misleading conclusions" (Melissa Clark, Diane Whitmore Schanzenbach, and Jesse Rothstein, "Selection Bias in College Admissions Test

Scores," NBER Working Paper 14265, National Bureau of Economic Research, Cambridge, Mass., August 2008, available at http://www.princeton.edu/~jrothst/published/crs_finalsubmit.pdf). Also reassuring is the fact that results based on data we have for four entire state systems are basically the same as the results we obtain for more limited populations.

19. A study by Allen and associates of the importance of "academic self-discipline" as a determinant of academic success comes to the same conclusion that we do; that study is based on a detailed study of students' personal behaviors (see J. Allen et al., "Third-Year College Retention and Transfer Effects of Academic Performance, Motivation, and Social Connectedness," *Research in Higher Education* 49 [2008]: 647–64). We are indebted to Ranjit Sidhu of ACT for directing us to this highly relevant piece of research, as well as to other studies conducted by ACT itself.

20. Recent work in California has attracted a great deal of attention and has provoked a spirited debate over both methods and findings. See Saul Geiser, "Back to the Basics: In Defense of Achievement (and Achievement Tests) in College Admissions," a paper prepared for the inaugural conference of the Center for Enrollment Research, Policy and Practice, August 2008, and subsequently published in *Change* (January–February 2009): 16–23, available at http://www.changemag.org/January-February%202009/full-back-to-basics.html. See also Saul Geiser and Roger Studley, "UC and the SAT: Predictive Validity and Differential Impact of the SAT I and SAT II at the University of California," Office of the President, University of California, Oakland, 2001, and S. Agronow and R. Studley, "Prediction of College GPA from New SAT Test Scores—A First Look," a paper presented at the annual meeting of the California Association for Institutional Research held in Monterey, California, on November 16, 2007, available at http://www.cair.org/conferences/CAIR2007/pres/Agronow.pdf. For discussions about the relationship between the SAT and SES in this context, see Rebecca Zwick and Jennifer Greif Green, "New Perspectives on the Correlation of SAT Scores, High School Grades, and Socioeconomic Factors," *Journal of Educational Measurement* 44 (2007): 23–45, and P. R. Sackett et al., "Does Socioeconomic Status Explain the Relationship between Admissions Tests and Post-secondary Academic Performance?" *Psychological Bulletin* 135 (2009): 1–22. Tempting as it is to plunge into this important discussion, we have made no independent investigation of the California data and do not know enough about the particular features of the California educational system to permit us to assess conflicting claims. Perusal of the references we have given should allow interested readers to come to their own conclusions.

For a summary of relevant studies by the College Board, see Krista D. Mattern et al., "Differential Validity and Prediction of the SAT," Research Report 2008-4, College Board, New York, October 2008, and Kobrin et al. For studies about using the ACT to predict readiness for college, see Jeff Allen and Jim Sconing, "Using ACT Assessment Scores to Set Benchmarks for College Readiness," ACT Research Report 2005-3, ACT, Iowa City, Iowa, 2005.

21. Roderick et al. (2006), especially pp. 68ff. Much of the "raw" relationship between graduation rates and both course rigor and test scores disappears after controlling for high school GPA. High school GPA, on the other hand, remains a powerful predictor of graduation rates after controlling for course rigor and test scores. See figure 3.3 on p. 69 of the report by Roderick et al.

22. We cannot present similar comparisons for the more selective universities because they admit very few students with high school GPAs below 3.0.

23. Roderick et al. (2006), p. 84.

24. The high school GPA coefficients for black men in Appendix Table 6.12 are especially interesting in that they are very much the same no matter which set of universities we look at. If black men with relatively low high school GPAs were doing particularly poorly at the most selective universities (where the competition is keener and there is, presumably, more risk of "mis-match"), we would expect to find larger high school GPA coefficients for them at, say, the SEL Is; in fact, the high school GPA coefficient for black men at the SEL Is is actually slightly lower than the high school GPA coefficients for black men at the less selective universities. One other interesting difference is that the high school GPA coefficients for students from the top quartile of the family income distribution are modestly larger at the less selective universities, which is consistent with our general impression that students from these families attending the less selective universities have surprisingly low graduation rates unless they have quite high high school GPAs (Appendix Table 6.13); we return to this question in Chapter 11. The reason for including Appendix Table 6.14, for all flagships taken together, is to give us enough observations for Hispanics to allow us to see if the coefficients for this important demographic group are noticably different from those for black students. They are not.

25. Lemann, pp. 66-67. The next quotation in this paragraph is from the same source.

26. The key statistician at ETS who worked on the Coleman Report (published in 1966), Alfred Beaton, was confident that northeastern Negroes would score higher than Southern whites on the basic ETS tests. This did not happen. According to Beaton, "The magnitude of the black/white difference and the uniformity over the country was mind-boggling. I can say it was a total surprise to me" (quotation in Lemann, p. 160, from Lemann's interview with Beaton). Lemann observes: "Because of how they had grown up, where they lived, and so on, Negroes as a group were in a uniquely bad position to perform well on tests designed to measure school-bred skills such as reading and vocabulary and mathematics." As Lemann points out, there was an inherent tension between the emerging meritocratic system and the cause of Negro advancement (p. 156).

27. We rely here on our North Carolina data because they are available for a large fraction of all high school seniors, regardless of where (or whether) they went to college. The students at our flagships, in particular, are too select a group to permit a proper assessment of these relationships.

28. Data from California also demonstrate that race and ethnicity are highly correlated with SAT scores in that state. Geiser (2009) reports: "When UC applicants were rank-ordered by SAT scores, roughly half as many Latino, African American and American Indian students appeared in the top third of the applicant pool than when the same students were ranked by high-school grades." The original study that produced these (and other) results is reported in Geiser and Santelices. Working with data for all California residents who applied to any of the University of California campuses for admission as regular freshmen for the 1993-94 academic year and seeking to predict first-year college GPA, Jesse Rothstein found that school-average SATs had considerable predictive power but that a substantial portion of the

predictive power of this measure derived from its association with the racial composition of high schools. He then observed: "One might conclude from [these findings] that colleges should give preferences to students from high-scoring schools." But, he added, "the predicted-performance-maximizing admissions rule amounts to affirmative action for socioeconomically advantaged students" (Rothstein, especially pp. 20–21). Along these same lines, there was an earlier report by Allan Nairn of ETS, published in 1980, in which, Lemann notes, "Nairn's central premise was that ETS, under a veneer of science, functioned as the opposite of a meritocratic force in American society. It provided an official way for people with money to pass on their status to their children" (Lemann, p. 227). In a chapter of his book on ETS, Nairn referred to "class in the guise of merit" (cited by Lemann, p. 271; the original source is Allan Nairn and Ralph Nader, *The Reign of ETS: The Corporation That Makes Up Minds* [Washington, D.C.: Ralph Nader, 1980]).

29. See Appendix Tables 6.1 and 6.2. See also the recent study by P. R. Sackett et al., pp. 1–22.

30. NACAC (2008), p. 39. This report also contains a long discussion of "uneven preparation for tests" ("coaching") and how it can give an advantage to students from families sufficiently affluent to afford test preparation. The report recommends further study of the extent to which coaching alters test scores (pp. 24ff).

31. Lemann, p. 39. In fact, 8 of the first 10 students chosen under Conant's new scholarship program, in part on the basis of test scores, were elected to Phi Beta Kappa. The Nobel laureate James Tobin was chosen two years later.

32. See, for example, College Board Research Reports 2008-4 (Mattern et al.) and 2008-5 (Kobrin et al.). The title of Research Report 2008-5 makes entirely clear the purpose to be served by this research program: "Validity of the SAT for Predicting First-Year College Grade Point Average." These two reports provide a careful explanation of the methodology used by the research scientists at the College Board, along with extended summaries of their findings. Other relevant work includes N. W. Burton and L. Ramist, "Predicting Success in College: SAT Studies of Classes Graduating since 1980," College Board Research Report 2001-2, College Board, New York, 2001; W. J. Camara and G. Echternacht, "The SAT I and High School Grades: Utility in Predicting Success in College," College Board Research Notes RN-10, College Board, New York, 2000; and W. J. Camara, "Score Trends, SAT Validity, and Subgroup Differences," paper presented at the Harvard Summer Institute, Boston, 2008.

33. We ran separate regressions for the overlapping set of students who took both the SAT and the ACT to see if there is any noticeable difference in the power of these two tests to predict rank-in-class. As in the case of graduation rates, the respective regression coefficients are strikingly similar.

34. In March 2005, the College Board introduced a revised ("new") SAT. The most notable change was the addition of a writing section (the SATW) that measures basic writing skills and includes a student-produced essay. The verbal section of the test was renamed the critical reading section; analogies were removed and replaced by questions on reading passages. The mathematics section was changed to include items from more advanced mathematics courses such as second-year algebra (see Kobrin et al., p. 1).

35. Kobrin et al., p. 6.

36. Christopher M. Cornwell, David B. Mustard, and Jessica Van Parys, "How Does the New SAT Predict Academic Achievement in College?" working paper, University of Georgia, Athens, last modified June 25, 2008, p. 11. The authors go on to say: "For example, one standard deviation in high school GPA corresponds to a 0.27-point higher first-year GPA, whereas a one standard deviation increase in the SATW score corresponds to a 0.05-point higher first-year GPA." The regressions used in this study include the same controls that we use: race/ethnicity, gender, parental education, and high school fixed effects.

37. Atkinson and Geiser (2009), p. 8.

38. In constructing our measure of SAT II test scores we simply averaged the scores on all tests taken by students who took at least one SAT II test (64 percent of students at the SEL Is and 49 percent at the SEL As). Too few students at the other flagships and at the state system SEL Bs and the HBCUs took these tests to permit us to carry out this analysis for students at these schools. Similarly, we averaged the AP test scores. This analysis of achievement test results includes all of the flagships except Rutgers and three of the four state systems with which we have worked. (The Ohio system, but not Ohio State, had to be excluded because of a lack of SAT II and AP scores.)

39. Additionally, AP scores are much less strongly correlated with SAT/ACT scores than are SAT II scores. The correlations between SAT/ACT scores and average AP scores are 0.58 at SEL Is, 0.53 at SEL IIs, 0.57 at SEL As, and 0.24 at SEL Bs.

40. An important caveat: it is scores earned on AP exams, not participation in AP courses, that predicts outcomes. Enrollment in AP courses per se is a poor predictor.

41. There has been a lively debate about the predictive power of SAT II scores versus regular SAT scores in California, which is the only state, to the best of our knowledge, that has required the SAT II for a long time. Geiser (2009) has argued in favor of the SAT II . Other scholars have criticized Geiser's work and, on the basis of a re-analysis of the same California data, have argued that the SAT I and the SAT II are very similar in predictive power (see R. Zwick, T. Brown, and J. C. Sklar, "California and the SAT: A Reanalysis of University of California Admissions Data," paper CSHE 8-04, Center for Studies in Higher Education, University of California–Berkeley, 2004). We should add that Geiser agrees with our conclusion that AP results are the best predictors of all of these tests.

42. Lemann, p. 38. In his memoirs, Conant also wrote, "Subject-matter examinations were of slight value. The aptitude, not the schooling, was what counted" (James B. Conant, *My Several Lives: Memoirs of a Social Inventor* [New York: Harper and Row, 1970], p. 424, as quoted in Eric Hoover, "Admissions Group Urges Colleges to 'Assume Control' of Debate on Testing," *Chronicle of Higher Education,* September 22, 2008, online edition).

43. Hispanic students, on the other hand, appear to make up about as high a percentage of AP test-takers as do high school students in general. See Steven Bushong, "Number of Students Doing Well on AP Tests Is Up, but Racial Gaps Persist," *Chronicle of Higher Education,* February 5, 2009, online edition, for a discussion of trends in AP test-taking. See also Tamar Lewin, "A.P. Program Is Growing, but Black Students Lag," *New York Times,* February 5, 2009, p. A19, for com-

ments by Gaston Caperton on the benefits of the AP tests in promoting speedy completion of degrees. We applaud the determined efforts of the College Board to expand the role of AP tests.

44. See N. R. Kuncel and S. A. Hezlett, "Standardized Tests Predict Graduate Student's Success," *Science* 315 (2007): 1080–81.

45. Richard C. Atkinson, "College Admissions and the SAT: A Personal Perspective," paper presented at the annual meeting of the American Educational Research Association, San Diego, California, April 14, 2004 (pp. 2–3), then published in *A Journal of the Association for Psychological Science Observer* 18 (2005). For a number of years Professor Michael Kirst at Stanford has also emphasized the importance of signaling and of aligning college admissions criteria with K–12 curricula. See, for example, Michael Kirst and Andrea Venezia, "Bridging the Great Divide between Secondary Schools and Postsecondary Education," *Phi Delta Kappan* 83, no. 1 (September 2001): 92–97.

46. Richard C. Atkinson and Saul Geiser, "Beyond the SAT," *Forbes*, August 13, 2008, online edition. Colleges and universities contemplating dropping requirements that applicants take the new SAT should carefully consider the benefit of the writing component—and not just to them but, through these signaling effects, to the educational system in general. It is also worth recalling that the AP English Language test has a writing component.

47. Geiser (2009).

48. The decision by the Board of Regents of the University of California to stop requiring SAT II tests (made at the time this book was in its near-final iteration) needs to be understood in the complex context of admissions policies at the University of California, where there is continuing concern about how to give more flexibility to local campuses. We are in no position to comment on the pros and cons of the overall set of new admissions policies recently announced (see Josh Keller and Eric Hoover, "U. of California to Adopt Sweeping Changes in Admissions Policy," *Chronicle of Higher Education,* February 5, 2009, online edition, and Scott Jaschik, "Unintentional Whitening of U. of California?" *Inside Higher Education,* February 5, 2009, online edition). These important changes in admissions policies have to be understood in the light of the implications for racial diversity of Proposition 209, which prohibited taking race into account in admissions to public institutions in California. Still, it would be unfortunate if this decision were interpreted nationally as a rejection of the value of content-based achievement tests. As the national data in this study show, such tests are valuable complements to high school grades.

Chapter 7   Transfer Students and the Path from Two-Year to Four-Year Colleges

1. Authors' calculations from the National Center for Education Statistics (NCES) *Digest of Education Statistics* 2007, table 189.

2. NCES *Digest of Education Statistics* 2007, table 321.

3. According to the 2004 National Postsecondary Student Aid Survey, the most recent edition of this NCES survey, among dependent students with family incomes below $40,000, the average tuition and fees at four-year public universi-

ties was $4,903, but net of grants it was $298. At public two-year colleges for the same income group, the average gross tuition and fees was $1,644 while the net was –$475 (i.e., grants were enough to pay all of students' tuition and part of their living costs on average). Thus, the gross difference was about $3,200, but the net difference was a little less than $800. Of course, students may not have been aware of these differences in grant aid, and community colleges may be closer and more convenient.

4. C. Lockwood Reynolds, "Where to Attend? Estimates of the Effects of Beginning at a Two-year College," mimeo, University of Michigan, Ann Arbor, October 25, 2006.

5. Some states, such as Maryland and California, have created programs specifically aimed at increasing the number of engineers, with an emphasis on recruiting members of underrepresented minority groups (Jeffrey Brainard, "Community Colleges Seen as Source of Engineers," *Chronicle of Higher Education,* October 10, 2008, online edition).

6. See program description at http://www.njstars.net/.

7. The transfer grants, which will first be made available to students in the fall 2007 entering cohort of freshmen if they transfer to a four-year college in fall 2009, are available only to students with a federally calculated expected family contribution of $8,000 or less. The standard award amount is $1,000 per year, with an additional $1,000 per year awarded to students enrolled in degree programs in engineering, mathematics, nursing, teaching, or science. In order to keep the award, students must earn at least a 3.0 GPA (State Council of Higher Education for Virginia, "Two-Year College Grant Transfer Program Fact Sheet," http://www.schev.edu/Students/factsheetTransferGrant.pdf, accessed November 17, 2008).

8. It is conceivable that this finding based on data from North Carolina would not hold up in other states. Specifically, it could be that the attainment gap between students who start at two- versus four-year institutions is smaller in states that have enacted policies to encourage transfers from two- to four-year colleges.

9. We also include students who did not answer that question or indicated that they were undecided about the highest level of education they planned to complete.

10. Specifically, from a probit model we estimate a propensity score as the predicted probability of starting at a two-year college based on the variables listed in the text. We drop students outside the region of common support; specifically, we drop two-year students with propensity scores greater than the maximum propensity score of the four-year students, and we drop four-year students with propensity scores lower than the minimum propensity score of the two-year students. Finally, we divide students into groups defined by the 10 deciles of the propensity score distribution of the remaining students.

11. Bachelor's degree attainment is calculated using the Clearinghouse degree data, which are not comprehensive in general but cover the vast majority (about 90 percent) of institutions attended by the 1999 North Carolina seniors.

12. Students who start at two- versus four-year colleges may still differ on their unobservable characteristics, which would bias these estimates. However, we believe it is extremely unlikely that such bias could explain all of the large negative effects that we find. Sensitivity analyses conducted by Reynolds in his study using

the NELS data support this proposition. Additionally, although an instrumental variables analysis conducted by Long and Kurlaender using data from Ohio produces a smaller (in magnitude) negative effect of starting at a two-year college on bachelor's degree attainment, it is still substantively and statistically significant— about 10 points on six-year graduation rates and 15 points on nine-year graduation rates (Bridget Terry Long and Michal Kurlaender, "Do Community Colleges Provide a Viable Pathway to a Baccalaureate Degree?" NBER Working Paper 14367, National Bureau of Economic Research, Cambridge, Mass., September 2008).

13. Among white students, 3,277 started at a two-year and 8,257 started at a four-year institution. Among black students, 623 started at a two-year college, 1,231 started at a PWI, and 2,013 started at an HBCU.

14. Long and Kurlaender.

15. These numbers combine white and black students in the North Carolina data and impose all of the same sample restrictions described earlier.

16. In order to identify and examine differences between transfers from two- and four-year institutions, we exclude from this analysis the five flagships and two state systems for which we lack sufficient data on the original institution attended. The excluded flagships are Pennsylvania State University, Purdue University, and the Universities of Michigan, Minnesota, and Washington. The excluded state systems are those of Ohio and Virginia.

17. We do not examine parental education due to a substantial amount of missing data for this variable among the transfer students.

18. Only a small part of this relationship is due to the presence of more low-income students at schools that take more two-year transfers. For example, at the flagships and state system SEL As, controlling for university attended reduces the difference between freshmen enrollees and two-year transfers in the percentage from the bottom income quartile only from 10 percentage points to 8 percentage points. Transfers from two-year colleges clearly come from lower-SES backgrounds relative to other students at the universities that they attend.

19. The average ages at graduation at the flagships and state system SEL As were 22.5 for freshmen enrollees, 23.4 for two-year transfers, and 23.1 for four-year transfers. At the state system SEL Bs, they were 22.5 for freshmen enrollees, 23.5 for two-year transfers, and 23.5 for four-year transfers.

20. Among four-year transfers, the pattern is similar at the state system SEL Bs but different at the flagships and state system SEL As, where the four-year transfers in each income quartile have graduation rates very similar to those of the freshmen enrollees.

21. When SAT/ACT scores are used instead of high school GPA, the results are similar (Appendix Table 7.4c).

22. Saul Geiser at the University of California has emphasized these points to us (in personal correspondence), and we independently had had the same thoughts. Having succeeded in the setting of a two-year college increases the odds that a student will succeed at a four-year institution, just as having done well in high school increases the odds that a student will do well in college (refer to Chapters 5 and 6).

23. The difference at the flagships and state system SEL As drops to 3 points if bachelor's degrees earned at subsequent institutions are counted.

24. The eight flagships for which transfer GPA data are available are: Iowa State University, the University of California–Berkeley and –Los Angeles, the University of Illinois at Urbana-Champaign, the University of North Carolina–Chapel Hill, and the Universities of Iowa, Maryland, and Oregon.

25. The corresponding differences are even larger at the state system SELBs.

26. California's master plan, adopted in 1960, aims to restrict eligibility for the University of California (UC) system to the top eighth of high school seniors and for the California State University (CSU) system to the top third.

27. Richard C. Atkinson and Saul Geiser, "UC Admissions, Proposition 209 and the California Master Plan," paper proposed for the conference Higher Education, Diversity and Access, UC–Berkeley, October 2006.

28. At these three universities, the graduation rate of four-year transfers is 93 percent, although these schools enroll only a small number of these students (3 percent compared to 17 percent two-year transfers and 81 percent freshmen).

29. Authors' calculations from the College Board's 2000–2001 Annual Survey of Colleges, which collected data describing the fall 1999 entering class. Institutions that did not provide transfer admissions data are excluded. Transfer admissions rates are also lower in California and Florida than in the rest of the nation: 63 percent in California, 70 percent in Florida, and 76 percent in the rest of the country.

30. To their credit, some community colleges have undertaken efforts to improve their retention rates, focusing on students "who couldn't have transferred or the ones for whom starting at a four-year institution wasn't an option," as one administrator put it (David Moltz, "Helping Community College Students Beat the Odds," *Inside Higher Education,* October 8, 2008, online edition).

Chapter 8   Financial Aid and Pricing on a National Level

1. See Bill and Melinda Gates, "A Bold Vision for Stimulus, Education Reform," *Roll Call,* February 10, 2009, online edition.

2. Throughout this chapter, we use the term "private institutions" to refer only to private non-profit institutions; for-profit institutions are largely outside the scope of this volume. Tuition and fees reflect the "direct costs" families pay for college, and these figures omit room and board and other costs such as those for books and transportation. These costs have risen in real terms, but at a considerably lower rate than those for tuition and fees. From an economic point of view, of course, living costs are not really costs of college (because one has to live anyway), but forgone earnings from being out of the full-time labor force are. Low-income students get, on average, enough grant aid to more than pay tuition and fees, providing some funding to offset living costs and other expenses. Many higher-income students and parents borrow to cover not only direct costs but living expenses as well.

3. See Thomas J. Kane and Peter R. Orszag, "Higher Education Spending: The Role of Medicaid and the Business Cycle," Brookings Institution Policy Brief 124, Brookings Institution, Washington, D.C., September 2003.

4. Because tax credits for college tuition are not received until the following year, when tax returns are filed, they do not directly improve students' immedi-

ate ability to pay. Furthermore, most low-income families benefit little from the program because (a) the credit can be applied only against a positive tax liability, (b) grants are offset against eligibility for the credit, and (c) the credit applies only to tuition rather than to the full cost of attendance.

5. Public universities generally need state legislative approval for any tuition increases, which are unsurprisingly unpopular among most legislators' constituencies. Many states also have merit scholarship programs for students who remain in state for college. Too often, funding for such programs is cut during economic downturns, times when families themselves can little afford to put more money toward college expenses (see Robert Tomsho, "States Weigh Cuts to Merit Scholarships," *Wall Street Journal,* January 13, 2009, online edition, which reports that at least five states are reconsidering their merit grant programs in response to the current recession). An example of this trend is the recent decision in New Jersey to make the state scholarship program (STARS) more selective, which will reduce the state's costs in the face of a budget shortfall but also redistribute aid to higher-income students, who tend to be more academically advantaged. This case displays the conflict in these scholarship programs between aiding those who need it and keeping "the best and the brightest" in the state (see David Moltz, "Cutting a Program—to Save It?" *Inside Higher Education,* December 18, 2008, online edition). After cuts to state financial aid, colleges are left to increase their institutional aid to financially struggling students, which can be heavily "front-loaded" on freshmen at the expense of older students (see Beckie Supiano, "Colleges Offer Extra Aid to Strapped Students," *Chronicle of Higher Education,* January 9, 2009, online edition).

6. In constant 2006 dollars, the median family income for families with a head aged 45 to 54 was $71,482 in 1986–87 and grew by only $1,400 in the ensuing 20 years (College Entrance Examination Board, *Trends in Student Aid,* Washington, D.C.: College Board, 2007). The National Center for Public Policy and Higher Education report "Measuring Up 2008" (National Center for Public Policy and Higher Education, San Jose, Calif., 2008) documents the same drop in college affordability; it calculates that the average net price at a public four-year insitution represented 55 percent of the average bottom-quintile family's yearly income in 2007.

7. See Appendix A of this volume. Historically, it has been difficult for students to borrow to finance education because, unlike investment in a physical asset, the value of a student's education cannot be posted as security for the loan. The classic argument for government intervention was made by Milton Friedman in a highly influential article from 1955 ("Economic Policy and Social Control: The Role of Government in Education," in *Economics and the Public Interest,* ed. R Solo [New Brunswick, N.J.: Rutgers University Press]).

8. In 1992 the federal government introduced an "unsubsidized" option for Stafford loans, available to all students (not just those who had financial need, a requirement under the subsidized program). Participation in this program has grown rapidly.

9. The Obama budget proposal is driven by the desire both to simplify the federal student loan system and to cut costs associated with subsidizing private lenders. Parents of students have been able to borrow for their children's college

education with a federal guarantee since 1980 under a program called Parent Loan for Undergraduate Students (PLUS).

10. Enrollment grew 23 percent between 1995–96 and 2005–06 (the latest years available), according to the NCES *Digest of Education Statistics,* available at http://nces.ed.gov/programs/digest/, accessed December 15, 2008.

11. College Entrance Examination Board, *Trends in Student Aid* (Washington, D.C.: College Board, 2008). The credit crisis that emerged in 2008 has raised significant doubts about the future of private lending to students by banks.

12. However, a recent change in the legislation has entirely severed the link between Pell awards and tuition levels. The gap between the cost of attending most colleges and the maximum award under this basic grant program has for some years been large enough that the cost of the college is no longer a significant factor in determining these awards.

13. Colleges' practices vary on these (sometimes consequential) details. Almost all colleges count a subsidized Stafford loan as part of the aid package. Some will also include unsubsidized loans or even private loans as "aid." Others will simply point out to parents that these borrowing options are available to families as one means of filling the gap between aid and the cost of attendance. These variations in practice are among the complexities that make it hard for families to get a clear picture of how to afford college.

14. These factors may not show up in something actually labeled a "merit award" but instead may simply be reflected in factors such as the relative amount of loan and grant included in an aid package (so-called preferential packaging).

15. In 2005–06, 86 percent of dependent students who received Pell Grants had family incomes under $40,000 per year (College Board 2008b).

16. Since the early 1990s, a number of states, concentrated for the most part in the South, have introduced broad-based "merit" grant programs aiming at students who remain in state for college. These programs have generous (or in some cases no) income limits and provide grants to all students who meet established grade-point or test-score standards. Studies of the effect of these programs are discussed later in this chapter.

17. Two important studies report no significant impact of the Pell Grant program on the college entry of low-income students: Lee W. Hansen, "The Impact of Student Financial Aid on Access," in *The Crisis in Higher Education,* ed. Joseph Froomkin, 84–96 (New York: Academy of Political Science, 1983), and Thomas J. Kane, "Rising Public College Tuition and College Entry: How Well Do Public Subsidies Promote Access to College?" NBER Working Paper, National Bureau of Economic Research, Cambridge, Mass., July 1995. However, Neil Seftor and Sarah Turner found significant effects of the Pell program on the enrollment of adult students in "Back to School: Federal Student Aid Policy and Adult College Enrollment," *Journal of Human Resources* 37, no. 2 (Spring 2002): 336–52.

18. Many students in these programs do not meet the college GPA requirement to maintain the scholarship (especially in Georgia, whose 3.0 GPA requirement is more restrictive than other programs), and this presumably attenuates the effect on persistence. Judith Scott-Clayton studies West Virginia's scholarship program, finding comparable effects on bachelor's degree attainment. She also finds that the unique incentive structure of the West Virginia scholarship

(which required a heavier course load than other similar state scholarships) had an important effect on time-to-degree ("On Money and Motivation: A Quasi-Experimental Analysis of Financial Incentives for College Achievement," draft, National Bureau of Economic Research, Cambridge, Mass., October 29, 2008, available at http://www.nber.org/~confer/2008/HIEDf08/scott-clayton.pdf, accessed December 15, 2008).

19. Susan Dynarski, "Building the Stock of College-Educated Labor," *Journal of Human Resources* 43, no. 3 (Summer 2007): 576–610; quote on p. 579.

20. Other examples of reliable studies include papers by Tom Kane examining, in one case, the impact of a program in the District of Columbia that permitted all D.C. students to qualify for in-state tuition at any public university in the country ("Evaluating the Impact of the D.C. Tuition Assistance Grant Program," NBER Working Paper 10658, National Bureau of Economic Research, Cambridge, Mass., July 2004), and, in another, the effect of a rule in the California state scholarship program that caused students who differed only very slightly in ability to pay to receive significantly different awards of aid ("A Quasi-Experimental Estimate of the Impact of Financial Aid on College-Going," NBER Working Paper 9703, National Bureau of Economic Research, Cambridge, Mass., May 2003).

21. For a useful survey of evidence about the effect of grants on college-going, with thoughtful attention to arguments for believing that simplicity and information are key, see David Mundel, "What Do We Know about the Impact of Grants to College Students?" in *The Effectiveness of Student Aid Policies: What the Research Tells Us,* ed. Sandy Baum, Michael S. McPherson, and Patricia Steele, 9–37 (Washington, D.C.: College Board, 2008).

22. Eric Bettinger, "How Financial Aid Affects Persistence," in *College Choices: The Economics of Where to Go, When to Go, and How to Pay for It,* ed. Caroline M. Hoxby, 207–38 (Chicago: University of Chicago Press, 2004).

23. Joshua Angrist, Daniel Lang, and Philip Oreopoulos, "Incentives and Services for College Achievement: Evidence from a Randomized Trial," Report IZA DP 3134, Institute for the Study of Labor, Bonn, October 2007.

24. For an apt summary of these findings, see David Deming and Susan Dynarski, "Interventions to Reduce College Costs," preliminary draft, in *Targeting Investment in Children: Fighting Poverty When Resources Are Limited,* ed. Philip Levine and David Zimmerman (Chicago: University of Chicago Press, forthcoming).

25. An overview of the proposed budget for the Department of Education, including these changes to the Pell Grant program, is available online at http://www.whitehouse.gov/omb/assets/fy2010_new_era/Department_of_Eduction.pdf, accessed March 9, 2009.

26. Carneiro and Heckman, cited earlier.

27. Ralph Stinebrickner and Todd R. Stinebrickner, "The Effect of Credit Constraints on the College Drop-Out Decision: A Direct Approach Using a New Panel Study," NBER Working Paper 13340, National Bureau of Economic Research, Cambridge, Mass., August 2007.

28. Thomas J. Kane, "College-Going and Inequality," in *Social Inequality,* ed. Kathryn M. Neckerman, 319–54 (New York: Russell Sage Foundation, 2004).

29. Lance J. Lochner and Alexander Monge-Naranjo, "The Nature of Credit Constraints and Human Capital," NBER Working Paper 13912, National Bureau of Economic Research, Cambridge, Mass., April 2008.

30. It is hard to get reliable information about the consequences of different choices families make about borrowing from most available data sets (including ours), in part because it is so difficult to have a complete picture of a family's financial situation. Among students who look similar in observable ways, one may borrow little because of "loan aversion," while another may simply have a generous grandmother. The Stinebrickners' studies at Berea College are promising from this point of view because they have remarkably detailed data about students' circumstances and choices, albeit at a rather unrepresentative institution.

31. Empirical evidence on the importance of loan aversion is sorely lacking. A recent unpublished survey paper by Bridget Terry Long ("The Effectiveness of Financial Aid in Improving College Enrollment: Lessons for Policy," draft, Harvard Graduate School of Education, National Bureau of Economic Research, and National Center for Postsecondary Research, Cambridge, Mass., January 2008) concluded that the evidence is "completely unclear."

32. Two papers provide credible evidence that term-time employment lowers college students' GPA: Ralph Stinebrickner and Todd R. Stinebrickner, "Working during School and Academic Performance," *Journal of Labor Economics* 21, no. 2 (April 2003): 473–91, and Jeffrey S. DeSimone, "The Impact of Employment during School on College Student Academic Performance," NBER Working Paper 14006, National Bureau of Economic Research, Cambridge, Mass., May 2008. Robert Bozick ties excessive student employment (and living with parents, another strategy for avoiding debt) to higher first-year drop-out rates ("Making It Through the First Year of College: The Role of Students' Economic Resources, Employment, and Living Arrangements," *Sociology of Education* 80, no. 3 [July 2007]: 261–84).

33. Leonhardt (2009a), p. 50.

34. Judith Scott-Clayton, "What Explains Rising Labor Supply among U.S. Undergraduates, 1970–2003?" draft, John F. Kennedy School of Government, Harvard University, Cambridge, Mass., November 8, 2007.

35. A wide array of examples is offered in Richard Thaler and Cass Sustein, *Nudge: Improving Decisions about Health, Wealth, and Happiness* (New Haven, Conn.: Yale University Press, 2008).

36. This proposed Access and Completion Incentive Fund would support the states in implementing, evaluating, and bringing to scale experimental programs aimed at increasing degree attainment rates. An overview of the proposed budget for the Department of Education is available at http://www.whitehouse.gov/omb/assets/fy2010_new_era/Department_of_Eduction.pdf, accessed March 9, 2009.

Chapter 9   Financial Aid at Public Universities

1. These other subgroups of students are of course important in their own right, and they deserve further attention in future work with these data. More detail on the sample restrictions for the various analyses in this chapter can be found in Appendix D.

2. The five flagships that are not included due to missing data on grants awarded in 1999–2000 are: Rutgers, the University of California–Berkeley, the University of Texas–Austin, and the Universities of Michigan and Washington.

3. A widely used federal data set, the National Postsecondary Student Aid Study (NPSAS), calculates net price differently. We subtract each student's total grant aid from his or her university's sticker price and present the average of each individual's net price, which may be negative. NPSAS calculates tuition minus grant aid for each student and sets the net price to zero for those whose grant aid exceeds their tuition before calculating the average. Thus, by definition, their reported net price can never be negative.

4. The average tuition is slightly different for students in different income groups because they are distributed differently across the institutions.

5. The differential in grant aid and in net price between whites on one hand and blacks and Hispanics on the other is present (although somewhat smaller) at higher income levels as well, but it makes much less difference in the average grant aid and net price because relatively few black and Hispanic students come from those higher income groups.

6. The "private loan" market—loans provided to students for college expenses without federal guarantees—has grown up for the most part since the time of the cohort in this study. Although private loans now amount to more than 20 percent of borrowing for college (see College Board 2008b), they represent less than 3 percent of loan value in our study. The 2008 financial crisis has cast doubt on the future of the private loan market.

7. Remember that some of this borrowing, particularly in the higher income groups, is by parents. As colleagues at Ohio State University noted when we visited there, one factor in explaining the lower amounts borrowed by lower-income students is that Pell Grants are available to them.

8. We focus on Virginia because, among the four states for which we have data on the public higher education system as a whole, Virginia's reporting on loan data is most consistent with the measures we have for the flagship/SEL A institutions. See Appendix D for further information.

9. One way that students may "fill" part of the gap is by living more cheaply than colleges estimate that they will (although the estimates provided by colleges are pretty "bare bones").

10. Remember that this gap we are examining is *not* "unmet need," which is a calculation based on an estimate by a financial aid officer, guided by a federally legislated formula, of what a particular family can afford to pay. "Unmet need" describes the size of any gap remaining after these family resources have been added in. We have reliable information on the "expected family contribution" (EFC) from only some of our institutions, and this information is necessarily restricted to those students who applied for aid. Therefore, we have not relied on it for the bulk of our analysis. However, we report some evidence based on that sub-set of students later in this chapter.

11. See Scott-Clayton (2007). As noted in Chapter 8, Scott-Clayton documents the trend of greater labor supply among U.S. university students and argues that "fuzzy" credit constraints, which are more often binding among low-income students, are driving this trend.

12. See Chapter 8, note 33.

13. When students are assigned a job as part of their financial aid package—so-called college work study—we have this information for some universities. But this work probably represents only a fraction (often a small fraction) of work hours even for those students, and it altogether misses the many students who work off-campus on jobs they find for themselves. According to anecdotal evidence, such off-campus work is sometimes quite time-consuming and affects both time-to-degree and completion rates.

14. The seven flagships included in this part of the analysis are: Iowa State, Ohio State and Stony Brook Universities, and the Universities of Florida, Iowa, Maryland, and Oregon.

15. Parents can borrow up to the full cost of attendance (including non-tuition costs), less other sources of aid their student has received.

16. College Board (2008b).

17. See Appendix Table 8.1.

18. The 11 flagship universities included in this part of the analysis are Iowa State, Ohio State, and Stony Brook Universities; the University of California–Los Angeles; and the Universities of Florida, Illinois, Iowa, Maryland, Minnesota, Nebraska, and Oregon.

19. Because these are all students who completed the Free Application for Federal Student Aid (FAFSA), we are able to learn the value of their EFC, which is a more complete estimate of their family financial circumstances than income alone provides. We therefore grouped these quartiles around the average value of the EFC for each student over the four-year period we examine.

20. However, anyone applying for an unsubsidized Stafford loan has to fill out the federal financial aid form, even though the student does not have to show need in order to get the loan. As Figure 9.9a shows, 17 percent of top-quartile students received this type of loan.

21. The maximum amount that students are allowed to borrow with federal support is lower in the first year of enrollment than in later years, and we suspect that a substantial portion of the increase in borrowing reflects students' increasing their loans in response to a higher ceiling.

22. Bottom-quartile students experienced a similar drop in outside awards, but in their case it was largely made up by a large increase in state grant awards, which go to a larger share of low-income students than of other students.

23. A November 2008 *New York Times* article reports on an "astonishing" decline in state revenues in California that is "without modern precedent here" and notes that change is equally dramatic in other states (Jennifer Steinhauer, "Facing Deficits, States Get Out Sharper Knives," *New York Times,* November 16, 2008, online edition). See also Josh Keller, "Cal State Campuses Are Forced to Reject Thousands," *Chronicle of Higher Education,* April 10, 2009, online edition, and Eric Bailey and Patrick McGreevy, "Poor Would Be Hard Hit by Proposed California Budget Cuts," *Los Angeles Times,* May 22, 2009, online edition. For the effect of similar budget cuts in Florida, see Paul Fain, "Budget Cuts Cast Shadow over Florida's Universities," *Chronicle of Higher Education,* May 29, 2009, online edition.

24. A qualification to this generalization is that some states offer "reciprocity" agreements with their surrounding states; in the Midwest, for example, students

residing in Wisconsin, Iowa, and Minnesota receive in-state tuition at public universities in any of the three states. Other reciprocity agreements may provide a price intermediate between the in-state and out-of-state tuition.

25. Our ability to hold "other things equal" in this analysis is far from perfect. These flagships differ from one another in a variety of ways, and ideally we would control for those differences in this analysis—but we cannot do this because of limitations in our data and in sample size. We are operating on the assumption that other differences across these institutions are largely uncorrelated with the pricing policy differences we focus on. Thus we cannot, for example, reject the hypothesis that institutions that provide more aid to low-income students also provide better opportunities to students in other ways, perhaps simply because they have more resources at their disposal. An illustration of the difficulty of establishing unambiguous evidence of causal effects in these data is that we find that flagship universities that provide more grant aid to low-income students have higher graduation rates not only for low-income students (as would be expected) but also for higher-income students, which suggests that the causal factors at work in this relationship go beyond simply the effect of providing more grant aid to highly needy students

26. The three universities that are excluded due to missing data on net price are: the University of California–Berkeley, the University of Texas–Austin, and the University of Washington.

27. See Sandy Baum, Michael McPherson, and Patricia Steele, *The Effectiveness of Student Aid Policies: What the Research Tells Us* (Washington, D.C.: College Board, 2008). Susan Dynarski's studies of the Georgia HOPE Scholarship program and of the Social Security Survivors' Benefits program, described in the previous chapter, provide quasi-experimental evidence on this point.

28. See Chapter 8, note 5, for some examples of how states and institutions are responding to the current recession.

29. The official Web site has further program details: www.unc.edu/carolina covenant, accessed December 23, 2008.

30. Serious efforts are under way to assess the effectiveness of the North Carolina and Virginia programs, but the programs are too new for their effect on graduation rates to be judged. Early results from an ongoing evaluation of the Covenant program in North Carolina indicate that Covenant Scholars are substantially less likely to temporarily stop out of college, more likely to persist into their fourth year of college, and more likely to graduate on time than similar students who enrolled in the year before the Covenant went into effect. These are significant findings in a field where reliable results are hard to come by.

31. College Board (2008b).

32. How institutions treat transfer students provides additional evidence on this point. We estimate that freshmen at flagship/SEL A institutions are given about $500 more in merit-based grant aid than observationally similar transfer students, suggesting active recruitment among these more selective universities for first-time students. That differential is only $200 at SEL Bs.

33. Shirley A. Ort, "The Impact of Tuition and Student Aid on College Access, Affordability and Success: A Practitioner's View," paper presented at the inaugural conference of the Center for Enrollment Research, Policy, and Practice, Uni-

versity of Southern California, Los Angeles, August 2008 (updated September 4, 2008).

Chapter 10   Institutional Selectivity and Institutional Effects

1. The relationship between institutional selectivity and four-year graduation rates is essentially the same. When we add four-year graduation rates to Figure 10.1 (not shown), the linear regression lines are parallel.

2. More specifically, we standardize the average high school GPAs and SAT/ACT scores (calculated from the student-level data) of the 57 public universities in our study so that each has a mean of zero and a standard deviation of one. We then average these two standardized measures to arrive at the combined selectivity index, which has a mean of zero and a standard deviation of one.

3. We first estimate institutional coefficients, which are marginal effects calculated from probit regressions of graduation status on institutional dummies and the control variables, holding the control variables at their mean values. We examine the two sets of institutions (flagships and SEL As versus SEL Bs) separately so that we are not making extreme comparisons (e.g., between a student at Berkeley and an "observationally equivalent" student at one of the least selective state system SEL Bs). We then calculate the adjusted graduation rates as the coefficient plus the unadjusted graduation rate at the university with the highest unadjusted graduation rate. Thus, the unadjusted and adjusted rates are the same by construction at the university with the highest unadjusted graduation rate.

4. When we add adjusted four-year graduation rates to Figures 10.3a and 10.3b (not shown), we find that the linear regression line is steeper for the four-year rates than for the six-year rates at the flagships and the state system SEL As. The lines are essentially parallel at the state system SEL Bs.

5. We acknowledge that some of these institutional differences likely reflect "selection on unobservables" that results from both institutional admissions decisions and students' decisions about where to go to college. However, we think it is highly unlikely that such selection bias explains more than a modest part of the substantial adjusted differences in graduation rates between institutions. Stacy Berg Dale and Alan Krueger, in their 2002 study "Estimating the Payoff to Attending a More Selective College: An Application of Selection on Observables and Unobservables" (*Quarterly Journal of Economics* 117, no. 4 [November]: 1491–1527), found that selection on unobservable characteristics explained the entire relationship between earnings and the average SAT score of the college attended. However, their findings are not relevant to our work because of the highly selective nature of the colleges and universities in the data they used compared to the far wider array of institutions included in our public university data. For example, two of the least selective universities in the Dale and Krueger study are the University of North Carolina–Chapel Hill and the University of Michigan–Ann Arbor, which are two of the most selective universities in our data. Anecdotal evidence suggests that, outside of the most selective private and public universities, admissions decisions are based largely on observables such as SAT and ACT scores and high school GPA; at places such as the state system SEL Bs that we study, selection on unobservables is unlikely to be important. Consequently, the fact that

the selectivity-graduation relationship holds for both less selective and more selective public institutions gives us added confidence in asserting that institutional selectivity per se (and the institutional characteristics that it reflects) has an independent impact on graduation rates.

6. Scott Jaschik, "Challenging the Measures of Success," *Inside Higher Education,* June 6, 2007, online edition.

7. It is possible that the less selective institutions would receive an additional "boost" to their graduation rates from rejecting applicants with weak academic credentials due to the resulting increase in their overall selectivity (average high school GPA and SAT scores), which we find is positively associated with adjusted graduation rates (Figures 10.3a and 10.3b). There is no way that we can estimate the magnitude of any such effect, but we are highly skeptical that taking into account such a change in the peer group would alter our main conclusion—to wit, that the "dipping-too-low" hypothesis explains only a small part of low graduation rates at less selective universities. It should not be used as an excuse for institutions to overlook low graduation rates among students with good credentials.

8. In Appendix Table 10.1b we examine the on-campus variable separately because it is missing for a handful of universities.

9. The institutions excluded due to missing data on whether students lived in a residence hall are: the University of California–Berkeley and –Los Angeles, the University of Maryland–Baltimore County, the University of Mary Washington, Miami University of Ohio, the University of Texas–Austin, and the Universities of Florida, Minnesota, Nebraska, Oregon, and Washington, as well as all state system SEL Bs in Maryland and Ohio.

10. We might have expected the on- versus off-campus differences to be larger for four-year graduation rates, but that is not the case (Appendix Table 10.1c).

11. At the 18 flagships and state system SEL As that we could include in this analysis, the coefficients on selectivity (in standard deviation units) and percentage living on campus (in units of 10 percentage points) are 0.067 and 0.038, respectively. Both are statistically significant from zero. At the 15 state system SEL Bs, the coefficients are 0.049 and 0.013, both of which are imprecisely estimated and consequently not statistically significant.

12. This finding is consistent with other research on this question. Astin explains how residence on campus leads to a greater sense of connectedness to one's own educational institution. This is the case because "students who live in residence halls have more time and opportunity to get involved in all aspects of campus life. . . . Residential students have a better chance than do commuter students of developing a strong identification and attachment to undergraduate life" (Alexander W. Astin, "Student Involvement: A Developmental Theory for Higher Education" *Journal of College Student Personnel* 25, no. 4 [July 1984]: 297–308; quote on p. 523). Such integration in turn allows a student to develop greater "institutional commitment," which lowers the probability that the student will drop out of the institution (Vincent Tinto, "Dropout from Higher Education: A Theoretical Synthesis of Recent Research," *Review of Educational Research* 45, no. 1 [Winter 1975]: 89–125; quote on p. 93).

13. Adjunct faculty also play an important role at many colleges and universities. In a recent study, Audrey J. Jaeger and M. Kevin Eagan Jr. found that stu-

dents at community colleges who took more courses with part-time faculty were less likely to transfer to a four-year institution (see A. J. Jaeger and K. Eagan, "Developing Emotional Intelligence as a Means to Enhance Academic Performance," *NASPA Journal* 44, no. 4 [2007]: 512–37, and A. J. Jaeger, K. Eagan, and L. G. Wirt, "Retaining Students in Science, Math, and Engineering Majors: Rediscovering Cooperative Education," *Journal of Cooperative Education and Internships* 42, no. 1 [2008]: 20–32). In an earlier study, the same authors found that first-year students at public four-year universities who were taught "gatekeeper" courses by part-time adjuncts, lecturers, or postdoctoral fellows were less likely to persist to their sophomore years (Peter Schmidt, "Studies Link Use of Part-Time Instructors to Lower Student Success," *Chronicle of Higher Education*, November 6, 2008, online edition).

14. William G. Bowen, Martin A. Kurzweil, and Eugene M. Tobin, in collaboration with Susanne C. Pichler, *Equity and Excellence in American Higher Education* (Charlottesville, Va.: University of Virginia Press, 2005).

15. We examine only the SEL I flagships because no other public universities had values of the selectivity index that were roughly comparable to those of the private institutions. The Ivy League Universities are Columbia, Dartmouth, Harvard, the University of Pennsylvania, Princeton, and Yale. The liberal arts colleges are Barnard, Bates, Bowdoin, Bryant, Carleton, Colby, Hamilton, Kenyon, Macalaster, Middlebury, Oberlin, Pomona, Smith, Swarthmore, Wellesley, Wesleyan, and Williams.

16. We are not able to control for high school GPA because it is unavailable for the private institutions.

17. The private institutions are classified into the same SEL groupings as the public institutions, using an average SAT cut-off of 1150. The Virginia SEL A private universities are the University of Richmond and Washington and Lee University. The Virginia private SEL Bs are Bridgewater College, Eastern Mennonite University, Ferrum College, Hollins University, Lynchburg College, Mary Baldwin College, Marymount University, Roanoke College, Shenandoah University, and Virginia Wesleyan College. The Virginia public institutions are listed in Table 1.2.

18. Tuition data are from the College Board.

19. Although the difference in sticker price is large, the difference in net tuition (sticker price minus financial aid) may be smaller, especially if institutions use merit aid to recruit academically able students from inside or outside Virginia.

20. The in-state versus out-of-state six-year graduation rates are 85 percent versus 82 percent at SEL A public, 87 percent versus 86 percent at SEL A private, 57 percent versus 53 percent at SEL B public, and 54 percent versus 53 percent at SEL B private institutions.

21. The 11 flagships included in this part of the analysis are: Ohio State and Stony Brook Universities, the University of California–Los Angeles, the University of Illinois at Urbana-Champaign, the University of North Carolina–Chapel Hill, the University of Texas–Austin, and the Universities of Iowa, Michigan, Nebraska, Oregon, and Virginia.

22. Variables taken into account in the propensity score analysis include SAT scores, adjusted high school GPA, gender, family income, parental education, and educational aspirations as reported on the SAT survey.

Chapter 11   Target Populations

1. As one reader pointed out, this discussion resonates with the themes in *Equity and Excellence in Higher Education* (Bowen, Kurzweil, and Tobin) as well as *The Shape of the River* (Bowen and Bok). The main difference is that in this book we have far more evidence concerning educational outcomes for all of these disadvantaged groups within the public sector of higher education.

2. Our decision to focus this discussion on black *men* is a direct reflection of the outcomes reported in this and other studies. Black women have somewhat lower graduation rates than white women (see Figures 3.12a and 3.12c), but these differences are much smaller than the differences between black men and white men. Thus, desirable as it would be to improve graduation rates for black women—and for students generally—by far the most pronounced race-gender disparity in outcomes is the low graduation rate of black men.

As we will indicate shortly, Hispanic men also graduate at relatively low rates. However, the limitations of our data prevent us from saying as much about them as a group as we can say about black men. In their *Advancing in Higher Education: A Portrait of Latina/o College Freshmen at Four-Year Institutions, 1975–2006* (Los Angeles: Higher Education Research Institute, 2008), Sylvia Hurtado and her colleagues at UCLA use their extensive data on entering freshmen from the Cooperative Institutional Research Program to demonstrate that the ratio of Hispanic men to Hispanic women among college freshmen has declined dramatically in recent years—from a high of 57.4 percent in 1975 to a low of 39.2 percent in 2006. The enrolled Hispanic population looks more and more like the enrolled black population in terms of the gender ratio.

3. Shaun R. Harper, "Black Male Students at Public Flagship Universities in the U.S.: Status, Trends, and Implications for Policy and Practice," Joint Center for Political and Economic Studies Health Policy Institute, Washington, D.C., 2006, p. 11. Harper also emphasizes the importance of looking separately at outcomes for black men and black women, and he is critical of the fact that in most research "black students have long been treated as a monolithic group" (Ibid., p. 1). According to Harper, data from the National Survey of Student Engagement (NSSE) show that black students were the group least satisfied with their college experiences (Harper, p. 1 and n. 6). See NSSE, "Exploring Different Dimensions of Student Engagement: 2005 Annual Survey Results," NSSE, Center for Post-secondary Research, Indiana University, Bloomington, 2005, especially p. 12. Harper also cites Michael J. Cuyjet's edited volume *African American Men in College* (San Francisco: Jossey-Bass, 2006) as a useful summary of a variety of support programs found to have been effective in retaining black male students (Harper, p. 11).

4. Michael A. Fletcher, "At the Corner of Progress and Peril," *Washington Post,* June 2, 2006, p. A01.

5. In their book *Come on People: On the Path from Victims to Victors* (Nashville, Tenn.: Thomas Nelson, 2007), Bill Cosby and Alvin Poussaint focus on family structures and parenting patterns. They argue: "A house without a father is a challenge. A neighborhood without fathers is a catastrophe. . . . A mother can usually teach a daughter how to be a woman. But as much as mothers love their sons, they have dif-

ficulty showing a son how to be a man" (pp. 3–4). They argue for a new model of fatherhood in which fathers would play a greater role in child rearing, and they also discuss the role of communities, the effects of trends in job markets, and many other factors. For a critical assessment of the Cosby-Poussaint book, see Ta-Nehisi Coates, "This Is How We Lost to the White Man," *Atlantic Monthly,* May 2008, online edition. Coates puts much more emphasis on environmental factors and public policies, as does Margaret C. Simms in her introduction to the Joint Center study by Shaun Harper cited earlier. For a discussion of the dynamics of black neighborhoods, see Frank F. Furstenberg Jr. et al., *Managing to Make It: Urban Families and Adolescent Success* (Chicago: University of Chicago Press, 1999), the work of Elijah Anderson on urban ethnography, and Kathy Edin's differences with Anderson on the attitudes and priorities of black women and black men (summarized in Julia M. Klein, "Man on the Street: How a Sharecropper's Son Deciphered the Code of the City," *Yale Alumni Magazine,* January–February 2008, online edition).

In an effort to examine the "family structure" aspect of this discussion, we obtained from the Higher Education Research Institute at UCLA a special set of tabulations comparing the family structures of black males attending a highly selective sub-set of our flagships (UCLA, UNC–Chapel Hill, and the University of Michigan) with black males at a less selective sub-set (the University of Iowa, Ohio State University, and Stony Brook University). The measure of family structure we use is the percentage of entering black male freshmen who come from "intact" families—with "intact" defined as both parents alive and living with each other. Relatively more black men at the highly selective sub-set come from intact families (just under 60 percent) compared to men at the less selective public universities (just under 50 percent). The data also indicate that the fraction of black male students from intact families has been quite constant since 1986 (when the question about family structures was first asked), but there has been some modest decline at the highly selective sub-set (from just over 60 percent in the late 1980s to roughly 55 percent in recent years). We do not have the data for earlier years that would be needed to test the Cosby-Poussaint hypothesis that there was a "seismic" shift in black family structures sometime in the 1960s. Nor do the data available permit us to test the proposition that the difference in black family structures between the more and less selective universities (which correlates with parental education and other factors) is big enough to have had an independent impact on graduation rates.

The family structures of white men are very different: in general, about 80 percent of white men come from intact families. Hispanic men are an in-between case: about 70 percent of those at the more selective universities come from intact families, as do about 60 percent at the less selective universities. The fraction of Hispanic male students from intact families at the less selective universities declined between the mid-1980s and the mid-1990s.

6. See Bowen and Bok, pp. xxxi–xxxii in the introduction to the paperback edition and pp. 59–65 in both the paperback and the original hard-cover edition.

7. In the corresponding analysis in *The Shape of the River,* black men were grouped by composite SAT scores due to the absence of data on high school grades. Our analysis in Chapter 6 of this book shows that high school GPAs are

far stronger predictors of graduation rates than are SAT scores. Nonetheless, we performed the same analysis using composite SAT score groups at the public universities and got very similar results.

8. Of course, we do not intend to suggest that the same result would have been obtained if the most selective universities had admitted random samples of students with high school GPAs below 3.0. Admissions staffs presumably selected students with high school GPAs below 3.0 whom they regarded as the most suitable candidates (but not always for strictly academic reasons, because there were surely some number of recruited athletes within this group!). Similarly, students were selecting universities at the same time that universities were selecting students, and it is entirely possible that black men with modest high school GPAs who opted to attend the more selective universities had above-average degrees of motivation and confidence in their ability to survive in competitive environments. Needless to say, the presence of these selection effects does not alter the fact that those black students with below-average high school GPAs who were selected (or who selected themselves) to attend the most selective universities graduated at high rates. It is possible, however, that some of these students who went to the SEL Is would have fared better at the less selective universities than did students with comparable credentials who actually went to the SEL IIIs and state system SEL Bs—which would mean that the "true" advantage of going to the SEL Is may be somewhat overstated by our inability to take account of such selection effects. But it seems highly improbable that "selection-on-unobservables" could have been anything like strong enough to switch the sign of the strong "net" relationship between selectivity and graduation rates that we report in the next paragraph.

9. This proposition holds regardless of race. We have presented here only data for black men in the interest of simplicity and in an effort to maintain our focus on this targeted group. We should add that the College and Beyond database on which the findings in *The Shape of the River* are based includes data on a number of other outcomes, including enrollment in graduate programs, later-life earnings, and satisfaction with one's undergraduate program of study. Looking at these outcomes only reinforces the basic conclusion stated here, namely, that students at the more selective universities did better on essentially all measures. As discussed in Chapter 10, these "institutional effects" could well be due to a number of factors, including the resources of the university in question, peer-group effects, and expectations. In general, the more selective universities are of course also the wealthier ones, and it would be disappointing indeed—and an indictment of how resources were being used—if students attending these privileged institutions did not have generally good outcomes.

10. Roderick et al. (2006), p. 74.

11. For a good discussion of these and other initiatives, see Schmidt (2008c). Shaun Harper, who is doing research on black men who are faring well in college, is quoted in this same story as noting that "there is no one pathway to success." Kevin Carey provides an excellent discussion of the CARE (Center for Academic Retention and Enhancement) program at Florida State University in his Education Sector report: "Graduation Rate Watch: Making Minority Student Success a Priority," Education Sector, Washington, D.C., April 2008, especially pp. 4–6.

12. See Carey, p. 4. Our more detailed tabulations of the Graduation Rate Survey data obtained from the National Center for Education Statistics show that many of the universities on Carey's list enroll more black women than black men and that the closing of the racial gap in graduation rates at many (though certainly not all) of these universities is due to the high graduation rates for black women. In the case of Maryland, recent data indicate that the graduation rate gap between black and white students has increased in spite of strong efforts to close it. There are not enough data, however, for us to know the reasons for this troubling development (see Stephen Kiehl, "Black Graduation Gap Grows at Maryland Universities," *Baltimore Sun,* March 11, 2009, online edition.

13. George D. Kuh, "High-Impact Educational Practices: What They Are, Who Has Access to Them, and Why They Matter," Association of American Colleges and Universities, Washington, D.C., 2008, especially pp. 17, 19.

14. Instituted in 1989 and now open to all students, the Meyerhoff Program still focuses on "producing high-achieving minority students in mathematics and science." See Freeman A. Hrabowski III, "The Meyerhoff Scholars Program: Producing High-Achieving Minority Students in Mathematics and Science," *Notices of the AMS* 48, no. 1 (January 2001): 26–28; and Freeman A. Hrabowski III, "The Access Imperative: The Robert H. Atwell Lecture," paper presented at the 89th annual meeting of the American Council on Education, Washington, D.C., February 11, 2007.

15. Data provided by Dr. Hrabowski in personal correspondence, December 22, 2008.

16. The "raw" coefficient in a regression predicting six-year graduation rates at UM–BC was 0.3 for those identified as Meyerhoff Scholars, which implies that Meyerhoff Scholars were 30 percentage points more likely to graduate within six years than were non-Meyerhoff students. When we control for differences in entering credentials and background characteristics, the coefficient falls to 0.21, implying that even including these controls for selection effects, Meyerhoff Scholars were 21 percentage points more likely to graduate than were other students. Of all black male Meyerhoff Scholars in the '99 entering cohort at UM–BC, the six-year graduation rate was 92 percent. For data on earlier cohorts, see Hrabowski (2001) and Chuck Salter, "It's Cool to Be Smart," *Fast Company* 57 (March 2002): 37.

17. However, the adjusted graduation rate for black women at UM–BC who were not part of the Meyeroff Program was higher, relative to the rate for white men, than the corresponding adjusted rate for black women at College Park.

18. Claude Steele and Joshua Aronson, "Stereotype Threat and the Intellectual Test Performance of African Americans," *Journal of Personality and Social Psychology* 69, no. 5 (1995): 797–811. See the Web site http://www.reducingstereo typethreat.org for a comprehensive discussion of this subject.

19. Geoffrey L. Cohen, et al., "Reducing the Racial Achievement Gap: A Social-Psychological Intervention," *Science* 313 (September 1, 2006): 1307–10; citation on p. 1308. A great many other interventions used to address stereotype vulnerabilities are described at the Web site identified in the previous note. See also Richard E. Nisbett, "Education Is All in Your Mind," op-ed contribution, *New York Times,* February 8, 2009, p. WK12. Professor Nisbett identifies a number

of other instances in which creative ways were found to overcome stereotype vulnerability.

20. Mikyung Ryu, *Minorities in Higher Education 2008*, 23rd annual status report (Washington, D.C.: American Council on Education, 2008), table 1. Hispanic women have a slightly higher educational attainment rate than do Hispanic men (13.7 percent versus 8.5 percent), but this gender gap is smaller than the corresponding gap for black women versus black men, and for that reason (and because of data considerations), we will work here with the overall Hispanic population.

21. The 2008 report of Excelencia in Education (Deborah A. Santiago, "Accelerating Latino Student Success at Texas Border Institutions," Excelencia in Education, Washington, D.C., October) emphatically states: "Neither Texas nor the United States can reach its human capital needs without accelerating Hispanic educational attainment" (p. 5). It is gratifying to see that this report stresses not only access to college but "timely completion." This report also contains a number of recommendations intended to increase the numbers of certificates and degrees awarded to Latino and Latina students and provides a number of examples of institution-specific initiatives designed to promote "success" in college.

22. See Consuelo Arbona and Amaury Nora, "The Influence of Academic and Environmental Factors on Hispanic College Degree Attainment," *Review of Higher Education* 30, no. 3 (Spring 2008): 247–69. This article is based on a detailed analysis of NELS data and also contains references to much other literature, including work by Richard Fry and Vincent Tinto. Alejandro Portes has done important ethnographic work on educational achievement among disadvantaged children of immigrants, and he stresses the importance of the human capital that immigrant families bring with them, the social context that receives them in America, and the composition of the immigrant family. See Alejandro Portes and Rubén G. Rumbaut, *Legacies: The Story of the Immigrant Second Generation* (Berkeley and New York: University of California Press and Russell Sage Foundation, 2001).

23. In comparison, 40 percent or less of students from other demographic groups in Chicago public schools reported that their mother had not attended college. See Roderick et al. (2006), pp. 21–22.

24. Hurtado et al., p. vi.

25. See the Chicago Consortium "Potholes" report (Roderick et al. 2008), pp. 74–75, especially figures 26 and 27. The Chicago report notes: "Only half of Latino students who planned to continue their education [beyond high school] enrolled in college and only 37 percent of Latino students who hoped to complete at least a four-year degree enrolled in a four-year college" (p. 15).

26. Roderick et al. (2008), pp. 75–86. Hurtado and associates comment on the relatively small number of Latino students attending their first-choice institution and argue that concerns about cost are a major driving force here: "Fewer Latina/os report they are attending their first choice college today. . . . This trend in not attending one's first choice college and concern for financing college may partially explain the rise in college application rates." They continue: "Although the majority of college students express some concern about their ability to pay for college, Latina/os are more likely to express concern about financing their college education compared to non-Hispanic White freshmen" (Hurtado et al. 2008, pp. 19–21).

27. These data were provided to us by the Posse Foundation. For a discussion of the Posse program, consult its Web site (http://www.possefoundation.org/, accessed October 14, 2008).

28. Kevin Carey's detailed explanation of the factors that have led the CARE program to be so successful at Florida State University assigns heavy weight to the careful and persistent nurturing of near-by at-risk students from sixth grade on. In effect, CARE has created "posse"-like groups of students. This strategy is obviously more practical when recruiting heavily from geographically proximate areas than it would be nationwide.

29. The differences in these gaps are explained only in small part (roughly 25 percent) by associated differences in SAT/ACT scores, high school GPA, state residency, and university attended. Regression analysis shows that the adjusted differences in graduation rates between low- and high-SES students are about 8 points at SEL I universities and 12–13 points at the other flagships and at the state system universities for which we have data on parental education. These patterns are strikingly similar to those we found earlier when we carried out a similar analysis that included black and Hispanic students within the low-SES group (refer back to Figures 3.4 and 3.7 and see the associated appendix tables). It is clear that the outcomes for low-SES students relative to high-SES students cannot be explained in any significant degree by the interactions between SES and race/ethnicity.

30. Bowen, Kurzweil, and Tobin, pp. 119–22.

31. Ibid., pp. 119–20 and 178 ff.

32. Note, however, that a recent study by John Aubrey Douglass and Gregg Thomson ("The Poor and the Rich: A Look at Economic Stratification and Academic Performance among Undergraduate Students in the United States," Research and Occasional Papers Series CSHE.15.08, Center for Studies in Higher Education, University of California–Berkeley, October 2008) finds surprisingly small differences in part-time work patterns between the "poor" and the "rich" students in the California system (p. 13). This study also finds that academic performance differs only slightly by SES—a finding consistent with our results. Unfortunately, this report does not have data on graduation rates.

33. If we add an estimate of how many went on to graduate from another four-year institution, this rate rises to 80 percent. When we impose an even stricter restriction on high school GPA and look only at students with GPAs of 3.33 and above, the results change only slightly. Now, 74 percent of these even better-qualified students graduated from the four-year institution they originally entered, and this graduation rate rises to 83 percent when we take account of those who transfer and then graduate from another college.

34. This point has serious real-world implications. We are told that there is a movement in Congress to allow undergraduate students (instead of only parents) to borrow, under what is now the parent loan program, up to the full costs of attending college, including room and board. This borrowing would be federally guaranteed and would likely result in significant numbers of parents' reducing their contributions, thereby transferring the burden to their children—and to federal guarantees.

35. Carey, pp. 8–9.

36. The Hawthorne effect, as defined in the *Dictionary of the Social Sciences,* edited by Craig Calhoun (New York: Oxford University Press, 2002), "describes the changes in behavior that result from being the subject of a behavioral study. The term derives from experiments carried out in the mid-1920s by the sociologists Fritz Roethlisberger and William J. Dickson at the Hawthorne Western Electric Company in Chicago. They set out to test theories of scientific management by measuring the impact of changes in working conditions on worker productivity —particularly variations in such factors as lighting, breaks, and compensation. They found that productivity increased no matter what they changed—a result attributed to the effect of the attention the researchers paid to the workers, which workers ostensibly interpreted as a sign of management concern and engagement."

37. See Lumina Foundation for Education, "A Stronger Nation through Higher Education: How and Why Americans Must Meet a Big Goal for College Attainment," Special Report, Lumina Foundation, Indianapolis, Ind., February 2009.

38. See Tinto (1993), p. 81. Two well-known social psychologists, Deborah Prentice and Nancy Cantor, are carrying out an in-depth analysis of the wide variety of personal and institutional factors leading students to withdraw from selected public universities in our study. This work, reflecting the disciplinary perspective of social psychology, should complement our research nicely.

39. Ibid., pp. 145–53; quotes on pp. 148 and 150.

Chapter 12   Looking Ahead

1. But we do acknowledge how hard it is to move "stubborn" numbers. A recent report in the United Kingdom notes that, in spite of many efforts and large expenditures, the university dropout rate in that country has remained steady at 22 percent for five years. See Polly Curtis, "University Dropout Steady at 22%," *Guardian,* February 20, 2008, p. 12. Of course, the optimal graduation rate is not 100 percent, but as Goldin and Katz emphasize (see Chapter 1), we are surely well below the optimal number today.

2. See Bill Gates, "A Forum on Education in America: Bill Gates," a speech delivered at the Forum on Education at the Bill and Melinda Gates Foundation, Seattle, for November 11, 2008, available at http://www.gatesfoundation.org/speeches-commentary/Pages/bill-gates-2008-education-forum-speech.aspx. The statements of President Obama and early initiatives of his administration are referenced in Chapter 1. As another sign of the times, in 2007 Texas lawmakers passed a budget that rewards colleges financially for improving graduation rates (Karin Fischer, "Texas Budget Rewards Retention," *Chronicle of Higher Education,* June 8, 2007, online edition).

3. See the comments by Lamar Alexander, reported by Sara Hebel in "Colleges Urged to Take Action as They Prepare to Reap Billions in Stimulus Bill," *Chronicle of Higher Education,* February 10, 2009, online edition. California's lieutenant governor has proposed a fast-track medical school that would cut three years from the time needed to become a physician (Katherine Mangan, "New Medical-

School Programs Put Students on a Fast Track to the White Coat," *Chronicle of Higher Education*, February 6, 2009, online edition). David Leonhardt (2009a) quotes a student at Shepherd University in West Virginia as saying, in discussing time-to-degree, "People don't push you" (p. 50). Leonhardt's article also describes the PROMISE (Providing Real Opportunities for Maximizing In-State Student Excellence) Scholarship Program in West Virginia.

4. Douglass and Thompson, cited earlier.

5. See Marjorie M. Shultz and Sheldon Zedeck, "Final Report: Identification, Development, and Validation of Predictors for Successful Lawyering," University of California, Berkeley, September 2008, available at http://www.law.berkeley .edu/files/LSACREPORTfinal-12.pdf. See also the report of the inaugural conference of the University of Southern California's Center for Enrollment Research, Policy, and Practice, including the comments by Wayne J. Camara, vice-president for research and analysis at the College Board, on the desirability of developing reliable measures of non-cognitive traits (Eric Hoover, "Admissions Experts Call for Broader Definition of College Readiness," *Chronicle of Higher Education*, August 6, 2008, online edition). We think it is encouraging that the College Board, long strongly identified with the standard SAT test, is actively working to promote greater use of Advanced Placement tests, as well as to develop reliable tests of non-cognitive skills. ACT has for many years put considerable focus on tests of "college readiness" and also on tests designed to measure workplace-related skills (see the ACT Web page).

6. See Helene Ragovin, "Amplified Application Will Provide Additional Cues about Prospective Students," *Tufts Journal*, May 2006, online edition, available at http://tuftsjournal.tufts.edu/archive/2006/may/features/index.shtml, accessed November 22, 2008.

7. Roderick et al. (2008), p. 24, and Roderick et al. (2009), figure 16, p. 53.

8. The Jack Kent Cooke Foundation's Undergraduate Transfer Scholarship Program addresses this question directly. Available at http://www.jkcf.org/ scholarships/undergraduate-transfer-scholarships/.

9. See Bowen, Kurzweil, and Tobin, especially chapter 4 and pp. 119–20.

10. For a good discussion of this entire set of issues, see Katherine Mangan, "Their Budgets Slashed, Public Colleges Share in Their Applicants' Economic Pain," *Chronicle of Higher Education*, November 19, 2008, online edition. Norma G. Kent, vice-president for communications at the American Association of Community Colleges, put it this way: "Turning away students is something of an anathema, but if your budgets are being cut and you don't have enough faculty or classes, it's a de facto closed door." According to this account: "For the first time in its history, California State University plans to cut systemwide enrollment—by 10,000 students—if the state doesn't provide more money" (see Katherine Mangan, "Rising Enrollments Buoy Some Colleges, Burden Others," *Chronicle of Higher Education*, November 28, 2008, online edition). Also see articles referenced in note 23, Chapter 9.

11. For a case study of the Amherst College experience with these issues, see Elizabeth Aries, *Race and Class Matters at an Elite College* (Philadelphia: Temple University Press, 2008). David Leonhardt (2009a) cites Peter Orszag, now director of

the Office of Management and Budget in Washington, as arguing that his fellow economists have made a mistake in paying so little attention to cultural norms (in the health care field, for example) and over-emphasizing market signals divorced from norms (p. 50). Education is full of examples of this tendency. Assumptions and expectations matter greatly.

Appendix A   The Modern Evolution of America's Flagship Universities

1. Martin A. Trow, "American Higher Education: Past, Present, and Future," *Educational Researcher*, 17, no. 3 (April 1988): 13–23; especially pp. 13, 15–16. See also Trow's contribution, "From Mass Higher Education to Universal Access: The American Advantage," in *In Defense of American Higher Education*, ed. Philip G. Altbach, Patricia J. Gumport, and D. Bruce Johnstone, 110–43 (Baltimore: Johns Hopkins University Press, 2001).

2. "An uncommon education for the common man" is from James Burrill Angell's inaugural speech (1879) as president of the University of Michigan, quoted by John Aubrey Douglass in *The Conditions of Admission: Access, Equity, and the Social Contract of Public Universities* (Stanford, Calif.: Stanford University Press, 2007), p. 5.

3. Douglass, pp. 7–9. Notes historian Allan Nevins: "Of the institutions benefited by the Morrill land grants, seventeen had been founded [often feebly] before 1862; eighteen more before the end of 1865 and sixteen others before the end of 1870." See Allan Nevins, *The State Universities and Democracy* (Urbana: University of Illinois Press, 1962), pp. 26, note 3, 27. Although "state colleges and universities" and "land-grant colleges and universities" are often used interchangeably, John Thelin reminds us that in many instances the historic state university predated the Morrill Act's passage and that state legislatures frequently created new, often rival, institutions to serve the land-grant function. This would be true of the University of Iowa and the land-grant Iowa State College (later University), the University of Michigan and land-grant Michigan State College (later University), Indiana University and the land-grant Purdue University, and the University of Oregon and the land-grant Oregon State College (later University). In still other instances, legislatures conferred land-grant status on private institutions, as in Massachusetts on the Massachusetts Institute of Technology and in New York on Cornell University. See John R. Thelin, *A History of American Higher Education* (Baltimore: Johns Hopkins University Press, 2004), pp. 75–78. In the South, the segregated historically black normal schools, many of which were created by or funded under the second Morrill Act (1890), were supported at much lower levels than were white institutions. See Robert L. Jenkins, "The Black Land-Grant Colleges in Their Formative Years, 1890–1920," *Agricultural History* 65, no. 2 (Spring 1991): 63–72.

4. This would change within a few years when the manpower demands of the nation's market-driven technologically innovative industries; the introduction of a more diverse high school curriculum to include vocational, technical, and manual training; and the enactment of compulsory school attendance laws combined to raise the intrinsic value of a high school diploma. See Claudia Goldin and Lawrence F. Katz, "Why the United States Led in Education: Lessons From Sec-

ondary School Expansion, 1910 to 1940," paper presented at the Rochester Conference in honor of Stanley Engerman: Factor Endowments, Labor and Economic Growth in the Americas, June 8–10, 2001. This is a revision of the earlier NBER Working Paper no. 6144 (National Bureau of Economic Research, Cambridge, Mass., August 1997). See also Claudia Goldin, "America's Graduation from High School: The Evolution and Spread of Secondary Schooling in the Twentieth Century," *Journal of Economic History* 58, no. 2 (June 1998): 345–74, and Claudia Goldin and Lawrence F. Katz, "The Shaping of Higher Education: The Formative Years in the United States, 1890 to 1940," *Journal of Economic Perspectives* 13, no. 1 (Winter 1999): 37–62, especially 49–52.

5. Trow (1988), p. 15, and Laurence Veysey, *The Emergence of the American University* (Chicago: University of Chicago Press, 1965), p. 339. By comparison, France's 16 universities had a total enrollment of about 40,000 students in 1910. In most European countries, including Britain, higher education enrollments did not surpass 5 percent until after the Second World War. See Hugh Davis Graham and Nancy Diamond, *The Rise of American Research Universities: Elites and Challengers in the Postwar Era* (Baltimore: Johns Hopkins University Press, 1997), p. 15.

6. Veysey, p. 339. Between 1908 and 1909, Edwin Slosson, the literary editor of the liberal weekly *The Independent,* visited 14 major academic institutions and wrote a series of articles, later published as *Great American Universities.* Slosson traveled to nine privately endowed universities—Harvard, Columbia, Chicago, Yale, Cornell, Princeton, the University of Pennsylvania, Stanford, and Johns Hopkins—and five public institutions—the Universities of Michigan, Minnesota, Wisconsin, California, and Illinois. After spending a week on each campus, attending classes and speaking with students, faculty, and administrators, Slosson did not shy away from identifying areas in which he saw room for improvement, particularly in undergraduate teaching. There was a desperate need for "more inspiring and stimulating lectures and fewer and shorter ones," he thought. As a former university professor, he was dismayed by faculty members' ignorance of basic pedagogical skills. "It would be well," he wryly observed, "if teachers did not know quite so much and if they knew how to tell what they did know better." Slosson's criticism of undergraduate education across these 14 privately endowed and publicly supported universities does not suggest that these leading institutions had reached consensus about the priority of research and the primacy of graduate and professional education, but the transition from teaching-centered to teaching and research–centered missions had clearly begun. See Edwin E. Slosson, *Great American Universities* (New York: Macmillan, 1910), pp. 517–18.

7. Roger L. Geiger, *To Advance Knowledge: The Growth of American Research Universities, 1900–1940* (New York: Oxford University Press, 1986), p. 108; Ernest H. Wilkins, "Major Trends in Collegiate Enrollments," *School and Society* 42 (1935): 442–48; and Historical Statistics of the United States Millennial Edition Online, table Bc523–536, "Enrollment in Institutions of Higher Education, by Sex, Enrollment Status, and Type of Institution: 1869–1995," available at http://hsus .cambridge.org/HSUSWeb/table/printTable.do?start=1&range=30&tableid=Bc52, accessed January 6, 2009.

8. Richard M. Freeland, *Academia's Golden Age: Universities in Massachusetts, 1945–1970* (New York: Oxford University Press, 1992), p. 90, and Thelin, pp. 252–53.

9. See Roger L. Geiger, "After the Emergence: Voluntary Support and the Building of American Research Universities," *History of Education Quarterly* 25, no. 3 (Autumn 1985): 369–81, especially p. 377, and Geiger (1986), appendix A, "Full-Time Fall Enrollments in Research Universities, 1894–1939," pp. 270–71.

10. Cambridge University Press, *Historical Statistics of the United States: Millennial Edition Online,* table Bc523–536, available at http://hsus.cambridge.org/ HSUSWeb/toc/hsusHome.do, accessed January 6. In 1950, the percentage of Americans aged 18–21 attending college and university stood at 16.5 percent; see Graham and Diamond, pp. 2, 21. See Nathan M. Pusey, *American Higher Education, 1945–1970: A Personal Report* (Cambridge, Mass.: Harvard University Press, 1978), p. 6.

11. James Lewis Morrill, president of the University of Minnesota, quoted by Stanford E. Lehmberg and Ann M. Pflaum in *The University of Minnesota, 1945–2000* (Minneapolis: University of Minnesota Press, 2000), p. 7.

12. Carnegie Commission on Higher Education, *Who Pays? Who Benefits? Who Should Pay? A Report and Recommendations* (New York: McGraw-Hill, 1976).

13. The Serviceman's Readjustment Act (1944) provided veterans with $500 (payable to the educational institution) for tuition for up to a maximum of four years, free textbooks, and a monthly living allowance of $50 for singles and $75 for married couples. Conceived as an anti-depression initiative that would mitigate the economic hardships of demobilization, championed most vigorously by the American Legion, and overseen by the Veterans Administration rather than the U.S. Office of Education, this imperfect measure—black veterans fell victim to continuing discrimination in the South and women were largely ignored—nonetheless created a remarkable precedent and foundation for the future expansion of educational opportunity. See Keith W. Olson, *The G.I. Bill, the Veterans, and the Colleges* (Lexington: University Press of Kentucky, 1974); Lizabeth Cohen, *A Consumers' Republic: The Politics of Mass Consumption in Postwar America* (New York: Knopf, 2003), pp. 156–60; Suzanne Mettler, "The Creation of the G.I. Bill of Rights of 1944: Melding Social and Participatory Citizenship Ideals," *Journal of Policy History* 17, no. 4 (2005): 345–74, especially p. 367; and Sarah E. Turner and John Bound, "Closing the Gap or Widening the Divide: The Effects of the G.I. Bill and World War II on the Educational Outcomes of Black Americans," *Journal of Economic History* 63, no. 1 (March 2003): 145–77.

14. Zook was an interesting and, in many respects, a logical choice to head the commission. With over four decades of experience in higher education, including stints as chief of the division of higher education at the U.S. Bureau of Education, president of the University of Akron, U.S. Commissioner of Education for one year before resigning in protest over President Franklin Roosevelt's refusal to include federal aid to education in the New Deal's economic recovery legislation, and president of the American Council on Education (ACE), he had developed into an accomplished politician and lobbyist. See "From A to Zook," *Time,* July 3, 1933, and "Zook," *Time,* August 12, 1946, available at http://www.time.com/time/magazine/article/0,9171,745755,00.html and http://www.time.com/time/magazine/article/0,9171,793162,00.html, accessed July 28, 2008. See also Freeland, pp. 73–75, and Ethan Schrum, "Establishing a Demo-

cratic Religion: Metaphysics and Democracy in the Debates over the President's Commission on Higher Education," *History of Education Quarterly* 47, no. 3 (August 2007): 277–301, available at http://www.sas.upenn.edu/dcc/workshops/documents/Schrum.pdf, accessed August 2, 2008, pp. 6–7.

15. Just as the decision to delegate responsibility for administering the educational program of the G.I. Bill to the Veterans Administration rather than the U.S. Office of Education provides some insight into the federal government's post-war thinking, so too did the Truman administration's use of the Office of War Mobilization and Reconversion in providing staff support for the President's Commission on Higher Education. See Janet C. Kerr, "From Truman to Johnson: Ad Hoc Policy Formulation in Higher Education," in *The History of Higher Education,* 2nd edition, ed. Lester F. Goodchild and Harold S. Wechsler (Boston: Pearson Custom Publishing, 1997), p. 629, and Schrum, pp. 5–6.

16. See Harry S. Truman, "Letter Appointing Members to the National Commission on Higher Education," July 13, 1946, in John T. Wooley and Gerhard Peters, *The American Presidency Project* (online), hosted by the University of California–Santa Barbara, Gerhard Peters database, available at http://www.presidency.ucsb.edu/ws/index.php?pid=12452, accessed July 24, 2008. Because this was the first presidential commission ever created for the purpose of examining higher education, contemporaries and later scholars have paid significant attention to the commission's membership. On one level, the civic leaders represented a cross-section of Democratic Party interest groups: religious organizations (the American Jewish Congress, National Catholic Welfare Congress, and Federal Council of Churches), organized labor (the International Ladies Garment Workers Union), and agriculture (the Ohio Farm Bureau). Though Eleanor Roosevelt initially agreed to serve, she withdrew after six months, citing a lack of time and voicing the National Education Association's (unfounded) concern that too much attention was being devoted to private rather than public education. Fourteen of the commissioners were college and university presidents, deans, and academic administrators, and they were drawn from the broadest spectrum of private and public institutions. Antioch and Vassar represented liberal arts and women's colleges. Tuskegee Institute represented historically black institutions. Emory, Stanford, Washington University, and the New School for Social Research represented private institutions. Kansas State College and the Universities of Arkansas, Illinois, Iowa, and Minnesota carried the public university and land-grant college banner. Catholic University (Washington, D.C.) represented sectarian institutions. Ball State (Indiana) spoke for public teachers colleges, and Webster Junior College (Utah) represented two-year colleges. Though a number of distinguished institutions participated, there was a notable absence of some of the nation's most influential and elite colleges and universities. Princeton University president Harold Dodds declined to serve, and major figures such as James Conant (Harvard) and Robert Maynard Hutchins (University of Chicago), each of whom had been publicly skeptical of the G.I. Bill's potentially adverse effects on academic standards, did not participate. See "Members of the Group Reporting on Education," *New York Times,* December 16, 1947, p. 44; Kerr, p. 629. Eleanor Roosevelt's correspondence with President Harry Truman on February

6, 11, and 12, 1947, can be found in Steve Neal, ed., *Eleanor & Harry: Correspondence of Eleanor Roosevelt and Harry S. Truman,* a joint project of the Franklin D. Roosevelt Presidential Library and the Harry S. Truman Presidential Library, available at http://www.trumanlibrary.org/eleanor/eleanordoctemplate.php?documentid=fdr19470206, accessed July 25, 2008.

17. Hugh Hawkins, *Banding Together: The Rise of National Associations in American Higher Education, 1887–1950* (Baltimore: Johns Hopkins University Press, 1992), p. 170; John Dale Russell, "Basic Conclusions and Recommendations of the President's Commission on Higher Education," *Journal of Educational Sociology* 22, no. 8 (April 1949): 493–508, especially p. 494. Not surprisingly, the commission's full-throated denunciation of the "separate but equal" principle produced a majority consensus, but four commissioners dissented. See President's Commission on Higher Education, *Higher Education for American Democracy,* 6 vols. (Washington, D.C.: U.S. Government Printing Office), vol. 2, pp. 25–29.

18. David D. Henry, *Challenges Past, Challenges Present: An Analysis of American Higher Education Since 1930* (San Francisco: Jossey-Bass, 1973), pp. 71–73. This study by the former president of the University of Illinois was part of the work of the Carnegie Council on Policy Studies in Higher Education, chaired by Clark Kerr and funded by the Carnegie Foundation for the Advancement of Teaching. Henry would also serve on the President's Committee on Education Beyond the High School (1956).

19. The commission's staff was remarkably accurate in its enrollment prediction. In 1960, the total undergraduate enrollment at degree-granting institutions was approximately 3.6 million students. See Bowen, Kurzweil, and Tobin, p. 34; President's Commission on Higher Education, vol. 1, pp. 40–41 and 25; and Seymour E. Harris, *A Statistical Portrait of Higher Education: A Report for the Carnegie Commission on Higher Education* (New York: McGraw-Hill, 1972), table 1.1-32, "Students Enrolled, Student Residents, and Students Remaining in Their Home States to Attend College, by Level of Enrollment and Control of Institutions, Aggregate United States, Fall 1963."

20. Russell, pp. 495–99, and Freeland, p. 76.

21. In *Banding Together,* Hugh Hawkins presents an insightful portrait of the national educational associations' reactions to the commission's report. Given its position as the major coordinating body for higher education and George Zook's role as commission chair, ACE tried to be as even-handed as possible, including opening its journal, the *Educational Record,* to critical judgments. The Association of Land Grant Colleges and Universities, whose public universities stood to gain immeasurably if the commission's opportunity agenda was adopted, made *Higher Education for Democracy* the centerpiece of its annual convention (1948). At the other end of the spectrum, the private institutional members of the Association of American Colleges (AAC), which included the majority of the nation's most distinguished liberal arts colleges, rejected the notion that their institutions' commitment to liberal education or selective admission standards was undemocratic or elitist. After Truman's victory in the 1948 election, AAC grew increasingly hostile toward the idea of offering federal aid to public institutions and community colleges. See Hawkins, pp. 170–75.

22. Diane Ravitch, *The Troubled Crusade: American Education, 1945–1980* (New York: Basic Books, 1983), p. 17, and Seymour Edwin Harris, *How Should We Pay for Education? Approaches to the Economics of Education* (New York: Harper, 1948). By the late 1940s, as higher education came to be perceived as an increasingly important contributor to the nation's welfare and national security, particularly through government-sponsored research, college and university faculties became targets for the same kind of allegations of disloyalty and subversive behavior that were directed at other prominent cultural and governmental organizations. Although no direct line connects the Zook Commission's calls for educational opportunity and racial and socioeconomic diversity with the kind of anti-Communist hysteria that led to the imposition and strengthening of mandatory loyalty oaths and speaker bans at a number of prominent public universities, including the Universities of California, Florida, Nebraska, North Carolina, and Washington and Rutgers, such tensions and conflicts were very much a part of higher education's growing prominence and visibility during the post-war years. See Ellen Schrecker, *No Ivory Tower: McCarthyism and the Universities* (New York: Oxford University Press, 1986); Thelin, pp. 274–77; Clark Kerr, *The Gold and the Blue: A Personal Memoir of the University of California, 1949–1967, 2 vols.* (Berkeley, Calif.: University of California Press, 2001–03), vol. 2, *Political Turmoil,* pp. 27–49; Julian M. Pleasants, *Gator Tales: An Oral History of the University of Florida* (Gainesville: University of Florida, 2006), pp. 49–51; Charles M. Gates, *The First Century at the University of Washington, 1861–1961* (Seattle: University of Washington Press, 1961), pp. 196–210; William D. Snider, *Light on the Hill: A History of the University of North Carolina at Chapel Hill* (Chapel Hill: University of North Carolina Press, 1992), pp. 271–73; and Richard P. McCormick, *Rutgers: A Bicentennial History* (New Brunswick, N.J.: Rutgers University Press 1966), pp. 293–96.

23. Robert Maynard Hutchins, "Double Trouble: Are More Studies, More Faculties, More Money the Key for Better Education?" in *Education for Democracy: The Debate over the Report of the President's Commission on Higher Education,* ed. Gail Kennedy, 82–86 (Boston: D. C. Heath, 1952). This article originally appeared under the title "The Report of the President's Commission on Higher Education" in the *Educational Record* 29, no. 2 (April 1948): 107–22.

24. The combination of Truman's reelection in 1948, the return of Democratic majorities in Congress, the potential impact of the G.I. Bill on the future expansion of educational opportunity, and the Zook Commission's unabashed emphasis on federal intervention reawakened the interest of privately endowed institutions in creating a systematic study of federal policies that would defend the private sector's prerogatives, autonomy, and traditions. Funded by the Rockefeller Foundation and the Carnegie Corporation of New York and with the cooperation of the Association of American Universities, the Commission on Financing Higher Education began its work in 1949 and completed two reports and published nine special studies within three years. Harvard provost Paul Buck served as chair, and John Millett, a professor of public administration at Columbia, played the leading role as executive director and principal spokesperson. The Zook and Millett commissions represented opposite ends of postwar higher education's public-private continuum, but they shared some com-

mon assumptions. Both agreed that the competitiveness, diversity, and pluralism of the nation's post-secondary institutions and the multiplicity of their funding sources were fundamental strengths of the U.S. system, and both supported a broadening of educational opportunity, though they fundamentally differed over the scale of that expansion. Where Zook's colleagues estimated that 32 percent of the college-age population should receive an opportunity to attend four years of college, Millett's colleagues thought that only the top 25 percent in ability deserved that opportunity. Unlike the Zook Commission's aggressively expansionist position aimed at eliminating economic barriers, the Rockefeller- and Carnegie-funded group argued that the most important objective was not increasing higher education's total enrollments but rather "getting better students into the existing facilities." The problem was less one of inequality, they suggested, than of motivation. Even if the financial barriers were removed, private sector advocates questioned whether the number of "intellectually able" students would approach the Presidential Commission's enrollment prediction. See Richard G. Axt, *The Federal Government and Financing Higher Education* (New York: Columbia University Press for the Commission on Financing Higher Education, 1952). George C. S. Benson reviewed the reports and monographs published by the Commission on Financing Higher Education in *American Political Science Review* 47, no. 3 (September 1953): 883–90.

25. Roger L. Geiger, *Research and Relevant Knowledge: America's Research Universities since World War II* (New York: Oxford University Press, 1993), pp. 46–47.

26. See Freeland, p. 87; Henry, pp. 86–87; Ronald B. Thompson, "The Impending Tidal Wave of Students: A Report," Committee on Special Projects, American Association of Collegiate Registrars and Admissions Officers, Washington, D.C., 1954.

27. Francis J. Brown, "A Long-Range View of Higher Education," *Annals of the American Academy of Political and Social Science* 301, no. 1 (September 1955): 1–6; quote on p. 5. Brown had served as executive secretary of the President's Commission on Higher Education and was the director of the ACE Leaders program.

28. Benjamin Fine, "Long-Term Financing Urged," *New York Times,* October 27, 1957, pp. 1, 54. See Clark Kerr, vol. 1, *Academic Triumphs,* p. 72, and Pusey, p. 57. In April 1956, President Dwight Eisenhower created the President's Committee on Education beyond the High School and appointed Devereux Josephs, president of the New York Life Insurance Company, as chair. A Philadelphia investment banker and graduate of Groton and Harvard, Josephs had served as chairman of the Carnegie Corporation of New York (1945–1948) and was a member in good standing of the "Episcopacy," the term Nicholas Lemann used to respectfully describe the families and individuals who dominated the country's elite educational, social, and philanthropic institutions before and immediately after World War II. Troubled by the absence of any long-term federal higher education policy that would be responsive to the demands of an expanding college-age population, the 34-member Josephs Committee, which represented college presidents, business leaders, school superintendents, and public officials, proposed incremental steps beginning with state-by-state surveys of future enrollments and facilities needs, as well as attention to the training of more able, qualified, and

better-paid teachers. When a lack of congressional funding brought the committee's work to an abrupt halt in the summer of 1957, Josephs and his colleagues limited their final report to calls for financial assistance to an ever-increasing number of students, better compensation of faculty, more women in the professoriate, and "federal leadership without federal control at state or local levels." The committee also proposed low-interest-rate loans for income-producing facilities and a program of work-study scholarships. See Lemann, pp. 12–16, 60–64. Press coverage of the President's Committee on Education beyond the High School can be found in these articles in the *New York Times:* Benjamin Fine, "Education in Review: Study of Post-High-School Training Needs Waits Now on Funds from Congress," July 15, 1956, p. 133; Bess Furman, "U.S. Urged to Set a College Policy: President's Committee Cites the Need for Expansion at the Higher Level," November 20, 1956, pp. 1, 28; and Benjamin Fine, "Education in Review: President's Committee Takes First Step in Plans for Expansion of Colleges," November 25, 1956, p. 221. See also Janet Kerr, pp. 634–35; Henry, pp. 102–4; Pusey, pp. 60–61; and Geiger (1993), pp. 164–65.

29. Christopher Jencks and David Riesman, *The Academic Revolution* (Garden City, N.Y.: Doubleday, 1969), p. viii.

30. Louis Menand, "The Marketplace of Ideas," Occasional Paper 49, American Council of Learned Societies, New York, available at http://archives.acls .org/op/49_Marketplace_of_Ideas.htm, accessed August 8, 2008.

31. HEW official, quoted by Elizabeth A. Duffy and Idana Goldberg in *Crafting a Class: College Admissions and Financial Aid, 1955–1994* (Princeton, N.J.: Princeton University Press, 1998), p. 170.

32. Duffy and Goldberg, p. 4, citing U.S. Department of Commerce, Bureau of the Census, *Current Population Reports,* Series P-25, Population Estimates and Projections, nos. 311, 519, 917, 100, 1022, 1095.

33. In December 1963, shortly after John F. Kennedy's assassination, President Lyndon B. Johnson signed into law the Higher Education Facilities Act of 1963, which provided matching funds to colleges and universities for the construction of classrooms, libraries, and laboratories. See Lyndon B. Johnson, "Remarks upon Signing the Higher Education Facilities Act," December 16, 1963, in Woolley and Peters, *The American Presidency Project* (online), available at http://www.presidency .ucsb.edu/ws/?pid=26387; Pusey, p. 106; and Wilson Smith and Thomas Bender, eds., *American Higher Education Transformed, 1940–2005: Documenting the National Discourse* (Baltimore: Johns Hopkins University Press, 2008), p. 5.

34. Lyndon B. Johnson, "Remarks at Southwest Texas State College upon Signing the Higher Education Act of 1965," November 8, 1965, in Woolley and Peters, *The American Presidency Project* (online), http://www.presidency.ucsb.edu/ws /index.php?pid=26729, accessed October 19, 2008.

35. Duffy and Goldberg, p. 174. The authors remind us that although the Higher Education Act (1965) was aimed at students from low-income families, the statute contained a provision that applicants were to "show evidence of academic or creative promise." In 1967 that language was eliminated in favor of a much broader recommendation for a study to determine the best means of "making available a post-secondary education to all young Americans who qualify and

seek it." See W. Lee Hansen, "Impact of Student Financial Aid on Access," in *The Crisis in Higher Education,* ed. Joseph Froomkin (New York: Academy of Political Science, 1983), pp. 88–89. The statute also included support for "developing institutions," part of the Johnson administration's broader Great Society vision that was intended to assist poor, under-resourced colleges and universities. In practical terms this meant that the historically black colleges and universities benefited, as did a large number of white, rural, sectarian institutions. See Graham and Diamond, p. 43.

36. Clark Kerr, "The American Mixture of Higher Education in Perspective: Four Dimensions," *Higher Education* 19, no. 1 (1990): 1–19, especially p. 1; American Council on Education, *Fact Book on Higher Education, 1986–1987* (New York: Macmillan, 1987), p. 57; U.S. Department of Education, National Center for Education Statistics, *120 Years of American Education: A Statistical Portrait* (Washington, D.C.: U.S. Department of Education, 1993), table 24, pp. 76–77; and Ravitch, pp. 182–84.

37. Between 1960 and 1970, 457 new community colleges opened their doors. See George B. Vaughan, *The Community College Story* (Washington, D.C.: American Association of Community Colleges, 2006), available at http://books.google.com/books?id=27iwNptunysC&pg=PA30&lpg=PA30&dq=community+colleges+and+the+1960s&source=web&ots=e8OTJKi51X&sig=ioKAiAv13-JxZ-QfhykZfnaiqrI&hl=en&sa=X&oi=book_result&resnum=7&ct=result.

38. Clark Kerr, *The Great Transformation in Higher Education, 1960–1980* (Albany: State University of New York Press, 1991), p. xii.

39. Graham and Diamond, pp. 44–47, and Freeland, p. 92.

40. Geiger (1993), p. 245.

41. Clark Kerr (2001–03), vol. 1, p. 78.

42. The California legislature's unusual decision to charter the University of California (UC, 1868) as a distinct branch of government—the University became a "public trust" in 1879—provided the institution with a rare degree of autonomy with respect to the establishment of academic programs and admissions standards, as well as the gradual development of new campuses. As early as 1910, tripartite agreements linking the University, state teachers colleges, and public junior colleges provided a foundation for the state's unusually bold and early commitment to educational opportunity. In 1919, the state assembly approved the creation of a two-year "Southern Branch" of the University in Los Angeles, and in 1927 construction began on the Westwood campus of the renamed University of California at Los Angeles. See Douglass, pp. 32–35, and Gary Orfield and Faith G. Paul, "*State Higher Education Systems and College Completion,*" Final Report to the Ford Foundation, New York, November 1992, p. 24, available at http://eric.ed.gov/ERICWebPortal/custom/portlets/recordDetails/detailmini.jsp?_nfpb=true&_&ERICExtSearch_SearchValue_0=ED354041&ERICExtSearch_SearchType_0=no&accno=ED354041, accessed September 29, 2008.

43. See Atkinson and Geiser, p. 3.

44. The Liaison Committee of the Regents of the University of California and the State Board of Education appointed a Master Plan Survey Team consisting of the UC president, the superintendent of public instruction, and four members

from each of the two boards. The survey team included two representatives each from UC, the state colleges and junior colleges, and the state's private colleges and universities. See T. C. Holy, "California's Master Plan for Higher Education, 1960–1975: A Factual Presentation of an Important Development," *Journal of Higher Education* 32, no. 1 (January 1961): 9–16. Arthur Coons, president of Occidental College, served as chairman. He was a wise arbitrator, and his representation of the private, independent sector also acknowledged the fact that the California State Scholarship Program could be used at the state's private and public institutions. Unlike Clark Kerr, Coons ultimately concluded that the Master Plan had more to do with controlling institutional rivalries and appetites than with education. See Arthur Coons, *Crises in California Higher Education: Experience under the Master Plan and Problems of Coordination, 1959 to 1968* (Los Angeles: Ward Ritchie, 1968).

45. Atkinson and Geiser, pp. 4–5. For an interesting early analysis of the community college's role in California, see Burton R. Clark, *The Open-Door College: A Case Study* (New York: McGraw-Hill, 1960), pp. 44–45.

46. John Rogers et al., "California Educational Opportunity Report 2006: Roadblocks to College," University of California/All Campus Consortium for Research Diversity and UCLA Institute for Democracy, Education, and Access, March 2006, p. 3, available at http://www.idea.gseis.ucla.edu/publications/eor06/fullreport/pdf/EOR-2006.pdf, accessed October 3, 2008, and Jeannie Oakes et al., "Removing the Roadblocks: Fair College Opportunities for All California Students," University of California/All Campus Consortium for Research Diversity and UCLA Institute for Democracy, Education, and Access, November 2006, p. ii, available at http://www.idea.gseis.ucla.edu/publications/roadblocks/pdf/ExecutiveSummary.pdf, accessed October 3, 2008.

47. Orfield and Paul, p. 29.

48. John Aubrey Douglass, *The California Idea and American Higher Education: 1850 to the 1960 Master Plan* (Stanford, Calif.: Stanford University Press, 2000), pp. 320–21.

49. Ibid., p. 324.

50. Peter Schrag, *Paradise Lost: California's Experience, America's Future* (New York: New Press, 1998), as quoted by Douglass (2000), pp. 324–25, and Brent Staples, "Editorial Observer; The 'Mississippification' of California Schools," *New York Times*, June 23, 2000, available at http://query.nytimes.com/gst/fullpage.html?res=9A01E7D61F31F930A15755C0A9669C8B63, accessed October 3, 2008.

51. This reflected, in part, the life experience of the state's governors and legislators, many of whom were educated at private colleges and universities, and, more particularly, the lack of interest among the Board of Regents of the University of the State of New York—not a university in the usual sense but a corporate policy-making and administrative body, elected by the legislature, with responsibility for all the elementary, secondary, and higher education institutions, private and public, approved by the state. Following passage of the Morrill Act (1862), the regents and the legislature did not take advantage of the federal government's incentives to establish land-grant programs in agriculture and engineering until State Senator Ezra Cornell offered to donate $500,000 to create a

new privately endowed university. The decision to designate Cornell University as the state's land-grant institution, while not unusual for the time, is suggestive of the state's convoluted attitudes toward public higher education. See Thelin, p. 77, and Sidney Gelber, *Politics and Public Higher Education in New York State: Stony Brook—A Case Study* (New York: Peter Lang, 2001), p. 13.

52. At the time of World War II, New York State's public higher education sector consisted of 34 previously unaffiliated institutions under the control of the regents: 11 four-year teachers colleges; 6 two-year agricultural and technical institutes; 7 professional colleges under contract with Syracuse, Cornell, and Alfred Universities; 6 two-year institutes of applied arts and science; and New York City's four municipal liberal arts colleges. See Judith S. Glazer-Raymo, "Nelson Rockefeller and the Politics of Higher Education in New York State," Nelson A. Rockefeller Institute of Government, State University of New York (SUNY), Albany, May 1989, p. 2. For a short history of SUNY, see State University of New York, "Short History of SUNY," 2008, available at http://www.suny.edu/student/university_suny_history.cfm, accessed September 1, 2008.

53. Gelber, pp. 65–67 and Glazer, p. 3.

54. In 1957–58, New York's per capita expenditure (state and local tax dollars) for higher education of $5.41 compared unfavorably with that of California ($15.17), Michigan ($11.82), Iowa ($10.29), Indiana ($8.55), Illinois ($8.08), Wisconsin ($7.65), and Texas ($7.61). See M. M. Chambers, "Higher Education in New York State: A Review Essay," *Journal of Higher Education* 32, no. 4 (April 1961): 222–26.

55. Heald had served as president of New York University. He was joined on the committee by Marion Folsom, a former secretary of Health, Education, and Welfare (HEW), and John Gardner, then president of the Carnegie Corporation and the Carnegie Foundation for the Advancement of Teaching, future HEW secretary during the Johnson administration, and later founder of two important non-profit organizations, Common Cause and the Independent Sector. Folsom had been intimately involved in drafting the National Defense Education Act, and in 1957 Gardner had served as chair of a Rockefeller Brothers–funded panel study on education. See Glazer, p. 5, and New York State Committee on Higher Education, "Meeting the Increasing Demand for Higher Education in New York State: A Report to the Governor and the Board of Regents," letter of transmittal, Board of Regents, State Education Department, Albany, November 1960.

56. Committee on Higher Education, p. 9.

57. Two critical elements of the Rockefeller administration's blueprint for SUNY's expansion involved compensatory assistance for the state's private colleges and a similar political and financial understanding with New York City's municipal colleges. The city's four senior liberal arts colleges were given independent status as part of a new, soon-to-be expanded City University of New York (CUNY), whose board of trustees was given control of finance and governance. CUNY was also granted the right to develop doctoral programs in exchange for introducing tuition at the graduate school level. The state's private colleges and universities benefited in two ways: first, access to the State Dormitory Authority's

low-cost loans for capital construction of academic buildings proved exceedingly important as institutions renovated or expanded their facilities, and second, later in the decade, over the objection of the regents and the state's Democratic legislators, Rockefeller used his political capital to win support for direct, unrestricted grants to private institutions based on the number of earned degrees conferred in the previous year on the assumption that independent colleges were educating a significant number of students who might otherwise add to the enrollment pressure at state college and university campuses. This program became known as "Bundy Aid" in honor of McGeorge Bundy, president of the Ford Foundation, who presided over a task force on financing higher education. See Glazer, pp. 7–8, 12–14.

58. Glazer, p. 14.

59. Gelber, p. 266

60. Graham and Diamond, p. 49.

61. Douglass (2007), p. 82.

62. Thelin, p. 304, and Geiger (1993), p. 257.

63. Glenwood C. Brooks and William E. Sedlacek, "Black Student Enrollment at the University of Maryland, College Park, 1968–1971," Research Report 1-72, Cultural Studies Center, University of Maryland, College Park, available at http://eric.ed.gov/ERICDocs/data/ericdocs2sql/content_storage_01/0000019b/80/39/03/0f.pdf, accessed August 27, 2008.

64. Dawn Elizabeth Reed, "'The Old University Is Dead': Activism and Change at the University of Virginia in the 1960s," *The Magazine of Albemarle County History* 60 (2002): 46–80; quote on p. 48.

65. Virginius Dabney, *Mr. Jefferson's Virginia* (Charlottesville: University of Virginia Press, 1981), p. 467, and Office of Institutional Assessment and Studies, "Historical Data: Admission," University of Virginia, Charlottesville, available at http://www.web.virginia.edu/IAAS/index.shtm, accessed August 27, 2008.

66. William A. Link, *William Friday: Power, Purpose, and American Higher Education* (Chapel Hill: University of North Carolina Press, 1995), pp. 162–63.

67. The Carlyle Commission subsequently recommended that the Woman's College at Greensboro be made coeducational and renamed the University of North Carolina at Greensboro and also that State College be renamed North Carolina State University at Raleigh.

68. University of North Carolina, "UNC Facts," available at http://www.northcarolina.edu/content.php/home/facts.htm, accessed August 28, 2008, and Geiger (1993), p. 264.

69. William H. Young, "The University's Supporting Resources, 1949–1974," p. 79; Karl F. Wendt, "The Growth of the University's Physical Resources, 1949–1974," p. 87; and F. Chandler Young, "On the Importance of Students, 1949–1974," p. 158, all in *The University of Wisconsin: One Hundred and Twenty-Five Years,* ed. Allan G. Bogue and Robert Taylor (Madison: University of Wisconsin Press, 1975).

70. Geiger (1993), pp. 265–66, and University of Wisconsin, "History and Organization of the University of Wisconsin System," available at http://wis.uwsa.edu/about/history.htm, accessed September 1, 2008.

71. Orfield and Paul, pp. 52–57.

72. Duffy and Goldberg, p. 11, and Eric D. Fingerhut, submitter, "The Strategic Plan for Higher Education, 2008–2017," Ohio Board of Regents, University System of Ohio, Columbus, March 2008, available at http://universitysystem.ohio.gov/pdfs/strategicPlan/USOStrategicPlan_ExecSummary.pdf, accessed August 27, 2008.

73. Francis P. Weisenburger, *The Fawcett Years, 1956–1972*, vol. 9 of *History of The Ohio State University* (Columbus: Ohio State University Press, 1975), p. 57.

74. Burton R. Clark, "The 'Cooling-Out' Function in Higher Education," *American Journal of Sociology* 65, no. 6 (May 1960): 569–76.

75. Thelin, p. 330.

76. John B. Gabel, *The Jennings Years, 1981–1990*, vol. 11 of *History of The Ohio State University* (Columbus, Ohio: Ohio State University Press, 1992), pp. 53–59.

77. Malcolm S. Baroway, *The Gee Years, 1990–1997*, vol. 12 of *History of The Ohio State University* (Columbus, Ohio: Ohio State University Press, 2002), p. 22.

78. Gabel, pp. 60–61.

79. Clark Kerr (1991), p. 146.

80. Clark Kerr (2001–03), vol. 2, pp. 20–21, 113.

81. Clark Kerr, *The Uses of the University* (Cambridge: Harvard University Press, 1963), p. 49. See also Clark Kerr, "The Frantic Race to Remain Contemporary," *Daedalus* 93, no. 3 (Fall 1964): 1051–70.

82. Clark Kerr (2001–03), vol. 1, p. 296, and Smith and Bender, p. 50.

83. Clark Kerr (2001–03), vol. 2, p. 20.

84. Jencks and Riesman, p. 40.

85. Geiger (1993), p. 234.

86. Jencks and Riesman, p. 151.

87. Ibid., p. 153.

88. Thelin, p. 315.

89. Jencks and Riesman, p. 37.

90. William J. Rorabaugh, *Berkeley at War: The 1960s* (New York: Oxford University Press, 189), pp. 22–46, and Sheldon W. Wolin, "Remembering Berkeley," in Smith and Bender, pp. 379–81.

91. Geiger (1993), p. 231.

92. Clark Kerr (1991), pp. 128–29, 147–48.

93. Geiger (1993), pp. 234–35.

94. Peter S. Van Houten and Edward L. Barrett, *Berkeley and Its Students: Days of Conflict, Years of Change, 1945–1970* (Berkeley: Berkeley Public Policy Press, Institute of Governmental Studies, University of California), pp. 42–43.

95. Thelin, pp. 318–19. In 1968, as Thelin notes, the federal government established the Higher Education General Information Survey, which provided basic information about enrollments, budgets, and degrees conferred, and it evolved into an expanded Integrated Postsecondary Education Data System. In 1973, the Carnegie Commission on Higher Education introduced a more nuanced, standardized classification system that, with periodic adjustments (in 1976, 1987, 1994, 2000, 2005, and 2008) and constant debate among institutions

over its categories and subcategories, continues to serve as an important reference for higher education research.

96. John Aubrey Douglass, "The Carnegie Commission and Council on Higher Education: A Retrospective," Research and Occasional Papers Series CSHE.14.05, Center for Studies in Higher Education, University of California, Berkeley, November 2005, pp. 1–2, available at http://64.233.169.104/search?q=cache: CdnEdR7hutIJ:cshe.berkeley.edu/publications/docs/ROP.Douglass.Carnegie.1 4.05.pdf+Clark+Kerr,+%22I+don%27t+expect+to+be+unemployed+very+long% 22&hl=en&ct=clnk&cd=1&gl=us, accessed August 27, 2008.

97. Douglass (2005), p. 3. The Carnegie Commission on Higher Education included a number of current and former college and university presidents, including Eric Ashby (Cambridge University), William Friday (University of North Carolina), David Henry (University of Illinois), Theodore Hesburgh (University of Notre Dame), Stanley Heywood (Montana State University), Katharine McBride (Bryn Mawr), James Perkins (Cornell), and Nathan Pusey (Harvard). The balance of the commission members included businessmen-philanthropists such as Ralph Besse and Norton Simon; academics such as Joseph Cosand (Michigan), Carl Kaysen (Institute for Advanced Study), Kenneth Keniston (Yale), and David Riesman (Harvard); and current or former public officials such as William Scranton (former governor of Pennsylvania) and Patricia Roberts Harris (Howard Law School professor and a future secretary of both Housing and Urban Development and later Health, Education and Welfare).

98. Mark E. Thompson, "Commissions and Zeitgeist: A Brief Critique of Commissions of Higher Education," *Peabody Journal of Education* 55, no. 4 (July 1978): 309–17, especially 312–13. Over the next 12 years, the commission (1967–1973) and its successor, the Carnegie Council on Higher Education (1973–1979), produced more than 80 studies, reports, and policy statements on such topics as federal funding, collective bargaining, expanding opportunity, community college development, purposes of higher education, academic reform, historically black colleges and universities, campus dissent, instructional technology, and the changing job market for college graduates.

99. Lewis B. Mayhew, *The Carnegie Commission on Higher Education* (San Francisco: Jossey-Bass, 1973), p. 16.

100. Carnegie Commission on Higher Education (1976), p. 99.

101. At the time of the task force's creation, Frank Newman was serving as an associate director of university relations at Stanford after a successful business career and an unsuccessful run as a Republican anti–Vietnam War candidate for Congress. One of his generation's most creative and innovative leaders in higher education, he would later serve as the president of the University of Rhode Island and the Education Commission of the States. See Karen Arenson, "Frank Newman, 77, Dies; Shaped Education," *New York Times,* June 4, 2004, online edition, available at http://query.nytimes.com/gst/fullpage.html?res=9F00E4DA1231F 937A35755C0A9629C8B63&scp=1&sq=Frank%20Newman,%20who%20shaped %20education,%20dies%20at%2077&st=cse, accessed November 19, 2008.

102. Frank Newman et al., *Report on Higher Education* (Washington, D.C.: U.S. Government Printing Office, 1971), p. 1, quoted in Douglass (2007), p. 102.

103. Thelin, p. 320.

104. Thompson, p. 314; Geiger (1993), p. 256; Andrew M. Greeley et al., "The Newman Report: Four Comments, "*Journal of Higher Education* 42, no. 7 (October 1971): 610–23; and Smith and Bender, p. 40.

105. Newman had sought persons who would "think about conventional problems in unconventional ways." The Newman Report panel included William Cannon, a vice-president and professor of public policy at the University of Chicago; Stanley Cavell, a professor of philosophy at Harvard University; and Audrey Cohen, an education reformer and founder of the College for Human Services (New York), an institution later re-named in her honor. Other panel members included Russell Edgerton, who served as special assistant to HEW secretaries Robert Finch and Elliott Richardson and would go on to play a key role as deputy director of the Fund for the Improvement of Postsecondary Education and to enjoy a productive career as the president of the American Association for Higher Education; Martin Kramer, who was director of higher education planning at HEW; Joseph Rhodes, who was a junior fellow in intellectual history at Harvard, a consultant to the Office of the Secretary of HEW, and a member of the Commission on Campus Unrest (1970); and Robert Singleton, who served as director of African American Studies at UCLA and later joined the business school faculty. See David E. Rosenbaum, "Panel Challenges U.S. College System," *New York Times*, March 9, 1971, p. 45, and Fred M. Hechinger, "Colleges: Ideas for Breaking the Lockstep," *New York Times*, August 8, 1971, p. E7.

106. Geiger (1993), p. 257.

107. Hechinger, p. E7.

108. Frank Newman et al., *The Second Newman Report: National Policy and Higher Education, Report of a Special Task Force to the Secretary of the U.S. Department of Health, Education, and Welfare* (Cambridge, Mass.: MIT Press, 1974), and Hechinger, p. E7.

109. Graham and Diamond, p. 84, and Carnegie Commission on Higher Education, *Quality and Equality: New Levels of Federal Responsibility for Higher Education* (New York: McGraw-Hill, 1968).

110. Earl F. Cheit, *The New Depression in Higher Education: A Study of Financial Conditions at 41 Colleges and Universities* (New York: McGraw-Hill, 1971), and Graham and Diamond, p. 84.

111. Thelin, p. 324.

112. Graham and Diamond, p. 89.

113. Harold J. Enarson, Ohio State University's president, reviewed *Priorities for Action: Final Report of the Carnegie Commission on Higher Education* in the *Journal of Higher Education* 45, no. 1 (April 1974): 311–12; quote on p. 312.

114. Douglass (2005), p. 7, and Graham and Diamond, p. 89.

115. Clark Kerr (1991), pp. xvii–xviii. The Second Newman Report had also recommended that federal support for post-secondary education flow directly to students rather than to colleges and universities. See Thompson, p. 315.

116. The 1972 amendments to the Higher Education Act of 1965 established Basic Educational Opportunity Grants (BEOGs) and State Student Incentive Grants (SSIGs). BEOGs, soon to be known as Pell Grants in honor of Senator Claiborne Pell (D-R.I.), were made directly to students whose families' resources

fell below an established need-based ceiling. They were portable and were awarded to individual students rather than to institutions. See Thelin, pp. 324–26. SSIGs provided incentives for states to start or expand grant programs and reflected Senator Jacob Javits' (R-N.Y.) efforts on behalf of SUNY, which wanted more federal participation in student aid in order to relieve the burden on New York State.

117. Thelin, pp. 324–26.

118. U.S. Department of Education, National Center for Education Statistics, Integrated Postsecondary Education Data System (IPEDS), Spring 2007 Enrollment component and Fall 2007 Completions component. Calculations were based on data for 91 flagship institutions identified by Michael J. Rizzo and Ronald G. Ehrenberg in "Resident and Nonresident Tuition and Enrollment at Flagship State Universities," NBER Working Paper 9516, National Bureau of Economic Research, Cambridge, Mass., February 2003, available at http://www.nber.org/papers/w9516.pdf, accessed January 20, 2009.

119. Christopher Newfield, *Unmaking the Public University: The Forty-Year Assault on the Middle Class* (Cambridge, Mass.: Harvard University Press, 2008), pp. 173–94.

120. In 2004, only 8 percent of the University of Virginia's operating budget came from the commonwealth, down from 28 percent 25 years earlier; Penn State received 12 percent of its annual budget from the Commonwealth of Pennsylvania; the state of Colorado provided 9 percent of the University of Colorado's operating expenses, and the University of Maryland received 27 percent of its support from the state, down from 43 percent in 1990. See William C. Symonds, "Should Public Universities Behave Like Private Colleges?" *Business Week,* November 15, 2004, p. 97.

121. Bowen, Kurzweil, and Tobin, pp. 206–10.

122. Douglass (2007), pp. 7–10, and George H. Callcott, *The University of Maryland at College Park: A History* (Baltimore: Noble House, 2005), p. 161.

123. "State Universities Getting Increasingly Selective," *Wall Street Journal,* November 13, 2006, p. A1.

124. Morton Owen Schapiro, Michael P. O'Malley, and Larry H. Litten, "Tracing the Economic Backgrounds of COFHE Students: Has There Been a 'Middle Income Melt?'" Discussion Paper 6, Williams Project on the Economics of Higher Education, Williamstown, Mass., November 1990, available at http://www.williams.edu/wpehe/DPs/DP-6.pdf, accessed September 22, 2008.

125. Michael S. McPherson and Morton Owen Schapiro, *The Student Aid Game: Meeting Need and Rewarding Talent in American Higher Education* (Princeton, N.J.: Princeton University Press, 1998), and Peter Passell, "Affluent Turning to Public Colleges," *New York Times,* August 13, 1997, p. B7.

126. Danette Gerald and Kati Haycock, "Engines of Inequality: Diminishing Equity in the Nation's Premier Public Universities," Education Trust, Washington, D.C., 2006, pp. 7, 18, available at http://www2.edtrust.org/NR/rdonlyres/F755E80E-9431-45AF-B28E 653C612D503D/0/EnginesofInequality.pdf, accessed September 22, 2008.

127. The quotation is from a paper by Shirley A. Ort, "The Impact of Tuition and Student Aid on College Access, Affordability and Success: A Practitioner's Views," presented at the inaugural conference of the Center for Enrollment Re-

search, Policy and Practice, University of Southern California, Los Angeles, August 2008. See also Amanda Pallais and Sarah E. Turner, "Opportunities for Low-Income Students at Top Colleges and Universities: Policy Initiatives and the Distribution of Students," *National Tax Journal* 59, no. 2 (June 2006): 357–86.

128. William G. Bowen and Derek Bok's *The Shape of the River* remains the seminal examination of what the authors delicately call "the long shadow of an 'unlovely history.'"

List of Figures

Chapter 4

List of Tables

List of Appendix Tables

The following tables are available at http://press.princeton.edu/titles/8971.html.

Chapter 5

Chapter 6

References

ACT. 2008. "Issues in College Success: What We Know about College Success; Using ACT Data to Inform Educational Issues." ACT Web site material. ACT, Iowa City, Iowa.

———. 2009. "The Forgotten Middle: Ensuring That All Students Are on Target for College and Career Readiness before High School." ACT Policy Report. ACT, Iowa City, Iowa, April 1.

Adelman, Clifford. 1999. *Answers in the Tool Box: Academic Intensity, Attendance Patterns, and Bachelor's Degree Attainment.* Washington, D.C.: U.S. Department of Education, Office of Educational Research and Improvement.

Agronow, Sam, and Roger Studley. 2007. "Prediction of College GPA from New SAT Test Scores—A First Look." Paper presented at the annual meeting of the California Association for Institutional Research, Monterey, California, November 16. Available at http://www.cair.org/conferences/CAIR2007/pres/Agronow.pdf.

American Council on Education. 1987. *Fact Book on Higher Education, 1986–1987.* New York: Macmillan.

Angrist, Joshua, Daniel Lang, and Phillip Oreopoulos. 2007. "Incentives and Services for College Achievement: Evidence from a Randomized Trial." Report IZA DP 3134. Institute for the Study of Labor, Bonn, October.

Arbona, Consuelo, and Amaury Nora. 2008. "The Influence of Academic and Environmental Factors on Hispanic College Degree Attainment." *Review of Higher Education* 30, no. 3 (Spring): 247–69.

Arenson, Karen W. 2004. "Frank Newman, 77, Dies; Shaped Education." *New York Times,* June 4, online edition. Available at http://query.nytimes.com/gst/fullpage.html?res=9F00E4DA1231F937A35755C0A9629C8B63&scp=1&sq=Frank%20Newman,%20who%20shaped%20education,%20dies%20at%2077&st=cse. Accessed November 19, 2008.

Aries, Elizabeth. 2008. *Race and Class Matters at an Elite College.* Philadelphia: Temple University Press.

Astin, Alexander W. 1984. "Student Involvement: A Developmental Theory for Higher Education." *Journal of College Student Personnel* 25, no. 4 (July): 297–308.

Atkinson, Richard C. 2004. "College Admissions and the SAT: A Personal Perspective." Paper presented at the annual meeting of the American Educational Research Association, San Diego, California, April 14. Later published in *A Journal of the Association for Psychological Science Observer* 18 (2005).

Atkinson, Richard C., and Saul Geiser. 2006. "UC Admissions, Proposition 209 and the California Master Plan." Paper proposed for the conference Higher Education, Diversity and Access, University of California–Berkeley, October.

———. 2008. "Beyond the SAT." *Forbes,* August 13, online edition.

———. 2009. "Reflections on a Century of College Admission Tests." Research and Occasional Paper CSHE.4.09. Center for Studies in Higher Education, University of California–Berkeley, April.

Attewell, Paul, and David E. Lavin. 2007. *Passing the Torch: Does Higher Education for the Disadvantaged Pay Off across Generations?* New York: Russell Sage Foundation.

Avery, Christopher, and Sarah E. Turner. 2008. "Playing the College Application Game: Critical Moves and the Link to Socio-Economic Circumstances," preliminary draft, December 29, 2008.

Axt, Richard G. 1952. *The Federal Government and Financing Higher Education.* New York: Columbia University Press for the Commission on Financing Higher Education.

Bailey, Eric, and Patrick McGreevy. 2009. "Poor Would Be Hard Hit by Proposed California Budget Cuts." *Los Angeles Times,* May 22, online edition.

Baroway, Malcolm S. 2002. *The Gee Years, 1990–1997.* Vol. 12 of *History of The Ohio State University.* Columbus, Ohio: Ohio State University Press.

Baum, Sandy, and Jennifer Ma. 2007. *Education Pays: The Benefits of Higher Education for Individuals and Society.* New York: College Board.

Baum, Sandy, Michael S. McPherson, and Patricia Steele. 2008. *The Effectiveness of Student Aid Policies: What the Research Tells Us.* Washington, D.C.: College Board.

Benson, George C. S. 1953. Untitled review of reports and monographs published by the Commission on Financing Higher Education. *American Political Science Review* 47, no. 3 (September): 883–90.

Bernanke, Ben S. 2008. "Remarks on Class Day 2008 at Harvard University, June 4, 2008." Speech delivered at Harvard University. Board of Governors of the Federal Reserve System, Washington, D.C. Available at http://www.federal reserve.gov/newsevents/speech/bernanke20080604a.htm.

Bettinger, Eric. 2004. "How Financial Aid Affects Persistence." In *College Choices: The Economics of Where to Go, When to Go, and How to Pay For It,* ed. Caroline M. Hoxby, 207–38. Chicago: University of Chicago Press.

Bound, John, Michael Lovenheim, and Sarah Turner. 2007. "Understanding the Increased Time to the Baccalaureate Degree." SIEPR Discussion Paper 06-43. Stanford Institute for Economic Policy Research, Stanford, Calif., August 23.

Bowen, William G., and Derek C. Bok. 1998. *The Shape of the River: Long-Term Consequences of Considering Race in College and University Admissions.* Princeton, N.J.: Princeton University Press.

Bowen, William G., Martin A. Kurzweil, and Eugene M. Tobin, in collaboration with Susanne C. Pichler. 2005. *Equity and Excellence in American Higher Education.* Charlottesville, Va.: University of Virginia Press.

Bozick, Robert. 2007. "Making It through the First Year of College: The Role of Students' Economic Resources, Employment, and Living Arrangements." *Sociology of Education* 80, no. 3 (July): 261–84.

Brainard, Jeffrey. 2008. "Community Colleges Seen as Source of Engineers." *Chronicle of Higher Education,* October 10, online edition.

Brooks, David. 2008. "The Biggest Issue." *New York Times,* July 29, p. A19.

Brooks, Glenwood C., and William E. Sedlacek. 1981. "Black Student Enrollment at the University of Maryland, College Park, 1968–1971." Research Report 1-72. Cultural Study Center, University of Maryland, College Park. Available at http://eric.ed.gov/ERICDocs/data/ericdocs2sql/content_storage_01/00000 19b/80/39/03/0f.pdf. Accessed August 27, 2008.

Brown, Francis J. 1955. "A Long-Range View of Higher Education." *Annals of the American Academy of Political and Social Science* 301, no. 1 (September): 1–6.

Burton, Nancy W., and Leonard Ramist. 2001. "Predicting Success in College: SAT Studies of Classes Graduating since 1980." College Board Research Report 2001-2. College Board, New York.

Bushong, Steven. 2009. "Number of Students Doing Well on AP Tests Is Up, but Racial Gaps Persist." *Chronicle of Higher Education*, February 5, online edition.

Calhoun, Craig J., ed. 2002. *Dictionary of the Social Sciences.* New York: Oxford University Press.

Callcott, George H. 2005. *The University of Maryland at College Park: A History.* Baltimore: Noble House.

Camara, W. J. 2008. "Score Trends, SAT Validity, and Subgroup Differences." Paper presented at the Harvard Summer Institute, Boston.

Camara, W. J., and G. Echternacht. 2000. "The SAT I and High School Grades: Utility in Predicting Success in College." College Board Research Notes RN-10, College Board, New York.

Cambridge University Press. 2009. *Historical Statistics of the United States: Millennial Edition Online.* Available at http://hsus.cambridge.org/HSUSWeb/toc/hsus Home.do. Accessed January 6.

Card, David E. 2001. "Estimating the Return to Schooling: Progress on Some Persistent Econometric Problems." *Econometrica* 69, no. 5 (September): 1127–60.

Carey, Kevin. 2008. "Graduation Rate Watch: Making Minority Student Success a Priority." Education Sector report. Education Sector, Washington, D.C., April.

Carnegie Commission on Higher Education. 1968. *Quality and Equality: New Levels of Federal Responsibility for Higher Education.* New York: McGraw-Hill.

———. 1973. *Higher Education: Who Pays? Who Benefits? Who Should Pay? A Report and Recommendations.* New York: McGraw-Hill.

Carneiro, Pedro, and James J. Heckman. 2002. "The Evidence on Credit Constraints in Post-Secondary Schooling." *Economic Journal* 112, no. 482 (October): 705–34.

Chambers, M. M. 1961. "Higher Education in New York State: A Review Essay." *Journal of Higher Education* 32, no. 4 (April): 222–26.

Cheit, Earl F. 1971. *The New Depression in Higher Education: A Study of Financial Conditions at 41 Colleges and Universities.* New York: McGraw-Hill.

Clark, Burton R. 1960a. "The 'Cooling-Out' Function in Higher Education." *American Journal of Sociology* 65, no. 6 (May): 569–76.

———. 1960b. *The Open-Door College: A Case Study.* New York: McGraw-Hill.

Clark, Melissa, Jesse Rothstein, and Diane Whitmore Schanzenbach. 2009. "Selection Bias in College Admissions Test Scores." *Economics of Education Review* 28, no. 3 (June): 295–307.

Coates, Ta-Nehisi. 2008. "'This Is How We Lost to the White Man.'" *Atlantic Monthly,* May, online edition.

Cohen, Geoffrey L., Julio Garcia, Nancy Apfel, and Allison Master. 2006. "Reducing the Racial Achievement Gap: A Social-Psychological Intervention." *Science* 313 (September 1): 1307–10.

Cohen, Lizabeth. 2003. *A Consumers' Republic: The Politics of Mass Consumption in Postwar America.* New York: Knopf.

Coleman, James S. 1966. *Equality of Educational Opportunity.* Washington, D.C.: U.S. Department of Health, Education, and Welfare, Office of Education.

College Entrance Examination Board. 1999. *Trends in College Pricing.* Washington, D.C.: College Board.

———. 2007. *Trends in Student Aid.* Washington, D.C.: College Board.

———. 2008a. *Trends in College Pricing.* Washington, D.C.: College Board.

———. 2008b. *Trends in Student Aid.* Washington, D.C.: College Board.

Conant, James B. 1970. *My Several Lives: Memoirs of a Social Inventor.* New York: Harper and Row.

Coons, Arthur G. 1968. *Crises in California Higher Education: Experience under the Master Plan and Problems of Coordination, 1959 to 1968.* Los Angeles: Ward Ritchie.

Cornwell, Christopher M., David B. Mustard, and Jessica Van Parys. 2008. "How Does the New SAT Predict Academic Achievement in College?" Working paper, University of Georgia, Athens, June 25.

Cosby, Bill, and Alvin F. Poussaint. 2007. *Come On, People: On the Path from Victims to Victors.* Nashville, Tenn.: Thomas Nelson.

Council of Graduate Schools. 2008. "Findings from the 2008 CGS International Graduate Admissions Survey, Phase III: Final Offers of Admission and Enrollment." Research report. Council of Graduate Schools, Washington, D.C., November. Available at http://www.cgsnet.org/portals/0/pdf/R_IntlEnrl08_III .pdf.

Coyle, Thomas R., and David R. Pillow. 2008. "SAT and ACT Predict College GPA after Removing *g.*" *Intelligence* 36: 719–29.

Crawford, Claire, Stephen Machin, and Anna Vignoles. 2008. "Closing the Gap in University Participation: Reaching Out to High Achieving Disadvantaged Pupils." Unpublished paper. Centre for the Economics of Education, London, September.

Curtis, Polly. 2008. "University Dropout Steady at 22%." *Guardian,* February 20, p. 12.

Cuyjet, Michael J., ed. 2006. *African American Men in College.* San Francisco: Jossey-Bass.

Dabney, Virginius. 1981. *Mr. Jefferson's University: A History.* Charlottesville: University Press of Virginia.

Dale, Stacy Berg, and Alan B. Krueger. 2002. "Estimating the Payoff to Attending a More Selective College: An Application of Selection on Observables and Unobservables." *Quarterly Journal of Economics* 117, no. 4 (November): 1491–527.

Dee, Thomas S. 2004. "Are There Civic Returns to Education?" *Journal of Public Economics* 88, no. 9–10 (August): 1697–720.

Deming, David, and Susan Dynarski. Forthcoming. "Interventions to Reduce College Costs." In *Targeting Investment in Children: Fighting Poverty When Resources Are Limited,* ed. Philip Levine and David Zimmerman. Chicago: University of Chicago Press.

DeSimone, Jeffrey S. 2008. "The Impact of Employment during School on College Student Academic Performance." NBER Working Paper 14006. National Bureau of Economic Research, Cambridge, Mass., May.

Dorans, Neil J. 1999. "Correspondences between ACT and SAT I Scores." College Board Report 99-1, ETS RR 99-2. College Entrance Examination Board, New York.

Douglass, John Aubrey. 2000. *The California Idea and American Higher Education: 1850 to the 1960 Master Plan*. Stanford, Calif.: Stanford University Press.

———. 2005. "The Carnegie Commission and Council on Higher Education: A Retrospective." Research and Occasional Papers Series CSHE.14.05. Center for Studies in Higher Education, University of California, Berkeley, November. Available at http://64.233.169.104/search?q=cache:CdnEdR7hutIJ:cshe .berkeley.edu/publications/docs/ROP.Douglass.Carnegie.14.05.pdf+Clark+K err,+%22I+don%27t+expect+to+be+unemployed+very+long%22&hl=en&ct=c lnk&cd=1&gl=us. Accessed August 27, 2008.

———. 2007. *The Conditions for Admission: Access, Equity, and the Social Contract of Public Universities*. Stanford, Calif.: Stanford University Press.

Douglass, John Aubrey, and Gregg Thomson. 2008. "The Poor and the Rich: A Look at Economic Stratification and Academic Performance among Undergraduate Students in the United States." Research and Occasional Papers Series CSHE.15.08. Center for Studies in Higher Education, University of California–Berkeley, October.

Duffy, Elizabeth A., and Idana Goldberg. 1997. *Crafting a Class: College Admissions and Financial Aid, 1955–1994*. Princeton, N.J.: Princeton University Press.

Dynarski, Susan M. 2008. "Building the Stock of College-Educated Labor." *Journal of Human Resources* 43, no. 3 (Summer): 576–610.

Ellwood, David T., and Thomas J. Kane. 2000. "Who Is Getting a College Education? Family Background and Growing Gaps in Enrollment." In *Securing the Future: Investing in Children from Birth to College*, ed. Sheldon Danziger and Jane Waldfogel, 283–324. New York: Russell Sage Foundation.

Enarson, Harold L. 1974. "Review [of *Priorities for Action: Final Report of the Carnegie Commission on Higher Education*]." *Journal of Higher Education* 45, no. 4 (April): 311–12.

Fain, Paul. 2009. "Budget Cuts Cast Shadow over Florida's Universities." *Chronicle of Higher Education*, May 29, online edition.

Fine, Benjamin. 1956a. "Education in Review: Study of Post-High-School Training Needs Waits Now on Funds from Congress ." *New York Times*, July 15, p. 133.

———. 1956b. "Education in Review: President's Committee Takes First Step in Plans for Expansion of Colleges." *New York Times*, November 25, p. 221.

———. 1957. "Long-Term Financing Urged." *New York Times*, October 27, pp. 1, 54.

Fingerhut, Eric D., submitter. 2008. "The Strategic Plan for Higher Education 2008–2017." Ohio Board of Regents, University System of Ohio, Columbus, March. Available at http://universitysystem.ohio.gov/pdfs/strategicPlan/USO StrategicPlan_ExecSummary.pdf. Accessed August 27.

Fischer, Karin. 2007. "Texas Budget Rewards Retention." *Chronicle of Higher Education*, June 8, online edition.

Fletcher, Jason M., and Marta Tienda. 2008. "High School Peer Networks and College Success: Lessons from Texas." Paper presented at the NBER Higher Education Working Group Meeting, Washington, D.C., May 2.

Fletcher, Michael A. 2006. "At the Corner of Progress and Peril." *Washington Post*, June 2, p. A01.

Freeland, Richard M. 1992. *Academia's Golden Age: Universities in Massachusetts, 1945–1970.* New York: Oxford University Press.

Freeman, Richard B., Emily Jin, and Chia-Yu Shen. 2004. "Where Do New U.S.-Trained Science-Engineering PhDs Come From?" NBER Working Paper 10554. National Bureau of Economic Research, Cambridge, Mass., June.

Friedman, Milton. 1955. "Economic Policy and Social Control: The Role of Government in Education." In *Economics and the Public Interest,* ed. Robert A. Solo, 123–44. New Brunswick, N.J.: Rutgers University Press.

"From A to Zook." 1946. *Time,* August 12, online edition. Available at http://www.time.com/time/magazine/article/0,9171,745755,00.html. Accessed July 28, 2008.

Furman, Bess. 1956. "U.S. Urged to Set a College Policy: President's Committee Cites the Need for Expansion at the Higher Level." *New York Times,* November 20, pp. 1, 28.

Furstenberg, Frank F. Jr., Thomas D. Cooke, Jacquelynne Eccles, Glen H. Elder Jr., and Arnold Sameroff. 1999. *Managing to Make It: Urban Families and Adolescent Success.* Chicago: University of Chicago Press.

Gabel, John B. 1992. *The Jennings Years, 1981–1990.* Vol. 11 of *History of The Ohio State University.* Columbus, Ohio: Ohio State University Press.

Gates, Bill. 2008. "A Forum on Education in America: Bill Gates." Speech delivered at the Forum on Education at the Bill and Melinda Gates Foundation, Seattle, November 11. Available at http://www.gatesfoundation.org/speeches-commentary/Pages/bill-gates-2008-education-forum-speech.aspx.

Gates, Bill, and Melinda Gates. 2009. "A Bold Vision for Stimulus, Education Reform." *Roll Call,* February 10, 2009, online edition.

Gates, Charles M. 1961. *The First Century at the University of Washington, 1861–1961.* Seattle: University of Washington Press.

Geiger, Roger L. 1985. "After the Emergence: Voluntary Support and the Building of American Research Universities." *History of Education Quarterly* 25, no. 3 (Autumn): 377.

———. 1986. *To Advance Knowledge: The Growth of American Research Universities, 1900–1940.* New York: Oxford University Press.

———. 1993. *Research and Relevant Knowledge: American Research Universities since World War II.* New York: Oxford University Press.

Geiser, Saul. 2009. "Back to the Basics: In Defense of Achievement (and Achievement Tests) in College Admissions." *Change* (January–February): 16–23. Available at http://www.changemag.org/January-February%202009/full-back-to-basics.html.

Geiser, Saul, and Maria Veronica Santelices. 2007. "Validity of High-School Grades in Predicting Student Success beyond the Freshman Year: High-School Record vs. Standardized Tests as Indicators of Four-Year College Outcomes." Research and Occasional Paper Series CSHE.6.07. Center for Studies in Higher Education, University of California–Berkeley, June.

Geiser, Saul, and Roger Studley. 2001. "UC and the SAT: Predictive Validity and Differential Impact of the SAT I and SAT II at the University of California." Office of the President, University of California, Oakland, Calif.

Gelber, Sidney. 2001. *Politics and Public Higher Education in New York State: Stony Brook—A Case History.* New York: Peter Lang.

Gerald, Danette, and Kati Haycock. 2006. "Engines of Diminishing Equity in the Nation's Premier Public Universities." Education Trust, Washington, D.C. Available at http://www2.edtrust.org/NR/rdonlyres/F755E80E-9431-45AF-B28E 653C612D503D/0/EnginesofInequality.pdf. Accessed September 22, 2008.

Gerwertz, Ken. 1999. "COACHing the High-Jump to Higher Education." *Harvard Gazette,* September 30, online edition.

Glazer-Raymo, Judith. 1989. "Nelson Rockefeller and the Politics of Higher Education in New York State." Nelson A. Rockefeller Institute of Government, State University of New York, Albany, May.

Goldin, Claudia. 1998. "America's Graduation from High School: The Evolution and Spread of Secondary Schooling in the Twentieth Century." *Journal of Economic History* 58, no. 2 (June): 345–74.

Goldin, Claudia, and Lawrence F. Katz. 1997. "Why the United States Led in Education: Lessons from Secondary School Expansion, 1910 to 1940." NBER Working Paper 6144, National Bureau of Economic Research, Cambridge, Mass., August.

———. 1999. "The Shaping of Higher Education: The Formative Years in the United States, 1890 to 1940." *Journal of Economic Perspectives* 13, no. 1 (Winter): 37–62.

———. 2002. "Why the United States Led in Education: Lessons from Secondary School Expansion, 1910 to 1940." Paper presented at the Rochester Conference in honor of Stanley Engerman: Factor Endowments, Labor and Economic Growth in the Americas, June 8–10, 2001. A revision of the 1997 NBER paper.

———. 2008. *The Race between Education and Technology.* Cambridge, Mass.: Belknap Press of Harvard University Press.

Graham, Hugh Davis, and Nancy Diamond. 1997. *The Rise of American Research Universities: Elites and Challengers in the Postwar Era.* Baltimore: Johns Hopkins University Press.

Greeley, Andrew M., Alexander W. Astin, Joseph Katz, and David C. Epperson. 1971. "The Newman Report: Four Comments." *Journal of Higher Education* 42, no. 7: 610–23.

Greene, Jay P., and Marcus Winters. 2006. "Leaving Boys Behind." Civic Report 48. Manhattan Institute, New York, April.

Grutter v. Bollinger et al. 2003. 539 U.S. 306.

Gudrais, Elizabeth. 2008. "Unequal America." *Harvard Magazine* 110, no. 6 (July–August): 22–29.

Hacker, Jacob S. 2006. *The Great Risk Shift: The Assault on American Jobs, Families, Health Care, and Retirement and How You Can Fight Back.* New York: Oxford University Press.

Hansen, W. Lee. 1983. "The Impact of Student Financial Aid on Access." In *The Crisis in Higher Education,* ed. Joseph Froomkin, 84–96. New York: Academy of Political Science.

Harper, Shaun R. 2006. "Black Male Students at Public Flagship Universities in the U.S.: Status, Trends, and Implications for Policy and Practice." Joint Center for Political and Economic Studies Health Policy Institute, Washington, D.C.

Harris, Seymour E. 1972. *A Statistical Portrait of Higher Education.* New York: McGraw-Hill.

Harris, Seymour Edwin. 1948. *How Shall We Pay for Education? Approaches to the Economics of Education.* New York: Harper.

Hart, Betty, and Todd R. Risley. 1995. *Meaningful Differences in the Everyday Experience of Young American Children.* Baltimore: Brookes.

Hawkins, Hugh. 1992. *Banding Together: The Rise of National Associations in American Higher Education, 1887–1950.* Baltimore: Johns Hopkins University Press.

Hebel, Sara. 2009a. "Americans Increasingly See College as Essential and Worry More about Access, Poll Finds." *Chronicle of Higher Education,* February 4, online edition.

———. 2009b. "Colleges Urged to Take Action as They Prepare to Reap Billions in Stimulus Bill." *Chronicle of Higher Education,* February 10, online edition.

Hebel, Sara, and Jeffrey J. Selingo. 2009. "Obama's Higher Education Goal Is Ambitious but Achievable, College Leaders Say." *Chronicle of Higher Education,* March 6, 2009, online version.

Hechinger, Fred M. 1971. "Colleges: Ideas for Breaking the Lockstep." *New York Times,* August 8, p. E7.

Henry, David D. 1975. *Challenges Past, Challenges Present: An Analysis of American Higher Education since 1930.* San Francisco: Jossey-Bass.

Holy, T. C. 1961. "California's Master Plan for Higher Education, 1960–1975: A Factual Presentation of an Important Development." *Journal of Higher Education* 32, no. 1 (January): 9–16.

Hoover, Eric. 2008a. "Admissions Group Urges Colleges to 'Assume Control' of Debate on Testing." *Chronicle of Higher Education,* September 22, online edition.

———. 2008b. "Admissions Experts Call for Broader Definition of College Readiness." *Chronicle of Higher Education,* August 6, online edition.

Hoxby, Caroline M. 1998. "The Return to Attending a More Selective College: 1960 to the Present." Mimeo, Department of Economics, Harvard University.

———. 2000a. "Testimony Prepared for U.S. Senate, Committee on Governmental Affairs, Hearing on 'The Rising Cost of College Tuition and the Effectiveness of Government Financial Aid.'" In Senate Committee on Governmental Affairs, *Rising Cost of College Tuition and the Effectiveness of Government Financial Aid: Hearings,* pp. 120–28. 106th Cong., 2d. sess., S. Hrg. 106-515, February 9.

———. 2000b. "The Effects of Geographic Integration and Increasing Competition in the Market for College Education." Revision of NBER Working Paper 6323. Harvard University, Cambridge, Mass., May.

Hoxby, Caroline, and Sarah E. Turner. 2008. "Improving Outcomes for High-Achieving Low-Income Students through Collective Action." Unpublished paper prepared for the Windsor Group conference, Charlottesville, Va., October 28.

Hrabowski, Freeman A. III. 2001. "The Meyerhoff Scholars Program: Producing High-Achieving Minority Students in Mathematics and Science." *Notices of the American Mathematical Society* 48, no. 1 (January): 26–28.

———. 2007. "The Access Imperative: The Robert H. Atwell Lecture." Paper presented at the 89th annual meeting of the American Council on Education, Washington, D.C., February 11.

Hurtado, Sylvia. 2008. *Advancing in Higher Education: A Portrait of Latina/o College Freshmen at Four-Year Institutions, 1975–2006.* Los Angeles: Higher Education Research Institute.

Hutchins, Robert Maynard. 1952. "Double Trouble: Are More Studies, More Faculties, More Money the Key for Better Education?" In *Education for Democracy: The Debate over the Report of the President's Commission on Higher Education,* ed. Gail Kennedy, 82–86. Boston: Heath.

Hvistendahl, Maria. 2008. "China Moves Up to Fifth as Importer of Students." *Chronicle of Higher Education,* September 19, online edition.

Jack Kent Cooke Foundation. 2008. "Undergraduate Transfer Scholarships." Available at http://www.jkcf.org/scholarships/undergraduate-transfer-scholarships/. Accessed November 22.

Jaeger, A. J., and K. Eagan. 2007. "Developing Emotional Intelligence as a Means to Enhance Academic Performance." *NASPA Journal* 44, no. 4: 512–37.

Jaeger, A. J., K. Eagan, and L. G. Wirt. 2008. "Retaining Students in Science, Math, and Engineering Majors: Rediscovering Cooperative Education." *Journal of Cooperative Education and Internships* 42, no. 1: 20–32.

Jaeger, David A., and Marianne E. Page. 1996. "Degrees Matter: New Evidence on Sheepskin Effects in the Returns to Education." *Review of Economics and Statistics* 78, no. 4 (November): 733–40.

Jaschik, Scott. 2007. "Challenging the Measures of Success." *Inside Higher Education,* June 6, online edition.

———. 2008. "The Graduation Rate Gap." *Inside Higher Education,* April 21, online edition.

———. 2009. "Unintentional Whitening of U. of California?" *Inside Higher Education,* February 5, online edition.

Jencks, Christopher, and David Riesman. 1968. *The Academic Revolution.* Garden City, N.Y.: Doubleday.

Jenkins, Robert L. 1991. "The Black Land-Grant Colleges in Their Formative Years, 1890–1920." *Agricultural History* 65, no. 2 (Spring): 63–72.

Johnson, Lyndon B. 1963. "Remarks upon Signing the Higher Education Facilities Act," December 16. In John T. Woolley and Gerhard Peters, *The American Presidency Project* (online). Hosted by the University of California–Santa Barbara, Gerhard Peters database. Available at http://www.presidency.ucsb.edu/ws/?pid=26387.

———. 1965. "Remarks at Southwest Texas State College upon Signing the Higher Education Act of 1965," November 8. In John T. Woolley and Gerhard Peters, *The American Presidency Project* (online). Hosted by the University of California–Santa Barbara, Gerhard Peters database. Available at http://www.presidency.ucsb.edu/ws/?pid=27356.

"Just Name, Rank and SAT Number." 2008. Letters to the editor, *New York Times,* November 24, p. A24.

Kane, Thomas J. 1995. "Rising Public College Tuition and College Entry: How Well Do Public Subsidies Promote Access to College?" NBER Working Paper 5164. National Bureau of Economic Research, Cambridge, Mass., July.

———. 2003. "A Quasi-Experimental Estimate of the Impact of Financial Aid on College-Going." NBER Working Paper 9703. National Bureau of Economic Research, Cambridge, Mass., May.

————. 2004a. "College-Going and Inequality." In *Social Inequality*, ed. Kathryn M. Neckerman, 319–54. New York: Russell Sage Foundation.

————. 2004b. "Evaluating the Impact of the D.C. Tuition Assistance Grant Program." NBER Working Paper 10658. National Bureau of Economic Research, Cambridge, Mass., July.

Kane, Thomas J., and Peter R. Orszag. 2003. "Higher Education Spending: The Role of Medicaid and the Business Cycle." Brookings Institution Policy Brief 124, Brookings Institution, Washington, D.C., September.

Kane, Thomas J., Cecelia Elena Rouse, and Douglas Staiger. 1999. "Estimating Returns to Schooling When Schooling Is Misreported." NBER Working Paper 7235. National Bureau of Economic Research, Cambridge, Mass., July.

Keller, Josh. 2008. "U. of California Report Offers New Push and Gauges for Accountability." *Chronicle of Higher Education,* September 22, online edition.

————. 2009. "Cal State Campuses Are Forced to Reject Thousands." *Chronicle of Higher Education,* April 10, online edition.

Keller, Josh, and Eric Hoover. 2009. "U. of California to Adopt Sweeping Changes in Admissions Policy." *Chronicle of Higher Education,* February 5, online edition.

Kerr, Clark. 1963. *The Uses of the University.* Cambridge: Harvard University Press.

————. 1964. "The Frantic Race to Remain Contemporary." *Daedalus* 93, no. 4 (Fall): 1051–70.

————. 1990. "The American Mixture of Higher Education in Perspective: Four Dimensions." *Higher Education* 19, no. 1: 1–19.

————. 1991. *The Great Transformation in Higher Education, 1960–1980.* Albany: State University of New York Press.

————. 2001–03. *The Gold and the Blue: A Personal Memoir of the University of California, 1949–1967.* 2 vols. Berkeley: University of California Press.

Kerr, Janet C. 1997. "From Truman to Johnson: Ad Hoc Policy Formulation in Higher Education." In *The History of Higher Education,* 2nd edition, ed. Lester F. Goodchild and Harold S. Wechsler, 628–52. Boston: Pearson Custom Publishing.

Kiehl, Stephen. 2009. "Black Graduation Gap Grows at Maryland Universities." *Baltimore Sun,* March 11, online edition.

Kirst, Michael, and Andrea Venezia. 2001. "Bridging the Great Divide between Secondary Schools and Postsecondary Education." *Phi Delta Kappan* 83, no. 1 (September): 92–97.

Klein, Julia M. 2008. "Man on the Street: How a Sharecropper's Son Deciphered the Code of the City." *Yale Alumni Magazine,* January–February, online edition.

Kobrin, Jennifer L., Brian F. Patterson, Emily J. Shaw, Krista D. Mattern, and Sandra M. Barbuti. 2008. "Validity of the SAT for Predicting First-Year College Grade Point Average." College Board Research Report 2008-5. College Board, New York, October.

Kuh, George D. 2008. "High-Impact Educational Practices: What They Are, Who Has Access to Them, and Why They Matter." Association of American Colleges and Universities, Washington, D.C.

Kuncel, N. R., and S. A. Hezlett. 2007. "Standardized Tests Predict Graduate Student's Success." *Science* 315 (2007): 1080–81.

Labi, Aisha. 2008. "As World Economies Struggle, Competition Heats Up for Students from Abroad." *Chronicle of Higher Education,* November 21, p. A22.

Lederman, Doug. 2008. "A Dent in the Data." *Inside Higher Education,* December 22, online edition.

Lehmberg, Stanford E., and Ann M. Pflaum. 2001. *The University of Minnesota, 1945–2000.* Minneapolis: University of Minnesota Press.

Lemann, Nicholas. 1999. *The Big Test: The Secret History of the American Meritocracy.* New York: Farrar, Straus and Giroux.

Leonhardt, David. 2009a. "The Big Fix." *New York Times Magazine,* February 1, online edition.

———. 2009b. "Casualties of the Recession." *New York Times,* March 4, p. B4.

Lewin, Tamar. 2009. "A.P. Program Is Growing, but Black Students Lag." *New York Times,* February 5, p. A19.

Link, William A. 1995. *William Friday: Power, Purpose, and American Higher Education.* Chapel Hill: University of North Carolina Press.

Lochner, Lance J., and Alexander Monge-Naranjo. 2008. "The Nature of Credit Constraints and Human Capital." NBER Working Paper 13912. National Bureau of Economic Research, Cambridge, Mass., April.

Long, Bridget Terry. 2008. "The Effectiveness of Financial Aid in Improving College Enrollment: Lessons for Policy." Draft. Harvard Graduate School of Education, National Bureau of Economic Research, and National Center for Postsecondary Research, Cambridge, Mass., January.

Long, Bridget Terry, and Michal Kurlaender. 2008. "Do Community Colleges Provide a Viable Pathway to a Baccalaureate Degree?" NBER Working Paper 14367. National Bureau of Economic Research, Cambridge, Mass., September.

Lowenstein, Roger. 2007. "The Inequality Conundrum." *New York Times Magazine,* June 10, pp. 11–14.

Lumina Foundation for Education. 2009. "A Stronger Nation through Higher Education: How and Why Americans Must Meet a Big Goal for College Attainment." Special Report. Lumina Foundation, Indianapolis, Ind., February.

Mangan, Katherine. 2008a. "Their Budgets Slashed, Public Colleges Share in Their Applicants' Economic Pain." *Chronicle of Higher Education,* November 19, online edition.

———. 2008b. "Rising Enrollments Buoy Some Colleges, Burden Others." *Chronicle of Higher Education,* November 28, online edition.

———. 2009. "New Medical-School Programs Put Students on a Fast Track to the White Coat." *Chronicle of Higher Education,* February 6, online edition.

Mattern, Krista D., Brian F. Patterson, Emily J. Shaw, Jennifer L. Kobrin, and Sandra M. Barbuti. 2008. "Differential Validity and Prediction of the SAT." College Board Research Report 2008-4. College Board, New York, October.

Mayhew, Lewis B. 1973. *The Carnegie Commission on Higher Education.* San Francisco: Jossey-Bass.

McCormack, Eugene. 2008a. "Growth Rate Lags Again in Graduate Schools' International Admissions." *Chronicle of Higher Education,* August 21, online edition.

McCormick, Richard P. 1966. *Rutgers: A Bicentennial History.* New Brunswick, N.J.: Rutgers University Press.

McPherson, Michael S., and Morton Owen Schapiro. 1998. *The Student Aid Game: Meeting Need and Rewarding Talent in American Higher Education.* Princeton, N.J.: Princeton University Press.

"Members of the Group Reporting on Education." 1947. *New York Times,* December 16, p. 44.

Menand, Louis. 2001. "The Marketplace of Ideas." Occasional Paper 49. American Council of Learned Societies, New York. Available at http://archives.acls .org/op/49_Marketplace_of_Ideas.htm. Accessed August 8, 2008.

Mettler, Suzanne. 2005. "The Creation of the G.I. Bill of Rights of 1944: Melding Social and Participatory Citizenship Ideals." *Journal of Policy History* 17, no. 4: 345–74.

Moltz, David. 2008a. "Helping Community College Students Beat the Odds." *Inside Higher Education,* October 8, online edition.

———. 2008b. "Cutting a Program—to Save It?" *Inside Higher Education,* December 18, online edition.

Mundel, David S. 2008. "What Do We Know about the Impact of Grants to College Students?" In *The Effectiveness of Student Aid Policies: What the Research Tells Us,* ed. Sandy Baum, Michael S. McPherson, and Patricia Steele, 9–37. Washington, D.C.: College Board.

Murray, Charles. 2008. "Down with the Four-Year College Degree!" *Cato Unbound,* October 6. Available at http://www.cato-unbound.org/2008/10/06/charles-murray/down-with-the-four-year-college-degree/.

Nairn, Allan, and Ralph Nader. 1980. *The Reign of ETS: The Corporation That Makes Up Minds.* Washington, D.C.: Ralph Nader.

National Association for College Admission Counseling. 2008. "Report of the Commission on the Use of Standardized Tests in Undergraduate Admission." National Association for College Admission Counseling, Alexandria, Va., September.

National Center for Public Policy and Higher Education. 2008. "Measuring Up 2008." National Center for Public Policy and Higher Education, San Jose, Calif.

National Science Board. 2004. *Science and Engineering Indicators 2004.* Arlington, Va.: National Science Foundation.

National Survey of Student Engagement. 2005. "Exploring Different Dimensions of Student Engagement: 2005 Annual Survey Results." National Survey of Student Engagement, Center for Postsecondary Research, Indiana University, Bloomington.

Neal, Steve, ed. 2008. *Eleanor & Harry: Correspondence of Eleanor Roosevelt and Harry S. Truman.* Joint project of the Franklin D. Roosevelt Presidential Library and the Harry S. Truman Presidential Library. Available at http://www.truman library.org/eleanor/eleanordoctemplate.php?documentid=fdr19470206. Accessed July 25.

Nevins, Allan. 1962. *The State Universities and Democracy.* Urbana: University of Illinois Press.

New Jersey Student Tuition Assistance Reward Scholarship (NJ STARS). 2008. Web site. Available at http://www.njstars.net/.

New York State Committee on Higher Education. 1960. "Meeting the Increasing Demand for Higher Education in New York State: A Report to the Governor and the Board of Regents." Letter of transmittal. Board of Regents, State Education Department, Albany, November.

Newfield, Christopher. 2008. *Unmaking the Public University: The Forty-Year Assault on the Middle Class*. Cambridge, Mass.: Harvard University Press.

Newman, Frank, et al. 1971. *Report on Higher Education*. Washington, D.C.: U.S. Government Printing Office.

————. 1973. *The Second Newman Report: National Policy and Higher Education, Report of a Special Task Force to the Secretary of the U.S. Department of Health, Education, and Welfare*. Cambridge, Mass.: MIT Press.

Nisbett, Richard E. 2009. "Education Is All in Your Mind." Op-ed contribution. *New York Times*, February 7, p. WK12.

Niu, Sunny Xinchun, Marta Tienda, and Kalena Cortes. 2006. "College Selectivity and the Texas Top 10% Law." *Economics of Education Review* 25, no. 3 (June): 259–72.

Noble, Julie, and Richard Sawyer. 2002. "Predicting Different Levels of Academic Success in College Using High School GPA and ACT Composite Score." ACT Research Report 2002-4. ACT, Iowa City, Iowa.

Oakes, Jeannie, John Rogers, David Silver, Siomara Valladares, Veronica Terriquez, Patricia McDonough, Michelle Renée, and Martin Lipton. 2006. "Removing the Roadblocks: Fair College Opportunities for All California Students." University of California/All Campus Consortium for Research Diversity and UCLA Institute for Democracy, Education and Access, November. Available at http://www.idea.gseis.ucla.edu/publications/roadblocks/pdf/ExecutiveSummary.pdf. Accessed October 3, 2008.

Obama, Barack. 2009a. "Remarks of President Barack Obama—Address to Joint Session of Congress." Text of a speech released by the White House Press Office, February 24.

————. 2009b. "Restoring American Leadership in Higher Education." From President Obama's Fiscal 2010 Budget Overview. Text released by the Office of Management and Budget, Washington, D.C., February. Available at http://www.aacrao.org/federal_relations/2010budget4.pdf.

————. 2009c. "Remarks by the President to the Hispanic Chamber of Commerce on a Complete and Competitive American Education." Text of a speech released by the White House Press Office, March 10.

Office of Institutional Assessment and Studies. 2008. "Historical Data: Admission." Office of Institutional Assessment and Studies, University of Virginia, Charlottesville. Available at http://www.web.virginia.edu/IAAS/index.shtm. Accessed August 27.

Olson, Keith W. 1974. *The G.I. Bill, the Veterans, and the Colleges*. Lexington: University Press of Kentucky.

Orfield, Gary, and Faith G. Paul. 1992. "State Higher Education Systems and College Completion." Final Report to the Ford Foundation, New York, November. Available at http://eric.ed.gov/ERICWebPortal/custom/portlets/record Details/detailmini.jsp?_nfpb=true&_&ERICExtSearch_SearchValue_0=ED35 4041&ERICExtSearch_SearchType_0=no&accno=ED354041. Accessed September 29, 2008.

Organisation for Economic Co-operation and Development. 2002. *Education at a Glance 2002: OECD Indicators*. Paris: Organisation for Economic Co-operation and Development.

―――. 2003. *Education at a Glance 2003: OECD Indicators*. Paris: Organisation for Economic Co-operation and Development.

―――. 2008. *Education at a Glance 2008: OECD Indicators*. Paris: Organisation for Economic Co-operation and Development.

Ort, Shirley A. 2008. "The Impact of Tuition and Student Aid on College Access, Affordability and Success: A Practitioner's View." Paper presented at the inaugural conference of the Center for Enrollment Research, Policy, and Practice, University of Southern California, Los Angeles, August (updated September 4, 2008).

Osterman, Paul. 2008. "College for All? The Labor Market for College-Educated Workers." Center for American Progress, Washington, D.C., August.

Pallais, Amanda, and Sarah E. Turner. 2006. "Opportunities for Low-Income Students at Top Colleges and Universities: Policy Initiatives and the Distribution of Students." *National Tax Journal* 59, no. (June): 357–86.

Passell, Peter. 1997. "Affluent Turning to Public Colleges." *New York Times*, August 13, p. B7.

Planty, Michael, William Hussar, Thomas Snyder, Stephen Provasnik, Grace Kena, Rachel Dinkes, Angelina KewalRamani, and Jana Kemp. 2008. *The Condition of Education 2008*. NCES 2008-031. Washington, D.C.: National Center for Education Statistics, Institute of Education Sciences.

Pleasants, Julian M. 2006. *Gator Tales: An Oral History of the University of Florida*. Gainesville: University of Florida.

Portes, Alejandro, and Rubén G. Rumbaut. 2001. *Legacies: The Story of the Immigrant Second Generation*. Berkeley and New York: University of California Press and Russell Sage Foundation.

Posse Foundation. 2008. Web site. Available at http://www.possefoundation.org. Accessed October 14.

President's Commission on Higher Education. 1947. *Higher Education for American Democracy*. 6 vols. Washington, D.C.: U.S. Government Printing Office.

Prochnik, George. 2007. "Hail to the Analysand." *New York Times*, May 6, online edition.

Pusey, Nathan M. 1978. *American Higher Education, 1945–1970: A Personal Report*. Cambridge, Mass.: Harvard University Press.

Ragovin, Helene. 2006. "Amplified Application Will Provide Additional Cues about Prospective Students." *Tufts Journal*, May, online edition. Available at http://tuftsjournal.tufts.edu/archive/2006/may/features/index.shtml. Accessed November 22, 2008.

Ravitch, Diane. 1983. *The Troubled Crusade: American Education, 1945–1980*. New York: Basic Books.

ReducingStereotypeThreat.org. 2008. Web site. Available at http://reducing stereotypethreat.org.

Reed, Dawn Elizabeth. 2002. "'The Old University Is Dead': Activism and Change at the University of Virginia in the 1960s." *Magazine of Albemarle County History* 60: 46–80.

Reynolds, Curtis Lockwood. 2006. "Where to Attend? Estimates of the Effects of Beginning at a Two-Year College." Mimeo, University of Michigan, Ann Arbor, October 25.

Richard, Alison. 2008. "Quality, Talent and Diversity in the UK University System." Speech delivered at the Universities UK annual conference, Cambridge, September 10. Available at http://www.admin.cam.ac.uk/offices/v-c/speeches/20080910.html.

Rizzo, Michael J., and Ronald G. Ehrenberg. 2003. "Resident and Nonresident Tuition and Enrollment at Flagship State Universities." NBER Working Paper 9516. National Bureau of Economic Research, Cambridge, Mass., February. Available at http://www.nber.org/papers/w9516.pdf. Accessed January 20, 2009.

Roberts, Sam. 2008. "A Generation Away, Minorities May Become the Majority in U.S." *New York Times,* August 14, p. A1.

Roderick, Melissa, Jenny Nagaoka, Elaine Allensworth, Vanessa Coca, Macarena Correa, and Ginger Stoker. 2006. "From High School to the Future: A First Look at Chicago Public School Graduates' College Enrollment, College Preparation, and Graduation from Four-Year Colleges." Consortium on Chicago School Research, Chicago, April.

Roderick, Melissa, Jenny Nagaoka, Vanessa Coca, Eliza Moeller, Karen Roddie, Jamiliyah Gilliam, and Desmond Patton. 2008. "From High School to the Future: Potholes on the Road to College." Consortium on Chicago School Research, Chicago, March.

Roderick, Melissa, Jenny Nagaoka, Vanessa Coca, Eliza Moeller. 2009. "From High School to the Future: Making Hard Work Pay Off." Consortium on Chicago School Research, Chicago, April.

Rogers, John, Veronica Terriquez, Siomara Valladares, and Jeannie Oakes. 2006. "California Educational Opportunity Report 2006: Roadblocks to College." University of California/All Campus Consortium for Research Diversity and UCLA Institute for Democracy, Education, and Access, March. Available at http://www.idea.gseis.ucla.edu/publications/eor06/fullreport/pdf/EOR-2006.pdf. Accessed October 3, 2008.

Rorabaugh, William J. 1989. *Berkeley at War: The 1960s.* New York: Oxford University Press.

Rosenbaum, David E. 1971. "Panel Challenges U.S. College System." *New York Times,* March 9, p. 45.

Rothstein, Jesse. 2005. "SAT Scores, High Schools, and Collegiate Performance Predictions." Working paper, Princeton University, Princeton, N.J., June. Available at http://www.princeton.edu/~jrothst/workingpapers/rothstein_CB volume.pdf.

Russell, John Dale. 1949. "Basic Conclusions and Recommendations of the President's Commission on Higher Education." *Journal of Educational Sociology* 22, no. 8 (April): 493–508.

Ryu, Mikyung. 2008. *Minorities in Higher Education 2008.* 23rd annual status report. Washington, D.C.: American Council on Education.

Sackett, P. R., N. R. Kuncel, J. J. Arneson, S. R. Cooper, and S. D. Waters. 2009. "Does Socioeconomic Status Explain the Relationship between Admissions Tests and Post-secondary Academic Performance?" *Psychological Bulletin* 135: 1–22.

Salins, Peter D. 2008. "The Test Passes, Colleges Fail." *New York Times,* November 18, p. A27.

Salter, Chuck. 2002. "It's Cool to Be Smart." *Fast Company* 57 (March), online edition.

Santiago, Deborah A. 2008. "Accelerating Latino Student Success at Texas Border Institutions: Possibilities and Challenges." Excelencia in Education, Washington, D.C., October.

Sawyer, Richard. 2008. "Benefits of Additional High School Course Work and Improved Course Performance in Preparing Students for College." ACT Research Report 2008-1. ACT, Iowa City, Iowa.

Schapiro, Morton Owen, Michael P. O'Malley, and Larry H. Litten. 1990. "Tracing the Economic Backgrounds of COFHE Students: Has There Been a 'Middle-Income Melt'?" Discussion Paper 6. Williams Project on the Economics of Higher Education, Williamstown, Mass., November. Available at http://www.williams.edu/wpehe/DPs/DP-6.pdf. Accessed September 22, 2008.

Schmidt, Peter. 2008a. "Studies Link Use of Part-Time Instructors to Lower Student Success." *Chronicle of Higher Education,* November 6, online edition.

———. 2008b. "Mismatches Found between Student Achievement and Parents' College Expectations in Federal Survey." *Chronicle of Higher Education,* April 23, online edition.

———. 2008c. "Colleges Seek Key to Success of Black Men in Classroom." *Chronicle of Higher Education,* October 10, A1.

Schrag, Peter. 1998. *Paradise Lost: California's Experience, America's Future.* New York: New Press.

Schrecker, Ellen W. 1986. *No Ivory Tower: McCarthyism and the Universities.* New York: Oxford University Press.

Schrum, Ethan. 2007. "Establishing a Democratic Religion: Metaphysics and Democracy in the Debates over the President's Commission on Higher Education." *History of Education Quarterly* 47, no. 3 (August): 277–301. Available at http://www.sas.upenn.edu/dcc/workshops/documents/Schrum.pdf. Accessed August 2, 2008.

Scott-Clayton, Judith E. 2007. "What Explains Rising Labor Supply among U.S. Undergraduates, 1970–2003?" Draft. John F. Kennedy School of Government, Harvard University, Cambridge, Mass., November 8.

———. 2008. "On Money and Motivation: A Quasi-Experimental Analysis of Financial Incentives for College Achievement." National Bureau of Economic Research, Cambridge, Mass., October 29. Available at http://www.nber.org/~confer/2008/HIEDf08/scott-clayton.pdf. Accessed December 15, 2008.

Seftor, Neil S., and Sarah E. Turner. 2002. "Back to School: Federal Student Aid Policy and Adult College Enrollment." *Journal of Human Resources* 37, no. 2 (Spring): 336–52.

Shultz, Marjorie M., and Sheldon Zedeck. 2008. "Final Report: Identification, Development, and Validation of Predictors for Successful Lawyering." University of California, Berkeley, September. Available at http://www.law.berkeley.edu/files/LSACREPORTfinal-12.pdf.

Sidhu, Ranjit. 2009. "Comparing the Validity of ACT Scores and High School Grades as Predictors of Success in College." Executive report. ACT, Iowa City, Iowa, April 3.

Slosson, Edwin Emery. 1910. *Great American Universities*. New York: Macmillan.

Smith, Wilson, and Thomas Bender, eds. 2008. *American Higher Education Transformed, 1940–2005: Documenting the National Discourse*. Baltimore: Johns Hopkins University Press.

Snider, William D. 1992. *Light on the Hill: A History of the University of North Carolina at Chapel Hill*. Chapel Hill: University of North Carolina Press.

Staples, Brent. 2000. "Editorial Observer: The 'Mississippification' of California Schools." *New York Times*, June 23, online edition. Available at http://query.nytimes.com/gst/fullpage.html?res=9A01E7D61F31F930A15755C0A9669C8 B63. Accessed October 3, 2008.

State Council of Higher Education for Virginia. 2008. "Two-Year College Transfer Grant Program Fact Sheet." State Council of Higher Education for Virginia, Richmond. Available at http://www.schev.edu/Students/factsheetTransfer Grant.pdf. Accessed November 18.

"State Universities Getting Increasingly Selective." 2006. *Wall Street Journal*, November 13, p. A1.

State University of New York. 2008. "Short History of SUNY." Available at http://www.suny.edu/student/university_suny_history.cfm. Accessed September 1.

Steele, Claude, and Joshua Aronson. 1995. "Stereotype Threat and the Intellectual Test Performance of African Americans." *Journal of Personality and Social Psychology* 69, no. 5: 797–811.

Steinhauer, Jennifer. 2008. "Facing Deficits, States Get Out Sharper Knives." *New York Times*, November 16, online edition.

Stinebrickner, Ralph, and Todd R. Stinebrickner. 2003. "Working during School and Academic Performance." *Journal of Labor Economics* 21, no. 2 (April): 473–91.

Stinebrickner, Todd R., and Ralph Stinebrickner. 2007. "The Effect of Credit Constraints on the College Drop-Out Decision: A Direct Approach Using a New Panel Study." NBER Working Paper 13340. National Bureau of Economic Research, Cambridge, Mass., August.

Supiano, Beckie. 2009. "Colleges Offer Extra Aid to Strapped Students." *Chronicle of Higher Education*, January 9, online edition.

Swanson, Christopher B. 2008. "Cities in Crisis: A Special Analytic Report on High School Graduation." Editorial Projects in Education Research Center, Bethesda, Md., April 1.

Symonds, William C. 2004. "Should Public Universities Behave Like Private Colleges?" *Business Week*, November 15, p. 97.

Thaler, Richard H., and Cass R. Sunstein. 2008. *Nudge: Improving Decisions about Health, Wealth, and Happiness*. New Haven, Conn.: Yale University Press.

Thelin, John R. 2004. *A History of American Higher Education*. Baltimore: Johns Hopkins University Press.

Thompson, Mark E. 1978. "Commissions and Zeitgeist: A Brief Critique of Commissions on Higher Education." *Peabody Journal of Education* 55, no. 4 (July): 309–17.

Thompson, Ronald B. 1954. "The Impending Tidal Wave of Students: A Report." Committee on Special Projects, American Association of Collegiate Registrars and Admissions Officers, Washington, D.C.

Tinto, Vincent. 1975. "Dropout from Higher Education: A Theoretical Synthesis of Recent Research." *Review of Educational Research* 45, no. 1 (Winter): 89–125.

———. 1993. *Leaving College: Rethinking the Causes and Cures of Student Attrition.* 2nd edition. Chicago: University of Chicago Press.

Tomsho, Robert. 2009. "States Weigh Cuts to Merit Scholarships." *Wall Street Journal,* January 13, online edition.

Trow, Martin. 1988. "American Higher Education: Past, Present, and Future." *Educational Researcher* 17, no. 3 (April): 13–23.

———. 2001. "From Mass Market Higher Education to Universal Access: The American Advantage." In *In Defense of American Higher Education,* ed. Philip G. Altbach, Patricia J. Gumport, and D. Bruce Johnstone, 110–43. Baltimore: Johns Hopkins University Press.

Truman, Harry S. 1963. "Letter Appointing Members to the National Commission on Higher Education," July 13, 1946. In John T. Woolley and Gerhard Peters, *The American Presidency Project* (online). Hosted by the University of California–Santa Barbara, Gerhard Peters database. Available at http://www .presidency.ucsb.edu/ws/?pid=12452.

Turner, Sarah E. 2004. "Going to College and Finishing College: Explaining Different Educational Outcomes." In *College Choices: The Economics of Where to Go, When to Go, and How to Pay for It,* ed. Caroline M. Hoxby, 13–56. Chicago: University of Chicago Press.

Turner, Sarah, and John Bound. 2003. "Closing the Gap or Widening the Divide: The Effects of the G.I. Bill and World War II on the Educational Outcomes of Black Americans." *Journal of Economic History* 63, no. 1 (March): 145–77.

University of North Carolina. 2008. "UNC Facts." Available at http://www .northcarolina.edu/content.php/home/facts.htm. Accessed August 28.

University of Wisconsin System. 2008. "History and Organization of the University of Wisconsin System." Available at http://wis.uwsa.edu/about/history.htm. Accessed September 1.

U.S. Census Bureau and U.S. Bureau of Labor Statistics. 2008. *Current Population Survey.* Washington, D.C.: U.S. Census Bureau. Available at http://www.census .gov/cps/.

U.S. Department of Education. 2008. "35 CFR Part 99 Family Educational Rights and Privacy: Final Rule." *Federal Register* 73, no. 237 (December 9).

U.S. Department of Education, National Center for Education Statistics. 1993. *120 Years of American Education: A Statistical Portrait.* Washington, D.C.: U.S. Department of Education.

U.S. Department of Education, National Center for Education Statistics, Institute of Education Sciences. 2003. *Digest of Education Statistics 2002.* NCES 2003-060. Washington, D.C.: U.S. Department of Education, National Center for Education Statistics, Institute of Education Sciences.

———. 2008. *Digest of Education Statistics 2007.* NCES 2008-022. Washington, D.C.: U.S. Department of Education, National Center for Education Statistics, Institute of Education Sciences.

Van Houten, Peter S., and Edward L. Barrett. 2003. *Berkeley and Its Students: Days of Conflict, Years of Change, 1945–1970.* Berkeley: Berkeley Public Policy Press, Institute of Governmental Studies, University of California.

Vaughan, George B. 2006. *The Community College Story*. Washington, D.C.: American Association of Community Colleges. Available at http://books.google.com/books?id=27iwNptunysC&pg=PA30&lpg=PA30&dq=community+colleges+and+the+1960s&source=web&ots=e8OTJKi51X&sig=ioKAiAv13-JxZ-Qfhyk ZfnaiqrI&hl=en&sa=X&oi=book_result&resnum=7&ct=result.

Veysey, Laurence R. 1965. *The Emergence of the American University*. Chicago: University of Chicago Press.

Weisenburger, Francis P. 1975. *The Fawcett Years, 1956–1972*. Vol. 9 of *History of The Ohio State University*. Columbus: Ohio State University Press.

Wendt, Karl F. 1975. "The Growth of the University's Physical Resources, 1949–1974." In *The University of Wisconsin: One Hundred and Twenty-Five Years*, ed. Allan G. Bogue and Taylor Robert, 87–98. Madison: University of Wisconsin Press.

Western Interstate Commission for Higher Education. 2008. "Knocking at the College Door: Projections of High School Graduates by State and Race/Ethnicity, 1992 to 2022." Western Interstate Commission for Higher Education, Boulder, Colo., March.

Wilkins, Ernest H. "Major Trends in Collegiate Enrollments." *School and Society* 42 (1935): 442–48.

Wirt, John, Patrick Rooney, Susan Choy, Stephen Provasnik, Anindita Sen, and Richard Tobin. 2004. *The Condition of Education 2004*. NCES 2004-077. Washington, D.C.: National Center for Education Statistics, Institute of Education Sciences.

Wolin, Sheldon. 2008. "Remembering Berkeley." In *American Higher Education Transformed, 1940–2005: Documenting the National Discourse*, ed. Wilson Smith and Thomas Bender, 379–81. Baltimore: Johns Hopkins University Press.

Woolley, John T., and Gehard Peters. 2008. *The American Presidency Project* (online). Hosted by the University of California–Santa Barbara. Gerhard Peters database. Available at http://www.presidency.ucsb.edu/.

Young, F. Chandler. 1975. "On the Importance of Students, 1949–1974." In *The University of Wisconsin: One Hundred and Twenty-Five Years*, ed. Allan G. Bogue and Taylor Robert, 131–56. Madison: University of Wisconsin Press.

Young, William H. 1975. "The University's Supporting Resources, 1949–1974." In *The University of Wisconsin: One Hundred and Twenty-Five Years*, ed. Allan G. Bogue and Robert Taylor, 79–86. Madison: University of Wisconsin Press.

"Zook." 1933. *Time*, July 3, online edition. Available at http://www.time.com/time/magazine/article/0,9171,793162,00.html. Accessed July 28, 2008.

Zwick, Rebecca, Terran Brown, and Jeffrey C. Sklar. 2004. "California and the SAT: A Reanalysis of University of California Admissions Data." Paper CSHE 8-04, Center for Studies in Higher Education, University of California–Berkeley.

Zwick, Rebecca, and Jennifer Greif Green. 2007. "New Perspectives on the Correlation of SAT Scores, High School Grades, and Socioeconomic Factors." *Journal of Educational Measurement* 44: 23–45.

Index

Page numbers for entries occurring in figures are suffixed by an f; those for entries in notes, by an n, with the number of the note following; and those for entries in tables, by a t.